SOCIAL JUSTICE AND ECHOES OF PAUL

Grimké's Evangelical Emancipatory Homiletic

Eric J. Freeman, PhD

The Freeman Institute
FOR INTEGRATIVE RESEARCH

Published by
The Freeman Institute for Integrative Research
201 Columbia Mall Blvd.
Columbia, SC 29223

ISBN 979-8-9929512-4-0

First Edition

The Freeman Institute for Integrative Research

This volume is a publication of The Freeman Institute for Integrative Research, a multidisciplinary center committed to advancing rigorous theological scholarship that speaks to the moral, spiritual, and social challenges of our time. Rooted in a tradition of evangelical conviction and intellectual inquiry, the Institute prioritizes historically grounded research, doctrinal clarity, and the amplification of voices often overlooked in theological discourse.

With a particular emphasis on homiletics, ethics, and ecclesial engagement, the Institute produces accessible, research-driven resources that bridge biblical theology with lived experience. This work on Francis James Grimké exemplifies the Institute's mission: to cultivate integrative scholarship that harmonizes theological fidelity with emancipatory praxis, equipping gospel leaders to proclaim truth with conviction, courage, and contextual awareness.

I am not

an island unto myself.

Every jot and tittle is an echo of those

who love and loved me.

Thank you.

+EJF

PREFACE

The life and ministry of Francis James Grimké (1850–1937) present a profound challenge and a prophetic invitation to those who preach, teach, and live the gospel in contexts fractured by division and injustice. This volume, *Social Justice and Echoes of Paul: Grimké's Evangelical Emancipatory Homiletic*, is born from the conviction that Grimké's preaching offers not only a historical case study but a living homiletical framework for the present age.

At the heart of this study is a simple but urgent question: how can gospel preaching confront ethnic prejudice in a way that is both biblically faithful and socially transformative? In response, this work proposes and defines Grimké's distinct preaching ministry as an *Evangelical Emancipatory Homiletic* (EEH). Rooted in Reformed evangelical theology, shaped by the lived experience of emancipation, and informed by the Apostle Paul's pastoral imagination, Grimké's homiletic presents a gospel that is not only proclaimed but embodied—a gospel that does not flinch before the hostile divisions of its age.

Through textual and thematic echoes of Paul, Grimké preached a message that aimed to liberate both heart and society, challenging the church to reflect more faithfully the reconciling love of Christ. His sermons confront the spiritual forces underlying ethnic prejudice while offering a vision of communal transformation grounded in the cross of Christ.

What follows is not merely a biographical or historical analysis, but a theological excavation of how Grimké's preaching integrated scripture, doctrine, and justice into a singular evangelical witness. In an era increasingly marked by polarization and mistrust, his voice—echoing Paul's—calls us to recover a gospel that reconciles, a pulpit that convicts, and a church that heals.

This book is offered to pastors, students, and scholars who long for a deeper integration of biblical fidelity and social responsibility. It is also a tribute to a preacher who, in the face of profound hostility, dared to say what others would not and lived what many still struggle to believe: that in Christ, there is no partiality, and no division that love cannot mend.

TABLE OF CONTENTS

PUBLIC DOMAIN STATEMENT vi

PREFACE vii

CHAPTER 1

GOSPEL FOUNDATIONS:
EVANGELICAL PREACHING IN A DIVIDED WORLD 1

Why This Study Matters: Clarifying the Evangelical Response to Prejudice 4

Approach and Disciplinary Framework 5

Understanding Grimké's Emancipatory Echo of Paul 5

Why Grimké Matters 7

Biblical Theology in Action: Foundations for Grimké's Emancipatory Preaching 9

Living the Text: A Working Definition of Biblical Theology 11

Breaking Dividing Walls: Paul and Grimké on Unity in the Church 12

When Preaching Becomes Protest: Embodied Christianity and Moral Witness 13

Echoes Beyond the Church: Apostolic Vision and Evangelical Engagement 15

Pulling the Threads Together: EEH as Theological Praxis 18

Setting the Stage: History, Theology, and Context 21

Post-Civil War America: The World Grimké Preached In 21

Grimké and Paul: Echoes of Gospel Conviction 22

Preaching Amid Prejudice: The Culture Grimké Confronted 22

The Church Divided: Evangelism's Mixed Witness 22

Grimké's Pauline Imprint: From Epistles to Pulpit....................23

Why Grimké's Voice Still Speaks 23

Challenging Normative Ecclesiastical Perspectives 24

Contributions to Ecclesiastical and Social Understanding....................24

Homiletical and Theological Innovation 24

Practical Implications for Contemporary Evangelical Thought....................25

Reconsidering Evangelical Social Activism....................25

Academic and Cultural Relevance 26

Emancipatory Pedagogical Processes....................26

Boundaries of Focus: What This Study Covers—and What it Doesn't....................27

Focus on Grimké's Distinctive Approach 27

Historical Period 28

Theological Scope 28

Geographical and Cultural Context....................28

Homiletical and Public Ministry 28

Theoretical Framework 29

Recognizing the Study's Limits: Harmonizing Echoes in the "Key of Dissonance" 29

Exploring Grimké's Voice: Method, Movement, and Meaning....................32

Chapter Outline 34

CHAPTER 2

SOCIALLY CHARGED ECHOES:
THE GOSPEL WITNESS, PAUL, GRIMKÉ, ET AL. 39

Section 1—Echoes: A Biblical Precedence 39

Section 2—Survey of Pivotal Historical Pauline Echoers 40

Section 3—Grimké, the Emancipated "Echoer" 41

Section 1—Echoes: A Biblical Precedence 42

Theoretical Foundations...................................44

Echoes in the Teachings of Jesus, Paul, and Others 53

Echoes in the Writings of Other NT Authors....55

Contemporary Application and Conclusion 56

Section 2—Survey of Pivotal Historical Pauline Echoers 57

John Chrysostom (c. 349–407) 58

Augustine of Hippo (354–430) 60

John of Damascus (675 or 676–749).................62

Peter Abelard (1079–1142) 64

Thomas Aquinas (1225–1274)..........................67

Martin Luther (1483–1546).............................69

John Calvin (1509–1564) 72

Daniel Alexander Payne (1811–1893) 75

Alexander Crummell (1819–1898)....................77

Conclusion...79

Section Three—Grimké, the Emancipated "Echoer" 80

Whispers of a Powerful Activism: A Historiographical Preview 81

Conclusion 88

CHAPTER 3

THE MAKING OF AN EVANGELICAL EMANCIPATOR.... 91

The Early Years 92

Frank—A Big Bite........ 96

Familial Betrayal and "Re-Enslavement" 97

From Emancipation to Education 100

Dissonance in the Postbellum South 100

The Journey Northward........ 101

Another Emancipation 102

The Lincoln Years 104

Emergence as a Leader........ 105

From Law School to Seminary 106

Princeton Halls and Echoes of Paul........ 107

From the Pulpit to the Public Square 111

The Fifteenth Street Presbyterian Church, Washington City........ 114

Marriage to Lottie 115

Jacksonville and the Moody Controversy........ 116

A Return to Washington: Beyond the Four Walls........ 118

An Emancipated Evangelical Echoer........ 124

Conclusion........ 126

CHAPTER 4

THE PAULINE PRAXIS: SUBVERSIVE EMANCIPATORY ECHOES OF A HEBREW PROPHET ... 127

Christoformity and Social Change: Embodying the Pauline Hermeneutic and Heart 128

Tactical Echoes of a Hebrew Prophet 130

Unmasking the Subversive Echoes of Paul's "Homiletic" 132

Defining a Subversive Homiletic 134

The Element of Hierarchy in Subversion 135

Hierarchy, Authority, and Power in the Pauline Epistles 136

The Epistle to the Romans and Philemon: Context, Themes, and Agendas 138

Historical and Cultural Context of Early Christianity 139

Contextual Agendas in Early Christianity 141

Textual Analysis and Interpretation: A Synopsis 142

Romans 13:1: Unveiling Subversive Dimensions 142

Philemon: Unveiling A Subversive Gospel 151

Synthesizing the Praxis 155

CHAPTER 5

THE GRIMKÉ ECHO: COURAGEOUS EMANCIPATORY ECHOES OF A HEBREW POET 157

Overview of the Penitential Psalms 158

The Seven Penitential Psalms 159

An Echoic History of Interpretation and Activism 162

Themes and Principles: Preaching the Penitential Elements of a Psalm 172

Synopsis Overview 173

Poetic Gospel Echoes: A Sermonic Witness 174

Additional Consideration 175

Conclusion 177

CHAPTER 6

THE ECHO CONTINUED: TOWARD AN EVANGELICAL EMANCIPATORY HOMILETIC 179

Overview 180

Objective 182

Defining "Echoes" in Preaching 182

Echoes: An Activist Pneumatological Phenomena 183

The Gospel Echo Heard: Contextuality in Discerning the Hearers' Ear 184

The Gospel Echo Received: Discerning and Engaging the Hearers' Heart ... 187

The Gospel Echo Response: Let the Church Say Amen 189

Conclusion: Theology of an Evangelical Emancipatory Homiletic 194

CHAPTER 7

PREACHING THAT TRANSFORMS: KEY INSIGHTS AND THE WAY FORWARD 197

Key Reflections 198

Gospel Preaching as Holistic Transformation .. 198

Conversionism and Activism as Gospel Indicatives 199

The Preacher as a Conduit of Personal and Social Change 200

Teasing Out the Distinctions 201

Summary of Research Contributions: Closing the Gap 203

Grounding the Theoretical Framework 207

Directions for Future Research 207

Implications for Homiletics:
Blind Spots and the Way Forward....................209

Final Thoughts....................212

SCHEDULE OF DIAGRAMS

Evangelical Emancipatory Homiletics....................214

The Evangelical Priorities of Gospel Preaching....................215

Cultural Contexts of Paul and Grimké's Ministries....................216

APPENDIX I

TABLES CHAPTER TWO....................217

Table 1. Textual Echoes—Jesus....................217

Table 2. Thematic Echoes—Jesus....................220

Table 3. Textual Echoes—Paul....................223

Table 4. Thematic Echoes—Paul....................225

Table 5. Textual Echoes—Other NT Examples....................227

Table 6. Thematic Echoes—Other NT Examples....................229

APPENDIX II

TABLES CHAPTER FIVE....................231

TABLE 1. *Five-Fold Principles for Preaching Penitential Psalms*....................231

TABLE 2. *Analysis: Five-Fold Principles for Preaching Penitential Psalms*....................233

APPENDIX III

MANUSCRIPT: GOD, AND PRAYER AS FACTORS IN THE STRUGGLE....................239

APPENDIX IV

HISTORICAL ARCHIVE:
SERMONS OF FRANCIS JAMES GRIMKÉ....................259

A Thirty-Year Survey: Socially Charged Sermons of an Evangelical Activist....................259

Grimké, the Evangelical Activist: Common Notes in the Corpus 261

Seven Pivotal Sermons: Two Decades of Activist Preaching 262

Summary 265

Sermon 1 The Remedy for the Present Strained Relations Between the Races in the South 266

Sermon 2 A Resemblance and a Contrast between the American Negro and the Children of Israel in Egypt, or the Duty of the Negro to Contend Earnestly for His Rights Guaranteed under the Constitution 288

Sermon 3 God and the Race Problem 309

Sermon 4 The Atlanta Riot 327

Sermon 5 The Paramount Importance of Character, or Character, the True Standard by Which to Estimate Individuals and Races 343

Sermon 6 Evangelism and Institutes of Evangelism 361

Sermon 7 The Race Problem as it Respects the Colored People and the Christian Church, in the Light of the Developments of the Last Year 367

BIBLIOGRAPHY 389

Figure 1 Nancy Weston, mother, c. 1885

Figure 2 The Grimké brothers—from left, Frank, Archie, and John, c. 1875

Figure 3 Charlotte Forten Grimké, n.d.

Figure 4 Francis James Grimké, n.d.

Figure 5 Fifteenth Street Presbyterian Church
in Washington, DC, c. 1899

All images courtesy of the Moorland Spingarn Research Center, Howard University, and the Schomburg Library, New York Public Library.

CHAPTER 1

GOSPEL FOUNDATIONS: EVANGELICAL PREACHING IN A DIVIDED WORLD

The present [day] is a good time . . . to consider the subject upon which I desire to speak this morning. It isn't of race prejudice, in general . . . but [specifically] of Christianity and Race Prejudice.
Francis James Grimké[1]

Throughout its history, the evangelical church has sought to engage the Pauline mandate to faithfully interpret and preach the timeless truths of the gospel to a world divided by hostilities.[2] Francis James Grimké, a twice-enslaved Presbyterian pastor, stands as a faithful

---

[1] Francis James Grimké, *The Works of Francis J. Grimke*, vol. 1, ed. Carter G. Woodson (Washington, DC: Associated, 1942), 442. Hereafter cited as Grimké, *Works I.* Reader's note: This was the opening proposition of the sermon Grimké delivered on May 29, 1910, following "an exhibition of race prejudice" at the Sixth World's Sunday School Convention held in Washington DC, May 19–24. The convention was a global gathering and included an address from President William Howard Taft.

[2] D. W. Bebbington, *Evangelicalism in Modern Britain: A History from the 1730s to the 1980s,* Revised ed. (London: Taylor & Francis Group, 2005), 2–4. While vulnerable to critiques of oversimplification, cultural and historical limitations, neglect of social and political factors, theological assumptions, static definition, exclusion of other important elements, and interpretational variability, the Bebbington Quadrilateral remains a widely used tool in the study of evangelicalism. Bebbington writes, "Variations there have certainly been in statements by Evangelicals about what they regard as basic. There is nevertheless a common core that has remained remarkably constant down the centuries. Conversionism, activism, biblicism, and crucicentrism form the defining attributes of Evangelical religion. Each characteristic can usefully be examined in turn." The characteristic of evangelical activism is the primary operative of this project. Reader's notes: The use of the locution "divided in hostilities" echoes Paul—Ephesians 2:14–16 ESV.

example of evangelical gospel preaching in a nation fractured by the Civil War. His message echoed the first-century church's struggles against unchristian ethnic and cultural hierarchies.[3] Like the Apostle Paul, Grimké courageously challenged the social conventions of his era, both in the church and beyond, recognizing the inimical spiritual forces at work behind them. For nearly fifty years, he preached the gospel and proclaimed the prophetic truth, "For God shows no partiality."[4]

Grimké, the second-born enslaved son of Henry W. Grimké, a white "aristocratic" plantation owner, and Nancy Weston, an enslaved mother of European and African descent, was reared in Charleston, South Carolina, under the arduous conditions of a nation and a family divided in animus.[5] He was introduced to the Christian faith under the careful hands of his mother, an avowed Baptist, and the Second Presbyterian Church.[6] Nancy and these early missionaries laid the religious foundation for young Frank that the ardent reformed traditions of Lincoln University and Princeton Seminary would ultimately shape.[7] As such, the crescendoed teachings of the Apostle

---

[3] Carolyn R. Calloway, "A Rhetorical Analysis of the Persuasion of Francis J. Grimké" (PhD diss., Indiana University, 1976), Xerox University Microfilms, v. Calloway's preface argues, "Grimké was one of the most controversial and militant black [preachers] of the nineteenth and twentieth centuries; he raised his voice in protest against race prejudice and the hypocrisy of the Christian Church at a time when Negroes felt a racial sting that deprived them of their political and social rights. . . . Yet, in spite of his efforts, he has been largely ignored by both black and white historians and by speech critics."

[4] Romans 2:11 ESV. Paul saw hostile spiritual forces at work behind the unjust social conventions and conflicts of his time. In other words, he viewed the societal wrongs and divisions not just as human issues but as manifestations of deeper, spiritual forces working against God's will. Cf. Ephesians 6:12; 2 Corinthians 10:3–4; Colossians 2:8; 1 Corinthians 2:12.

[5] Henry J. Ferry, "Francis James Grimké: Portrait of a Black Puritan" (PhD diss., Yale University, 1970), University Microfilms, 2–3.

[6] Ibid., 21–24.

[7] Ibid., 86. Reader's note: The heart of this enterprise is not to narrow Grimké to a reformed "Paulinist" persona. Instead, it is to examine him as a principled

Paul, though interpreted through a distinctly African American marginalized hermeneutic, were inescapable.[8] We hear the profound effects on Grimké best in the following,

> "Whenever I think of the pulpit, of the ministry [of the gospel], and of what it is capable of becoming and of achieving, instantly I think of the Apostle Paul—of his zeal, his earnestness, his steady, unswerving devotion to Jesus Christ and the interest of his kingdom. What a record he made for himself! What a glorious record. Let us all . . . [embody] his noble spirit."[9]

Noting the Apostle Paul's impact upon Grimké's ministry, this work excavates the social and cultural topography of Grimké's era. Furthermore, it describes the praxis and implications of Grimké's theological and homiletical engagement with the issue of ethnic prejudice, ultimately presenting an evangelical preaching ethos that anticipated the gospel's transformational or emancipatory essence (the emotive response of the heart to the preached word of the gospel with social intimations) as prescribed in the Pauline corpus.[10] In short, Grimké, like Paul, understood the gospel to be the announcement of

---

student of the reformed tradition, shaped by multiple reformed educational institutions. To do this efficiently, we will focus on distinct streams of the Pauline tradition and its practical influence on the homiletical ethos of Grimké. Moreover, because Grimké was a comprehensive Bible preacher, this study suggests a paradigm for researching additional particularities in Grimké's *evangelical emancipatory homiletic* [emphasis].

[8] Cleophus James LaRue, *The Heart of Black Preaching* (Louisville, KY: Westminster John Knox Press, 2000), 79. LaRue carefully and systematically analyzes Grimké's biblical hermeneutic of "a God who acts mightily on behalf of the marginalized and powerless."

[9] Francis James Grimké. *Meditations on Preaching* (Minneapolis: Log College Press, 2018), 16–17.

[10] Ibid., 4. Grimké journals, "The truths that we present ought first of all to lay hold of our own hearts. . . . My constant prayer to God is that he would help me to preach . . . not mainly to the intellect, but to the heart." Note: This theme recurs throughout the Grimkéan corpus.

the good news that, *through* [emphasis] the life, death, and resurrection of Jesus Christ, God has reconciled sinners to Himself and to one another, breaking down all divisions to create one united people in Christ.[11]

Why This Study Matters: Clarifying the Evangelical Response to Prejudice

This investigation focuses on Grimké's preaching and his engagement with the public square in relation to the evangelical church's response to ethnic prejudice, particularly in the context of post-Civil War America. It examines Grimké's homiletical practices through a Pauline–Grimkéan hermeneutic—an interpretive approach that intertwines the pastoral ethos of the Apostle Paul with Grimké's embodiment of these teachings in his ministry.

Additionally, this study seeks to provide an enhanced understanding of how the evangelical tradition, as exemplified by Grimké, can inform the development of an evangelical emancipatory homiletic.[12] Such a homiletic emphasizes spiritual salvation and social

---

[11] Ibid., vi; Ephesians 4:14–16; Galatians 3:28. Throughout this work, the gospel is defined as follows: "The gospel is the good news that, through the life, death, and resurrection of Jesus Christ, God has reconciled sinners to Himself and to one another, breaking down all divisions to create one united people in Christ."

[12] Maxine Green, *The Dialectic of Freedom* (New York: Teachers College Press, 1988), 3. Hereafter, Green, *Dialectic*. Green writes, "Celebrations of the Constitution and the Bill of Rights continue, but day after day their complex affirmations dwindle into slogans. . . . Young and old alike find it hard to shape authentic expressions of hopes and ideals. Lacking embeddedness in memories and histories they have made their own, people feel as if they are rootless subjectivities. . . . And yet, those of us committed to education are committed not only to effecting continuities but to preparing the ground for what is to come." Appending the latter, this body of work asserts that the artful and committed presentation of the gospel (homiletics) is a head and heart transformational emancipatory instrument empowering its hearers to activism, in assent and act, over and against the world's hostilities.

reconciliation as the fully embodied expression of Christ's redemptive work.[13] By addressing and challenging unchristian prejudice, it aims to emancipate its hearers from the spiritual forces of sin, death, Satan, and the fear of God's wrath that underlie these injustices.[14]

Ultimately, this work addresses the central clarifying inquiry: what are the *evangelical priorities* [my emphasis] that define a historically resonant gospel response to ethnic prejudice?

Approach and Disciplinary Framework

As a qualitative historical and theological preaching treatise, this exercise explores the intersection of history and theology in Grimké's preaching, examining how his homiletic was shaped by his experiences of enslavement, emancipation, conversion, and evangelical education. By investigating the historical context and theological foundations of Grimké's ministry, the treatise presents a unique perspective on his Reformed biblical theology and his distinctly evangelical preaching and activism.

Understanding Grimké's Emancipatory Echo of Paul

Francis James Grimké, in his embodiment of the Pauline tradition, offers a model for how the evangelical preacher, through the lens of the Bebbington Quadrilateral, confronts ethnic prejudice with the gospel of Jesus Christ. This study proposes that Grimké's ministry did not merely *echo* [emphasis] the epistolary notes of the apostle but also adapted, embodied, and lived its principles and ethos to directly address the divisive issue of ethnic prejudice in a post-Civil War American context, especially within the church.[15]

---

[13] Cf. Leviticus 19:18; Matthew 22:37–39; Mark 12:30–31; Luke 10:27; Romans 13:9; Galatians 5:14; James 2:8.

[14] Channing L. Crisler, "Interview 1," interviewed by Eric J. Freeman, May 19, 2023.

[15] In Chapter 2, we will explore the theoretical constructs that shape the use of the term "echo" in literature. For our purposes, however, we will define

Grimké's approach suggests a distinct synthesis of biblical fidelity, doctrinal soundness, spiritual sensitivity, and sociocultural relevance in response to the divine power of the gospel.[16] His commitment to preaching "the whole counsel of God" as the answer to the complex realities of racial inequality and injustice positions his ministry as an apt case study in the history of evangelical social engagement with issues of prejudice and discrimination.[17] He journaled:

> Whether popular or not, it is our duty to declare the whole counsel of God. Only thus will our skirts be clean and our title to be called ambassadors of God be fully vindicated. No cowardly minister who is afraid to declare the whole word of God lest he give offense, or interfere with his popularity, has any right in any Christian pulpit. He is simply a disgrace to it and a stench in the nostrils of Jehovah.[18]

Through his pulpit ministry and public life, Grimké employed a *gospel-embodied* approach to challenge and "subvert" the hierarchical ethnic and social constructs prevalent in his time.[19] His interpretation

---

echo in its most general sense as—*whenever what one does is inspired by something someone else has done* [my emphasis].

[16] Francis James Grimké, *The Works of Francis J. Grimke*, vol. 3, ed. Carter G. Woodson (Washington, DC: Associated, 1942), passim. Hereafter cited as Grimké, *Works III.* Note: Woodson documents more than ninety-eight Grimkéan statements, 1914–1934, betraying Paul's influence on Grimké's synthesis and praxis.

[17] Acts 20:27 ESV.

[18] Grimké, *Works III*, 580–81.

[19] The term *subvert* is used occasionally throughout this discourse to frame the subversive nature of the gospel message, as embodied by the apostle Paul and Grimké. In this context, *subversive* refers to the intentional (though not always) and tactical use of religious discourse within oral or written communications to challenge, question, and disrupt unrighteous or unjust social constructs. The phrase *gospel-embodied* is preferred over *gospel-centered* in this discourse to emphasize the holistic nature of the gospel

of the gospel as responsive to societal issues of his day set a framework for future evangelical leaders to address systemic social injustices.

This enterprise is grounded in a Pauline–Grimkéan hermeneutic and homiletic that sets out the theological basis and practical outworkings of Grimké's approach. It examines how his interactions with Paul's epistles and ethos informed his response to ethnic prejudice and how this response was manifested in his preaching and activism. By intersecting Grimké's ministry with the four dimensions of the Bebbington Quadrilateral—biblicism, crucicentrism, conversionism, and activism—the study evinces a method for evangelical gospel preaching that intrepidly confronts social ills.[20]

It is also part of this thesis that Grimké's ministry provides a motif for contemporary evangelical homiletics. This suggests that understanding and emulating Grimké's heart-challenging approach to the gospel can instigate a robust and effective evangelical response to the ongoing issue of ethnic prejudice in the modern world.[21] Overall, this research examines how Grimké's life and work exemplified an evangelicalism deeply rooted in scripture and passionately committed to social activism, mirroring the apostolic zeal of Paul and offering a courageous model for gospel preaching in a world divided in hostilities.

Why Grimké Matters

There are apparent theoretical, practical, archival, and pedagogical gaps in understanding how historical figures, particularly within the evangelical tradition, "harmonized" biblical theology and social activism in response to the divine power of the gospel.[22] This

---

mandate and its lived manifestations. For example, social activism is not an add-on to the gospel but a necessary outworking of its embodiment.

[20] Bebbington, *Evangelicalism*, 2–4.

[21] Note: The author contends that Grimké's homiletic, with echoes akin to the Apostle Paul's, was primarily driven towards the heart or affective domain first. See footnote 12.

[22] The term *harmonization* in this work denotes the integration of theological constructs as distinct expressions of a single, unified message rather than as

treatise addresses these gaps by examining how Grimké's distinct interpretation of *Pauline praxis* [emphasis added] provided a framework for confronting ethnic prejudice and advocating for justice.[23]

Theoretical Gap: This gap arises from the lack of theoretical frameworks that connect biblical theology, particularly Pauline interpretive practices, with social activism. This treatise fills this gap by examining how Grimké historically modeled Paul's reliance on scriptural sources to confront social injustices, providing a fresh theoretical framework for the practical implications of biblical theology in homiletics.

Practical Knowledge Gap: There is a lack of practical knowledge on how historical figures like Grimké connected theological insights from the gospel to real-world social issues. This treatise addresses this gap by providing examples of Grimké's harmonization of biblical theology, evangelical gospel preaching, and social activism. In doing so,

---

separate or divisible elements. This idea parallels musical harmony, where individual notes form a cohesive chord, each distinct but essential to the larger composition. Similarly, the components discussed here contribute uniquely yet integrally to a unified expression of the gospel, as opposed to functioning as isolated theological constructs.

[23] The operative *Pauline praxis* refers to the practical integration of the Apostle Paul's teachings in the life of a Christian community or individual. It emphasizes the embodiment of Paul's theological ideas, translating them into everyday actions and behaviors, particularly within the context of Christian ministry, ethics, and community life. This praxis also involves Paul's OT interpretive practices, where he reinterprets and adapts OT scriptures to guide the ethical and theological life of the Christian community. We explore the activist component (activism) of the Pauline praxis in later chapters. See Hays, *Letters*, 35. Hays clarifies his emphasis on intertextual examination rather than exploring the text's historical context, stating, "Anyone still so disposed may ask at the end of such a reading what pastoral problems Paul is confronting as he writes; however, such questions are not the primary concern of our present inquiry." While Hays focuses on intertextual analysis, this study explores the intertextual implicative notes on Pauline praxis, as implied in the initial clause of his delimitation. To ensure clarity and consistency throughout our analysis, we utilize this operative as a guiding framework.

it offers a valuable resource for preachers and theologians who seek to embody the gospel's divine power unto salvation and respond to it through advocacy for social reform.

Archival Preservation Gap: There is a gap in the archival preservation and analysis of Grimké's sermon manuscripts.[24] Existing studies appear to overlook the importance of preserving these sermons as primary sources. This treatise fills this gap by preserving key Grimké manuscripts and providing an analysis that highlights their relevance.

Pedagogical Process Gap: This study aims to build awareness of how the evangelical tradition, as exemplified by Grimké, can facilitate a homiletical pedagogy capable of confronting and addressing all forms of unchristian prejudice and its inimical forces through the gospel in a liberating or emancipatory manner—evangelical emancipatory homiletics. This gap underscores the need for practical strategies and teaching methodologies that preachers and educators can use to address contemporary issues of prejudice and discrimination within the framework of evangelical preaching.[25]

Biblical Theology in Action: Foundations for Grimké's Emancipatory Preaching

Understanding the practical aspect of the theoretical framework that undergirded Grimké's ministry is essential to grasping his evangelical emancipatory homiletic (EEH), particularly its intersection with biblical theology, gospel proclamation, and social activism.[26]

---

[24] Carter G. Woodson, ed., *The Works of Francis J. Grimké*, 4 vols. (Washington, DC: Associated, 1942). Woodson's collection remains the only intentional archival compilation of Grimké's sermons.

[25] C. Müller-Bloch and J. Kranz, "A Framework for Rigorously Identifying Research Gaps in Qualitative Literature Reviews," in *Proceedings of the International Conference on Information Systems*, ed. T. Carte, A. Heinzl, and C. Urquhart (Fort Worth, TX, December 16, 2015).

[26] The use of the acronym *EEH* in this study is for efficiency and clarity, not necessarily to coin a new homiletical construct, but to streamline references to Grimké's "evangelical emancipatory homiletic" throughout the text. This

These interactions are also crucial for understanding how his Reformed tradition, *social or contextual awareness*, and embodiment of *Paul's hermeneutic and heart* [emphasis added] shaped his preaching.[27] In this section, we will develop these foundational theories, focusing primarily on biblical theology, to establish a common language for what is meant by biblical theology, in the context of gospel preaching and social activism. This biblical emphasis reflects Paul's and Grimké's pervasive reliance on the truth of God's word in proclaiming the gospel. As Grimké journaled:

> The apostle [Paul] tells us, 'The world by wisdom knew not God,' and, therefore, any attempt to win men to Christ by appealing to their intellects, is a fool's project. Men are not won in that way. The old way, and the Bible way, of winning men is by the simple

---

abbreviation allows for concise reference to the historical description of Grimké's distinct homiletical approach.

[27] By "social or contextual awareness," we refer to Grimké"s ability to remain committed to the belief that salvation comes only through Jesus Christ, while simultaneously addressing racial prejudice through the indicatives of the gospel, particularly within the church, but also beyond. This reflects Grimké's capacity to embody the gospel faithfully in both spiritual and social dimensions, though it is doubtful that Grimké or Paul would have strictly separated the two. Grimké writes, "Besides, is it not singular, that with all the horrible things that are going on within our own borders—with colored men and women being lynched, burnt, tortured—there has never been, even a single day, set apart for prayer to God that this horrible race prejudice, out of which all these evils have come, might cease. And why? Because these very Christians who are anxious to get the aid of Almighty God in the war against Germany, are the very ones, in large measure, who are helping, either actively, or by their silence, to make possible these wrongs at home. They want to beat Germany, but have no desire to conquer their prejudices." See Grimké, *Works* III, 46. Furthermore, "Paul's hermeneutic and heart" is a phrase coined here to extend the concept of Pauline praxis (defined in footnote 22), capturing moments when Grimké reflects Paul's interpretive method, theology, or ethos. The phrase may at times be used interchangeably with Pauline praxis to denote Grimké's alignment with Paul's hermeneutic and heart.

presentation of the truth of God, in dependence upon the Holy Spirit to make the truth effectual. He alone can open blind eyes, unstop deaf ears, soften hard hearts. No other kind of preaching has ever been effectual and ever will be.[28]

Living the Text: A Working Definition of Biblical Theology

J. P. Gabler, in his 1787 inaugural address, *An Oration on the Proper Distinction between Biblical and Dogmatic Theology*, argued for a "historical concept" of biblical theology.[29] His distinction emphasized the historical nature of biblical theology. While this is helpful, the approach in this enterprise aligns more closely with the distinctions noted by Edward W. Klink III and Darian R. Lockett in *Understanding Biblical Theology: A Comparison of Theory and Practice*. They describe biblical theology as "the theology contained in the Bible, the theology of the Bible itself," distinguishing between descriptive theology (what the Bible says) and prescriptive theology (how it relates to today).[30]

Though the nuances of research defining biblical theology are more far-reaching than the general constructs presented here, this treatment focuses on the prescriptive aspect of biblical theology to highlight Grimké's EEH and its embodiment of scripture in addressing the ethnic prejudices of his time. While we recognize this is not an exhaustive approach to New Testament (NT) scholarship, we argue that its application, though limited in scope, effectively frames the intrinsic social context of gospel preaching.[31] As Klink and Lockett

---

[28] Grimké, *Meditations*, 20.

[29] Edward W. Klink III and Darian R. Lockett, *Understanding Biblical Theology: A Comparison of Theory and Practice* (Grand Rapids, MI: Zondervan, 2012), 14–15.

[30] Ibid., 14.

[31] Jared E. Alcántara, *The Practices of Christian Preaching: Essentials for Effective Proclamation* (Grand Rapids, MI: Baker Academic, 2019), 89–90. Alcántara notes that the preached gospel, though universal in its implications, historically "incarnates itself as a localized word in the language and culture of time and space."

aver, "Even those who affirm the Bible's divine inspiration and normativity must acknowledge that its message requires interpretation and application in each new generation."[32] This broader understanding of biblical theology aligns with what Grimké practiced: a theology that not only described God's salvific work but also demanded active responses to oppose and resist sin, especially interpersonal hostilities within the church.[33]

Breaking Dividing Walls: Paul and Grimké on Unity in the Church

It is important to emphasize that for both Paul and Grimké, the sociological notes or activism within their biblical theology was primarily focused on addressing social injustices and hostilities among fellow believers. This was not the whole of their hermeneutic and ethos, but an important note in their expression and embodiment of the gospel and its indicatives for the Christian. Their understanding of the gospel rejected divisions within the body of Christ, especially along ethnic lines. Paul's letters, particularly Galatians and Romans, emphasized the gospel's rejection of ethnic divisions among believers: "There is neither Jew nor Greek . . . for you are all one in Christ Jesus."[34] Similarly, Grimké's preaching, deeply impressed by Paul, confronted racial and social hostilities within the church and beyond.

---

[32] Klink, *Biblical Theology*, 14.

[33] Grimké, *Works III*, 151. Responding to race prejudice within his denomination and community, and in language that is anything but passive, Grimké writes, "In thinking of the things which race prejudice is constantly putting in the way of our progress, and by which it seeks to annoy and humiliate us, it is a comforting thought that nothing that it may do can prevent us from maintaining our self-respect, and from going forward, intellectually, morally and spiritually. In spite of all that is done against us, we can, if we really desire, keep on the even tenor of our way, towards the things that are true and just, and pure, and lovely, and of good report." Note the latter Pauline echo as he asserts this conviction to believer and nonbeliever alike.

[34] Galatians 3:28 ESV.

Grimké saw these prejudices, as enemies of the gospel, echoing Paul's conviction that "For there is no respect of persons with God."[35]

Paul's emphasis on confronting ethnic and social barriers within the body of believers is further demonstrated in passages like Ephesians 2:14–15, where Paul explains that Christ "has broken down in his flesh the dividing wall of hostility" between Jews and Gentiles, creating "one new man in place of the two, so making peace." This reflects Paul's consistent effort to engage divisions within the church, as seen also in Romans 11:17–18, where he urges Gentile believers not to boast against the Jews, emphasizing that they were grafted into the same olive tree of God's covenant.

When Preaching Becomes Protest: Embodied Christianity and Moral Witness

Grimké's EEH echoes Paul's approach in addressing ethnic divisions within the church, yet he also confronted broader societal prejudices, which were often tacitly or directly perpetuated by Christians beyond the church.[36] As Grimké observed, many Christians who professed faith did not live in accordance with the gospel's call to reconciliation, particularly regarding racial issues. He pointedly wrote:

> A great deal of discussion is going on through the papers, books, and periodicals about Christianity, what it is, what it requires, which may be all right, but what is most important, and about which we don't seem to care very much, is [embodying] it. It is more important that we should live it, should square our lives by its teachings than that we should be talking and writing about it. However much we may be talking and writing about it, if we are not living it, it will have but little influence. Words are cheap; it is easy to speak; it is not so easy to live, to show by our example what we really believe about it. How many, many there are among

---

[35] Romans 2:11 KJV. See Sermon 5 in Appendix IV.

[36] Grimké, *Works III*, 103.

> us who can talk well and eloquently about Christianity, but whose lives are but poor commentaries upon the faith which we profess. A Christianity that is [embodied], in its simplicity and power, is what is most sorely needed everywhere. The most of us who profess to be Christians are nothing but hypocrites; we know that we are not what we profess to be; and that we are not half trying to be. Think of Christian men and women drawing the color line on a brother or sister! Think of Christian men and women standing idly by, and often taking part in the murder of a fellow human being by a band of lynchers! Think of Christian men and women sanctioning the Jim Crow car and all the other forms of segregation practiced against colored people![37]

Grimké's words highlight the moral inconsistency he saw among Christians who tolerated or participated in racial injustice. His criticism paralleled Paul's challenge to Peter in Galatians 2:11–14, where Paul confronted Peter for withdrawing from Gentile believers out of fear of judgment from the Jewish Christians. Paul rebuked Peter because his actions were "not in line with the truth of the gospel," suggesting that the gospel's truth requires the active rejection of ethnic divisions within the church.

Preaching to Preserve Life: Extending the Gospel's Reach

While Grimké's activism, as he embodied the ethos of his EEH, clearly echoed Paul's stance on ethnic unity within the church, he expanded the gospel's indicatives to address social injustices that reached beyond Christian converts. For Grimké, his activism was an expression of "practical piety."[38] Some might conclude that this marks a departure from the Pauline praxis; however, if it is a departure, it is a limited one, as most Americans in 1900 were professed Christians. Scholars such as Scott W. Sunquist, Todd M. Johnson, and Gina A.

---

[37] Ibid., 103–4.

[38] Ferry, "Puritan," 83.

Zurlo estimate that more than ninety percent of the U.S. population at the time identified as Protestant Christians.[39] The point here is that given Grimké's historical context, it is likely that much of his social activism was still directed toward professed Christians, even if they were not members of his denomination or local church.

Nevertheless, while Paul is often understood to have focused on tearing down ethnic divides for the gospel's sake within Christian communities, Grimké extended these gospel imperatives more broadly. He was convinced that many who claimed to be Christians were not true believers.[40] Faced with rampant lynching and systemic violence against African Americans, Grimké acted on the conviction that, in so many words, "you can't preach the gospel to a dead man."[41] His social activism, therefore, sought to intervene in acts of violence to preserve life and dignity, thereby ensuring that the opportunity to receive the gospel remained available. In this way, Grimké's activism and EEH, while rooted in the same gospel indicatives Paul articulated within early church communities, expanded to address the urgent social realities of his time.

Echoes Beyond the Church: Apostolic Vision and Evangelical Engagement

Paul's broader mission to the Gentiles provides another example of the gospel's social indicatives. Luke records him preaching to the Gentiles at the Areopagus in Athens, declaring that God "made from one man every nation of mankind to live on all the face of the earth . . .

---

[39] See Scott W. Sunquist, *The Unexpected Christian Century: The Reversal and Transformation of Global Christianity, 1900–2000* (Grand Rapids, MI: Baker Academic, 2015); Todd M. Johnson and Gina A. Zurlo, *World Christian Encyclopedia*, 3rd ed. (Edinburgh: Edinburgh University Press, 2019).

[40] Grimké, *Works III*, 103. Also, Crisler notes that there are limited examples of Paul insisting on the gospel's indicatives outside the Christian communities he served. Channing L. Crisler, "Interview 5," interviewed by Eric J. Freeman, October 24, 2024.

[41] Grimké, *Works I*, 291–303.

that they should seek God."[42] Paul's statement arguably challenged the ethnic and religious boundaries of the time, extending God's offer of salvation to all people, not just the Jews. In this context, Paul's proclamation inherently disrupted societal and ethnic divisions beyond the church, presenting to an audience of unbelievers the gospel's vision of a reconciled humanity under God's redemptive plan.

Grimké similarly embraced this expansive vision, though with a focus shaped by his own context.[43] He extended the gospel's social implications further by confronting racial injustice and systemic violence both within and beyond the church. In Grimké's view, this wasn't just about Christian unity among Christians—it was about literally preserving lives to ensure that the message of salvation could reach all.[44] His activism aimed to uphold human dignity and ensure that the gospel's transformative power could be fully realized in a world marred by racial violence.

Defining EEH: A Framework for Gospel-Rooted Emancipation

The term EEH, as used in this work, is not intended as a theological concept but rather functions as a historical construct that frames the unique contextual dimensions of Grimké's preaching. This construct encompasses two central elements:

1. **Evangelical** – This element highlights Grimké's identity as a well-trained, self-identified Reformed evangelical Presbyterian pastor.[45] His theology was firmly rooted in Reformed evangelical doctrine, emphasizing the authority of Scripture, the necessity of personal faith in Christ, and the transformative power of the gospel.[46]

---

[42] Acts 17:26–27 ESV.

[43] Grimké, *Meditations*, 8.

[44] Grimké, *Works III,* 579–80.

[45] Grimké, *Works III*, 86–92, 371.

[46] Ferry, "Puritan," 136. Ferry noted, "Grimké presented a pietistic gospel, calling for total personal commitment to Christ. [Grimké] wrote, 'In God's

2. **Emancipatory** – The *emancipatory* aspect reflects Grimké's experience of liberation, having been emancipated through the Emancipation Proclamation following his complex experience with enslavement. [47] In this context, *emancipatory* is used as a historical descriptor to capture the social realities of Grimké's context and his personal narrative of emancipation. This experience deeply influenced his engagement with social issues, framing freedom and justice as essential indicatives of the gospel message. The term *emancipatory* is not used polemically or in opposition to terms like *liberation*; rather, it is employed to signify the historical impact of his emancipation.[48]

While EEH serves primarily as a historical descriptor, it also carries theological implications, particularly within practical and pastoral theology—topics that will be explored further in Chapters 5 through 7. Grimké's approach underscores the inherent contextual nature of gospel preaching, whether consciously or subconsciously. Jared Alcántara refers to this dynamic when well executed as "contextualization" with content fidelity, suggesting that awareness of

---

sight, there are only two classes of persons—those who are in Christ, and those who are not. Those who are in Christ are safe; but for those who are not... there is no salvation.'"

[47] Ibid., 38–39.

[48] Readers note: This usage of "emancipatory" is distinct from the theological and philosophical concept of *liberation* as it appears in *liberation theology*, which focuses on systemic injustice, often within frameworks developed by scholars like James Cone (*A Black Theology of Liberation*) and Paulo Freire (*Pedagogy of the Oppressed*). Here, *emancipatory* refers specifically to Grimké's own experience of literal emancipation from enslavement and how that personal history influenced his approach to gospel preaching and social engagement, particularly in addressing issues of justice, unity, and activism within his context. Cf. James H. Cone, *A Black Theology of Liberation* (Maryknoll, NY: Orbis Books, 1990); Paulo Freire, *Pedagogy of the Oppressed* (New York: Bloomsbury, 2000).

contextual factors strengthens the gospel's message, ensuring its relevance and relational impact across diverse cultural contexts.[49] In many ways, this is an echo of the apostle Paul, who said, "I have become all things to all men."[50] Alcántara further argues that ignoring this phenomenon creates a dissonance that can hinder the personal encounter necessary for gospel recipients outside the preacher's cultural sphere.[51]

Similarly, Cleophus LaRue, in his discussion of "communal interpretative strategies," points to African American preaching as a model of this awareness, while noting that every preacher brings a cultural lens to their homiletical praxis, whether they recognize it or not.[52] LaRue also asserts that marginalized voices, often more attuned to such biases due to their position in discourse, are more sensitive to these blind spots.[53] Grimké embodied this awareness fully, crafting his distinct EEH with an understanding that his homiletical approach was no more biased than others'. In his view, the "blindness" claimed by some was often selective and "hypocritical."[54]

Pulling the Threads Together: EEH as Theological Praxis

In summary, Grimké's ministry was shaped by three constructs that provide a common language for understanding the relationship between his theological framework and social activism.

Biblical Theology: As defined, biblical theology seeks to understand the theology contained within the Bible itself.[55] It tracks the progressive revelation of God throughout scripture, discerning the narrative arc that links various texts and periods. Both Paul and Grimké practiced a biblical theology that was not merely descriptive of God's

---

[49] Alcántara, *Preaching*, 99–100.
[50] Cf. 1 Corinthians 9:22 ESV.
[51] Alcántara, *Preaching*, 117–20.
[52] LaRue, *Heart*, 34.
[53] Ibid., 37–38.
[54] Ferry, "Puritan," 356–57.
[55] Klink, *Biblical Theology*, 14.

work but also demanded action. They believed that the message of scripture calls for an application that speaks to the present social realities. For Grimké, this meant engaging scripture to confront racial injustice in his time, while for Paul, it involved addressing the divisions and hostilities that threatened the early church.

Gospel Preaching: Gospel preaching is the announcement of the good news that, through the life, death, and resurrection of Jesus Christ, God has reconciled sinners to Himself and to one another, breaking down all divisions to create one united people in Christ.[56] Paul and Grimké emphasized that this reconciliation extends beyond personal salvation and carries pronounced ethical implications within the Christian community. Paul's letter to Philemon, which will be explored in Chapter 4, is a notable example of how this reconciliation affected social relationships. Beyond Philemon, Paul's letters often addressed broader social ethics, such as in Galatians 3:28, where he proclaimed that there is "neither Jew nor Greek . . . for you are all one in Christ Jesus," and in Romans 12:10, urging believers to "honor one another above yourselves." Their preaching centered on how believers should relate to one another, particularly in rejecting ethnic divisions and fostering unity in Christ. Paul's letters to the Galatians and Romans provide foundational examples of his insistence on gospel-embodied unity, while Grimké's sermons, embodying the same ethos, confronted the racial divides and injustices within the American church.[57]

Social Activism: Activism is the intentional proclamation and embodiment of the gospel's indicatives. In other words, it is to "live what you preach."[58] Social activism is defined as organized efforts to

---

[56] Cf. Romans 5:10–11; 2 Corinthians 5:18–20; Galatians 3:28; Ephesians 2:13–16, 4:3–6; Colossians 1:20–22.

[57] Reader's note: Like Paul, Grimké embodied the gospel's indicatives beyond racial prejudice. He was equally adamant in his activism for marriage, temperance, and women's suffrage. See Ferry, "Puritan," 126, 164.

[58] Grimké, *Works III*, 103–104. Grimké writes, "Words are cheap; it is easy to speak; it is not so easy to live, to show by our example what we really believe about it. How many, many there are among us who can talk well and

effect social change, grounded in biblical justice, mercy, and human dignity, as implied in Jesus' echoed commandment to "love your neighbor as your [equal]."[59] With this backdrop, Grimké extended Paul's gospel indicatives to confront broader societal issues such as lynching, segregation, and systemic violence against African Americans. He believed that these social injustices not only violated human dignity but also compromised the church's witness to the gospel.[60] For Grimké, social activism was not an add-on to the gospel but a necessary outworking of it, aimed at preserving life and dignity so that the opportunity to receive the gospel message could be made available to all.

These foundational concepts—biblical theology, gospel preaching, and social activism—demonstrate that Paul's and Grimké's ministries were concerned not only with the spiritual life of the church but also with addressing the social realities that jeopardized the integrity of the gospel and the well-being of those who needed to hear it. While Paul's pushback against ethnic divisions is often interpreted as limited to the Christian community, his broader mission to the Gentiles shows that his message inherently disrupted societal and ethnic boundaries beyond the church.[61] Grimké, deeply aligned with this vision, extended the gospel's social implications even further,

---

eloquently about Christianity, but whose lives are but poor commentaries upon the faith which we profess. A Christianity that is lived, in its simplicity and power, is what is most sorely needed everywhere."

[59] Cf. Leviticus 19:18; Matt. 22:39; Mark 12:31. Scholars such as N.T. Wright and Craig Keener argue that "as yourself" carries an implication of loving others with equal regard, going beyond mere empathy to a standard of equality that holds others' welfare as closely as one's own. See Craig S. Keener, *The Gospel of Matthew: A Socio-Rhetorical Commentary* (Grand Rapids: Wm. B. Eerdmans, 2009), 200–201; N.T. Wright, *Matthew for Everyone, Part 2: Chapters 16–28* (Louisville: Westminster John Knox Press, 2004), 95.

[60] Grimké, *Works III*, 19.

[61] Cf. Romans 1:5, 13–14; Galatians 3:28; Ephesians 2:11–14, 3:6; Colossians 3:11; Acts 17:26. Also, Crisler, "Interview 5."

confronting racial injustice both within and beyond the church to uphold human dignity and ensure that the message of salvation could reach all.

By defining these terms early on, we establish a common language that enables us to articulate more clearly the theological and practical dimensions of Grimké's EEH as this treatise progresses.

Setting the Stage: History, Theology, and Context

This treatise concerns events at a crucial juncture in American history, exploring the interplay between evangelical, Pauline-patterned preaching and social activism as exemplified in the life and ministry of Grimké. In short, this is an interdisciplinary study that intersects history and biblical studies through Grimké's life narrative, his homiletic as a gospel preaching social activist, and his use of echoes from the Apostle Paul and the Old Testament (OT) Hebrew poets to catalyze his audience.[62]

Post-Civil War America: The World Grimké Preached In

Grimké's ministry unfolded during a pivotal era in American history, marked by the aftermath of the Civil War and the ensuing struggles of post-Reconstruction. This period was characterized by violence and profound ethnic and economic schisms that deeply

---

[62] Chapters 4 and 5 of this treatise will further develop this exploration of the interplay between evangelical, Pauline-patterned preaching and social activism. Chapter 4, "The Pauline Praxis: Subversive Echoes of a Hebrew Prophet," analyzes Paul's theological framework and his subversive challenge to social norms, while Chapter 5, "The Grimké Echo: Courageous Emancipatory Echoes of a Hebrew Poet," demonstrates how Grimké's preaching echoes Paul's approach and incorporates OT penitential themes to confront racial injustices and inspire social change. The two chapters are closely connected, as Chapter 5 shows how Grimké builds upon the theological and social model established by Paul in Chapter 4.

divided the nation.[63] The treatise examines how these historical realities influenced Grimké's preaching and activism. Understanding this era's complex dynamics is essential for appreciating Grimké's response to the challenges of his time and the broader evangelical engagement with social issues.

Grimké and Paul: Echoes of Gospel Conviction

Grimké wittingly and unwittingly echoed Paul's pastoral fervor, earnestness, and devotion to the gospel throughout his fifty years of ministry in the pulpit and public square. This treatment explores how Grimké's admiration for Paul shaped his approach to preaching and how he embodied Pauline thought to address the racial issues of his day.[64]

Preaching Amid Prejudice: The Culture Grimké Confronted

Grimké ministered in a society grappling with the legacy of slavery, entrenched (or systemic) ethnic prejudices, and the struggle for civil rights. This treatise parses how these sociocultural factors influenced Grimké's pastoral and public responses to ethnic prejudice. It examines how he navigated the cultural landscape of his time, using the gospel to challenge unchristian societal practices while concomitantly advocating for an end to ethnic prejudice.

The Church Divided: Evangelism's Mixed Witness

The study also considers the ecclesiastical environment in which Grimké operated. Much like today, the evangelical church wrestled

---

[63] Carter G. Woodson, "Fifty Years of Negro Citizenship as Qualified by the United States Supreme Court," *Journal of Negro History* 6, no. 1 (January 1921): 1–53, https://www.jstor.org/stable/271387. The cultural milieu of the nation surrounding race prejudice and civil rights was complex and dynamic. Woodson's post-Civil War analysis provides an incisive overview of the structural realities that informed the nation's hostilities and divisions.

[64] Grimké, *Works III*, 40.

with its role in addressing social injustices during this period.[65] Grimké's ministry provides a lens through which to view the broader evangelical response to the social issues of the era. The treatise explores how Grimké's approach to these issues reflected and influenced the evangelical church's stance on racial equality and justice.

Grimké's Pauline Imprint: From Epistles to Pulpit

Last, the research situates Grimké within the Pauline tradition, exploring how his preaching and social engagement, in his estimation, echoed the apostolic example of Paul.[66] This involves a detailed examination of how Grimké, consciously and subconsciously, embodied *Pauline praxis* [emphasis] in his context, particularly concerning ethnic prejudice.

In sum, the general context for this study is multifaced, encompassing the historical, theological, sociological, and ecclesiastical dimensions of Grimké's ministry. This approach provides a backdrop against which to examine Grimké's evangelical confrontation of ethnic prejudice, offering insights into the practical application of Pauline thought in a divided nation and its implications for present-day evangelical thought and practice.

Why Grimké's Voice Still Speaks

The ensuing study has seven observable implications. An overview of each contribution follows:

---

[65] Robert F. Schwarzwalder, Jr., "'For a Real, Not a Sham Christianity': Francis J. Grimké on Racial Strife and World Peace in the Early Twentieth Century," *Fides et Historia* 53, no. 2 (Summer/Fall 2021): 21.

[66] Grimké, *Works III*, 453. Quoting Dr. Robert E Speer, Grimké journaled, "The Holy Spirit can do today for the modern Church what he did for the Apostolic Church. The only personnel we need is the lives of men and women, with few talents or many, surrendered to and controlled by the Holy Spirit. . . . [T]hen the Church will move outward, and forward as a unity . . . with full efficiency."

Challenging Normative Ecclesiastical Perspectives

This treatise carries significance as it details the unique positioning of Francis James Grimké's ministry, which is distinct from the typical stances of his contemporary white clergy in the Presbyterian denomination and divergent from certain conservative, "accommodationist" African American preachers. [67] By assessing Grimké's pulpit and public square discourse, the study sheds light on how his echoed embodiment of the Pauline tradition engaged and often upset (subverted) the prevalent ecclesiastical perspectives of his time.

Contributions to Ecclesiastical and Social Understanding

Furthermore, this research fosters a richer understanding of the complexities of the ecclesiastical response to ethnic and social issues in post-Civil War America. Grimké's approach provides an insightful case study for understanding how evangelical thought and practice can diverge from mainstream denominational positions when addressing societal issues. Even more, this study highlights how a critical voice thoughtfully demonstrated evangelical doctrinal integrity *by* [my emphasis] addressing the pressing social injustices of the era and framing their source as enemies of the gospel.

While there are significant descriptive accounts concerning the evangelical response to racism in America, there are no known scholarly instructive examples, particularly in homiletics. This study aims to fill that gap.

Homiletical and Theological Innovation

This study offers insights into integral, innovative homiletical practices and theological interpretations. Grimké's incisive approach to

---

[67] Mark Sidwell, "Francis Grimké and the Value and the Limits of Carter Woodson's Model of the Progressive Black Pastor," *Fides et Historia* 32, no. 1 (Winter/Spring 2000): 111.

the pulpit and public discourse, which resonated with the Pauline tradition yet stood in contrast to his contemporaries' typical narratives, endows the homiletics field by providing a paradigm for preaching that is firmly established in scripture while boldly addressing societal realities.

Practical Implications for Contemporary Evangelical Thought

The practical implications of this study for modern evangelicalism are curiously compelling. Grimké's ministry is an example of how studied biblical and theological convictions inform active social engagement. This research is a resource for gospel adherents seeking to navigate the complex historical dynamics of faith, *race* [emphasis added], and justice in contemporary society.[68]

Reconsidering Evangelical Social Activism

This treatise frames an expanded theological discourse by reexamining evangelical social activism.[69] It invites contemporary ecclesial leaders to reflect critically on the historical roots and

---

[68] Monroe N. Work, "The Passing Tradition and the African Civilization," *Journal of Negro History* 1, no. 1 (January 1916): 34, https://www.jstor.org/stable/2713514. Work astutely observes, "The bringing of the first Negroes from Africa as slaves was justified on the grounds that they were heathen. It was not right, it was argued, for Christians to enslave Christians, but they could enslave heathen, who as a result would have an opportunity to become Christians. These Negro slaves did actually become Christians and as a result the colonists were forced to find other grounds to justify their continuation of the system. The next argument was that they were different from white people. Here we have a large part of the beginnings of the doctrine of the inferiority of the Negro." This article scientifically delineates the cultural ideologies that have historically driven ethnic hostilities in America.

[69] Timothy Larsen, *Every Leaf, Line, and Letter: Evangelicals and the Bible from the 1730s to the Present* (Downers Grove, IL: IVP Academic, 2021), 196–217. Ref. Chapter 9, Malcolm Foley, "'The Only Way to Stop a Mob': Francis Grimké's Biblical Case for Lynching Resistance."

trajectories of their engagement with social issues, encouraging them to consider how exemplars like Grimké can inform present practices and approaches.

Academic and Cultural Relevance

Academically, this study advances research in Pauline studies, American church history, practical theology, and homiletics by analyzing the distinct approach of a notable figure in the evangelical tradition. In particular, the contribution to Pauline studies focuses on *Reception History*—how subsequent interpreters, like Grimké, engaged Paul's teachings within their own unique historical situations.[70] Culturally, this work addresses broader conversations about race, justice, and the role of the gospel in societal change, inviting a nuanced understanding of ecclesial approaches to societal challenges.

Emancipatory Pedagogical Processes

This study underscores Grimké's homiletic, akin to the Apostle Paul's, as primarily driven towards the heart or affective domain, facilitating emancipatory learning and homiletics. Drawing from Greene's assertion in *The Dialectic of Freedom* that authentic expressions of hope and ideals are grounded in embedded memories and histories, this work asserts that the artful and committed presentation of the gospel is a head and heart transformational instrument.[71] It empowers preachers to activism over and against the world's hostilities, highlighting the role of gospel preaching as an emancipatory tool capable of confronting and impacting all forms of unchristian prejudice.

---

[70] Channing L. Crisler, "Interview 3," interviewed by Eric J. Freeman, November 16, 2023.
[71] Green, *Dialectic*, 3.

Overall, this treatise underscores the enduring resonance of a gospel-embodied approach to social justice as exemplified in the life and ministry of Francis James Grimké.

Boundaries of Focus: What This Study Covers—and What it Doesn't

While panoramic in its approach to exploring the pulpit and public ministry of Francis James Grimké, this treatise is delineated by specific boundaries that focus on and define its scope. These delimitations are registered to maintain a clear and targeted exploration of Grimké's unique contribution to the evangelical response to ethnic prejudice within the specified historical, theological, and cultural contexts.

Focus on Grimké's Distinctive Approach

The primary delimitation of this study is its concentration on Grimké's specific approach to preaching and public ministry, particularly in how it aligns with and diverges from the Pauline tradition. While Grimké was a part of the broader Presbyterian denomination, this study delineates explicitly his ministry as distinct from the typical positions of his white clergy contemporaries and divergent from certain conservative, "accommodationist" African American preachers of his time.

Moreover, this study necessarily emphasizes Grimké's engagement with Pauline praxis, particularly in ways that echo the scope of this research. Although Grimké's entire body of preaching spans the breadth of biblical scripture—a scope not fully accessible in this study—we capture an important dimension of it through Paul's characteristic use of OT scripture in his epistles.[72] In short, while this

[72] Richard B. Hays, *Echoes of Scripture in the Letters of Paul*, new ed. (New Haven, CT: Yale University Press, 1993), 29–33. Reader's note: Hays's seven tests for hearing echoes will serve as an approximator in assessing Pauline echoes in Grimké.

study maintains a narrow focus, those limitations do not compromise the essence of either the Apostle Paul's teachings or Grimké's ethos.

Historical Period

The treatise is delimited to the historical period surrounding Grimké's most active years in ministry, primarily the post-Civil War era in America from 1878 to 1928. This period is critical for understanding the social and cultural dynamics that shaped Grimké's approach. The study does not extend into a thorough historical analysis beyond this era, except where directly relevant to providing context for Grimké's ministry.

Theological Scope

The study is delimited to examining Grimké's theological embodiment of the Pauline tradition as an African American Reformed Presbyterian pastor. While acknowledging that Grimké's theological perspectives may have been influenced by various other theological traditions and contemporary religious thought, the focus remains on how he integrated Pauline thought into his response to ethnic prejudice and its inimical forces.

Geographical and Cultural Context

The treatise is geographically and culturally confined to Grimké's experience and ministry within the United States, particularly in the context of the societal aftermath of the Civil War. This delimitation provides a specific cultural and social backdrop against which Grimké's ministry is analyzed without extending into a comparative study of similar figures in different cultural or national contexts.

Homiletical and Public Ministry

Another key delimitation is the focus on Grimké's preaching and public ministry activities. This study emphasizes his sermons, speeches, and writings, specifically analyzing how he utilized these media to address the issue of ethnic prejudice. Other aspects of his ministry, such as pastoral care or church administration, are not the primary focus of this study unless they directly contribute to understanding his approach to preaching and public engagement.

Theoretical Framework

Finally, the research is framed within a Pauline–Grimkéan hermeneutic, a specific interpretive lens that combines Paul's homiletical ethos with Grimké's homiletical praxis through the matrix of the Bebbington quadrilateral. This delimitation means the study's findings and conclusions are primarily derived from and relevant to this particular hermeneutical approach.

These delimitations are set to warrant that the treatise remains focused on its core aim of exploring Francis James Grimké's unique approach to addressing ethnic prejudice within the evangelical context, as influenced by Pauline thought, and its pedagogical implications for contemporary evangelical thought and practice in homiletics.

Recognizing the Study's Limits: Harmonizing Echoes in the "Key of Dissonance"

This study anticipates, acknowledges, and addresses the potential challenges and complexities of its intended course—in short, its limitations. While the goal is to harmonize the homiletical ethos of Francis James Grimké with that of the Apostle Paul, certain methodological decisions—such as limiting the depth of sermon analysis in the main body—reflect strategic choices aimed at maintaining thematic clarity while presenting opportunities to enhance the study's rigor through supplementary materials.

1. **Complex Hermeneutic Interpretations**: Synthesizing a Pauline–Grimkéan hermeneutic requires careful navigation between two complex theological and historical landscapes. The risk of oversimplification or misinterpretation of these

perspectives is appreciable. This research employs a meticulous and reflexive approach to ensure that both Paul's and Grimké's voices are represented with fidelity and depth.

2. **Primary Source Constraints**: The reliance on Grimké's sermons, speeches, and writings presents challenges regarding the availability and completeness of these sources. This study represents a thorough review of the available archives and collections, acknowledging that the limitations in primary sources may also shape the study's scope and depth.

3. **Historical Contextualization**: While rich in historical significance, the post-Civil War American context is fraught with complexities. The research is grounded in an interdisciplinary reflective understanding of this era to foster a careful contextual and historical analysis.

4. **Theological Neutrality and Bias**: Given the theological nature of this study, maintaining an objective stance is challenging. Recognizing personal biases and theological viewpoints through peer review processes is essential to safeguard a balanced interpretation of Grimké's and Paul's theological positions and their implications for addressing ethnic prejudice.

5. **Generalizability of Findings**: The specific focus on Grimké within a historical context poses questions about the relevance and applicability of findings to contemporary issues. Differences in social, political, and cultural contexts between Grimké's time and today—such as changes in racial dynamics, activism methods, and church practices—may limit the direct correlation of his praxis. This research critically analyzes how Grimké's principles can be codified and adapted

to modern contexts to ensure the study's present-day relevance and implications.

6. **Integrating Doctrinal and Sociocultural Relevance**: This study explores how Grimké harmonized doctrinal integrity with sociocultural responsiveness. Operating this parity requires a piercing understanding of theological doctrines and the sociocultural dynamics of his time.

7. **Theoretical Framework Limitations**: Adopting a specific hermeneutical framework provides a focused lens but limits the scope to alternative theological interpretations. This research takes account of these limitations, exploring and acknowledging diverse perspectives where relevant.

8. **Focused Sermon Analysis in the Main Body**: This study strategically limits detailed sermon analysis in the main body to one pivotal sermon, using it as a representative example of Grimké's homiletic methodology and alignment with Pauline echoes. While this approach provides thematic clarity and narrative focus, it may risk underrepresenting the breadth of Grimké's homiletical contributions. To address this limitation, additional analyses of Grimké's sermons spanning multiple decades are included in the appendix, ensuring that readers have access to a more comprehensive resource for further exploration.

The complexities and challenges of an enterprise of this nature are anticipated and will continue to be acknowledged as presented. Doing so sets the stage for a study that contributes meaningfully to historical and theological understanding and engages critically with its own methodological and interpretive frameworks.

Exploring Grimké's Voice: Method, Movement, and Meaning

This book employs a structured, three-stage research design to examine how Francis James Grimké's preaching, shaped by Pauline theology, offers a faithful and contextually responsive model for evangelical engagement with ethnic prejudice. Using a comparative critical analysis, this approach situates Grimké within the broader historical narrative of evangelicalism's public witness, particularly in response to social injustice. Following a three-stage research technique, the proposed treatise adopts a comparative critical analysis method to explore the evangelical church's response to ethnic prejudice through Grimké's preaching. This approach situates Grimké's voice within the broader historical narrative of evangelicalism's engagement with social issues, drawing parallels with the Apostle Paul's motif of challenging unrighteous social conventions through the gospel.

Stage 1: Exploratory Research (Literature Review and Biographical Sketch)

The initial phase, executed in Chapters 2 and 3, involves an exploratory literature review and biographical sketch to establish a theoretical foundation and contextual background for the study. This phase begins with defining key concepts such as scriptural echoes, Pauline theology, and evangelical homiletics, while reviewing the theoretical foundations of the literary phenomenon known as the aural metaphor of "echo" and its relevance in biblical theology.[73] It continues with a historical survey of key figures who echoed Pauline theology in their preaching and writings, including John Chrysostom, Augustine of Hippo, Martin Luther, John Calvin, and others, analyzing their contributions and how they utilized Pauline themes to address contemporary issues. Finally, this stage provides an overview of Grimké's personal biography, early life, education, and conversion

[73] A full treatment of this phenomenon will be provided in Chapter 2, Section 1.

experience, examining his pastoral tenure with a focus on his reliance on scriptures, emphasis on Christ's crucifixion, and advocacy for social justice. The analysis also explores how Grimké's personal piety influenced his approach to addressing ethnic prejudice and social injustices through a Pauline praxis.

Stage 2: Descriptive Comparative Research (Chapters 4 and 5)

The second stage of the methodology employs a descriptive comparative analysis to examine the theological expressions and homiletical strategies of the Apostle Paul and Grimké. In Chapter 4, the study begins with an exploration of Paul's subversive homiletic as depicted in his epistles. This involves defining key terms such as subversion, praxis, and social and hierarchical ethics to contextualize Paul's approach to challenging social norms. The chapter then delves into a detailed examination of Paul's writings, specifically the interpretations and misinterpretations of Romans 13:1 and the Epistle to Philemon. By analyzing various historical and modern perspectives on these texts, this study uncovers how Paul's teachings were used to address issues of obedience, authority, and social justice. This analysis sets the stage for appreciating how Paul's subversive use of OT textual and thematic echoes and hierarchical ethics influenced his broader theological framework and public ministry.

In Chapter 5, the focus shifts to Grimké, whose sermons and public addresses are analyzed through the lens of the penitential psalms and within the context of the reformed tradition. This chapter provides an overview of the penitential psalms and their historical interpretations across Jewish, early Christian, medieval, and reformed traditions, highlighting their theological and homiletical significance. The chapter then presents a detailed examination of how Grimké integrated themes from these psalms into his preaching, particularly in his sermons on Psalm 27. By drawing parallels between Grimké's homiletical strategies and Paul's use of scriptural echoes, the study reveals how Grimké employed Pauline interpretive methods to address racial injustices and promote social reform. This comparative analysis not only highlights the continuity between Paul's and Grimké's approaches, but also demonstrates how Grimké adapted these methods to confront the specific social and racial challenges of his time.

Stage Three: Causal–Comparative Synthesis and Implications (Chapters 6 and 7)

The final stage of the methodology involves a causal–comparative synthesis and implications analysis to understand why Grimké's evangelical approach was effective in addressing ethnic prejudice and social injustices. In Chapter 6, the treatise explores echoes as an activist evangelical emancipatory homiletic (EEH), examining how Grimké's life experiences, theological training, and personal piety shaped his unique approach to preaching. This chapter analyzes how Grimké creatively employed Pauline theological themes such as biblicism, crucicentrism, conversionism, and activism to craft sermons that resonated deeply with his congregation and broader society. By investigating the causal factors behind Grimké's interpretive practices and their impact, the study uncovers the underlying theological principles and contextual dynamics that made his homiletic so powerful in confronting racial injustices. Chapter 7 provides an overview of the findings and implications of the research conducted in Chapters 2 through 6.

Chapter Outline

1. **Gospel Foundations: Evangelical Preaching in a Divided World.** This chapter introduces the historical, theological, and sociocultural context that shaped Francis James Grimké's ministry. It outlines the book's central claim—that Grimké's preaching embodied a Pauline-inspired evangelical response to ethnic prejudice—and introduces key concepts such as Evangelical Emancipatory Homiletics (EEH). The chapter also highlights gaps in existing scholarship and explains the

methodological approach, providing a foundational understanding of how Grimké's post-Civil War context and Reformed convictions informed his vision of gospel-centered justice.

2. **Socially Charged Echoes: The Gospel Witness, Paul, Grimké, et al.** Chapter 2 surveys the biblical and historical tradition of using scriptural "echoes" to proclaim the gospel in times of crisis. An examination of how the Apostle Paul, Francis Grimké, and other influential figures, such as Augustine, Luther, and Calvin, employed Pauline themes in ways that addressed the spiritual and social challenges of their respective contexts. This chapter situates Grimké within that interpretive tradition, emphasizing how gospel echoes function as both theological proclamation and moral confrontation.

3. **The Making of an Evangelical Emancipator.** This chapter explores the formative experiences that shaped Francis Grimké's identity as both preacher and activist. It introduces his early life under slavery, his theological training at Lincoln University and Princeton Seminary, and his emergence as a leading Reformed evangelical voice. Grimké's lived experiences, academic formation, and historical context converge to form a gospel witness defined by doctrinal fidelity and a resolute commitment to social emancipation.

4. **The Pauline Praxis: Subversive Emancipatory Echoes of a Hebrew Prophet.** Chapter 4 explores how Paul's epistles model a subversive homiletic that disrupts social hierarchies and ethnic hostilities. By examining how Paul's pastoral letters challenged systems of power within the early church and laid the groundwork for gospel-embodied activism, this chapter pays special attention to Paul's use of Hebrew prophetic

themes and scriptural reinterpretation to confront injustice, offering a theological framework that Grimké would later echo in his own preaching.

5. **The Grimké Echo: Courageous Emancipatory Echoes of a Hebrew Poet.** Building on the previous chapter, this section analyzes Grimké's sermons through the lens of penitential psalms and Pauline echoes. Through lament, repentance, and poetic expression, Grimké called his audience to moral clarity and social responsibility. The chapter offers an in-depth look at his sermon on Psalm 27, revealing how his integration of biblical poetry and Pauline theology became a powerful instrument for confronting ethnic prejudice in the American church.

6. **The Echo Continued: Toward an Evangelical Emancipatory Homiletic (EEH).** This chapter draws together key insights to define the structure and purpose of Grimké's Evangelical Emancipatory Homiletic. Readers will learn how Grimké's preaching incorporated Pauline emphases—biblicism, crucicentrism, conversionism, and activism—to create a gospel witness that spoke both to the soul and to society. The chapter concludes by articulating how Grimké's EEH offers a practical and theological model for preaching that engages the spiritual and social crises of today.

7. **Preaching the Transforms: Key Insights and the Way Forward.** This chapter draws together key insights to define the structure and purpose of Grimké's Evangelical Emancipatory Homiletic. His preaching incorporated Pauline emphases—biblicism, crucicentrism, conversionism, and activism—to create a gospel witness that addressed both soul and society. The chapter concludes by articulating how Grimké's EEH offers a practical and theological model for

preaching that faithfully engages the spiritual and social crises of the present day.

Appendix I: Textual and Thematic Echoes in the Preaching of Jesus and Paul. This appendix provides Tables of the textual and thematic echoes used by Jesus, Paul, and other NT writers, as referenced in Chapter 2.

Appendix II: Emancipatory Echoes of a Hebrew Poet. This appendix outlines five key principles for preaching Penitential Psalms, focusing on divine presence, contemporary relevance, prayer, hope, and community, as detailed in Table 1: Five-Fold Principles for Preaching Penitential Psalms. These principles are analyzed in Table 2: Analysis: Five-Fold Principles for Preaching Penitential Psalms, using Grimké's sermons to show their relevance to personal and communal struggles. Table 3: Linguistic Analysis of Psalm 27 provides an analysis of the language and themes within the Psalm. Each Table supports references in Chapter 5.

Appendix III: God and Prayer as Factors in the Struggle. This appendix presents Grimké's sermon manuscript with annotations detailing its unique attributes as a sermon on Psalm 27 with a social activist focus, as referenced in Chapter 5.

Appendix IV: Prominent Notes of an Evangelical Activist: Three Decades of Activist Preaching. This appendix provides a timeline of Grimké's socially charged sermons from 1892–1921, annotating and archiving seven manuscripts for future research.

Through this structured methodology, the treatise contributes a nuanced understanding of Grimké's theological and homiletical approach to ethnic prejudice, situating it within the legacy of the Apostle Paul's gospel mission. This investigation articulates a response grounded in the evangelical tradition while addressing one of America's most enduring social challenges—race prejudice.[74]

[74] Reader's Note: The idiom "race prejudice" is used by Grimké throughout his corpus and thereby employed in this analysis.

CHAPTER 2

SOCIALLY CHARGED ECHOES: THE GOSPEL WITNESS, PAUL, GRIMKÉ, ET AL.

We come now to an exploration of the dynamic interplay between the biblical witness and engagement with contemporary social issues, as articulated through Grimké's homiletic. Following the apostolic example of Paul, Grimké used the biblical text to confront the pressing social and pastoral challenges of his time—particularly ethnic and racial tensions. This literature review traces the theological and historical continuities that frame such engagements. By examining the use of scriptural echoes from biblical times to Grimké's era, this analysis underscores the enduring relevance and transformational power of scripture in addressing societal challenges through a gospel-embodied homiletic—or, more succinctly, through the gospel. Three sections structure this dialogue.

Section 1—Echoes: A Biblical Precedence

Section 1 of this discourse explores the OT's intrinsic role in shaping NT discourse, illustrating how the Apostle Paul, Jesus (as reported in the gospels), and other NT writers routinely engaged the Hebrew scriptures.[1] These scriptural echoes were more than strategic or rhetorical devices but principled patterns deeply embedded and embodied within the ethos of the early Christian church. In this review

---

[1] Note: The "echoes" of "Jesus (as reported in the gospels)" are observed to establish a general pattern of OT scriptural echoes amidst the earliest Christ followers. The extended discourse surrounding the Jesus of history versus the Christ of the faith is beyond the scope of this work, as our primary focus is the Pauline corpus and its interaction with Grimké. For more on this, see Craig S. Keener, *The Historical Jesus of the Gospels* (Grand Rapids, MI: Eerdmans, 2009); John P. Meier, *A Marginal Jew: Rethinking the Historical Jesus,* 5 vols. (New Haven, CT: Yale University Press, 1991–2016); E. P. Sanders, *Jesus and Judaism* (Philadelphia: Fortress Press, 1985).

portion, an echo is defined as either a direct or indirect reference made by NT writers to OT texts, manifesting as explicit textual quotations or subtler thematic and narrative reflections resulting in the embodiment of OT wisdom to address NT realities. Such reverence for the OT reflects a continuation and affirmation of the faith traditions established by the earliest Christians, who identified the written word of God as authoritative and directly applicable to the challenges and circumstances of NT communities. Moreover, this practice betrays a high view of scripture as a living, breathing guide whose teachings, though historical, were dynamically relevant to the ongoing spiritual and communal life of the early church.

Through this lens, Section 1 sets the stage for understanding Francis James Grimké's similar use of biblical echoes, highlighting his alignment with a long-standing tradition of scriptural engagement to address and challenge his time's social and ethical issues. This dual framework of examining textual and thematic echoes—direct citations or allusions and the adoption of similar thought patterns and themes—guides our analysis to facilitate a more structured exploration of the intertextual connections employed both within the biblical canon and within the interpretive and homiletical traditions of the church.

Section 2—Survey of Pivotal Historical Pauline Echoers

Section 2 surveys the enduring legacy of Pauline echoes deployed by seminal theologians across numerous crucial epochs in church history. By offering an overview of the interpretive practices of Chrysostom, Augustine, John of Damascus, Peter Abelard, Aquinas, Luther, Calvin, and contemporaries of Grimké, this exploration highlights how these figures adapted Paul's teachings to meet their times' spiritual and communal demands. Each theologian and homiletician represents a pivotal period in developing Western Christian thought, illustrating the broad and evolving engagement with Pauline scriptures that has shaped theological discourse and church practices throughout the centuries.

1. John Chrysostom (c. 349–407)
2. Augustine of Hippo (354–430)
3. John of Damascus (675 or 676–749)
4. Peter Abelard (1079–1142)
5. Thomas Aquinas (1225–1274)
6. Martin Luther (1483–1546)
7. John Calvin (1509–1564)
8. Daniel Alexander Payne (1811–1893)
9. Alexander Crummell (1819–1898)

By surveying these church leaders and theologians' engagement with Paul's teachings, this section illustrates the persistent presence of Pauline echoes throughout church history, setting the stage for understanding how Francis James Grimké later embodied these historical and theological precedents to confront the social and ethical challenges of his time. This historical survey highlights the influence of Pauline motifs through critical moments in church history—culminating in their use by Grimké.

Section 3—Grimké, the Emancipated "Echoer"

This section details the corpus that documents Francis James Grimké's pastoral tenure, highlighting his biography and reformed evangelical licitness—and their influence on his Pauline-patterned pulpit and public discourse as he addressed ethnic or racial tensions. Additionally, Grimké's commitment to personal piety markedly shaped his homiletic. This portion demonstrates that Grimké's puritanical inclinations were not isolated from the broader social context but were intrinsically causal in his responses to social injustices and his advocacy for civil rights.[2]

---

[2] The author contends that Grimké's experiences with enslavement, emancipation, and evangelical education distinctly shaped his Pauline-patterned gospel homiletic, developing it into an "evangelical emancipatory

Section 1—Echoes: A Biblical Precedence

Every Scripture is God-breathed and profitable for teaching, for reproof, for correction, and for instruction in righteousness.

2 Timothy 3:16

A careful examination of NT writings reveals a pronounced presence of OT scriptural references. These episodes of intertextual engagement are literary operatives, generally, but not always technically, referred to as echoes.[3] The execution of these echoes extends beyond repeating or reciting the Hebrew Bible or simply reinterpreting the ancient text; more principally, it suggests an underlying ethos of how

homiletic" (EEH). The author further proposes that this EEH represents an activist approach to preaching that embodies and echoes the *Pauline praxis* [emphasis]. Importantly, the EEH is presented here as a historical descriptor of Grimké's distinct, contextual embodiment of Paul's *hermeneutic and heart* [my emphasis].

[3] Richard B. Hays, *Echoes of Scripture in the Gospels* (Waco, TX: Baylor University Press, 2016), 2–10. Hereafter cited as Hays, *Gospels*. A detailed treatment of the criticism and various voices that characterize literary echoes is beyond the purview of a preaching treatise. Because the objective of this exercise is to establish biblical precedence for scripturally based proclamation (we argue that the earliest preachers of the gospel of Jesus Christ ordinarily and reflexively used OT scripture to support their claims), the term echo in this body operates as an umbrella term to capture what Hays "approximates" as "scriptural citations, allusions, and echoes." For clues to further investigation, see Stanley Porter, "The Use of the Old Testament in the New Testament: A Brief Comment on Method and Terminology," in *Early Christian Interpretation of the Scriptures of Israel: Investigations and Proposals*, eds. Craig A. Evans and James A. Sanders (Sheffield: Sheffield Academic Press, 1997), 79–96, and Stanley Porter, "Further Comments on the Use of the Old Testament in the New Testament," in *The Intertextuality of the Epistles: Explorations of Theory and Practice*, eds. Thomas L. Brodie, Dennis R. MacDonald, and Stanley E. Porter (Sheffield: Sheffield Phoenix Press, 2006), 98–110. See also note 14 in Chapter 1.f

the earliest preachers of the Gospel of Jesus Christ understood, proclaimed, and lived their faith.[4]

Referencing the criticism of NT scholar Richard B. Hays, this phenomenon of echoes in the NT is most apparent through a cataloged display of the application and embodiment of scriptural echoes by Jesus (as reported in the gospels) and the Apostle Paul—noting how they employed echoes to engage the particularities of their communities dialectically.[5] Their *reflexive and creative instinct* [my emphasis] in doing so demonstrated an implicit inclination to the contextual engagement and embodiment of the Hebrew scriptures to herald the gospel's soteriological and, simultaneously, sociological indicatives.[6] Moreover, for both Jesus and Paul, the gospel's saving power boasted a vertical (theological) and horizontal (sociological) delta. Consequently, Jesus and the Apostle Paul epitomized and established their gospel announcement on God's expressed word as it dwelt among the individual and the corporate body.[7]

This work proposes that understanding these patterned and patented scriptural echoes, as modeled by Jesus, the Apostle Paul, and others within the NT writ, is foundational in developing a homiletic or preaching praxis that is biblical, socially relevant, and soteriologically sound. Borrowing from Alcántara's *The Practices of*

---

[4] Ibid., 1–3. Note Hays's commentary on Luther's "figural reading" of the gospels.

[5] Ibid., 7–8. Hays writes, "I do not want to be understood as suggesting that the Evangelists were engaged in fanciful Promethean poetic creativity. . . . As long ago as my book *Echoes of Scripture in the Letters of Paul*, I was fumbling toward articulating something like this by arguing that Paul's interpretation of the Old Testament was an instance of 'dialectical,' rather than 'heuristic,' intertextuality." See Tables 1–4.

[6] Hays, *Letters*, x–xii. Reader's note: Hays is not primarily concerned with the historical contexts of Paul's letters but with their literary characteristics. We extend Hays's investigation by considering the historical context of Paul's pastoral letters and examining the pragmatic sociological implications of their dialectic.

[7] Cf. John 1:14; Romans 1:15–17.

Christian Preaching, we ultimately assert that all constructive gospel preaching relevant to the day's issues requires a scriptural foundation.[8] Or, as Grimké journaled, "Our duty is to preach what the Bible teaches, its ideals, principles, great truths concerning God and man, sin and righteousness, never mind what others may think or say."[9]

Theoretical Foundations

The construct of echoes in biblical interpretation is central to demonstrating how scriptural actors engaged with, interpretively adapted, and embodied OT scriptures. This hermeneutical approach, primarily shaped within the disciplines of literary criticism and NT scholarship by Hollander and Hays, offers key insights that bridge literary theory and biblical scholarship to advance critical research on scriptural intertextuality. Applying such an apparatus to homiletics, especially the homiletic of Grimké, is the anticipated contribution of this pragmatic study.

In his formative works *Echoes of Scripture in the Letters of Paul* and *Echoes of Scripture in the Gospels*, Hays parses the nuanced ways NT authors, particularly Paul and the gospel writers (for this review, primarily gospel writings attributed to the sayings of Jesus), invoke and transform OT texts to articulate fresh theological assertions.[10] Building upon John Hollander's "trope of metalepsis," Hays constructs a robust analytical framework for examining how these echoes function as textual reproductions and prophetic–pastoral recontextualizations to encounter the unfolding theological and communal needs of nascent Christian communities.[11]

---

[8] Alcántara, *Preaching*, 81.

[9] Grimké, *Meditations*, 110.

[10] Hays, *Letters*, x. Hays states, "if we are to arrive at a properly nuanced estimate of Paul's theological stance toward his own people and their sacred texts, we must engage him on his own terms, by following his readings of the texts in which he hears the word of God."

[11] Hays, *Gospels*, 370. For more study on Hollander's "trope of metalepsis," see note 19.

With this in mind, assessing the presence of echoes in scriptural texts moves beyond simply cataloging references (though such an exercise can prove meaningful in and of itself); it involves a critical analysis to uncover the underlying patterns and ethos that drive these intertextual interactions. Hays puts forth that these interactions reveal biblical texts' dynamic and ever-relevant nature, showcasing how they are recontextualized and theologically reframed to address contemporary doctrinal and ethical challenges.[12]

Though this composition does not probe the broader deliberations and challenges surrounding the theory of echoes within NT or literary scholarship, a general understanding of its origins and applications is informative. Therefore, an appreciation of its basic tenets will ground our discussion and amplify the methodological approach used in this investigation, ultimately guiding the application of the echoes concept to Grimké's homiletic to effectuate the theoretical framework of this study.

Hollander and Hays in Brief

John Hollander (1929–2013), a distinguished poet and literary critic, held the coveted position of Sterling Professor Emeritus of English at Yale University.[13] His magnum opus, *The Figure of Echo: A Mode of Allusion in Milton and After*, catalyzed modern research on echoes within numerous traditions in literary criticism.[14] He described echoes as a sophisticated form of allusion that, while typically subtle,

[12] Ibid., 11–12.

[13] Carole Bass, "John Hollander, Poet & Professor," *Yale Alumni Magazine*, August 19, 2013, accessed August 7, 2024, https://yalealumnimagazine.org/blog_posts/1543-john-hollander-poet-professor.

[14] Channing L. Crisler, "Interview 4," interviewed by Eric J. Freeman, June 13, 2024. Reader's note: For the remainder of the study this interview will be referred to as Crisler, "Interview 4." Also, John Hollander, *The Figure of Echo: A Mode of Allusion in Milton and After* (Berkeley: University of California Press, 1981).

carries profound interpretative power within a literary work.[15] For Hollander, echoes help to create conversations between texts, allowing earlier texts within a literary work to take on new life and applications in the context of a developing story.[16] As such, his interpretation has appreciably impacted the role of literary criticism in NT studies.[17]

As an extension of Hollander's work, Hays's treatises on biblical intertextuality provide a crucial approach to detecting and interpreting scriptural echoes. His method develops a nuanced perspective on how NT writers incorporate and re-form OT texts to address new theological and communal realities.[18] Hays introduces several criteria for analyzing echoes: volume (the clarity of the reference across the canon), frequency (repetition of themes or citations), resonance (depth of thematic connections), and appropriateness (contextual fit within the new narrative).[19] Hays's analysis is not exact, yet for this study and application, its qualities help to shape a practical instrument to identify echoes.[20]

---

[15] Hays, *Gospels*, 370n21.

[16] Hollander, *Figure of Echo*, 62. Consider the following observation from Hollander, "When we speak metaphorically of echoes between texts, we imply a correspondence between a precursor and, in the acoustical actuality, a vocal source. What is interesting and peculiar about this is that whereas in nature, the anterior source has a stronger presence and authenticity, the figurative echoes arise from the later, present text. But it has many sorts of priority over what has been recalled in it. In one way, the relation of echo and source is like the curious dialectic of 'true' meanings of words: the etymon and the present common usage each can claim a different kind of authority. (The dialectic might be called the field of combat between synchrony and diachrony. That field is the domain of poetry as well.)"

[17] Hays, *Letters*, 19–21. Hays writes, "We will have great difficulty understanding Paul, the pious first-century Jew, unless we seek to situate his discourse appropriately within what Hollander calls the 'cave of resonant signification' that enveloped him."

[18] Hays, *Gospels*, 9–14.

[19] Hays, *Letters*, 1–33, passim.

[20] See footnote 3.

While Hollander and Hays set the die for the trajectory of this project, it is necessary peripherally to review the contributions of others in acknowledging the difficulty of defining echoes. Since literary scholar Julia Kristeva's theory of intertextuality was first considered in Biblical studies, it has been exploited for various reasons and in sundry ways—so much so that "almost everybody who uses it understands it somewhat differently." [21] Porter attempts to bring clarity and consistency to the often loosely defined and haphazardly used terms. In his essay, "The Use of the Old Testament in the New Testament: A Brief Comment on Method and Terminology," Porter sought to clarify Hays's usage of the term "echo."[22] Realizing the limitations of his initial treatment, Porter expanded his clarifying efforts in a contributing chapter of *The Intertextuality of the Epistles: Explorations of Theory and Practice*, aiming to address what he perceived as expanded abuses. Porter notes that literary allusions are particularly complicated to define, and that the line between allusion and echo is often indeterminate; some even use the term "allusive echo," which further blurs the distinction.[23] Porter makes his clearest characterization in the composition "Allusions and Echoes," where he identifies allusions as referring to specific people, places, or works, while echoes invoke

---

[21] Julia Kristeva, "The Bounded Text," in *Desire in Language: A Semiotic Approach to Literature and Art*, ed. Leon S. Roudiez, trans. Thomas Gora, Alice Jardine, and Leon Roudiez, 36–63 (New York: Columbia University Press, 1980), 36, originally published 1969; Heinrich F. Plett, "Intertextualities," in *Intertextuality* (Berlin: de Gruyter, 1991), 3. Reader's note: Kristeva, who coined the term "intertextuality," actually came to prefer the term "transposition" due to the way some had misappropriated her work. She writes, "The term inter-textuality denotes this transposition of one (or several) sign system(s) into another; but since this term has often been understood in the banal sense of 'study of sources,' we prefer the term transposition because it specifies that the passage from one signifying system to another demands a new articulation of the thetic—of enunciative and denotative positionality." Julia Kristeva, *Revolution in Poetic Language* (New York: Columbia University Press, 1984), 59–60.

[22] Porter, "Use of the Old Testament," 79–96.

[23] Porter, "Further Comments," 98–110.

broader thematic language or general concepts.[24] However, he admits that the latter category may be too diffuse to offer any meaningful way forward. Keesmaat contributes to the discussion by distinguishing between allusions (intentional) and echoes (unintentional) based on the author's intent.[25] While these distinctions appear helpful, they ultimately remain subjective to the reader, as Hays also recognized.[26] Finally, Christoph Heilig's work extends the concept of echoes, shifting the focus from OT echoes to identifying critical "imperial echoes" of the Roman Empire in Paul's letters. This shift highlights the flexibility and broader applicability of the construct. Heilig argues that while these echoes are present, the hypothesis must be refined to account for their complexity and limitations. He emphasizes the need for a more nuanced approach, encouraging scholars to reevaluate Pauline texts in light of Paul's engagement with Roman imperial ideology.[27]

Limitations aside, and language notwithstanding, the pragmatic intimations of Hollander's and Hays's work support the case for employing the concept of echoes to assess a Pauline–Grimkéan homiletical praxis. Hollander's literary theories provide a foundation for viewing scriptural references as dynamic and impactful elements of narrative construction. Hays's analytical framework offers specific tools for dissecting and appreciating these echoes in the biblical text. Together, they cultivate an appreciation for how NT actors used OT

---

[24] Stanley Porter, "Allusions and Echoes," in *As It Is Written: Studying Paul's Use of Scripture*, eds. Stanley E. Porter and Christopher D. Stanley, (Atlanta: Society of Biblical Literature, 2008), 29–40.

[25] Sylvia Keesmaat, "Exodus and the Intertextual Transformation of Tradition in Romans 8:14–30," *Journal for the Study of the New Testament* 54 (1994): 32.

[26] Hays, *Letters*, xii. Hays unfolds here his most comprehensive apparatus for understanding intertextuality in Paul's letters. Yet, while he uses the tools of literary critics as "hearing aids" for interpreting Paul, he does not always employ these tools exactly as they were designed to be used.

[27] Christoph Heilig, *Hidden Criticism? The Methodology and Plausibility of the Search for a Counter-Imperial Subtext in Paul* (Tübingen: Mohr Siebeck, 2015), 35–45, 125–138.

writings to support their arguments and mobilize a living word that resonated with relevant significance in the Christian discourse.

In conclusion, establishing the biblical and apostolic foundation for scriptural echoing, particularly in the employ of public discourse, is the chief priority of this treatise. By understanding the general theories of literary echoes, we set a practical and purposeful platform for applying these concepts to homiletics. With this in mind, we use the term *echo* as the interpretive tool for engaging scripture to communicate the gospel responsibly and relevantly [my emphasis]. We broadly classify echoes within this homiletical enterprise as either textual (explicit reliance on a biblical text) or thematic (embodied reliance upon a biblical text).[28,29]

Echoes and Homiletics: A Pauline Example

Hays's concept of scriptural echoes betrays how the earliest preachers of the gospel of Jesus Christ relied on scripture to convey their messages within their social contexts. For example, in examining the Apostle Paul's approach to scriptural interpretation, as demonstrated in his recontextualization of Deuteronomy 30:11–14 in

---

[28] Ellen F. Davis and Richard B. Hays, eds., *The Art of Reading Scripture* (Grand Rapids, MI: Eerdmans, 2003), 1. For a clear explanation of metanarrative in a postmodern context, see Richard Bauckham, "Reading Scripture as a Coherent Story," in *The Art of Reading Scripture*, ed. Ellen Davis and Richard Hays (Grand Rapids, MI: Eerdmans, 2003), 38–53. Bauckham's essay is particularly notable for his application of Gerard Genette's distinction between story and narrative, illustrating that narratives are varied performances of a central story. This author contends that gospel preaching, from Paul to Grimké, is *metanarrative contextual scripturalizing* to the extent that it is the instrumentation or performance of a central story to a particular end—the gospel of Jesus Christ [emphasis added]. In sum, gospel preaching involves interpreting and performing the central story of the gospel of Jesus Christ in various contexts, using scripture meaningfully to convey this overarching message.

[29] Crisler, "Interview 4." Crisler suggested that echo theory might serve pragmatically within the field of homiletics as a general construct for identifying explicit textual overtures and embodied textual allusions.

Romans 10:6–8, Hays disinters the depth and complexity inherent in Pauline exegesis.[30] According to Hays, Paul's adaptation of Moses' exhortation about the law is a prime example of how NT writings often engage with the Hebrew Scriptures through direct citation and a transformative lens that introduces new theological insights. Hays observes that, in this instance, Paul shifts the focus from the law being physically and intellectually accessible to emphasizing the nearness and accessibility of the word of faith. For Hays, Paul's innovative use of scripture underscores a deeper theological move—his use of the authority and familiarity of the OT to introduce and validate new doctrinal points central to the Christian faith, effectively making the old text preach in new ways that resonate with his audience's current experience and understanding. We will observe Grimké doing something very similar in his sermon, "God and Prayer as Factors in the Struggle," in Chapter 5.

Channing L. Crisler further explores Paul's engagement with Deuteronomy 30 in Romans 10:6–8, offering a detailed analysis of Paul's partial citation of Deuteronomy 30:12.[31] Crisler notes that Paul omits certain elements of the Septuagint (LXX) version, including the pronoun ἡμῖν ("to us") and the phrase Οὐκ ἐν τῷ οὐρανῷ ἐστιν λέγων ("It is not in heaven, saying"), possibly for stylistic reasons or because Paul does not include himself with Israel at this point. Paul's use of the phrase Τοῦτ' ἔστιν Χριστὸν καταγαγεῖν ("This means to bring Christ down") immediately after his partial citation functions as a kind of *pesher* [emphasis] (interpretive commentary), interpreting Deuteronomy 30:12–14 in light of Christ's role in bringing salvation.[32] Crisler highlights how Paul's use of Τοῦτ' ἔστιν ("This means") in Romans 10:6–8 introduces Christ as the fulfillment of these pre-texts, reframing the accessibility of the law as the nearness of Christ.[33]

---

[30] Hays, *Letters,* 1.

[31] Channing L. Crisler, *An Intertextual Commentary on Romans, Volume 3: Romans 9:1–11:36* (Eugene, OR: Pickwick Publications, 2022), 258.

[32] Ibid.

[33] Ibid., 259.

To fully understand Paul's interpretation, Crisler emphasizes the need to recognize the "contextual consistency" between Deuteronomy 30:12 and Paul's usage. Deuteronomy 30 is part of Moses' "covenant address," which contrasts Israel's future judgment and exile with its repentance and restoration, emphasizing heartfelt love and obedience to God.[34] Crisler notes that Paul's use of this passage in Romans shifts from a focus on Mosaic law obedience to a focus on Christ's nearness as the fulfillment of these covenant promises. This transformation highlights the broader theological movement within Paul's writings, as he adapts OT texts to reveal new covenant realities in Christ.

Mark A. Seifrid builds on this approach by highlighting the unifying thread of Paul's engagement with OT revelation throughout the epistle to the Romans. Seifrid points out that "Paul claims his gospel was promised beforehand through the prophets (Rom 1:2; 2:9–11; 3:2, 21; 4:11, 23–24)," demonstrating how Paul continually ties his message back to Jewish scripture. This theme reaches a climactic development in Romans 9–11, where Paul addresses the faithfulness of God in relation to the promises given to Israel.[35] Seifrid emphasizes how Paul's numerous "citations of the OT . . . in [these chapters] (cf. 9:24–33; 10:11–13)" reinforce the continuity of Paul's gospel with prior revelation, particularly in the "question of God's faithfulness . . . (Rom 3:3–4; 9:6-9; 11:25–32)."[36] Seifrid's analysis affirms that Paul's gospel is not a departure from the OT but its fulfillment, a claim Paul consistently revisits throughout Romans.

Hays, Crisler, and Seifrid illustrate the broader pattern of Pauline echoes throughout the epistles. While a comprehensive analysis of this phenomenon, including the subtler allusions in Paul's writings, exceeds the scope of this initial review, it is important to recognize the general connection between Paul's proclamation of the gospel and the OT

---

[34] Ibid.

[35] Mark A. Seifrid, "Paul's Approach to the Old Testament in Rom 10:6-8," *Trinity Journal* 6, no. 1 (Spring 1985): 4.

[36] Ibid.

narratives. This section establishes that foundational link, with a deeper exploration of Pauline echoes through two specific examples—Romans 13:1 and Philemon—to follow in Chapter 4.

A Taxonomy of the Pauline Echo

To simplify the extensive textual connections and nuances outlined in Hays's theoretical framework, this study classifies echoes into two general categories for analyzing NT scriptural engagement: textual echoes and thematic echoes. The former includes instances like Paul's use of Deuteronomy, in which he explicitly cites and recontextualizes an OT text to support an NT doctrine. This form of echo directly engages the original text but develops its application to espouse a new covenant theology. On the other hand, thematic echoes harmonize the essence and themes of OT scriptures into the melody of NT narratives without direct quotation.[37] These echoes might manifest in the actions or teachings of Jesus and other figures who embody OT prophecies or typologies, bringing to life the scriptural promises in a personified form. We demonstrate this interpretive taxonomy in Tables 1–6 of Appendix I.

Applying the Pauline Echo to Homiletics

A bilateral interpretative approach to identifying scriptural echoes—both textual and thematic echoes—simplifies the identification of echoes in biblical texts and avails accessible practices for contemporary homiletics. [38] In consequence, the anticipated application of the taxonomy is two-fold:

---

[37] Hays, *Letters*, 23. Hays writes, "Hollander's principle that 'the interpretation of a metalepsis entails the recovery of the transumed material' [is applicable]. At the explicit literal level of the discourse, Paul [in Philippians 1:15–17] simply borrows a phrase from Job [13:7–16] to express confidence amidst trying circumstances. But when the source of the phrase is read in counterpoint with the new setting into which it has been transposed, a range of resonant harmonics becomes audible."

[38] Crisler, "Interview 4."

1. Equip homileticians to identify examples of echoes in the scriptures readily.
2. Equip homileticians to embody the long-standing biblical and historical tradition of scriptural echoing to address social ills faithfully.

Applying this modified research-specific taxonomy of echoes to our analysis of echoes in the NT reveals the prolific nature of the biblical tradition of scriptural echoing. In the sections below, a focused examination of this phenomenon in the teachings of Jesus, Paul, and other NT writers broadens our assessment of scriptural echoes and their intersection with contemporary homiletical practices.

Echoes in the Teachings of Jesus, Paul, and Others

This section illustrates how Jesus, the Apostle Paul, and other NT actors engaged with OT texts. Using a schedule of tables, we illuminate patterns that suggest an underlying driving ethos by categorizing their scriptural interactions into textual and thematic echoes, as defined in the prior section. These patterns demonstrate a dynamic recontextualization of ancient texts, deliberately or subconsciously employed to address the contemporary issues of their time. We aim to highlight the deep respect for and reliance on scriptural authority that characterized and still characterizes their teachings to underscore its enduring relevance and vital role in shaping Christian doctrine and practice. We begin the assessment with a representative sample of Jesus and His scriptural echoes, as accorded in the gospels.

Jesus and Scriptural Echoes

The gospels portray Jesus as a masterful interpreter of scripture, adept at using the Hebrew Scriptures to articulate His teachings and define His mission.[39] His engagements with the OT are integral to understanding His messianic role and ethical instructions. In Tables 1 and 2 of Appendix I, we categorize a representative sampling of these interactions into two types: textual echoes, where Jesus cites scripture directly, and thematic echoes, where He infuses OT principles into His teachings and actions in a more nuanced manner. These examples are not necessarily mutually exclusive. There are many instances of overlap in the distinct echoes. However, the delineation gives rise to the pronounced presence of Jesus' use of scriptural echoes to announce His message.

One striking example is Jesus' direct citation of Isaiah 61:1–2 in Luke 4:18–19. After reading from the scroll in the synagogue, Jesus declares, "The Spirit of the Lord is upon me, because he has anointed me to proclaim good news to the poor . . . to proclaim the year of the Lord's favor."[40] Here, Jesus concomitantly cites and fulfills Isaiah's prophecy, framing His mission in light of the OT's vision of liberation and restoration.

These textual and thematic scriptural echoes enrich our understanding of Jesus' teachings, demonstrating His deep engagement with and reverence for the OT as He embodied its wisdom and prophecies in His ministry. His reflexive use of scripture informs contemporary homiletical practices by illustrating the biblical text's perennial pertinence. We now examine how Paul does the same.

Paul and Scriptural Echoes

The Apostle Paul's epistles also demonstrate a sophisticated and instinctive theological engagement with the OT that reflects his background as a Pharisee and his transformative encounter with Christ.[41] His writings employ scriptural references as foundational

---

[39] Cf. Matthew 4:4–10; Matthew 22:29–32; Mark 12:10–11; Luke 4:16–21; Luke 10:25–28; Luke 24:25–27; John 5:39–40; John 7:38; John 10:34–35.
[40] Luke 4:18–19 ESV.
[41] Hays, *Letters*, 122.

elements for constructing theological arguments and guiding the moral and communal life of the early Christian churches. We examine these interactions in Tables 3 and 4 of Appendix I.

A compelling example of Paul's scriptural echo is found in Romans 4:3, where he directly cites Genesis 15:6: "Abraham believed God, and it was counted to him as righteousness."[42] Paul uses this citation to support his argument about justification by faith, showing that righteousness is credited based on faith, not works of the law. This reference forms the basis of Paul's theological discussion on the relationship between faith, grace, and the promises given to Abraham, echoing the foundational role of the OT in his teaching.

Paul's textual and thematic scriptural echoes expand our understanding of his teaching and inferred preaching ethos. They demonstrate a reflexive reliance on the OT as he embodied its wisdom and prophecies to guide and shape early Christian communities. Paul's intense reliance on scripture informs contemporary homiletical practices by illustrating the contextual relevance and adaptability of the biblical text. In the section below, we observe a similar ethos in other NT authors.

Echoes in the Writings of Other NT Authors

The NT, beyond the gospels and the writings of Paul, contains a symphony of references to and engagements with the OT. These scriptural echoes are employed by various authors to affirm the continuity of God's redemptive plan, to establish doctrinal foundations, and to guide the moral and communal life of early Christian communities.[43] As in our prior samplings, authors such as Peter, James,

---

[42] Romans 4:3 ESV.

[43] Christopher D. Stanley, "The Social Environment of 'Free' Biblical Quotations in the New Testament," in *Early Christian Interpretation of the Scriptures of Israel: Investigations and Proposals*, eds. Craig A. Evans and James A. Sanders (Sheffield: Sheffield Academic Press, 1997), 18. Stanley asserts that "the authors of the documents that we call the New Testament drew most of

John, and the writer of Hebrews interact with scripture by making direct citations (textual echoes) and contextually harmonizing OT principles (thematic echoes). See Tables 5 and 6 in Appendix I.

One noteworthy example comes from 1 Peter 2:6, where Peter cites Isaiah 28:16: "Behold, I am laying in Zion a stone, a cornerstone chosen and precious, and whoever believes in him will not be put to shame."[44] By referencing this OT passage, Peter affirms Jesus as the prophesied cornerstone, foundational to the faith of early Christian believers. This textual echo not only connects Jesus to Israel's redemptive history but also underscores His central role in the formation of the new Christian community.

Contemporary Application and Conclusion

The discipline of echoing scriptural texts has a solid biblical precedence. Drawing from the example of NT echoers, scripturally sound gospel sermons that address contemporary social and ethical issues can be developed within the broader narrative of God's work throughout history. The rich interplay of texts showcases how foundational scriptures remain vibrant and relevant in effectively addressing today's issues. This tradition ranges from direct quotations to subtler thematic links, proving the Bible is not an outdated relic but a living word that continues to resonate in modern contexts.

For contemporary preachers, understanding these echoes is crucial for connecting ancient biblical truths with the complexities of today's world. Furthermore, engaging scriptural echoes enrich theological discussions as they charge refined conversations around ethics, community life, and personal spirituality. By integrating the Bible's historical contexts with pressing contemporary issues, preachers

---

their argumentative methods from contemporary rhetorical practice. One of the more common techniques they used to seal an argument was to adduce a verse from the Jewish Scriptures that could be read as supporting or at least illustrating their position."

[44] 1 Peter 2:6 ESV.

offer insightful analyses and provide guidance and inspiration for living faithfully today. This approach underscores the emancipating power of God's word across different ages and cultures, setting the stage for a deeper exploration of Pauline echoes that have significantly shaped theological and homiletical traditions. To that end, we begin our next section of the literature review.

Section 2—Survey of Pivotal Historical Pauline Echoers

Preachers and theologians have drawn on the Pauline echo across numerous epochs in church history. This section surveys how these figures interacted with Pauline themes and texts in their work. These interactions were primarily through homilies, commentaries, and pastoral practices. Rather than providing an exhaustive analysis, this survey offers a general overview of research on the preaching, teaching, and sociocultural milieu of Chrysostom, Augustine, John of Damascus, Peter Abelard, Aquinas, Luther, Calvin, and contemporaries of Grimké, this study provides a summary of crucial textual and thematic connections.[45] Each subject represents a significant period for Western Christian thought. Their biographies suggest or, in some cases, explicitly demonstrate Paul's influence on their theological framework for preaching and social engagement.

While this historical overview provides essential context, the primary focus of this research is not on theological interactions but on the homiletical implications of Pauline interpretative practices.[46] The

---

[45] Note: This work is an interdisciplinary presentation on Grimké's activist EEH and does not engage in historical analysis as its primary focus. Instead, our goal in this assessment is to establish an approximate continuity with historical Pauline interpretive practices.

[46] For a broad sweep of perspectives on the theological interaction of Pauline interpretive practices, see E. P. Sanders, *Paul and Palestinian Judaism* (Minneapolis: Fortress Press, 1977); N. T. Wright, *Paul and the Faithfulness of God* (Minneapolis: Fortress Press, 2013); James D. G. Dunn, *The Theology of Paul the Apostle* (Grand Rapids, MI: Eerdmans, 2006); Hays, *Letters*; Douglas J. Moo, *The Epistle to the Romans* (Grand Rapids, MI: Eerdmans, 1996);

detailed exploration of these theological engagements is thus reserved for scholarship in NT biblical theology, as this project aims to explore how the Pauline tradition impacted Grimké's activism and preaching.

John Chrysostom (c. 349–407)

Scholars recognize Chrysostom, the "Golden Mouth," as one of Paul's most influential early interpreters. Known for his homilies on the Pauline epistles, Chrysostom approached Paul's writings with a strong emphasis on moral exhortation and practical application.[47] He highlighted the ethical indicatives of Paul's teachings, focusing on how Christians should live in response to the gospel.[48] For example, Chrysostom emphasizes Paul's lack of attachment to worldly honors, describing how "Paul set no store by the things that fill our visible world" and considered tyrants and hardships as insignificant as "gnats."[49] He continues with admiration of Paul's joy in the face of adversity, stating, "When he saw death imminent, he bade others share

---

Channing L. Crisler, *Reading Romans as Lament: Paul's Use of Old Testament Lament in His Most Famous Letter* (Eugene, OR: Pickwick, 2016), Kindle edition.

[47] O. C. Edwards, *The History of Preaching*, vol. 1 (Nashville: Abingdon Press, 2004), Kindle edition, Location 2172. Describing Chrysostom's homiletic, Edwards writes, "On occasion he would make one moral appeal in the introduction and another in the conclusion. His one overriding interest was in persuading the people of God to live consistently with their calling."

[48] Stephen Westerholm, *Romans: Texts, Readers, and the History of Interpretation* (Grand Rapids, MI: Eerdmans, 2022), 121–33. Westerholm, noting Chrysostom's penchant for interpretive application, writes, "Finally, it must be remembered that Chrysostom was a preacher. . . . Even while explicating a text, he included in his sermons whatever he thought his congregation needed to hear. Though the greater part of each of the sermons on Romans was devoted to Paul's text, in nearly every case Chrysostom ended by exhorting his congregation" (132).

[49] John Chrysostom, *Homilia II de laudibus sancti Pauli*, in *Patrologiae Cursus Completus: Series Graeca*, vol. 50, ed. J.-P. Migne (Paris: Garnier Fratres, 1857), 477–480.

his joy: 'Rejoice and be glad with me!'"[50] He finally declares, "Paul, more than anyone else, has shown us what man really is, and in what our nobility consists."[51] With these interactions in mind, the ensuing review of Chrysostom's interaction with the apostle Paul reveals a definite engagement with Pauline praxis, mainly through Chrysostom's homilies on Paul's epistles.[52]

Margeret M. Mitchell's work, *John Chrysostom on Paul: Praises and Problem Passages*, is a mammoth analysis of Chrysostom's sermons that highlights the centrality of Paul's teachings in Chrysostom's theological reflections and moral exhortations.[53] Mitchell further emphasizes the "monumental importance" of Chrysostom's interaction with the Pauline corpus, noting its prominent influence on patristic and later Christian exegesis. Her work ultimately attempts to demonstrate how Chrysostom's legacy set a precedent for how Pauline texts were interpreted and embodied within the Christian tradition.[54]

In her translation of *The Cult of the Saints: John Chrysostom's Homilies on Saints*, Wendy Mayer highlights Chrysostom's employment of Pauline teachings to shape his homilies, emphasizing the indicatives of the ethical and spiritual lessons derived from Paul's letters.[55] David Rylaarsdam's treatise, *John Chrysostom on Divine Pedagogy: The Coherence of His Theology and Preaching*, investigates how Chrysostom's interpretation of Paul's letters informed his pastoral care, particularly in moral and ethical instruction.[56] Blake Leyerle's study,

---

[50] Ibid.

[51] Ibid.

[52] For a definition of "Pauline praxis," see note 21 in Chapter 1.

[53] Margeret M. Mitchell, *John Chrysostom on Paul: Praises and Problem Passages* (Atlanta: SBL Press, 2022).

[54] Margeret M. Mitchell, *The Heavenly Trumpet: John Chrysostom and the Art of Pauline Interpretation* (Louisville, KY: Westminster John Knox Press, 2002), preface.

[55] Wendy Mayer, trans., *The Cult of the Saints: John Chrysostom's Homilies on Saints* (Crestwood, NY: St. Vladimir's Seminary Press, 2006).

[56] David Rylaarsdam, *John Chrysostom on Divine Pedagogy: The Coherence of His Theology and Preaching* (Oxford: Oxford University Press, 2014).

The Narrative Shape of Emotion in the Preaching of John Chrysostom, also examines how Chrysostom's emotional appeals in his sermons were often grounded in Pauline exegesis, reflecting his intimate pirouette with Paul's writings.[57] Greek Orthodox professor Karl Donfried's lecture at the 2008 Pauline Symposium in Istanbul, Turkey, explored Chrysostom's spiritual connection with Paul and its effect upon his pastoral care and preaching.[58] Chrysostom's interactions with Paul's teachings shaped his pastoral work and set a lasting example for how Pauline theology would be interpreted, expressed, and embodied in Christian thought for generations. Building on the weightiness of Chrysostom, we review Augustine's interpretive legacy next.

Augustine of Hippo (354–430)

Augustine's interpretative engagement with Paul, especially in the apostle's letter to the Romans, is foundational to Western Christian thought. His theological reflections often engaged the Apostle Paul, especially his epistle to the Romans. On grace and justification, Augustine's *Confessions* highlight his struggle with sin through the lens of Paul's words in Romans 7:24: "I read . . . that Paul 'was delighted with the law of God according to the inner man,' but he saw 'another law in his members warring against the law of his mind.'"[59] This struggle underscores Augustine's view of the indispensable role of grace in overcoming sin. Augustine's writings also underscore the tension between faith and works, as seen in *On Nature and Grace*, where he echoes Paul's exhortation to "put on the Lord Jesus Christ."[60]

---

[57] Blake Leyerle, *The Narrative Shape of Emotion in the Preaching of John Chrysostom* (Berkeley: University of California Press, 2020).
[58] Karl Donfried, "The Relationship between Paul and John Chrysostom," lecture at the 2008 Pauline Symposium, Istanbul, Turkey, October 9–17, 2008, accessed August 9, 2024, https://www.youtube.com/watch?v=FoI5MAawd7M.
[59] Augustine, *Confessions*, trans. Henry Chadwick (Oxford: Oxford University Press, 2009), Book VII, Chapters 21.
[60] Cf. Romans 13:14.

Augustine states, "For Paul commands us to 'put on the Lord Jesus Christ,' and thus our own efforts do not achieve this, but grace itself," emphasizing the Pauline praxis and ethos of grace over human striving.[61]

Moreover, Augustine reflects on Paul's doctrine of original sin, particularly Romans 5:12, in *City of God*, noting, "The apostle says, 'By one man sin entered into the world, and death by sin,' showing how the whole human race shares in Adam's sin."[62] This interpretation affirms Paul's teaching on the universal implications of sin and forms a critical element of Augustine's doctrine. Known for the internal tug-of-war within his texts, Augustine resonantly expanded the Pauline themes of grace, sin, and predestination.[63] Furthermore, his reading of Paul was formative in shaping the theological debates of the Reformation.[64]

Michael Cameron, in *Christ Meets Me Everywhere: Augustine's Early Figurative Exegesis*, argues that Augustine's interactions with Pauline praxis are foundational to his exegetical methods, particularly in the areas of grace, predestination, and original sin. [65] Paula Fredriksen, in her book *Augustine and the Jews: A Christian Defense of Jews and Judaism*, explores how Augustine employed Paul's epistles, especially Romans, to construct his theological arguments concerning Jews and the interpretation of Jewish law within Christian theology. Fredriksen highlights the complexity of Augustine's engagement with

---

[61] Augustine, *On Nature and Grace*, trans. Peter Holmes, in *Nicene and Post-Nicene Fathers*, First Series, vol. 5, ed. Philip Schaff (Buffalo, NY: Christian Literature Publishing Co., 1887), 53.

[62] Augustine, *The City of God*, trans. Marcus Dods (New York: Modern Library, 1950), 13.3.

[63] Westerholm, *Romans*, 152–71. See also, Augustine, *Confessions*, Book VIII, Chapters 5, 10, 11, 12; Book VII, Chapter 10.

[64] Ibid., 42.

[65] Michael Cameron, *Christ Meets Me Everywhere: Augustine's Early Figurative Exegesis* (Oxford: Oxford University Press, 2012).

Paul, noting its significance in his broader theological framework.[66] Known for his powerful sermons, Peter Sanlon points out Augustine's unique ability to distill complex theological ideas into contextually provocative messages that resonated with his audience—a distinct Pauline practice.[67] Much more could be said about Augustine, but the body of research documenting Augustine's interaction with Pauline texts and themes is vast and impractical for this overview. Nevertheless, this sample of studies provides a synoptic of the centrality and context of Paul's influence on Augustine's interpretive praxis.

John of Damascus (675 or 676–749)

The Western tradition does not cover John of Damascus as extensively as Augustine—but in Eastern Orthodox scholarship, he is more broadly acknowledged, especially for his engagement with the Apostle Paul's letters.[68] His works, notably, helped to ground the Byzantine understanding of Paul's teachings, especially concerning the nature of Christ and the role of icons in worship.[69] John frequently engaged with the teachings of the Apostle Paul, particularly in his defense of religious images and icons. He saw Paul's teachings on the incarnation and the divine image of Christ as theological foundations for the veneration of icons. For instance, in *On Holy Images*, John of Damascus argues that Christ's incarnation enables the representation of divine realities through material images, a view he believes is

---

[66] Paula Fredriksen, *Augustine and the Jews: A Christian Defense of Jews and Judaism* (New Haven, CT: Yale University Press, 2010).

[67] Peter Sanlon, "Depth and Weight: Augustine's Sermon Illustrations," *Churchman* 122, no. 1 (Spring 2008): 61–76.

[68] Eirini Artemi, "John of Damascus and the Use of the Letters of Paul in His Writing: *An Exact Exposition of the Orthodox Faith*," *Mirabilia* 24 (2017): 23–39.

[69] John of Damascus, *Pro Sacris Imaginibus Orationes Tres*, PG 94:1227–419, referenced in Artemi, "John of Damascus," 24n2.

supported by Paul's teachings on Christ's visible humanity.[70] John stresses that the material world, including icons, can point believers to spiritual truths, mirroring Paul's assertion that "the invisible things of Him from the creation of the world are clearly seen, being understood by the things that are made."[71]

Investigations into John of Damascus's interactions with Pauline praxis convey a palpable reliance on Paul's doctrinal and Christological arguments. In her article, "John of Damascus and the Use of the Letters of Paul in His Writing: *An Exact Exposition of the Orthodox Faith*," Eirini Artemi astutely excavates how John integrated Pauline praxis into his theological framework, particularly in his work *An Exact Exposition of the Orthodox Faith*. Artemi notes that John, in the heritage of the patristics, relied heavily on Paul's letters.[72] She argues that the Pauline letters sourced his capacity to effectively communicate core theological concepts like the nature of sin, Christ's role in redemption, and the establishment of the New Covenant.[73] By drawing on Paul's teachings, John constructed a systematic and comprehensive presentation of Christian doctrine that aligned with the theological traditions of the Eastern Orthodox Church. Artemi's succinct analysis demonstrates the centrality of John's traditioned interpretive interactions with Pauline praxis through the apostle's letters.[74] In "John

---

[70] John of Damascus, *On the Divine Images: Three Apologies Against Those Who Attack the Divine Images*, trans. David Anderson (Crestwood, NY: St. Vladimir's Seminary Press, 1980), 15–18. Cf. Romans 1:20.

[71] Ibid., 22–23, on the use of the material world to reveal spiritual truths.

[72] Artemi, "John of Damascus," 26–28.

[73] John of Damascus, *Expositio Accurata Fidei Orthodoxae*, 4.11, PG 94:961C. See Romans 7:17, referenced in Artemi, "John of Damascus," 37n87.

[74] Artemi, "John of Damascus," 26. Artemi notes, "John had understood that the tradition was part of the Byzantine theological and political history. He believed that Christians should not overpass the divine tradition, which was the pillar of theology and Christian Church. He adopted the theological tradition and explained it [in] this way . . . to be clarified for other Christians and scholars that [sought] to identify the conditions under which Christianity was likely to be perceived as relevant to contemporary political and theological

of Damascus, *On the Faith against the Nestorians*," Scott Ables explores John's use of Pauline texts in his polemical works against the Nestorians. Ables emphasizes that Paul's writings were capable *accomplices* [my emphasis] in shaping John's theological defenses against heretical views.

Moreover, in *St. John Damascene: Tradition and Originality in Byzantine Theology*, Andrew Louth provides a helpful exploration of John's theological contributions. He focuses on how John balanced tradition with innovative theological thought to operate his activism against heresies. Louth also surveys John's engagement with Pauline praxis in his defense of Christian doctrine, particularly in Byzantine theological debates.[75]

John of Damascus, a significant and ardent activist against doctrinal heresies, represents an essential link in Pauline interpretive practices. Next, we review a controversial character in the Pauline interpretive tradition who was on the receiving end of anti-heresy activism—the eclectic medieval French scholastic cleric and philosopher Peter Abelard.

Peter Abelard (1079–1142)

Peter Abelard, one of the foremost medieval theologians, frequently referenced Paul's epistles to defend his views, particularly around grace, free will, and ethics. Using Paul, Abelard famously wrote, "The Apostle says, 'For it is God who works in you both to will and to

---

problems. He followed Paul's advice [in the] Second Epistle to Thessalonians, in which Paul urges: 'Stand firm, then brethren, and hold by the traditions you have learned, in word or in writing from us.' So, John presented through his teaching that the analyses of the theological tradition should be without innovations and interpretations that opposed . . . the Holy Scripture and fathers' and Councils' sacred deposit of faith." Here, I appreciate Artemi's point. She does not interpret John as opposing "innovations and interpretations." She frames John's position as one opposed to "innovations and interpretations" that "opposed . . . the Holy Scripture and fathers' and Councils' sacred deposit of faith."

[75] Andrew Louth, *St. John Damascene: Tradition and Originality in Byzantine Theology* (Oxford: Oxford University Press, 2002), passim.

act according to His good purpose,'"[76] which Abelard interpreted as evidence that grace works cooperatively with human will in a person's ethical life. Abelard's understanding of free will and human cooperation with divine grace contrasted with stricter Augustinian views, as he contended that while divine grace initiates, it does not compel, leaving room for human freedom.

Abelard also turned to Paul's teachings on love in 1 Corinthians 13 to underpin his concept of ethical intention over mere action. He interpreted Paul's statement, "If I give all I possess to the poor and surrender my body to the flames, but have not love, I gain nothing," to mean that the moral value of an action lies in the love and intent behind it, rather than the act itself. [77] This view challenged contemporaneous interpretations and underscored his emphasis on intention as essential to moral evaluation.

These Pauline quotes were central to Abelard's writings in *Ethica* and *Theologia Scholarium*, where he elaborates on grace, free will, and moral philosophy, using Paul's words as foundational evidence for his theological positions. Abelard's innovative readings of Paul reveal his attempts to harmonize Christian ethics with philosophical rigor, positioning love and intention as pivotal in moral judgment.

In his book *Romans: Texts, Readers, and the History of Interpretation*, Westerholm introduces Abelard as a "flamboyant" figure in his personal life and teaching. [78] Westerholm details how Abelard's dramatic personality and provocative ideas led to significant controversy, including charges of heresy from William of Saint Thierry and Bernard

[76] Peter Abelard, *Ethica*, trans. D. E. Luscombe (Oxford: Clarendon Press, 1971), 90. Abelard references Philippians 2:13, emphasizing Paul's view that "it is God who works in you both to will and to act according to His good purpose."

[77] Ibid., 102. Abelard interprets Paul's famous passage on love in 1 Corinthians 13:3 to mean that the true worth of any action depends on the love or intention motivating it.

[78] Westerholm, *Romans*, 179.

of Clairvaux.[79] According to Westerholm, the accusations culminated in Abelard's second condemnation at the Council of Sens in 1140, an event that curiously did nothing to diminish Abelard's popularity.[80] These episodes set the stage for understanding how Abelard's engagement with Pauline praxis was a dissonant mix of innovation and contention.

There is little doubt that Abelard's interactions with the apostle Paul were consequential in shaping his theological and philosophical work. John Marenbon, in *The Philosophy of Peter Abelard*, discusses how Abelard grappled with issues of grace, free will, and original sin, relying extensively on Pauline praxis to develop his theological positions.[81] Constant J. Mews, in *Abelard and Heloise*, highlights Abelard's interpretation of Paul and its influence on his views on ethics and redemption.[82] In *Beginning to Read the Fathers*, Bonaventure Ramsey notes Abelard's contribution to medieval scriptural exegesis and emphasizes his innovative use of Paul's letters to formulate theological arguments.[83] In *The School of Peter Abelard*, David Luscombe explores how Abelard's engagement with Pauline praxis influenced subsequent medieval thinkers.[84] Rita Copeland's *Pedagogy, Intellectuals, and Dissent in the Later Middle Ages* examines how Abelard used (echoed) Pauline teachings as an activist argument for integrating faith and reason in intellectual inquiry.[85] As we pivot from this brief

---

[79] Ibid.

[80] Ibid, 179–81.

[81] John Marenbon, *The Philosophy of Peter Abelard* (Cambridge: Cambridge University Press, 1997).

[82] Constant J. Mews, *Abelard and Heloise* (Oxford: Oxford University Press, 2005).

[83] Bonaventure Ramsey, *Beginning to Read the Fathers* (New York: Paulist Press, 1985).

[84] David Luscombe, *The School of Peter Abelard: The Influence of Abelard's Thought in Medieval Europe* (Cambridge: Cambridge University Press, 1969).

[85] Rita Copeland, *Pedagogy, Intellectuals, and Dissent in the Later Middle Ages: Lollardy and Ideas of Learning* (Cambridge: Cambridge University Press, 2001).

assessment, the latter two entries on Abelard—the "flamboyant" cleric—prove a fitting segue to our next medieval interpreter, St. Thomas Aquinas, the "Dumb Ox" Angelic Doctor of the Church.[86]

Thomas Aquinas (1225–1274)

Aquinas provided a scholastic interpretation of Paul, most notably through his *Commentary on the Epistles of Paul.*[87] In Pauline fashion, he integrated Aristotelian logic into Paul's theology, offering a systematic and philosophical reading that shifted Catholic doctrine concerning the nature of grace and justification.[88] He writes, for instance, on grace in relation to Romans 11:6, "If it is by grace, it is not now by works," that, "grace excludes the merit of works, because grace is not from works but from the will of God."[89] Here, Aquinas emphasizes that divine grace, according to Paul, does not arise from human merit but is freely given by God, thus reinforcing his doctrine of divine initiative.

In his *Commentary on Romans*, Aquinas explores Romans 1:20, where Paul writes of the visible world revealing God's invisible qualities, interpreting it to mean that "the creation of the world manifests the power of God."[90] He sees Paul's words as supporting the view that natural reason leads to a knowledge of God, which forms the basis of natural theology.

Aquinas also discusses Paul's teachings on love in his *Commentary on 1 Corinthians*, especially on 1 Corinthians 13. He interprets Paul's "faith, hope, and charity" as the theological virtues, concluding that

---

[86] G. K. Chesterton, *Saint Thomas Aquinas: The Dumb Ox* (New York: Image Books, 1974), 1–2.

[87] Thomas Aquinas, *Commentary on the Letters of Saint Paul: Complete Set (Latin–English Opera Omnia)*, ed. The Aquinas Institute (Emmaus Academic, 2012).

[88] Westerholm, *Romans*, 188–205.

[89] Thomas Aquinas, *Commentary on Saint Paul's Letter to the Romans*, trans. F. R. Larcher and Edward C. Miller (Steubenville, OH: Emmaus Academic, 2018), 11:6.

[90] Ibid., 1:20.

"charity is the form of the virtues," suggesting that love is the animating force of all Christian virtues.[91] Aquinas thus uses Paul to articulate his view that love, or charity, is the highest expression of Christian life and the root of moral action.

Reflecting on these passages, Aquinas's *Commentary on the Letters of Saint Paul* emerges as a classic interpretive work that systematically exegetes Paul's writings, focusing on key theological themes.[92] His regard for Paul as an authoritative key to understanding Christian doctrine and moral action highlights Aquinas's dedication to grounding both theological and moral instruction within the Pauline framework. Through this approach, he establishes a continuity between faith and action, which deeply influences later Catholic theology, bridging doctrinal fidelity and practical devotion in the Christian life.

Matthew Levering's *Paul in the Summa Theologiae* offers a compelling examination of how Aquinas intricately weaves Pauline theology into his magnum opus, the *Summa Theologiae.* Levering carefully analyzes Aquinas's interpretative methods in approaching Paul's teachings on faith, charity, and the continuity between the Old and New Testaments, amplifying the apostle's resonant effects on Aquinas' theological constructs.[93] Joseph Wawrykow, in *The Westminster Handbook to Thomas Aquinas*, presents an overview of Aquinas's theological landscape. He explores how Aquinas's readings of Paul inform his perspectives on predestination, the sacraments, and

---

[91] Thomas Aquinas, *Commentary on the Letters of Saint Paul to the Corinthians*, trans. Fabian Larcher and Daniel Keating (Steubenville, OH: Emmaus Academic, 2018), 13:13.

[92] Thomas Aquinas, *Commentary on the Letters of Saint Paul*, trans. Fabian Larcher, O.P., and ed. J. Mortensen (Lander: Aquinas Institute, 2012).

[93] Matthew Levering, *Paul in the Summa Theologiae* (Washington, DC: Catholic University of America Press, 2014), ix-xiii.

moral theology, providing another witness to the apostle's role in shaping Aquinas's thought and ethic.[94]

As in several prior treatments in this exercise, notwithstanding the limited scope of this sweeping historiography, more could and should be said of Aquinas. Yet, few works are more pronounced in demonstrating his interaction with Pauline praxis than those just visited. Given our core interest in the immediate context that shaped Grimké's activism and preaching, we reserve the larger body of this work to examine the Pauline interpretative practices of Reformed and African American examples pertinent to Grimké. That said, the course is set for our survey of Pauline interpretive practices in the Reformation. We start with Martin Luther.

Martin Luther (1483–1546)

Luther is known for his revolutionary reading of Paul, most explicitly his interpretation of Romans. His emphasis on justification by faith alone is a central doctrine of the Protestant Reformation. Through his reading of Romans, Luther's understanding of Paul's stance against legalism directly influenced his challenge to Catholic doctrines and the development of Reformation thought.[95] Luther's Pauline praxis is most apparent in his interaction with Paul's epistle to the Romans.[96] For instance, in Luther's *Commentary on Romans*, he underscores the idea that "salvation lies outside ourselves," emphasizing Paul's stance in Romans that righteousness comes from divine grace, not human merit.[97] Luther also reflects on faith's transformative role in the Christian life, describing it as "a living, daring confidence in God's

---

[94] Joseph Wawrykow, *The Westminster Handbook to Thomas Aquinas* (Louisville, KY: Westminster John Knox Press, 2005).

[95] Westerholm, *Romans*, 217–35.

[96] Crisler, *Romans*, Locations 1670–71.

[97] Martin Luther, *Commentary on Romans*, trans. J. Theodore Mueller (Grand Rapids, MI: Kregel Publications, 1976), 18. "Salvation lies outside ourselves, and thus righteousness is given by God, not as something that can be achieved through human efforts." Cf. Romans 9:16.

grace," powerful enough that he would "stake his life on it" multiple times—a perspective directly inspired by Paul's teachings on salvation and grace.[98] Additionally, Luther interprets Paul's counsel in Romans on the sinful nature of humanity, noting that the Apostle's reflections on human incapacity without divine grace reinforce the need for justification by faith alone.[99]

Research on Luther's interpretative approach to the Pauline oeuvre portrays the intense influence of Paul's writings on Luther's theology and the Reformation movement in general. Westerholm, in *Perspectives Old and New on Paul: The "Lutheran" Paul and His Critics*, provides an in-depth analysis of Luther's engagement with Pauline praxis, echoing Luther's revolutionary interpretation of Romans again. He traverses how Luther's doctrine of justification by faith alone became a cornerstone of the Protestant Reformation. Luther's application of Paul, Westerholm argues, positioned the apostle himself as a staunch opponent of the legalism Luther lamented in the Catholic Church. Additionally, Westerholm's broader analysis further complements the scholarly consensus that Luther's engagement with Paul's letters, especially Romans and Galatians, was the bedrock of the theological and doctrinal shifts that defined the Reformation.[100]

Erik Herrmann, through his article "Luther's Journey with Paul," leads an investigation into how Luther's engagement with Paul's epistles, particularly around the concept of justification by faith, was transformative personally and doctrinally. Herrmann draws distinct

---

[98] Martin Luther, *Commentary on Romans*, trans. J. Theodore Mueller (Grand Rapids, MI: Kregel Publications, 1976), 24. "Faith is a living, daring confidence in God's grace, so sure and certain that a man could stake his life on it a thousand times."

[99] Martin Luther, *Lectures on Romans*, in *Luther's Works*, vol. 25, ed. Hilton C. Oswald (St. Louis: Concordia Publishing House, 1972), 276. "Paul's point in showing the limits of the law is to highlight the absolute need for grace. By faith alone, and not by our efforts, are we made right with God."

[100] Stephen Westerholm, *Perspectives Old and New on Paul: The "Lutheran" Paul and His Critics* (Grand Rapids, MI: Eerdmans, 2003), passim.

parallels between Luther's struggles and those of Paul.[101] Luther undergirds this connection in his *Commentary on Paul's Epistle to the Galatians*, a tour de force of Pauline praxis, as he articulates his views on law, grace, and Christian life.[102] The significance of Luther's interpretation of Paul is emphasized again in "The Apostle Paul: Polling Our Sources," which examines how Luther's exegesis of Romans became foundational to his activism and reformation theology.[103]

N. T. Wright's contribution to the conversation, especially his work on the historical context of Paul's letters and the doctrine of justification, has experienced broad influence but has also sparked mixed reactions, most notably within evangelical circles. While many appreciate Wright's commitment to the authority of scripture and his contributions to NT studies, his reinterpretation of justification has caused indigestion among those who adhere to traditional Reformed theology.[104] Nevertheless, through the intimations of works like *Justification: God's Plan and Paul's Vision*, Wright's Pauline praxis challenges the classic Protestant understanding of justification by faith alone, expanding the bounds of Pauline interpretive activism.[105]

Additional studies, such as David C. Steinmetz's *Luther in Context*, offer a nuanced perspective on Luther's interpretative practices,

---

[101] Erik Herrmann, "Luther's Journey with Paul," *Lutheran Witness*, June/July 2008, accessed May 3, 2024, https://witness.lcms.org/2008/luthers-journey-with-paul-6-2008/.

[102] Martin Luther, *Commentary on Paul's Epistle to the Galatians*, trans. Theodore Graebner (Grand Rapids, MI: Zondervan, 1949).

[103] Bart D. Ehrman, "The Apostle Paul: Polling Our Sources," in *Peter, Paul, and Mary Magdalene* (New York: Oxford University Press, 2006), 89–100.

[104] See John Piper, *The Future of Justification: A Response to N. T. Wright* (Wheaton, IL: Crossway, 2007).

[105] N. T. Wright, *Justification: God's Plan and Paul's Vision* (Downers Grove, IL: IVP Academic, 2009), passim. For more studies on this, see Piper, *Future* and Guy Prentiss Waters, *Justification and the New Perspectives on Paul: A Review and Response* (Phillipsburg: P&R Publishing, 2004).

particularly concerning his interactions with Paul.[106] Steinmetz situates Luther within his time's broader historical and intellectual currents by demonstrating how Luther's engagement with the apostle was concomitantly a continuation of and a departure from earlier theological traditions.[107] Through a close examination of Luther's writings and sermons, Steinmetz catalogs how the Pauline concepts of justification by faith, the nature of the law, and the role of grace were central to Luther's reformative efforts.[108] Wrapping on this note, John Calvin, another storied Reformer, comes to the fore.

John Calvin (1509–1564)

Calvin, noted for his comprehensive and systematic interpretation of Paul's epistles through his commentaries, reflects a rigorous engagement with Pauline praxis—primarily on issues of predestination, the sovereignty of God, and the Christian life. Calvin's exegesis of Paul was foundational for Reformed theology and has had a lasting influence on Protestant thought.[109] He argues, "Paul, however, shows that all are shut up to a miserable slavery unless they are liberated by God's mercy; for they are kept fast bound by the chains of sin till they are set free by Christ" in his commentary on Romans 6:17, showing his view on God's sovereignty in liberation from sin through grace alone.[110] Calvin emphasizes this further in his commentary on Ephesians 1:4, saying, "Paul testifies that we were chosen in Christ before the foundation of the world, that we might not glory in

---

[106] David C. Steinmetz, *Luther in Context* (Bloomington: Indiana University Press, 1986).
[107] Steinmetz, *Luther in Context*, 85–97.
[108] Steinmetz, *Luther in Context*, 10, 18, 29–31.
[109] Westerholm, *Romans*, 248–60.
[110] John Calvin, *Commentary on the Epistle of Paul to the Romans*, trans. John Owen (Grand Rapids, MI: Christian Classics Ethereal Library, 1947), 6:17.

ourselves."[111] Calvin views this as an assurance of salvation rooted in God's sovereign choice, aligning with Paul's teaching that all glory belongs to God, not humanity. Calvin's interpretations reveal an *echoey* [my emphasis] engagement with Pauline doctrine, shaping his theological stance on election and human dependency on divine grace alone.

Scholarly examinations of Calvin's interactions with the Apostle Paul reveal a multifaceted engagement with Pauline praxis that extends across his commentaries, doctrinal writings, and pastoral practices. His commentaries and expositions on the Epistles to the Romans, Ephesians, Hebrews, Galatians, and others demonstrate Calvin's systematic approach to Pauline praxis in addressing critical issues of grace, law, and Christian living.[112] These commentaries were pivotal in shaping Reformed theology and highlight Paul's central role in Calvin's Pauline *hermeneutic and heart-embodied* [emphasis added] theological framework.

Beyond his commentaries, Calvin's engagement with Paul is evident in his broader theological and pastoral work. David C. Steinmetz, in his analysis of Calvin's doctrine, illustrates how Pauline praxis influenced Calvin's broader theological vision. In *Calvin in Context*, Steinmetz emphasizes how Calvin's interpretation of Pauline themes, such as justification by faith, predestination, and the church's role in society, shaped his doctrinal formulations and pastoral strategies. Steinmetz situates Calvin's exegesis within the broader Reformation context by highlighting how Calvin's engagement with Paul was integral to his efforts to reform the church and establish a coherent theological framework that resonated with the spiritual needs of his

---

[111] John Calvin, *Commentary on the Epistle of Paul to the Ephesians*, trans. William Pringle (Grand Rapids, MI: Christian Classics Ethereal Library, 1947), 1:4.

[112] John Calvin, *Commentaries on the Epistles of Paul to the Galatians and Ephesians*, trans. William Pringle (Grand Rapids, MI: Eerdmans, 1948). See also John Calvin, *Commentaries on the Epistle of Paul the Apostle to the Hebrews*, trans. and ed. John Owen (Edinburgh: Calvin Translation Society, 1853).

time.[113] Elsie Anne McKee and B. A. Gerrish present a collection of Calvin's writings in *John Calvin: Writings on Pastoral Piety*, part of the *Classics of Western Spirituality* series, that showcases his dogged commitment to pastoral care and spiritual formation. The volume compiles texts that reveal how Calvin's theological insights, especially those influenced by Pauline doctrine, were implemented in his pastoral ministry. McKee and Gerrish emphasize how Calvin's interpretation of Paul shaped his views on Christian piety, the role of the church, and the practical aspects of leading a Christian life. This collection is essential for understanding how Calvin's engagement with Paul went beyond academic exegesis and deeply informed his pastoral strategies.[114] Michael Horton's *Calvin on the Christian Life: Glorifying and Enjoying God Forever* explores John Calvin's personal piety and practical theology, emphasizing how his interpretive practices of Pauline praxis shaped his spiritual life and ministry. By drawing from Calvin's *Institutes*, biblical commentaries, and lesser-known writings, Horton reveals how Calvin's engagement with Pauline themes, such as grace and faith, informed his approach to Christian living and pastoral guidance.[115]

Further expanding on Calvin's interaction with Paul, T. H. L. Parker examines Calvin's sermons on Paul's letters to demonstrate how Calvin textually and thematically echoed Pauline praxis to address his congregation's spiritual and communal needs.[116] I. John Hesselink's exploration of *Calvin's Institutes of the Christian Religion* reveals the pervasive influence of Pauline themes such as grace, faith, and

---

[113] David C. Steinmetz, *Calvin in Context*, 2nd ed. (Oxford: Oxford University Press, 2010).
[114] Elsie Anne McKee and B. A. Gerrish, *John Calvin: Writings on Pastoral Piety* (New York: Paulist Press, 2002).
[115] Michael Horton, *Calvin on the Christian Life: Glorifying and Enjoying God Forever* (Wheaton, IL: Crossway, 2014).
[116] T. H. L. Parker, *Calvin's Preaching* (Edinburgh: T&T Clark, 1992), passim.

predestination throughout this seminal work.[117] Collectively, these studies illustrate how Calvin's engagement with Paul extended beyond his commentaries, influencing his doctrinal writings, pastoral practices, and ecclesiological views, making Paul a cornerstone of Calvin's theological legacy.

Daniel Alexander Payne (1811–1893)

Payne, a bishop in the African Methodist Episcopal (AME) Church and a prominent educator, is noted for his sermons that often focused on the theme of liberation and education as tools for empowerment. His preachment was significantly influenced by his belief in the power of education, both spiritually and socially, to uplift the African American community.[118] He famously proclaimed, "As Christ died to make men holy, so we must labor to make them wise," highlighting a Pauline theme of freedom through knowledge.[119] Drawing on Paul's writings, Payne preached that "where the Spirit of the Lord is, there is liberty," grounding his call for educational advancement in the liberating work of the Holy Spirit. His ministry echoed Paul's emphasis on unity and equality in the body of Christ, particularly referencing Galatians 3:28 to affirm the inherent dignity and equality of all believers, stating that "all are one in Christ Jesus."[120]

Scholarly discussions on Daniel Alexander Payne often explore the echoes of Pauline praxis in his leadership within the AME Church, particularly in his commitment to education and moral integrity. Authors like Richard S. Newman and Dennis Dickerson betray how Payne's theological and educational contributions were influenced by Pauline ethics, especially in his approach to church governance and

---

[117] I. John Hesselink, *Calvin's First Catechism: A Commentary* (Louisville, KY: Westminster John Knox Press, 1998).
[118] Larue, *Heart*, 92–102.
[119] Daniel Payne, *Recollections of Seventy Years* (Nashville: Publishing House of the A.M.E. Sunday School Union, 1888), 33.
[120] Ibid., 77.

ministerial training.[121] Carol V. R. George examines Payne's sermons, emphasizing his alignment with Paul's teachings on moral character and the orderly conduct of church affairs, which were pivotal in shaping the AME Church's clergy.[122] James T. Campbell and Mark A. Noll analyze Payne's writings and leadership style by drawing clear parallels with Paul's pastoral epistles, particularly in Payne's efforts to establish a well-educated and morally upright clergy.[123] Gayraud S. Wilmore and Lawrence W. Levine discuss Payne's educational philosophy, while Albert J. Raboteau and W. E. B. du Bois provide broader contextual analyses of Payne's ministry, noting the significant influence of Pauline praxis on his work within the African American religious community.[124] Additionally, LaRue, in his signature study of African American preaching, underscores Payne's strategic use of the pulpit to address the moral and intellectual needs of his congregation.

---

[121] Richard S. Newman, *Freedom's Prophet: Bishop Richard Allen, the AME Church, and the Black Founding Fathers* (New York: New York University Press, 2009); Dennis Dickerson, *African American Preachers and Politics: The Careys of Chicago* (Jackson: University Press of Mississippi, 2011).

[122] Carol V. R. George, *Segregated Sabbaths: Richard Allen and the Emergence of Independent Black Churches, 1760–1840* (New York: Oxford University Press, 1973).

[123] James T. Campbell, *Songs of Zion: The African Methodist Episcopal Church in the United States and South Africa* (Chapel Hill: University of North Carolina Press, 1998); Mark A. Noll, *God and Race in American Politics: A Short History* (New York: Oxford University Press, 2001).

[124] Gayraud S. Wilmore, *Black Religion and Black Radicalism: An Interpretation of the Religious History of African Americans* (Maryknoll, NY: Orbis Books, 1998); Lawrence W. Levine, *Black Culture and Black Consciousness: Afro-American Folk Thought from Slavery to Freedom* (New York: Oxford University Press, 30th anniversary ed., 2007); Albert J. Raboteau, *Slave Religion: The "Invisible Institution" in the Antebellum South* (New York: Oxford University Press, updated ed., 2004); W. E. B. du Bois, *The Souls of Black Folk*, unabridged ed. (Mineola, NY: Dover, 2016), originally published in 1903; V. P. Franklin, *Black Self-determination: A Cultural History of the Faith of the Fathers* (Westport, Conn.: L. Hill, 1984).

This practice resonates strongly with Paul's approach to pastoral care and guidance.[125]

Alexander Crummell (1819–1898)

Crummell was known for his sermons' intellectual rigor and his vision of African American destiny.[126] He often spoke of the "destined superiority" of African Americans, based on a theological framework that emphasized divine justice and racial uplift.[127] His sermons reflected an admiration for the Apostle Paul's character and spiritual depth, as well as a commitment to conveying the importance of a communal Christian identity shaped by personal integrity and divine inspiration. Crummell praised the "character" evident in Paul's Epistle to the Ephesians, seeing it as a "ground of excellence," especially in its depiction of the purity and steadfastness of the Ephesian church amid the "darkness of Ephesian pagan life."[128] Crummell's view of Paul went beyond admiration, highlighting him as a model of passionate spiritual life, describing him as "ardent, fiery, impulsive," and captivated by divine truth.[129]

Moreover, Crummell saw Paul's teachings as essential to fostering the principle of "brotherhood," which unites all believers in spiritual kinship. As he explains, the "principle of grace" transforms individual faith into a "corporate unity with the saints."[130] In Crummell's preaching, Paul's writings serve as a foundation for understanding how

---

[125] LaRue, *Heart*, 102.
[126] Ibid., 64–77. Crummell was an ordained priest of the Episcopal Church. He spent twenty years as a missionary in Liberia and later spent twenty-five years in Washington, DC. During his time in Washington, he worked alongside another influential pastor and preacher in the city, Francis James Grimké.
[127] Ibid., 70.
[128] Alexander Crummell, *The Greatness of Christ and Other Sermons* (New York: Thomas Whitaker, 2 and 3 Bible House, 1882), 135.
[129] Ibid., 82.
[130] Ibid., 141.

Christian love extends beyond personal salvation to include a communal harmony rooted in shared commitment to truth and righteousness.

Scholars like LaRue discuss Crummell's engagement with themes that align closely with Paul's teachings, allowing readers to draw connections between Crummell's moral and ethical focus and Pauline praxis. Similarly, William Henry Ferris in *Alexander Crummell: An Apostle of Negro Culture* and Wilson J. Moses in *Alexander Crummell: A Study of Civilization and Discontent* present Crummell in a way that invites comparisons to Paul, emphasizing his role in moral leadership and racial uplift without making overt references to Pauline scripture.[131]

James T. Campbell in *Songs of Zion: The African Methodist Episcopal Church in the United States and South Africa* and A. G. Miller in *Elevating the Race: Theophilus G. Steward, Black Theology, and the Making of an African American Civil Society, 1865–1924* offer analyses of Crummell's work that allow readers to draw thematic connections to Pauline praxis, though they do not explicitly make these connections themselves.[132] Similarly, Vincent Harding in *There is a River: The Black Struggle for Freedom in America* and George M. Fredrickson in *Black Liberation: A Comparative History of Black Ideologies in the United States and South Africa* provide contexts in which Crummell's adoption of ideas reminiscent of Pauline rhetoric becomes apparent, especially in his broader social justice efforts and advocacy for a more unified Christian body.[133]

---

[131] William Henry Ferris, *Alexander Crummell: An Apostle of Negro Culture* (Boston: Pilgrim Press, 1920); Wilson J. Moses, *Alexander Crummell: A Study of Civilization and Discontent* (New York: Oxford University Press, 1989).

[132] Campbell, *Songs of Zion*; A. G. Miller, *Elevating the Race: Theophilus G. Steward, Black Theology, and the Making of an African American Civil Society, 1865–1924* (Knoxville: University of Tennessee Press, 2003).

[133] Vincent Harding, *There is a River: The Black Struggle for Freedom in America* (New York: Harcourt Brace Jovanovich, 1981); George M. Fredrickson, *Black Liberation: A Comparative History of Black Ideologies in the United States and South Africa* (New York: Oxford University Press, 1995).

Edward J. Blum, in *Reforging the White Republic,* also offers perspectives that open the door to seeing Crummell as a modern interpreter of Pauline ethics, especially in his efforts to address social justice and racial equality.[134] These scholarly works do not explicitly link Crummell to Paul but instead provide a framework that encourages such connections, reflecting the broader impact of Pauline themes on Crummell's ministry and the African American religious experience in the nineteenth century.

Conclusion

The influence of the apostle Paul on the theological development and ministerial practices of early historical figures such as Chrysostom, Augustine, and Aquinas laid a robust foundation for later Christian leaders, including contemporaries of Grimké like Daniel Alexander Payne and Alexander Crummell. Each of these exemplars, to some measure, adapted Pauline teachings to the spiritual and communal needs of their times. Payne and Crummell, much like Grimké, drew from this tradition, particularly embodying Paul's focus on the gospel's indicatives concerning social interactions within the Christian community and beyond.

In conclusion, Grimké, Payne, and Crummell were contemporaries who shared a common heritage while addressing different aspects of African American religious life. Their ministries reflected meaningful and courageous engagement with the ethical, theological, and social dimensions of Paul's writings. With this as our foundation, we focus on the biographical elements of Grimké's activist EEH.

---

[134] Edward J. Blum, *Reforging the White Republic: Race, Religion, and American Nationalism, 1865–1898* (Baton Rouge: Louisiana State University Press, 2005).

Section Three—Grimké, the Emancipated "Echoer"

Grimké is a pivotal figure in the landscape of American religious history, particularly for his contributions to pastoral and public discourse during a time of significant racial and social upheaval. His eloquence in the pulpit and his forthrightness in public advocacy made him a vital voice for spiritual guidance and social justice. This section explores the depth and breadth of Grimké's impact, focusing on how his sermons and public addresses consistently reflected a robust engagement with Pauline praxis. By examining Grimké's life and ministry, we gain insight into how his Reformed evangelical perspective and commitment to personal piety shaped his responses to the pressing issues of his time.

Furthermore, one cannot overstate the providential irony of Grimké's Reformed evangelical perspective.[135] Rooted in the traditions of the Reformation, his theological approach characterized a firm adherence to the authority of scripture and the atonement of Christ, an emphasis on the doctrine of justification by faith, and a profound reliance on the transformative power of the Holy Spirit. This theological foundation and his personal piety informed every aspect of his ministry. Grimké's dedication to personal holiness was not merely a private endeavor, but also a public testament to his faith, influencing his homiletical tendencies and his fervent advocacy for civil rights. This section appraises how Grimké's puritanical inclinations were seamlessly integrated with his social activism, ultimately demonstrating his

---

[135] Larry E. Tise, *Proslavery: A History of the Defense of Slavery in America, 1701–1840* (Athens: University of Georgia Press, 1987), 112–98. The overwhelming majority of the extant examples of pro-slavery sermons from 1701–1840 were found among Presbyterian and Reformed Baptist clergy. This is particularly striking as a backdrop to Grimké's activism. Grimké does something different with his Reformed theological bent, suggesting a space to balance the tension of the gospel's indicatives over and against the implications of one's theological tribe. For Grimké, the gospel and its indicatives were the overriding factor in his theology. See Tables 5.1–6.23.

convictions' intrinsic link to his efforts to address and rectify social injustices.

Whispers of a Powerful Activism: A Historiographical Preview

This section surveys key scholarship on Grimké, emphasizing how historians and theologians have recognized his contributions to social justice and African American intellectual history. While a more thorough biographical treatment will be presented in Chapter 3, this literature review focuses on how Grimké's work has been analyzed across different historical and intellectual contexts.

Early Scholarship and Foundational Works

The historiographical exploration of Grimké reveals an evolving recognition of his profound contributions to social justice and African American intellectual history. Early scholarship, including Carter G. Woodson's seminal work, *The History of the Negro Church*, provides foundational insights into Grimké's pivotal role in developing the African American church and advocating for racial equality. [136] Woodson situates Grimké within the broader framework of African American religious leaders who utilized their platforms to combat segregation and discrimination, underscoring the importance of his sermons and writings in the larger struggle for civil rights.

Mid-Twentieth Century and Social Gospel Scholarship

As mid-twentieth century scholarship began to probe Grimké's theological and political thought with greater scrutiny, works like Ralph Luker's *The Social Gospel in Black and White: American Racial Reform, 1885–1912* illuminate Grimké's alignment with the Social Gospel movement.[137] Luker's analysis details how Grimké intertwined

---

[136] Carter G. Woodson, *The History of the Negro Church* (Washington, DC: Associated Publishers, 1921).

[137] Ralph Luker, *The Social Gospel in Black and White: American Racial Reform, 1885–1912* (Chapel Hill: University of North Carolina Press, 1991). It is

his religious beliefs with his activism, promoting social reforms that addressed systemic racial injustices. This period of historiographical inquiry underscores Grimké's dual identity as both a religious leader and a social reformer, emphasizing the interconnectedness of his spiritual convictions and political engagements—a critical theme in understanding his influence.

Legacy Preservation and Archival Work

Woodson's efforts in preserving and promoting Grimké's legacy are particularly noteworthy. Woodson's compilation and editing of *The Works of Francis J. Grimké* into four volumes, published in 1942, represents the most comprehensive repository of Grimké's primary source materials.[138] This collection, comprising Grimké's "Addresses," "Sermons," "Thoughts and Meditations," and "Letters," serves as a vital resource for scholars and activists, ensuring that Grimké's extensive body of work remains accessible for future generations. Woodson's dedication to this project solidifies Grimké's place as a prolific thinker whose writings continue to inform discussions on civil rights and social justice.

Contributions to African American Intellectual History

Recent decades have seen an expansion of Grimké studies, with scholars examining his contributions to African American literature and intellectual history. Patricia Hill Collins's *Black Feminist Thought: Knowledge, Consciousness, and the Politics of Empowerment* positions Grimké's writings within the broader intellectual tradition that shaped

---

pertinent to note that this is an ex post facto analytic that, in the author's considerations, potentially conflates and applies Grimké's activism beyond the heart of Grimké's theological bent. Luker, nonetheless, provides important practical details about the texture of Grimké's activism and its eventual effect in shaping the ministry of Martin Luther King, Jr. and other Christian civil rights activists.

[138] Woodson, *Works of Francis J. Grimké.*

later generations of African American thinkers.[139] Collins's work highlights how Grimké's ideas resonate within the continuum of African American intellectual history, influencing subsequent civil rights movements and underscoring the constant relevance of his thought in contemporary discourse on race and justice.

Rhetorical and Biographical Analyses

Specific works, such as Carolyn R. Calloway's *A Rhetorical Analysis of the Persuasion of Francis J. Grimké* and Henry Justin Ferry's *Francis James Grimké: Portrait of a Black Puritan*, provide deeper insights into Grimké's rhetorical style and personal philosophy.[140,141] Calloway's rhetorical analysis reveals Grimké's evocative use of language to advocate for civil rights.[142] At the same time, Ferry's biography comprehensively portrays Grimké's life through an emphasis on his adherence to Puritanical values and his relentless pursuit of social justice. These rare and pivotal research treatises contribute to a more nuanced understanding of Grimké's methods and motivations as they illustrate the complexity and depth of his activism.

---

[139] Patricia Hill Collins, *Black Feminist Thought: Knowledge, Consciousness, and the Politics of Empowerment* (New York: Routledge, 2000).

[140] Calloway, "Rhetorical."

[141] Ferry, "Puritan."

[142] Calloway, "Rhetorical," 177. Calloway observes, "Given [Grimké's] strident phrasing, it was easy for whites to interpret his rhetoric as a threat to their economic and social order, as a menace to their determination to 'keep the Negro in his place.' . . . Once, for example, he told the editor of *The Continent*, 'I agree with all you say under the first three general heads, but after I had finished reading under the last general head, I wrote on the margin, these words which spontaneously came to my lips, 'That man talks more like a heathen than a Christian.' He indicted white America's record on racial equality, calling it 'a failure, a pitiable failure.' And 'the shame of it all,' he said, 'is that it has failed not because of inability but because of the unfaithfulness of its professed followers, because the men and women who ought to stand up for the Christian principles have surrended [sic] them through weakness, through cowardice.'"

Interdisciplinary and Thematic Studies

Interdisciplinary approaches have further enriched the historiography of Grimké's legacy by integrating perspectives from gender studies, cultural history, and postcolonial theory. For example, *Lift Every Voice: African American Oratory, 1787–1900*, edited by Philip S. Foner and Robert James Branham, explores Grimké's oratorical techniques and his rhetorical tendencies in advocating for racial equality. [143] These studies emphasize the multifaceted nature of Grimké's activism, recognizing him as a central figure in America's broader struggle for social justice.

Articles and Focused Historical Analyses

Mark Sidwell's article, "Francis Grimké and the Value and Limits of Carter Woodson's Model of the Progressive Black Pastor," adds another layer of complexity to the historiography by analyzing Grimké's place within Woodson's conceptual framework. [144] Sidwell explores how Grimké's blend of conservative theology with radical social activism challenges the traditional dichotomy between conservative and progressive ideologies within the African American church. This analysis emphasizes the intersection of religious and social dimensions in Grimké's life, contributing to a more intricate understanding of his activism.

Malcolm Foley's chapter "The Only Way to Stop a Mob: Francis Grimké's Biblical Case for Lynching Resistance," in the book *Every Leaf, Line, and Letter: Evangelicals and the Bible from the 1730s to the Present*, critically examines Grimké's theological response to lynching.[145] Foley's

---

[143] Philip S. Foner and Robert James Branham, eds., *Lift Every Voice: African American Oratory, 1787–1900* (Tuscaloosa: University of Alabama Press, 1998).

[144] Sidwell, "Value," 99–117.

[145] Malcolm Foley, "The Only Way to Stop a Mob: Francis Grimké's Biblical Case for Lynching Resistance," in *Every Leaf, Line, and Letter: Evangelicals and the Bible from the 1730s to the Present*, ed. Timothy Larsen (Downers Grove, IL: InterVarsity Press, 2021), 196–217.

work reveals how Grimké utilized biblical exegesis to argue against lynching and to mobilize his congregation for resistance. By framing lynching as antithetical to Christian values, Grimké underscored the moral imperative for African Americans to defend themselves against such violence, adding depth to the understanding of his religious and social thought.

Robert F. Schwarzwalder, Jr.'s article, "For a Real, Not a Sham Christianity: Francis J. Grimké on Racial Strife and World Peace in the Early Twentieth Century," published in *Fides et Historia*, explores Grimké's theological perspective on Christianity as a foundation for racial equality and global peace.[146] Schwarzwalder's analysis situates Grimké's views within the broader context of his activism by illustrating how his religious convictions informed his critiques of both domestic and international policies, further demonstrating the relevance of Grimké's ideas in contemporary discussions on social justice.

Mark A. Noll's article, "Theology, Presbyterian History, and the Civil War," published in *Presbyterian History*, provides additional context by examining Grimké's theological commitments alongside his fierce opposition to racial injustice.[147] Noll underscores how Grimké maintained a traditional Presbyterian theology by advocating tirelessly for racial justice. His commitment to his faith's spiritual and social dimensions is evident in his substantial ministry at the Fifteenth Street Presbyterian Church in Washington, DC, where he consistently preached sermons grounded in scripture while supporting Black reform movements and civil rights causes. Noll's analysis further illustrates the depth of Grimké's influence within the Presbyterian tradition and his role as a bridge between religious conviction and social activism.

---

[146] Schwarzwalder, "For a Real, Not a Sham Christianity," 17–33.

[147] Mark A. Noll, "Theology, Presbyterian History, and the Civil War," *Presbyterian History* 89, no. 1 (Spring/Summer 2011): 5–15.

Noll further explores Grimké's theological and social impact in his book chapter, "Still Under a Bushel," from *America's Book: The Rise and Decline of a Bible Civilization, 1794–1911*.[148] Here, Noll portrays Grimké as a compelling example of the characteristic holism with which many African Americans approached the Scriptures. Grimké's career, marked by his long service at Washington's Fifteenth Street Presbyterian Church, exemplified a thoroughly traditional theology deeply intertwined with a commitment to racial justice. Noll highlights Grimké's unwavering belief in divine revelation, the unity of humankind, and the power of Christian redemption, which shaped his lifelong ministry. Despite the intense racial prejudices of his time, Grimké remained steadfast in his mission to advocate for both the spiritual and social elevation of African Americans. His sermons and writings reflect a consistent effort to fuse religious conviction with social activism. Through his examination, Noll provides a nuanced understanding of Grimké's legacy as a preacher who did not shy away from addressing the pressing social issues of his day.

Ferry's article "Patriotism and Prejudice: Francis James Grimké on World War I," published in *The Journal of Religious Thought*, delves into Grimké's complex views on patriotism during World War I.[149] Ferry highlights how Grimké balanced his advocacy for African American participation in the war effort with his criticism of the racial prejudices prevalent in the United States.[150]

---

[148] Mark A. Noll, "Still Under a Bushel," in *America's Book: The Rise and Decline of a Bible Civilization, 1794–1911* (New York: Oxford University Press, 2022; online ed, Oxford Academic, April 21, 2022), https://doi.org/10.1093/oso/9780197623466.003.0031.

[149] Henry Justin Ferry, "Patriotism and Prejudice: Francis James Grimké on World War I," *Journal of Religious Thought* 32 (Spring–Summer 1975): 86–94.

[150] See also Henry Justin Ferry, "Francis James Grimke: Prophet on a Tightrope," lecture notes, Reformed Institute of Metropolitan Washington, date unknown, accessed August 8, 2024, https://reformedinstitute.org/resources/.

W. B. Hesseltine's article "Some New Aspects of the Pro-Slavery Argument," published in *The Journal of Negro History*, adds valuable context to Grimké's work by examining the pro-slavery rhetoric that he consistently opposed. [151] Hesseltine discusses how pro-slavery advocates sought to justify the institution of slavery, which Grimké challenged through his sermons and writings. Notably, Hesseltine highlights Grimké's defense of Elizabeth Keckley, a formerly enslaved woman and author of *Behind the Scenes*, against claims questioning her existence and authorship. Grimké's accounts refuting these assertions provide crucial historical insights into his intellectual and moral battles against entrenched pro-slavery ideologies.

Contemporary Analyses and Relevance

Most recently, the chapter "Pandemics, the Rev. Francis J. Grimké, and Life Lessons" by Kathryn Freeman, Elise M. Edwards, Bertis D. English, and Stephanie C. Boddie, published in *Racialized Health, COVID-19, and Religious Responses*, draws clear parallels between Grimké's response to the 1918 influenza pandemic and the challenges posed by the COVID-19 pandemic.[152] The authors focus on Grimké's November 3, 1918, sermon, which addressed the spiritual and social implications of the influenza outbreak. In it, Grimké emphasized the importance of learning moral lessons from such crises and called for repentance and social unity—messages that resonate strongly with today's global struggles. This chapter highlights Grimké's present relevance in addressing public health crises through the lens of social justice and religious conviction, demonstrating how his historical activism continues to offer valuable guidance in modern times.

---

[151] W. B. Hesseltine, "Some New Aspects of the Pro-Slavery Argument," *Journal of Negro History* 21, no. 1 (1936): 1–59.

[152] Kathryn Freeman et al., "Pandemics, the Rev. Francis J. Grimké, and Life Lessons," in *Racialized Health, COVID-19, and Religious Responses: Black Atlantic Contexts and Perspectives*, ed. R. Drew Smith, Stephanie C. Boddie, and Bertis D. English (New York: Routledge, 2022), 99–109.

In *The Mount of Vision: African American Prophetic Tradition, 1800–1950*, the African American prophetic tradition is examined with a focus on its historical development and key figures, including Francis James Grimké.[153] The book investigates Grimké's significant role in interpreting divine will and advocating for justice within the context of his time. Hobson lifts Grimké's sermons and public addresses as vital components of his ministry, demonstrating a skillful mobilization of his religious convictions through social activism.

In summary, the small but growing body of scholarship on Grimké highlights his significant role in the fight for civil rights. More importantly, Grimke's stalwart commitment to the Pauline praxis of scripturally sound activism is a model that merits repeating. As scholars continue to explore his contributions, Grimké's legacy remains an essential component of American intellectual and cultural history, echoing the whispers of a powerful activism that still resonates today.

Conclusion

In conclusion, this chapter has explored how Pauline echoes have been utilized by theologians and preachers across history to address social and theological issues, culminating in the work of Grimké. These echoes were expressed through both direct quotations of Pauline texts and engagements with OT scriptures that followed the interpretive practices Paul modeled in his epistles. This phenomenon was sometimes a conscious execution of Pauline teachings and themes, but often it represented an unconscious embodiment of Pauline praxis. By surveying figures such as Chrysostom, Augustine, and Calvin, we have traced the persistent influence of Paul's teachings on key figures in church history. This foundation establishes the broader context in which Grimké's homiletical and social engagement with racial and social challenges can be understood.

---

[153] Christopher Z. Hobson, *The Mount of Vision: African American Prophetic Tradition, 1800–1950* (New York: Oxford University Press, 2012), passim.

As we move forward, Chapter 3 will provide a biographical sketch of Grimké, examining the formative influences on his thought and ministry. This deeper exploration will help illuminate how his unique historical and theological context shaped his approach to gospel preaching and social activism, particularly in the face of racial and social challenges.

CHAPTER 3

THE MAKING OF AN EVANGELICAL EMANCIPATOR

> *Twenty years ago, when I was a sophomore at Yale, men spoke the name "Dr. Grimké" with respect and reverence. And they do today . . . . Since the deaths of Bishop Daniel Payne 1893 and Dr. Alexander Crummell 1898, Dr. Grimké has remained the most potent figure in the Negro ecclesiastical world.*
>
> William H. Ferris, 1912[1]

In his 1970 Yale treatise concerning Ferris's trumpeted herald of Grimké, Dr. Henry Justin Ferry lamented, "Fifty years later [Grimké's] name was known but to a handful of scholars, black or white."[2] Whatever faint echoes might have remained in Ferry's day, they are greatly reduced now. To that end, we will reamplify through a biographical sketch the enchanted voice of one of the church's finest preachers—The Reverend Francis James Grimké.[3]

This biographical sketch will explore the key experiences and theological influences that shaped Grimké's distinctive evangelical emancipatory homiletic (EEH). By examining his life's journey—from his early years in enslavement to emancipation, theological training,

---

[1] William H. Ferris, *The African Abroad*, vol. 2 (New Haven, CT: Tuttle, Morehouse & Taylor, 1913), 888–89, cited in Ferry, "Puritan," ii. Ferry notes that Ferris initially made this acknowledgement of Grimké in 1912.

[2] Ferry, "Puritan," ii.

[3] Reader's note: The author acknowledges that the works documenting Grimké's biography are limited. Despite a narrow bounty, the existing body boasts reliability worthy of record. Though not the core overarching objective of the undertaking, the aim of this chapter is (1) to contribute additional documentation to an underrepresented voice in the history of the American church and (2) to verify and clarify the sourced materials of the existing works. As such, the author may be more generous than typical in quotes and citations to maintain an ongoing record of this important narrative.

and ministry—we see how his narrative informed his approach to gospel preaching and activism. His life and theological convictions fused into a voice that both echoed and expanded the apostle Paul's hermeneutic and heart, addressing not only racial and social injustices but also calling believers to embody gospel ethics within their communities.

Ultimately, this chapter provides a contextual foundation for later analyses of Grimké's homiletical framework, examining how his gospel-embodied activism engaged theological and social challenges that remain relevant for contemporary evangelical approaches to social issues.

The Early Years

The story begins with one of America's most stark contradictions: the coexistence of aristocratic privilege and the brutal reality of slavery. Amid the pine-forested ridges of the Charleston Colleton Districts in South Carolina's Lowcountry, "Caneacres" emerged among the nation's most productive rice plantations.[4] Located roughly twenty-five miles from Charleston, where the Grimké name was "synonymous with aristocracy," the widower Henry Grimké watched from a distance as his "mulatto servant girl," Nancy Weston, gave birth to the second son

---

[4] Ferry, "Puritan," 1, 2–5. The author visited the general region of the former "Caneacres" Plantation in the summer of 2024. The area was located off Cane Acre Road, and it seems that the name Caneacres might have been either a portmanteau of 'Cane' and 'Acre's' or Ferry's attempt to capture the unique dialect of the Gullah people recording the name phonetically in his treatise. For more on the latter practice, see Lorenzo Dow Turner, *Africanisms in the Gullah Dialect* (Chicago: University of Chicago Press, 1949), 254. Turner speaks of transcribing recordings from phonograph disks into phonetic notations to document the authentic expression of the people in his research. Perhaps, Ferry, in tribute to Grimké's African heritage, was doing something similar. Given Ferry's careful attention throughout this well-researched and rare treatise on Grimké, it is doubtful this is a typographical error.

of their growing contraband family.[5] It was a Monday, November 4, 1850, and they named the boy Frank, short for Francis—Francis James Grimké.[6]

The notes of a peppered pedigree marked the earliest years of young Frank's life.[7] Nancy was a progeny of African and European parentage and played an active role in the life of Henry's first family as a nurse before the death of his wife, Selina.[8] Henry was an Englishman

---

[5] Ibid., 2. The term "contraband" generally referred to enslaved people who escaped to Union lines during the Civil War, but here it alludes to the socially and legally precarious status of Henry Grimké's children with his enslaved "servant girl," Nancy Weston, due to the racial dynamics and laws of the time. For more on the term, see Ira Berlin, ed., *The Destruction of Slavery,* vol. 1 of *Freedom: A Documentary History of Emancipation, 1861–1867* (Cambridge: Cambridge University Press, 1985); Eric Foner, *Give Me Liberty! An American History*, vol. 1, 6th ed. (New York: W. W. Norton & Company, 2020); George W. Williams, *A History of the Negro Troops in the War of the Rebellion* (New York: Harper and Brothers, 1888), 69–71, 73, 98, 190, 344, 529–30, 532.

[6] Grimké, *Works I*, xii, as detailed in the editorial introduction by renowned African American historian Carter G. Woodson. See also Dickson D. Bruce, *Archibald Grimke: Portrait of a Black Independent* (Baton Rouge: Louisiana State University Press, 1993), 4. Bruce notes, "In an interesting reversal of one of the hoariest conventions of African-American autobiography, Archie recalled that his father named him. According to Archie, all the slave children of the plantation were automatically called James, and this applied to him as well. His father objected, however, changed his son's name to Archibald, calling him Archie." The same was ostensibly the case with his younger brother, Francis.

[7] For a significant portion of this chapter, the author heeds the following observation of Princeton scholar, Mary Nickel, "Because of what will become an obvious necessity, I will refer to the personalities treated in the following narrative according to their first names. Because virtually all of the individuals described are members of one family, it would be impractical to refer to them by their last name. This procedural point . . . is thus fitting to refer not to this or that Grimké—though the name does carry a certain significance—but of [Frank], [Archie], Henry, Nancy, Angelina." See Mary Nickel, "Incorporating Intimacy: The Evocative Story of Francis J. Grimké," *Journal of Black Religious Thought* 1, no. 2 (2022): 199n3, https://doi.org/10.1163/27727963-01020005.

[8] Bruce, *Archibald*, 2; Ferry, "Puritan," 3.

of the highest order whose family boasted lawyers, state supreme court justices, plantation owners, and, ironically, two of the most noted abolitionists in the world, the famous Grimké sisters, Angelina and Sarah. [9] Though illegal, Henry and Nancy's "common law" arrangement was later described by their boys as warm.[10]

If, in earnest, it was a warm "marriage," void of the power dynamics often prevalent in the illicit arrangements of that day, it did not last long.[11] In an unexpected turn of providence, Nancy, pregnant with their third son, John, bid her final goodbyes to Henry as he succumbed to a typhoid fever outbreak on September 29, 1852.[12] That woeful Wednesday ended Caneacres, and Nancy and her two young boys returned to Charleston, Henry, having left instructions in his will

---

[9] Ferry, "Puritan," 61. The Grimké brothers did not come to know their famous aunts until their post-emancipation teen years.

[10] Bruce, *Archibald*, 3. See also Archibald H. Grimké, "Memoirs of Archibald H. Grimké," 4, in Archibald H. Grimké Papers, Box 2, Folder 47, Moorland-Spingarn Research Center, Howard University, Washington, DC; Henry Grimké, "Letter to 'Dear Boys,'" n.d., in E. Montague Grimké Papers. Bruce notes, "In his letters to his sons [from his first wife, Selina], Henry always mentioned Nancy with affection. In one letter, he talked about an episode of fever that had put her in bed for over two weeks. Henry took her into his house and nursed her continuously. . . . Nancy, for her part, later told Archie that she had 'believed absolutely' in Henry." See also, Ferry, "Puritan," 1–3; Nickel, "Intimacy," 199.

[11] Ibid., 4. As was often the case, these "arrangements" were complex and nuanced. Bruce observed, "It would be a mistake, however, to assume that Henry shared his more famous abolitionist sisters' racial enlightenment. As a young man, he was a notably cruel master . . . he remained strongly attached to slavery and, whatever feelings he had for Nancy, to white supremacy. . . . In a letter to Montague, for instance, he professed his faith in the doctrines of equality proclaimed in the American Declaration of Independence but concluded, 'These remarks apply exclusively to the Caucasian race.'" Bruce further notes, "The relationship between Henry and the sons Nancy bore him, was distant but affectionate. Certainly, Henry considered them slaves, but he did not list them as such in the 1850 census of slaves on his plantation."

[12] Ibid., 5.

for them (though still legally enslaved) to be treated "as members of the family."[13]

Frank and his brothers, Archibald and John, were reared in this contradictory amalgam for the next several years. They straddled the bizarre divide between privilege and oppression as they wrestled with the dynamic interplay of bondage and freedom. The brothers later journaled their mother's faith-filled devotion and its pivotal role in nurturing them through the torn nature of their predicament. Archibald wrote:

> Well do I recall many an evening scene of this mother and her 95adies, recall her in her plain little sitting room, with a child on either side as she talked in her simple, earnest, Christian way of heaven and hell. Her description of the future home of the good made virtue appear beautiful to the boys and greatly to be desired, while her portrayal of the future abode of the wicked made sin seem hideous to them and above all things to be shunned. How she did it, I would fain put into words, but it was not what she said so much as how she looked and breathed and lived each day of life in the presence of her children.[14]

Frank's reflections were no less moving. He journaled in his later years:

> In the room where I am sitting, between my picture and that of dear Lottie [his wife], hangs the picture of my mother looking down upon me as I write. Hers is a strong, sweet, kind, benevolent face. Can I ever forget her? Never. Was there ever a better mother— a more loving, self-sacrificing, devoted mother? Never. . . . There never was a better mother—a mother more

---

[13] Calloway, "Rhetorical," 1. See also, Bruce, *Archibald*, 5–7; Ferry, "Puritan," 8–13.

[14] Archibald H. Grimké, "A Madonna of the South," *The Southern Workman* 29, no. 7 (July 1900): 392. Originally sourced in Ferry, "Puritan," 21n2.

> deeply and sincerely and intelligently devoted to the best interest of her children.[15]

As the brothers grew older, their mother's devotion increasingly shaped their character and aspirations. For Frank, these *sentinel lessons* [my emphasis] in resilience and perseverance were particularly formative. They laid the foundation for his eventual work as a gospel preacher and advocate for racial equality.[16] As he continued to build on her foundation, Frank's life became a testament to the power of a mother's principled love. Years later, the echoes of Nancy's teachings resonated far beyond their humble Charleston home as they amplified the voice and "prophetic bite" of one of the nation's most respected and influential preachers.[17]

Frank—A Big Bite

The bond between the Grimké brothers was one forged in adversity and loss. Like "latter-day Musketeers," they gained "dubious fame" on the streets of Charleston, where they became known as most formidable fighters among the local boys.[18] Each brother excelled in his own way: John, the youngest, was the champion "butter," known for his swift head butts; Frank, the middle son and most diminutive in

---

[15] Grimké, *Works III*, 610–11.

[16] Ferry, "Puritan," 21–24.

[17] Grimké, *Works III*, 94. On the occasion of his seventieth birthday, a reflective Grimké penned, "And among the blessings of these years that I can look back to, was that of a good mother,—one of the truest, best, noblest of women. No sacrifice was too great for her to make for her children; and the standard which she held ever before them, and to which she required them to conform, was always the highest. She strived, as earnestly as any mother ever did, to bring her children up right. And I feel that the blessings that have attended us have been due largely to her prayers on our behalf." See, Francis James Grimké, *The Works of Francis J. Grimke*, vol. 2, ed. Carter G. Woodson (Washington, DC: Associated, 1942), viii for Woodson's note on Grimké's fierce prophetic zeal.

[18] Ferry, "Puritan," 18.

stature, earned the title of champion "biter," a fierce and determined fighter who, fortuitously, had no problem using his mouth to win a battle; and Archibald, the oldest, was the champion "kicker," whose well-aimed strikes were both feared and respected. The trio always fought in unison, embodying the philosophy that "an attack on one was an attack on all."[19]

On one notable occasion, a group of "white boy toughs" attacked the three brothers. Refusing to back down, Frank stood his ground. When Archie returned, after initially scurrying for the younger John's safety, he found Frank on top of a boy, "pounding him for all he could give him!"[20] There was no doubt concerning Frank's nerve, and this reputation would follow him for the remainder of his life. Fearless and unrelenting, the young Frank was already packing a biting punch that would foreshadow his prophetic praxis and legacy as a gospel preacher and activist.

Familial Betrayal and "Re-Enslavement"

Henry's will made vague provisions for Nancy and their children. It, in effect, tendered a "quasi-free status" under the guardianship of his eldest son, Montague Grimké.[21] Henry assured Nancy that "though he would not free her, he would 'leave [her] better than free'" through Montague's oversight.[22] Nancy implicitly trusted Henry's words as a gesture of "good faith."[23]

Unfortunately, it did not take long for Nancy to see that Montague's guardianship starkly contrasted with her expectations. Although the auction liquidating Henry's estate did not result in a journey to the slave blocks, Montague's wardship quickly proved less

---

19 Ibid.

20 Angelina Weld Grimké, "A Biographical Sketch of Archibald H. Grimke," *Opportunity* 3 (February 1925): 46, as cited in Ferry, "Puritan," 17–18. Hereafter, A. W. G., "Sketch."

21 Bruce, *Archibald*, 6.

22 Ibid. See also Calloway, "Rhetorical," 1, 18n4.

23 Ibid., 5, 6.

protective than Henry promised.[24] The nebulous language of Henry's will left Nancy and her children vulnerable to the wiles of Montague, as they were technically his property.[25] Despite his father's directives, Montague did not handle his half-brothers and "foster mother" with the familial care promised, essentially leaving them destitute.[26]

The years that followed insisted grinding hardship upon them. Nancy, later described by Archie as "a poor mother, a defenceless [*sic*] woman, crippled in one arm," took on washing and ironing to support the family.[27] This period, which her elder son later described as "bitter years," was characterized by extreme deprivation. [28] Nancy relied heavily on the charity of her brothers, especially Isaac, a butcher who provided them with leftover victuals. [29] With the funds from the sale of her livestock with Henry's estate, she commissioned a first cousin of her mother, a free black drayman—Samuel O'Hear, to build a small three-room cottage on his back lot a few blocks north of Montague's house.[30]

By 1860, the situation for Nancy and the boys had taken a decided turn for the worse. Montague had taken a new wife, and his need for new servants landed squarely on his brothers. In a campaign to satisfy the new "Mistress's" need for house servants, he defaulted on his father's promise, effectively re-enslaving the boys.[31] Unsurprisingly, Frank resisted, making several attempts to escape.[32] However, his bids

---

[24] Ferry, "Puritan," 10, 12. Ferry write, "The oblique recognition of [Nancy's] 'property rights,' itself contrary to the slave code, represents tacit admission of the Montague's moral obligation to treat [her] and her children as members of the family. Yet Montague's attitude was ambiguous."

[25] Ibid., 12, 24–36.

[26] Ibid., 2–3.

[27] Ibid., 13–14.

[28] Bruce, *Archibald*, 7.

[29] Ibid.

[30] Ibid. See Ferry, "Puritan," 12.

[31] Calloway, "Rhetorical," 3. See Ferry, "Puritan," 26.

[32] Ferry, "Puritan," 27–30, 32–35.

for freedom were short-lived; he was bountied, soon recaptured, and returned to Montague.[33]

Finally tiring of his "irksome" half-brother, with Frank's return, Montague took the opportunity to rid himself of the "Tarter."[34] Ferry writes,

> In this sale, the last vestige of independence was stripped from Frank. Title to his person changed hands; he had, in fact been reduced to the status of chattel property. Thus, he remained until the fortunes of war actualized Lincoln's Emancipation Proclamation for those slaves in the "cradle of the Confederacy." [35]

Biographical Reflection. Grimké's early years, marked by stark contrasts of privilege and oppression, laid a unique groundwork for his ministry and his engagement with Paul's gospel message of reconciliation. Perhaps his biracial identity, much like Paul's dual citizenship, gave him an intimate perspective on the social and ethnic divisions around him and a personal stake in bridging these divides. Furthermore, the betrayal and re-enslavement he faced under his half-brother's guardianship likely deepened his commitment to justice and resilience, fueling his later activism against the racial inequities he encountered. Through his mother's faith and her own fortitude in adversity, Grimké gained a blueprint for a faith that would not only endure hardship but would also actively seek to rectify injustices. This complex combination of familial loyalty, betrayal, and a faith-centered upbringing laid a foundation for the future evolution of Grimké's

---

[33] Ibid., 35. The following appeared in the *Mercury* in 1863: "FIFTY DOLLARS REWARD FRANCIS (a brown boy) about 15 years old, 4 feet 9 inches high; ran away from the Charleston Hotel in July."
[34] Ibid., 27, 36; Bruce, *Archibald*, 16; Francis J. Grimké, "Letter to 'Dear Bro,'" January 24, 1887, in *Francis Grimké Papers*, Box 1, Folder 1.
[35] Ibid., 36.

EEH—a homiletic that would confront injustice with an unwavering commitment to gospel fidelity.

From Emancipation to Education

> *We need educated ministers, yes; we need men who know what is going on in the world about them, yes; but the great need is for men who believe firmly in the Scriptures as the word of God, and who faithfully preach the truth therein contained, in dependence upon the Holy Spirit to give efficacy to the truth, and not upon their training, their education, their ability to construct arguments in defence [*sic*] of the truth.*
>
> Francis James Grimké[36]

Dissonance in the Postbellum South

The Civil War's end was an inflection point for the Grimké brothers. The Confederacy's defeat legally freed them from the bonds of slavery. But, transitioning from enslaved to emancipated was no light affliction. The fallen South was in turmoil and struggling to rebuild war-torn cities as it adapted to a new reality.[37] Charleston was no exception. Harriet H. Ravenel, the famed nineteenth-century Charlestonian poet, author, and historian, wrote,

> Everything was overgrown with rank, untrimmed, vegetation. Not grass merely, but bushes, grew in the streets. The gardens looked as if the Sleeping Beauty might be within. The houses were indescribable: the gable was out of one, the chimneys fallen from the next; here a roof was shattered, there a piazza half gone; not a

---

[36] Grimké, *Works III*, 191. Reader's note: Grimké's pneumatological emphasis persisted throughout his ministry. His preaching and activism were inextricably tied to his "dependence upon the Holy Spirit." The author contends that an analysis of Grimké's work is most comprehensive against the backdrop of his pneumatology.

[37] Ibid., 37–40.

window remained. The streets looked as if piled with diamonds, the glass lay slivered so thick on the ground.[38]

As the dissonance of defeat abounded, a nascent hope emerged through educational initiatives for the newly emancipated. Among these was the Morris Street School, established by the Freedmen's Bureau to educate freed black children.[39] Here, Frank and his brothers came under the principalship of Frances Pillsbury, a dedicated abolitionist from the North.[40] Under "Mrs. Pillsbury," the brothers showed the early signs of intellectual prowess and conviction that would later define their life's work, their progress so impressive that it became evident the Grimké brothers needed a "more advantageous learning situation" if they were to reach their full potential in the "prosecution of [their] studies."[41]

The Journey Northward

With the constraints of the postbellum South ever pressing, Pillsbury sought more appropriate opportunities for the brothers. Leveraging her husband's weighty name and connections within abolitionist circles, she arranged their journey northward. "Frank was to go to Stoneham, Massachusetts, and study medicine with Dr. John Brown, who had been a surgeon with the 55th Colored Regiment. Archie was to study law with the Boston abolitionist, Samuel E. Sewall,

---

[38] Harriott H. Ravenel, *Charleston: The Place and the People* (New York: Macmillan, 1906), 505; Ferry, "Puritan," 37.

[39] Ferry, "Puritan," 42; Bruce, *Archibald*, 17. See also Joel Williamson, *After Slavery: The Negro in South Carolina During Reconstruction, 1861–1877* (Chapel Hill: University of North Carolina Press, 1965), 211; A. W. G., "Sketch," 45.

[40] Ferry, "Puritan," 45.

[41] Grimké, *Works I*, xi. See also Ferry, "Puritan," 45–46.

who was also an old friend of Sarah Grimke and Angelina Grimke Weld,"[42] but ended up with a family in Peacedale, Rhode Island.[43]

Frank's reception was chilling. Dr. Brown was not nearly as enlightened as one might suppose—housing Frank in a barn and relegating his sleeping quarters to a hayloft exposed to the bitter cold and damp. Frank later wrote, "During my whole stay with them, I was forced to sleep in the barn, in the hayloft, with no other mattress than the hay, and no other bedstead than the floor. . . . My treatment while with them was so different from what I had been led to expect that I would receive, that I soon left them."[44] The ill conditions quickly drove Frank's escape to a brief foray in the shoe business after "'learning of the . . . business' from his 'very warm friends,' Mr. and Mrs. [Lyman] Dyke" of Stoneham.[45]

Though slightly better, Archie faced challenges adjusting as well. The separation from his brothers and the strain of adapting to a new environment weighed on him.[46] It was increasingly apparent that the boys' circumstances were not conducive to successful studies, and soon, word of their declining progress would reach Pillsbury through the advocacy, once again, of their mother, Nancy.[47]

Another Emancipation

The toll on Frank and Archie was too drastic for Pillsbury to ignore. Concerned for their well-being, in the spring of 1866, she instructed the teens to "repair at once" for evacuation to Pennsylvania, confident they could resume their studies in a more supportive environment.[48] Her intuition was accurate.

---

[42] Ferry, "Puritan," 46.
[43] Bruce, *Archibald*, 18.
[44] Grimké, *Works I*, viii, as quoted in Ferry, "Puritan," 48.
[45] Ferry, "Puritan," 48–49.
[46] Bruce, *Archibald*, 18–19.
[47] Ibid., 19.
[48] Ibid.; Ferry, "Puritan," 49.

In Pennsylvania, the brothers found the stability they needed at Lincoln University.[49] Their youngest brother, John, joined them in 1868 but did not stay long. (The trauma of the earliest events of their lives had ostensibly wounded him—a struggle that would remain with John for the balance of his days.)[50] Frank and Archie, however, thrived, their resilience capturing the attention of their teachers and broader audiences. So compelling was their achievement that national publications began to feature them.[51] Through this publicity, their aunts, Sarah and Angelina Grimké, learned of their existence. Recognizing the family name, they reached out to their yet-not-disclosed nephews.[52] Archibald aptly responded, beginning what would become a powerful familial relationship.[53]

---

[49] Bruce, *Archibald*, 20. Bruce clarifies that Lincon's matriculation process involved two departments—a "Preparatory Department" and a "Collegiate Department." He writes, "Archie and Frank first entered the Preparatory Department, spending their first spring and then their first full academic year there, before going on to their college-level studies in the fall of 1867." A deeper dive into the brother's years at Lincoln would require understanding the distinction to portray specific timelines accurately.

[50] Ferry, "Puritan," 63, 65, 109.

[51] Ferry, "Puritan," 59.

[52] Ibid., 59–60. Here, Ferry shares the initial letter written by Angelina Grimké Weld to the brothers. See also A. G. Weld "Letter to Mr. Grimkie [*sic*]," February 15, 1868, Grimké Papers, Howard University.

[53] A. W. G., "Sketch," 46, as cited in Ferry, "Puritan," 62. Archibald's daughter later humorously wrote of the brothers' first meeting with their famous but modest aunts, "They often laugh now, over the picture they must have presented to the astonished eyes of the Weld family that was the simplest of the simple in manner, dress, and living. To the boys, this was a great occasion, the greatest in all their lives and, cost what it might, they were determined to live up to it. They were virtually penniless, but each carried a cane, wore a high silk hat which had been made to order, and boots that were custom-made. Whatever the aunts and the Welds thought, they were welcomed with wide-open arms and hearts and made at home. The simplicity here soon taught them their lesson."

From then on, the aunts became active mentors.[54]

The Lincoln Years

Founded as Ashmun Institute and later renamed Lincoln University in honor of President Abraham Lincoln, a group of "Presbyterians seeking [to find] middle ground between abolitionist and pro-slavery extremes" established an institution to prepare "free American Negroes 'for the missionary and Colonization work in Africa.'"[55] The curriculum focused on classical and theological studies and required students to learn Latin, Greek, mathematics, and the natural sciences. Religious instruction remained a core emphasis with perennial "study of the Westminster Catechism, the Bible, Biblical geography, and a more popular theological work, Charles Hodge's *Way of Life*." Frank and Archie relished the rigor, invariably finishing atop their class.[56]

In the summers, like many peers needing additional support, the brothers took on various jobs—often returning to the South to work in freedmen's schools teaching newly emancipated youth.[57] These episodes were not just practical, but also fomented an active commitment to the uplift of their people. In aggregate, through their summer duties and school activities, the early permeations of leadership had begun to emerge.

---

[54] Ferry, "Puritan," 65. Ferry avers, "Frank and Archie responded positively to their aunts' exhortations; thus 'Yankee' virtues joined evangelical piety and classical education in shaping their character."

[55] Ibid., 49–50. Author's note: The providence of God directing Grimké to an institute named for the architect of the Emancipation Proclamation is not lost on this researcher. Furthermore, the author acknowledges and affirms the irony of the university's initial mission. Ferry notes, "The school reflected the mediating bias of many Presbyterians in the ante-bellum era. . . . Basic to this view was a rather positive acceptance of American slavery as a beneficial part of God's plan for Africa."

[56] Ibid., 52, 56–58, 69.

[57] Ibid., 66.

Emergence as a Leader

Frank's unusual instinct in articulating ideas made him a leader amongst his peers. He was not a simple mouthpiece. He was thoughtful, and professors and fellow students alike increasingly recognized his reflective oratory prowess.[58] Actively participating in literary societies, such as the Philosophian Society and the Garnet Lyceum, he, no doubt, was fearless in engaging the most challenging issues of the day.[59] Frank's incisive way and biting wit were golden, and as his future wife would later declare, he spoke with the grace of a "colored Chrysostom."[60]

By graduation, the administration had selected him to share the "Valedictory Oration."[61] The future was promising as commencement approached, and the brothers were anxious to continue their education. Their aunts, though proud, advised Frank and Archie to take a "year of out-door [*sic*] manual labor" as a break. But the brothers did not relent.[62] The emerging leaders had set their eyes on law school.

---

[58] Ibid., 58. See also Nickel, "Intimacy," 209. The author notes, "Francis . . . quickly gained a reputation for . . . excellent scholarship and oration." The same was true for his elder brother, Archie.

[59] Ibid. See also Calloway, "Rhetorical," 16.

[60] Ibid., 177.

[61] Ibid., 69. Ferry reports, "When graduation day arrived, the Grimké name was well on the way to 'its place of honor among the princes of the land.' Both brothers spoke during the exercises. For his record in classical studies and literature, Archie was honored with the Latin Salutatory. Frank had 'maintained the highest general average of scholarship throughout the whole course,' and he was 'assigned the Valedictory Oration.'" Original source: Lincoln University, "Records of Ashmun Institute," June 14, 1870, 104, in Andrew E. Murray, *Presbyterians and the Negro: A History* (Philadelphia: Presbyterian Historical Society, 1966), 185; Grimké, *Works I*, viii, xi.

[62] Ibid., 69–70. The aunt's advice to take a one-year break should not be considered without context. This was not an unusual practice of the day, particularly considering Frank's recent bout with illness. See Ferry, "Puritan," 68. The aunts were unreservedly proud. Sarah in a letter to William Lloyd Garrison, wrote, "Is it not remarkable that these young men should far exceed in talents any of my other Grimké nephews; even their half brothers bear no

From Law School to Seminary

Frank's pursuit of the law met with several providential roadblocks. In just a few short years, he had enrolled in two law programs, with both closing due to a lack of funding.[63] "After due reflection," the meaning of these events crystalized for Frank. The unexpected turns signaled a divine intervention. From there, for Frank, the call was clear—the small boy with a big bite would place his voice in the service of the gospel.[64]

Growing relationships with influential mentors like George van Deurs, associate pastor of the Bethany Presbyterian Church in Philadelphia, Drs. John B. Reeve and Lorenzo Westcott, members of the Theological Department of Howard University, and his brother Archie's persistent encouragement reinforced this realization.[65] In the days ahead, he moved with more certitude.

Observing Frank's potential and what it meant for the denomination, on September 8, 1875, through his membership at the Central Presbyterian Church on Lombard Street, the church recommended him before Session, subsequently endorsing him before the Presbytery on October 4, and thereby sponsoring his theological education.[66] Soon after, Frank enrolled at Princeton Theological Seminary.

---

comparison with them, and my brother Thomas's sons, distinguished as he was, are far inferior to them in intellectual power."

[63] Ibid., 70–74. Grimké studied in the law departments at Lincoln and Howard University, which closed due to inadequate funding. The same redirects were not true for Archie, who became a Harvard-trained lawyer, publisher, and U.S. ambassador. See Bruce, *Archibald*, passim.

[64] Grimké, *Works I*, ix. Sourced at Ferry, "Puritan," 75.

[65] Ferry, "Puritan," 73–74. See also "Obituary for George van Deurs," *Philadelphia Inquirer*, September 17, 1906, 2. Accessed August 18, 2024, https://www.newspapers.com/article/the-philadelphia-inquirer-obituary-for-g/83378023/ for details on van Deurs.

[66] Ibid., 75–76. Frank first became acquainted with Central during his initial summer break at Lincoln. See Ferry, "Puritan," 53.

Princeton Halls and Echoes of Paul[67]

When Frank entered the hallowed halls of Princeton, the school was well established as a bastion of "scholastic Reformed orthodoxy," the seminary having "specifically" bound itself to "three broad areas of intellectual attainment—biblical, theological, and practical." [68] An emphasis on the Westminster Confession and Pauline praxis was prominent. [69] Among his classmates was Benjamin Breckinridge Warfield, who would become one of the leading theologians of the Reformed tradition.[70] Together, they were members of the last class to study under the venerable Charles Hodge.[71] Hodge's rigorous approach to biblical exegesis and his devotion to the authority of scripture "imprinted" Frank to the core.[72] Under Hodge, Frank now had a front-row seat for the theologian responsible for much of his religious formation at Lincoln, directly shaping Frank as he received a firsthand

---

[67] The author notes that the tone of the "Sketch" turns more technical as the biographical details in the following sections are particular in shaping the theoretical framework of this project.

[68] Ibid., 81, 86.

[69] Ibid., 86, 88.

[70] Ibid., 88.

[71] Ibid., 86, 100. Ferry observed that "In retrospect it seems most appropriate, even providential, that Frank and his fellow seniors had the additional time with the venerable Princetonian. The class of '78 was the last to sit as his pupils for the complete sequence of exegetical, didactic, and polemic. It was the last to undergo examination on the written Systematic by the author himself. In a sense teacher and students together would graduate from the academic study of God."

[72] Ibid., 86–87, 95–96, 100–01. Ferry notes, "an exalted view of the Bible's integrity was essential to the school because Scripture functioned as both cornerstone and keystone in the architecture of the Seminary's curriculum. The course of study through which Frank Grimké passed commenced and ended with the Bible. . . . For three years Frank was exposed to an intellectual climate under the hegemony of Charles Hodge, whose long experience teaching Old and New Testament courses provided the foundation for his particular expression of Reformed theology. . . . Frank later reflected this method in his preaching and polemical writings."

dose of the "Pauline–Augustinian–Calvinist tradition explicated by Hodge."[73]

Frank's tenure at Princeton was no less impressive than that at Lincoln. He excelled in all pursuits. Of his character and scholarship, Hodge "reckoned him equal to the ablest of his students."[74] Ferry captures the penetrating ethos of Frank's studies at Princeton by observing:

> From October 1877 to April 1878, Hodge addressed the Sunday afternoon meetings at least a dozen times. In the course of those talks, he treated basic themes: the nature of the Gospel, the necessity of agape love, stability and perseverance in faith; growth in grace. Underlying every discourse is the affirmation that "truth unto salvation" is revealed by God in Scripture. Thus, the Princeton ideal—the wedding of learning and piety—is realized for Hodge from the matrix of a Bibliocentric theology.[75]

Frank, no doubt, imbued the *Hodge Way* [my emphasis]. He later wrote:

> [We must] get hold of [this] great idea or truth and have it vitalized in our lives, that is, to so come under its influence as to be controlled by it, is of the greatest importance. Take the great truth which underlies the Gospel,—the truth as to the atoning sacrifice of Jesus Christ. The Bible teaches us that by his suffering and death, an atonement was made for the sin of the world, for your sin and mine, for all the sinful race of Adam. It is a

---

[73] Ibid., 100. See also 96–97. In observing Princeton's ethics department, Ferry notes, "Noticeably absent . . . was an emphasis on social ethics, due in part to the spiritual understanding of the Church prevalent at Princeton. That Grimké developed a method by which he could judge the race issue in America depended less on Aiken's [the ethics professor] teaching than on that of Charles Hodge."

[74] Grimké, *Works I*, x.

[75] Ferry, "Puritan," 101.

> stupendous fact, this dying of Jesus Christ for the sins of the world; and ought to have certain definite effects upon us.[76]

He continues:

> Whenever I think of the pulpit, of the ministry [of the gospel], and of what it is capable of becoming and of achieving, instantly I think of the Apostle Paul—of his zeal, his earnestness, his steady, unswerving devotion to Jesus Christ and the interest of his kingdom. What a record he made for himself! What a glorious record. Let us all . . . [embody] his noble spirit.[77]

In these statements, we discern four core Pauline resonant priorities in Frank's studies: an emphasis on the authority of scripture (biblicism), the work of Christ and the cross (crucicentrism), piety and the regenerative work of grace (conversionism), and an outward working of the indicatives of the gospel (activism)—a defining ethos that we will revisit later in this work.[78]

During the summer before Frank's final year at Princeton, the Fifteenth Street Presbyterian Church in Washington, DC, invited him

[76] Grimké, *Works III*, 55.

[77] Grimké, *Meditations*, 16–17.

[78] Reader's note: Though this observation is made with the benefit of Bebbington's historical critique of Evangelicalism, the author contends that this is not a case of historical revisionism, retrospective reinterpretation, or presentism for two reasons: 1. Bebbington's framework is based on extensive historical evidence and primary sources from the period in question, ensuring that his conclusions are grounded in the context of the time rather than imposed retroactively, and 2. Bebbington explicitly focuses on the development and characteristics of Evangelicalism as understood by contemporaries within their own historical setting, rather than applying modern concepts or values to interpret past events. In other words, Bebbington's work is inherently framed and interpreted within its historical context. See Bebbington, *Evangelicalism*, 2–4, passim.

to "occupy the pulpit . . . for a season . . . as their stated supply."[79] Though never confirmed, the call was likely at the urging of his mentor, Dr. Westcott.[80]

Again, Frank met the challenge—with documented efficiency in "the conduct of worship, preaching, [and] visiting the sick."[81] He excelled in the more intricate matters of church life, as well.[82] By summer's end, it was apparent that his time had become more than simple field experience. Returning to Princeton, he most likely sensed that his senior year at the seminary would become the capstone of his preparation to serve the Fifteenth Street Church.[83]

Frank's last year maintained what had already been a remarkable tenure. Graduating on a Tuesday, April 23, 1878, he had "convinced all the professors under whom he studied as a young man of a very high order of talent and of excellent character."[84]

Biographical Reflection. Here, it's reasonable to infer that Grimké's journey from enslavement to a Princeton Theological Seminary education contextualized his view of the gospel's redemption as a reality encompassing spiritual, intellectual, and social reconciliation. This perspective likely built his capacity to harmonize his Reformed evangelical convictions with a call to active engagement as he wielded sound biblical doctrine with a commitment to justice and dignity, especially within the church. His mistreatment by alleged sympathizers in his earliest years up north must also be noted. We will hear hints of the pain of the hypocrisy Grimké experienced throughout

---

[79] Ferry, "Puritan," 97.

[80] Ibid., 97–98. Ferry opines, "It is not certain that Lorenzo Westcott engineered Frank's return to Washington, but as moderator of the Session it is highly probable that his influence counted heavily in the body's deliberation."

[81] Ibid., 98.

[82] Ibid. Ferry reports Grimké's sensitive oversight of a member's excommunication for "causing scandal to the church and herself for violation of the seventh commandment."

[83] Ibid., 98–99.

[84] A letter of support from James McCosh, President of College of New Jersey, February 10, 1881. See Grimké, *Works I*, x–xi; Ferry, "Puritan," 102.

his sermon corpus. These watershed moments are important, as they seemingly shaped Grimké's EEH and invigorated him to preach a gospel that called for holistic transformation and reconciliation across ethnic and societal divides.

From the Pulpit to the Public Square

Frank (hereafter Grimké) transitioned from seminary to the pulpit during two of America's most socially disruptive epochs—Post-Reconstruction and the Gilded Age.[85] Given this critical context, his sermons, as he stepped into the lore of the Fifteenth Street Church in the summer of 1878, were steeped in a socially engaged orthodox praxis that was especially *noisy* [my emphasis] against the era's backdrop.[86] In Calloway's rhetorical analysis of "Grimké's audience," she notes the following:

> The abandonment of the Negro by the Republican Party and the abolitionists, who had crusaded on behalf of his freedom between 1830 and 1877, caused him to become disillusioned with politics. From 1890 to 1915, when lynching constituted one of the greatest shames in America, Negroes gave up their belief in justice and equality in American society. . . . As the Negro became increasingly disfranchised and denied his right to hold political office, he placed more stress on economic and moral development as a substitute for his treatment in American society. . . . As August Meier put it, "The strongly economic, materialistic, laissez-faire, and Social Darwinist cast of late nineteenth-century American thought was to have a large influence upon Negro thinking." . . . As a result of this influence, the Negro believed that if he improved himself morally and economically, the white man

[85] Calloway, "Rhetorical," 22–51, passim.
[86] Ferry, "Puritan," 133–36.

> would gradually admit him into the mainstream of American life.[87]

She further observes:

> Immediately following Reconstruction, however, the Negro was not as unified as previously around this common belief because of the class divisions that resulted from the antebellum era. There was a conflict between the former house servants and the former field hands about the most effective way to solve their problem. The former house servants, according to Frazier, "hoped that the federal government, through the Republican party, would coerce the South into according the Negro equality." In contrast, the former field hands gradually gave up hope that the government would grant them their rights. Despite the fact that this class division existed until the beginning of the twentieth century, during the Gilded Age, upper-class Negroes were forced to work with the masses because Southern and Northern whites treated both groups as "forgotten men" as they turned their attention toward the healing of their own wounds.[88]

Regarding the effects of the nation's social dynamics on Washington, Ferry adds:

> For Negroes, the capital city possessed more than the ordinary meaning as the seat of political power; it symbolized the mood and intent of the nation concerning their future. At least since the

---

[87] Calloway, "Rhetorical," 22, 35–36.

[88] Ibid., 36–37. For more on the Gilded Age and interactions of the African American community and Protestantism, see Joel Shrock, *The Gilded Age* (Westport: Greenwood Press, 2004), 184, 222; Herbert G. Gutman, "Protestantism and the American Labor Movement: The Christian Spirit in the Gilded Age," *The American Historical Review* 72, no. 1 (1966): 74–101, https://doi.org/10.2307/1848171.

> Civil War, — for the local community much longer — Negroes instinctively looked to Washington as the hub about which turned their fortunes as a people. As long as the federal government stood guard, the civil rights of Negroes appeared secure, and their opportunities relatively unlimited. Yet after 1877, Washington proved not to be a sentinel for racial justice but a weather-cock of political expediency blown by the winds of a nation undergoing a remarkable social alteration.[89]

This cultural milieu framed Grimké's initiation into full-time pulpit ministry at the Fifteenth Street Church. With his typical bite, in response to the nation's state, Grimké assessed that "until the Negro's manhood is recognized, and all his rights, civil and political, are accorded to him, he will never hold his peace, will never cease to cry aloud to agitate to make trouble." One might imagine how startling these subversive notes must have been, but alarming as his language sounded, "agitation" was not Grimké's end. Of his approach, Woodson observes with piercing clarity:

> Dr. Grimké often preached about the injustices heaped upon the race, especially the hypocrisy of those who called themselves Christians when denying the race liberty and freedom guaranteed the Negroes in the laws and the Constitution. . . . Yet, he never used his church as a center for agitation where anyone could hold a meeting for propaganda purposes. Dr. Grimké had a keen conception of the dignity of the church and in his ministry never permitted his congregation to diverge from these ideals. . . . [He] had no desire to devote his time to agitation, and he cannot be classified as such a leader. He was drawn into the battle for human rights because as a minister he was duty-bound to plead for

[89] Ferry, "Puritan," 133.

equality and justice in accordance with the teachings of the Bible.[90]

The Fifteenth Street Presbyterian Church, Washington City[91]

Known as "one of the most prestigious Negro churches in the nation," Fifteenth Street was the aesthete epicenter of religious and social life.[92] For Grimké, it provided the respected platform he required to cultivate his distinct gospel homiletic. As he navigated the delicate theological trill of grace and law, Grimké "presented a pietistic gospel, calling for total personal commitment to Christ. 'In God's sight,' Grimké preached, there are only two classes of persons—those who are in Christ and those who are not. Those who are in Christ are safe, but for those who are not . . . there is no salvation.'"[93] Grimké subscribed fully to the spiritual as well as the social indicatives of the gospel and, as such, did not suffer hypocrisy well.[94] His sermons promulgated the gospel as a spiritual *and* socially emancipatory claim.[95] His claim:

---

[90] Carter G. Woodson in Grimké, *Works I*, xiii.

[91] Grimké, *Works I*, ix; cf. legal and professional documents, Grimké Papers, Howard University. Grimké's call letter from the 15th St. Presbyterian Church: "The congregation of the 15th St. Presbyterian Church, Washington City, being on sufficient grounds, well satisfied of the ministerial qualifications of you, Frank J. Grimké, now of Princeton, N.J.; and having, from our past experience of your labors, good hopes that your ministrations in the gospel will be profitable to our spiritual interests, do earnestly call and desire you to undertake the pastoral office in said congregation, promising you in the discharge of your duty all proper support, encouragement, and obedience in the Lord."

[92] Ferry, "Puritan," 104, 136.

[93] Ferry, "Puritan," 136.

[94] Calloway, "Rhetorical," 99–100. Calloway writes, "An examination of his sermons and addresses reveals that he used personal pronouns to contribute to his ethos. They were, however, reserved largely . . . to denounce hypocrisy and to repudiate the Negro for his addiction to drink and immorality." Also, see Woodson's commentary in Grimké, *Works I*, xiii–xiv.

[95] Grimké, *Works III*, 149. Grimké expounds, "The true mission of a church in the community where it is located is to preach the Gospel, with the double

"From the beginning, all along, I have felt that my mission was to preach the gospel, to expound the bible as the word of God."[96] Of this claim, Calloway observes, "Whether the form of address was that of a eulogy, a letter, or an anniversary sermon, Grimké was drawn to traditional texts, [echoing] biblical characters, ideas, and events appropriate to the subject under discussion."[97] Grimké was a gospel preacher who categorically preached the Bible and the entire course of its indicatives, from temperance to race prejudice.[98] However, he did not do so without the support of an influential advocate—his wife, Lottie.

Marriage to Lottie

In 1878, Grimké married Charlotte Forten, a woman thirteen years his senior, who, foreshadowing her future role as his wife, had aided him in evacuating to Boston as a teen. Lottie hailed from a distinguished African American family in Philadelphia; her grandfather was a noted community leader, and she was a relatively well-known author with a storied abolitionist heritage.[99] Their marriage proved a personal union and potent partnership in gospel ministry and social

---

purpose, first, of winning men to an acceptance of Jesus Christ; and, second, of building them up in faith and holiness. In other words, its value to the community will be in proportion as it is helping to make its members, after they are brought in, better men and women, better Christians, getting them, in character and life, more conformed to the character and teachings of the Lord Jesus Christ." This is a common theme of Grimké's homiletic: the intersection of the personal and the communal, or, generally, what Bebbington identifies as "Conversionism" with "Activism." This also thematically echoes the Pauline praxis espoused in 1 Corinthians 9:23—I do all things for the sake of the gospel, so that I may become a fellow partaker of it. Sourced via Crisler, "Interview 3." A further investigation here would be interesting but is not practical for this exercise.

[96] Grimké, *Works III*, 265.

[97] Calloway, "Rhetorical," 102.

[98] Ferry, "Puritan," 164.

[99] Ibid., 47, 104–07.

activism. Ferry notes, "In Lottie, Frank . . . found a Christian woman who consistently confirmed his conviction. Moreover, life together provided the experience which corroborated Grimké's biblically derived principles for founding a marriage and making it succeed."[100]

Jacksonville and the Moody Controversy

The Grimkés spent most of their ministry years in the service of Fifteenth Street, save a formative three-year stint in Jacksonville, Florida, due to health concerns.[101] This period came after a particularly sorrowful chapter in their lives—the birth and subsequent loss of their only child, a daughter named Theodora Cornelia.[102] Lottie would later journal:

> O my darling, what unspeakable happiness it would be for us to have her with us today. She would be nearly six years old, our precious New Year's Gift—and how lovely and companionable I know she would have been. But I must not mourn. Father, it was Thy will. It must be for the best. I must wait.[103]

The personal loss predictably affected the Grimkés. But it did not sully their resolve. Not long after beginning their service at the Laura Street Church, Grimké's gospel convictions would encounter another hypocritical foe.[104]

Ferry notes, "One of the earliest figures to play Herod to Grimké's John the Baptist [in Jacksonville] was none other than the world-famous evangelist, Dwight L. Moody."[105] Learning of Moody's tepid posture in relegating the decision-making process concerning whether

---

[100] Ibid., 122.
[101] Ibid., 157–80.
[102] Ibid., 108.
[103] Ibid., 109.
[104] Ibid., 157, 168–70.
[105] Ibid., 168.

or not his revival meetings would be integrated or segregated to "local committees," Grimké, in a toothy editorial, cried loud and spared not, writing, "It is impossible to contemplate this man . . . without mingled feelings of pity and disgust."[106] In a manner akin to Paul's frustration with Peter in his letter to the Galatians, Grimké advances:

> It is surprising that colored people in the churches to which such men minister are either given to understand that they are not wanted at all, or when they venture in occasionally are shown to the galleries or special seats known as "nigger seats"? I cannot help thinking that much of the present feeling in the Church against the Negro is due to ministerial unfaithfulness and cowardice.[107]

Grimké further insinuated that the Christian church, by "remaining silent" or "acquiescing" in the practice of segregation, was giving its nod to the most hideous corporate wrong in the land.[108]

Grimké's position could not be more apparent. A preacher must uphold the indicatives of the gospel's premier claim, "God hath made of one blood all nations of men."[109] He would not suffer the forces of racism co-opting a gospel that, by definition, must remain an uncompromised nonpartisan instrument of righteous justice. [110] Ultimately, Grimké's campaign was unsuccessful, the winds of expediency being the order of the day. But his claim was nonetheless unrelenting, and in a few short years, he would return to the nation's capital.

---

[106] Ibid., 169; Callow, "Rhetorical," 68.

[107] Francis James Grimké, "Mr. Moody and the Color Question in the South," *Independent*, 38, no. 1964 (Thursday, July 22, 1886): 7. Originally reported in *The Laura Morning News*, March 7, 1886. Cf. Galatians 2:11–14..

[108] Ibid., 6 (912).

[109] Ibid., 7 (913); See also Grimké, *Works I*, xvi. Cf. Acts 17:26.

[110] Ibid.

A Return to Washington: Beyond the Four Walls

When Grimké returned to Fifteenth Street in the early spring of 1889, his influence had extended far beyond the four walls of the church. The lighter demands of a smaller congregation in Jacksonville provided him the liberty to expand his ministry, as non-Presbyterian denominational leaders, especially Bishop Daniel Payne of the African Methodist Episcopal Church, invited Grimké to speak before their regional and national gatherings.[111] Booker T. Washington, and other notable educators, sought his services as a chapel preacher at several of the "predominantly Negro colleges in the South."[112]

It was no surprise that Grimké increasingly explored his interest in education as a tool for "not only training . . . young men and women to think, and to be industrious, but [also] to be virtuous."[113] This conviction led him to work and serve at the pleasure of several leading institutions, including Howard University.[114] He found in these efforts a strategic and powerful activist outlet for his conception of a church and nation fully affected by the gospel. Like his preaching, his involvement was in spirit and matter. Still, as we will soon witness, he never allowed his interactions to distract him from his main task—preaching the gospel and living out its indicatives.

Howard University, Board of Trustees. For several decades, Grimké committed himself to supporting programs emphasizing character development and rigorous academic discipline at Howard University and others.[115] However, these efforts did not come without challenges. One instance was the controversial administration of John

---

[111] Ferry, "Puritan," 158.

[112] Ibid., 158, 162–63.

[113] Ibid., 161–62. In addressing the ethos of Tuskegee Institute in its earliest days, Grimké continues with a Pauline echo, "The emphasis which [education] lays on character—the pains which it takes to inspire them with a love for the things that are true and just and good and lovely and of good report is one of the most delight features about it."

[114] Ibid., 162, 251.

[115] Ibid., 265.

Gordon, marked by insensitivity and race prejudice during his tenure as president (1903–1906), which thoroughly tested Grimké's mettle.[116] The situation escalated so much that it became a point of national debate, with Grimké's brother, Archie, leading the charge against Gordon. The *New York Age*, a prominent African American newspaper, ran a series of articles by Archie exposing Gordon's discriminatory practices, eventually leading to successful calls for his resignation.[117]

Meanwhile, many saw Grimké as the ideal candidate to replace Gordon, given his long-standing commitment to the university and distinguished character.[118] The *Washington Post* even editorialized that "a colored president for a colored university is not only an appropriate idea, but it means an opportunity for some intelligent and able negro [*sic*] in a sizable position."[119]

Despite the widespread support for his potential candidacy, Grimké declined to pursue the presidency. In a letter to the *Age*, he expressed his gratitude for the endorsement but firmly stated, "I am

---

[116] Walter Dyson, *Howard University: The Capstone of Negro Education, A History: 1867–1940* (Washington, DC: Graduate School, Howard University, 1941), 390–91, 415. See Ferry, "Puritan," 266nn1–3.

[117] Archibald H. Grimké, "Troubles of Howard: Executive Raids Upon Other Departments' Finances," *New York Age* 18, no. 39, May 11, 1905, 1; "Colorphobia in Howard: Under New Pilot, Old Ship Now Heads Due South," *New York Age* 18, no. 40, May 18, 1905, 1; "Snubbed Coleridge-Taylor: His Reception at Boston and Howard Contrasted," *New York Age* 18, no. 41, May 25, 1905, 1; "Dr. Gordon Faces a Crisis: Said He Should Right-About-Face or Abdicate," *New York Age* 18, no. 42, June 1, 1905, 1; "Alumni Petition Trustees: Indict Gordon and Pray for His Dismission," *New York Age* 18, no. 43, June 8, 1905, 1. Jerome B. Peterson, Editor, New York, as cited in Ferry, "Puritan," 267n2. Accessed August 18, 2024, https://dds.crl.edu/crldelivery/8217. The author finds particularly interesting the biting titles leveraged by A. Grimké, the elder brother and fellow board member, to expose the "colorphobia" of the white president and his administration. Ferry notes that Francis was unapologetically in lockstep with his brother in this fight for Gordon's "dismission." Once again, the brothers' concerted efforts proved triumphant. See also Ferry, "Puritan," 266–67.

[118] Ferry, "Puritan," 269.

[119] Ibid., 268n2.

not a candidate, and would not, if the position were offered to me by the trustees, accept it." Grimké's decision was rooted in his definitive sense of call. He viewed his work as a minister as unreservedly vocational, saying, "I am doing the work now that I love most of all, and shall continue to pursue it to the end of my days."[120]

Grimké's refusal to seek the presidency betrayed a core conviction characteristic of his manner, but as the board of trustees nominating committee secretary, his resolve did not hamper his involvement. He ultimately led the charge in appointing William Patterson Thirkield, a Methodist minister with a strong record of working among African Americans, later remarking, "his coming to be president of Howard University was due largely to my influence."[121]

Denominational Activism and Beyond. On April 11, 1905, the Presbytery of Washington City met in the Westminster Church to discuss the merits of reunion between the Cumberland Presbyterian Church and the Presbyterian Church, USA. The gathering was a high mark in a series of merger discussions dating back to 1866.[122] Grimké vehemently opposed the reunion on the grounds that the chief bartering chip for the merger—the separation of the races within the church—was an unchristian reinstitution of a "color line" in the family of God.[123] His challenge was not a solo effort but part of a broader alliance with a powerful friend who had come to appreciate his "rousing addresses"—Justice John Marshall Harlan, the Supreme Courts lone dissenter in the infamous *Plessy v. Ferguson* case.[124]

---

[120] T. Thomas Fortune, "Howard's Next President," *New York Age* 19, no. 19, January 4, 1906, 4. Accessed August 18, 2024. https://dds.crl.edu/crldelivery/8217. Cited originally in Ferry, "Puritan," 270nn1–2; cf. Grimké, *Works*, I, xviii.

[121] Ferry, "Puritan," 270–71.

[122] Ibid., 253.

[123] Ibid., 264.

[124] Ibid., 264–65, 264n3. Ferry records the following episode after Grimké's prophetic address to the Presbytery, "Applause burst from the audience; Grimké had 'touched with tongue of flame the conscience of Presbytery and for one fleeting moment quickened it to life.' Many white presbyters were on

Despite being a white Southerner, Harlan stood firmly against racial segregation, both legally and socially. As such, Grimké's accord with Harlan was serviceable in his broader campaign to challenge the church's resegregation efforts. Harlan's opposition to the "separate but equal" doctrine inspired Grimké with legal and moral stamina—the justice having famously argued that "Our Constitution is color blind, and neither knows nor tolerates classes among citizens." Grimké echoed this sentiment in his critique of the church's reunion plans.[125] Like the Constitution, Grimké insisted that the church should be blind to race, pointing to Harlan's dissent as a moral compass for the church.[126]

In their shared efforts, Grimké and Harlan echoed the Apostle Paul as they contended that the church is a model of unity, not a perpetrator and perpetuator of "insidious distinctions." [127] Their overtures were valiant but, in the end, they failed. Once again, the winds of expediency and apathy were too great a force. Ferry wrote:

> Despite . . . Harlan's prestige and Grimké's passion, the Presbytery voted forty-one to twenty-three in favor of the merger. In a sense, the affirmative vote was a rebuke from which Grimké never recovered. In 1906, final action effecting the reunion signified a

---

their feet seeking to gain the floor to respond. . . . Among the most venerable was Justice John Harlan. He went on record against the overture because Christianity 'has nothing to do with race, but only with men.' 'Let us,' Harlan urged, 'stand in the way of the fathers, and say to the world that as far as our church is concerned, we are race blind and color blind.'" See also Peter S. Canellos, *The Great Dissenter: The Story of John Marshall Harlan, America's Judicial Hero* (New York: Simon & Schuster, 2021), 3–4.

[125] Canellos, *The Great Dissenter*, 3.

[126] Ferry, "Puritan," 264n3.

[127] Ibid., 175. See Charlotte L. Forten and Anna J. Cooper, *Life and Writings of the Grimke Family* (Published by Anna J. Cooper, 1951), 52–53, https://xtf.lib.virginia.edu/xtf/view?docId=chadwyck_aap/uvaGenText/tei/chaap_D045.xml (accessed August 18, 2024). Cf. Galatians 3:28.

salient victory for the "Lost Cause" and the bitter defeat for those, who like Grimké, had "dreamed the impossible dream."

The Founding of the NAACP. With the increasing rise of Jim Crow tyranny, the African American community needed a response. Once again, Grimké was on the frontline of the fight, moving quietly and decisively. Many historiographies of the NAACP's formation expatiate voices like W. E. B. Du Bois, Ida B. Wells, and Mary Church Terrell; Grimké's contributions were no less significant. Andrew Martin, one of the few noted scholars on Grimké, similarly observes:

> [Most] narratives of the NAACP's formation rightly emphasize Du Bois, along with Ida B. Wells, Mary Church Terrell, Moorfield Storey, William English Walling, and others. Yet, contemporary evidence indicates that the roles played by Francis Grimké and his brother Archibald were also crucial, though they have been underappreciated, especially Francis's. . . . In the months leading up to the famous Carnegie Hall Conference in January 1904, which led to the break between Booker T. Washington and Du Bois, Francis Grimké received confidential letters from both men. . . . Notably, of the 28 names Du Bois listed, he placed only four—besides his own and Grimké's—as solidly aligned with his cause. Grimké was a trusted member of this small circle. . . . In 1909, a call was issued for a national conference to address the unequal treatment of people of color in the United States and to advocate for civil liberties. Francis Grimké was one of seven African Americans to sign this call, which led to the Negro National Conference held on May 31 of the same year. Out of that conference, a steering committee was created to form the NAACP.[128]

[128] Andrew Martin, "The Civil, Political, Religious, and Moral: Francis Grimké, W.E.B. Du Bois, and the Early NAACP," presented at the 73rd annual meeting of the Evangelical Theological Society, with the theme

Documentation thoroughly records Grimké's activism leading up to the NAACP's formation. His correspondence with Washington and Du Bois reflects the high regard of both leaders, who sought his counsel during a pivotal time in the struggle for African American rights.[129] As highlighted by Martin, Grimké's alignment with Du Bois's vision underscores his influential role in shaping the direction of the civil rights movement. In 1909, Grimké was recorded as one of the few African Americans to sign the call for an "Emancipation Conference" to address the systemic injustices faced by African Americans.[130] His courageous endorsement carried weight, and the executions of the conference laid the groundwork for the NAACP, cementing his role in the organization's formation.

Biographical Reflection. Grimké's journey from the pulpit to the public square unfolded amid sweeping social changes that likely impacted his EEH. Confronted with the post-Reconstruction and Gilded Age's systemic racial inequities and institutional betrayals, Grimké unapologetically saw his call to the gospel as inseparable from his call to confront social injustice. In his marriage to Charlotte, a committed abolitionist and intellectual equal, we see an aspect of his biography that likely reinforced his dedication to a gospel-embodied activism that distinctly echoed Paul's hermeneutic and heart. The shared grief of losing their only child may also have deepened Grimké's sense of compassion and resolve in preaching a gospel that addressed tangible suffering. Through this unique synthesis, we observe a ministry shaped by biblical fidelity and social engagement.

"Wealth and Poverty," Fort Worth, TX, November 16–18, 2021, in the section "American Christianity Topics in 20th Century American Christianity: 1) Presbyterian Conflict and 2) African American Advance," 00:06:24–00:09:11 on audio, accessed August 17, 2024, https://www.wordmp3.com/details.aspx?id=40528.

[129] Ferry, *Puritan*, 282–92.

[130] Ibid., 288.

An Emancipated Evangelical Echoer

Grimké's pastoral approach was reflexively rooted in Reformed evangelical theology, which emphasized the authority of Scripture, the sovereignty of God, and the necessity of personal conversion and piety. His sermons exercised a rigorous exegesis of biblical texts, which he used to address spiritual and social issues. He believed that true faith must manifest in one's living. Grimké's sermons often highlighted themes of personal holiness, ethical integrity, and social responsibility; their rigor and moral clarity provided a solid foundation for his ministry.

Concerning the "Social Gospel," Grimké took exception and drew sharp distinctions. Ferry excursed:

> For many, especially among the colored clergy, the teaching of Christianity provided an effective critique of the predominant cultural outlook of late nineteenth-century America. More specifically, the rise of the Social Gospel movement after the Civil War did not influence only white men. The movement placed great emphasis on the application of Christian faith to social problems on a corporate basis, *although it largely overlooked the Negro and the problem of race prejudice* [my emphasis]. Consequently, it remained for those most affected to draw out the implications of this emphasis for the removal of Jim Crow laws and other racist accoutrements [*sic*]. Francis Grimké took his place in the vanguard of such activity.[131]

Nonetheless, beyond the selective applications of the Social Gospel movement as observed by Ferry, Grimké saw no dichotomy

---

[131] Ibid., 184–85. See also Charles H. Hopkins, *The Rise of the Social Gospel in American Protestantism 1865–1915* (New Haven, CT: Yale University Press, 1967), passim; Grace R. Gwaltney, "The Negro Church and the Social Gospel from 1877 to 1914" (MA thesis, Howard University, Washington, DC), passim. Sourced from Ferry, "Puritan," 185n1.

between preaching the gospel and advocating for civil rights within his theological and interpretative framework. He viewed them as complementary aspects of his ministry, setting a precedent for integrating Reformed theology with social justice in a praxis not easily dismissed. He vehemently believed this and supported it with his talent, time, and treasure.[132] His effectiveness as a preacher and activist was so great that his congregation refused to accept his resignation even at a late age.[133] Of his incisive legacy, Woodson wrote:

> All who knew of him and read after him were not his followers. He alienated the genuflecting, compromising, and hypocritical leaders of both races. Dr. Grimké was an unyielding advocate of righteousness. He was a man of high ideals. He walked circumspectively, lived above reproach and bore an honorable name even among those who did not agree with him and charged him with being bitter and narrow. Persons who knew him well often referred to him as the "Black Puritan."[134]

On October 11, 1937, Francis James Grimké, the little boy with the big bite, graduated from the church militant to the church triumphant, his life echoing his heralded sentiments of the Apostle Paul, "What a record he made for himself! What a glorious record. Let us all . . . catch his noble spirit."[135]

---

[132] Grimké, *Works I*, xv. Of Grimké's commitment, Woodson notes, "In order to expose this unbrotherly attitude of the so-called Christian church, Dr. Grimke delivered lectures and preached sermons not only from his own pulpit, but wherever the opportunity offered. What he preached, moreover, he had printed and at his own expense widely distributed his messages in pamphlet form. He sent these especially to the clergymen of both races, called upon them to stand up and fight for righteousness—never to compromise with any such evil as that of treating the Negro other than as a brother."

[133] Ibid., xxi.

[134] Ibid., xiii.

[135] Grimké, *Meditations*, 16–17.

Conclusion

In this chapter, we explored Grimké's life—from his birth in bondage to his education at Princeton Theological Seminary, his leadership as a minister, and his outspoken advocacy against racial injustice—and how these experiences shaped his Evangelical Emancipatory Homiletic (EEH). His journey, marked by formative influences such as his mother's resilient faith, early betrayals by supposed allies, and confrontations with racial prejudice in Northern institutions, provided him with a contextualized view of the gospel as addressing both spiritual renewal and social transformation. These influences informed his commitment to Reformed theology and a gospel praxis that echoed the apostle Paul's hermeneutic and heart in confronting ethnic and social hostilities, particularly within the church. Grimké's ministry exemplifies a model of socially engaged evangelicalism that harmonizes sound biblical doctrine with a commitment to equality and reconciliation.

We now go upstream in Chapter 4 to review an example of Paul's gospel praxis and its challenge of the status quo before moving to a Chapter 5 analysis of one of Grimké's most piercing preachments—"God, and Prayer as Factors in the Struggle."[136]

---

[136] Ibid., 274–90.

CHAPTER 4

THE PAULINE PRAXIS: SUBVERSIVE EMANCIPATORY ECHOES OF A HEBREW PROPHET[1]

Grimké's ministry was notably influenced by his admiration for the apostle Paul, especially Paul's unwavering commitment to the gospel amid social and religious challenges. Grimké reflected on Paul's "zeal, his earnestness, his steady, unswerving devotion to Jesus Christ and the interest of his kingdom," seeing in Paul a model or pattern of ministry that harmonized doctrinal fidelity with social engagement.[2] As we observed in Grimké's Princeton studies in the previous chapter, this synthesis foreshadowed the complexities he would confront in his own ministry. This chapter, therefore, examines Paul's gospel ethos and praxis, particularly how he tactically used the epistolary form to advance a transformative gospel message that opposed entrenched social hierarchies (interpersonal and communal sins) within the church and beyond as a representative form of what Grimké likely would have interpreted as social activism.[3]

Additionally, Paul's letters embody a subversive, emancipatory praxis that challenges the status quo of both individual and systemic

---

[1] Reader's note: The author uses the terms subversion and praxis as follows: Subversion describes a strategic approach aimed at challenging and transforming established hierarchical social systems of authority or dominance from within. It involves undermining prevailing power dynamics while maintaining a careful balance between opposing extremes. The term acknowledges the need to navigate hierarchical frameworks adeptly, leveraging the effects of scripture, the cross, conversion, and the Holy Spirit. Praxis is the intentional or intuitive alignment of beliefs, values, and theological convictions with concrete actions and behaviors. It is the pragmatic embodiment of one's faith ethic.

[2] Grimké. Meditations,16–17.

[3] Jeffrey A. D. Weima, *Paul, The Ancient Letter Writer* (Grand Rapids, MI: Baker Academic, 2016), 92.

sin through politically charged language and gospel proclamations that boldly confront the inimical forces of sin, death, Satan, and the fear of God's wrath. His example has inspired generations to courageously embrace his hermeneutic and heart, proclaiming the gospel's transformative indicatives to both believers and the world alike, echoing his message in the hearing of all creation. In the following chapter, we will see this phenomenon reflected in Grimké, who courageously echoes and embodies Paul's praxis in his own context.

While this analysis is more technically driven by form and genre analysis, the intent of this exercise is singular: to demonstrate that Paul's pastoral letters intentionally or coincidentally carried pronounced calls for a new social order in response to the lordship and redemptive work of Jesus Christ, particularly among believers. As Paul himself stated, this gospel "he promised beforehand through his prophets in the holy Scriptures," indicating that his work did not simply imitate but also fulfilled the Hebrew prophetic tradition.[4]

Christoformity and Social Change: Embodying the Pauline Hermeneutic and Heart

Save Jesus Christ, Paul is arguably the greatest proponent of the gospel's indicatives. As such, Stanley Porter notes the tension of the traditional interpretations of Paul's corpus. He observes that Paul's ethical praxis, on the surface, appears to reinforce established social structures but, in actuality, harbors subtle and subversive elements that challenge prevailing norms and suggest remarkable sociological displacements in light of the "good news."[5] This chapter illuminates echoes of subversive tactics in Paul's writings, ultimately revealing how his hierarchical ethic is a subtextual tool for frustrating and reforming

---

[4] Romans 1:2 ESV.

[5] Stanley E. Porter and Cynthia Long Westfall, "Paul Confronts Caesar with the Good News," in *Empire in the New Testament* (Eugene, OR: Pickwick, 2011), 97–98.

societal power structures in early Christian communities—in essence, social activism.[6]

Furthermore, this chapter demonstrates how Paul's praxis transcends its historical context and remains relevant as a pattern for proclaiming the gospel and its inherent indicatives, offering a paradigm for Grimké's EEH to accomplish something similar in a distinctively contextualized manner.[7] We study two Pauline texts, Romans 13:1, because of its similarities to Grimké's interactions with the government's support of Jim Crow laws, and the book of Philemon, because of its radical intimations of a Christian kinship that eradicates the bonds of slavery. By discerning and interpreting the contextually driven layers of subversion within these texts, we evaluate Paul's dissident maneuvers and the implications for modern ethical dilemmas.

Moreover, akin to our work in the last chapter on Grimké, an awareness of the contextual milieu that encountered Paul's praxis amplifies the activist nature of his engagements.[8] In sum, we argue that

---

[6] Heilig, *Hidden*, 35–45, 125–38. Christoph Heilig concludes that the hypothesis of identifying critical "echoes" of the Roman Empire in Paul's letters must be modified to be maintained. Heilig emphasizes the need to refine this approach and acknowledge its limitations while also encouraging a re-evaluation of Pauline texts in light of Paul's interaction with Roman ideas. Our use of the term in this chapter refers to subtle characteristics in Paul's writings that suggest directly or indirectly a criticism of exploitative social dynamics. We have three general constructs for using the term echoes: 1. Textual Echoes, 2. Thematic Echoes, and 3. Subversive Echoes. These constructs often interact with one another to characterize an NT prophetic thrust in proclaiming the new gospel. The author asserts that Paul's interactions with Roman culture or ideas were akin to the way of the Hebrew prophets of the OT. Furthermore, the author contends that Paul's frequent use of OT texts was a strategy, though not necessarily an intentional one, for doing so.

[7] Scott McKnight, *Reading Romans Backward: A Gospel of Peace in the Midst of Empire* (Waco, TX: Baylor University Press, 2019), 73.

[8] Craig Keener, "Romans Session 1: Introduction," lecture series produced by Ted Hildebrandt from biblicalelearning.org, Wilmore, KY, February 15, 2016, YouTube video, 13:13, accessed July 9, 2023, https://www.youtube.com/watch?v=hPQZOexILag.

Paul's gospel ethic and praxis are a catalyst for subverting sinful societal norms and facilitating emancipatory change through what McKnight calls "Christoformity"—one's embodiment of the gospel's indicatives, personally and corporately. [9]

Interestingly, McKnight's language is constructive in aligning the *ultimate end* [emphasis] in the ethical praxis of Paul and Grimké.[10] Like Paul, whose praxis was bathed in the spirit of the ancient Hebrew prophets, Grimké ardently challenged unrighteous and unjust societal constructs—mainly his frustration with the hypocritical practices within the white Presbyterian church and the examples of decadence within his own community. But he did not leave it there. He echoed the emancipatory notes of the gospel's end—Christoformity. In other words, he followed the Pauline gospel pattern and tactic of emancipation through subversion.

The sections below analyze examples of Paul's praxis, but first, we must apply an extended treatment to define the phenomena—a process that forms the bulk of this chapter.

Tactical Echoes of a Hebrew Prophet

McKnight argues that Paul's praxis was a "tactic" designed to subvert the strategy of the Roman Empire's way of life. He declares, "If the strategy of the empire was conquer, the tactic of Paul was surrender. If the image of the empire was sword, the image of Paul was the cross. The strategy was a sword. The tactic was the cross."[11] McKnight is not describing a Pauline "dictatorship of the proletariat" version of subversion—dethroning the strong and enthroning the weak—but

[9] Scott McKnight, "The Apostle Paul: 'No One Knows the Trouble I've Seen,'" lecture presented at Lanier Theological Library Lecture Series, Houston, TX, October 26, 2019, video, 15:29, YouTube, https://youtu.be/TC3eqZbTkos (accessed July 12, 2023). Hereafter referred to as McKnight, "L1."
[10] By "ultimate end," we refer to the "ultimate amen," as defined in Chapter 6: "lives transformed to show forth the glory of God actively." Cf. Romans 15:6; 2 Corinthians 1:20; Philippians 1:11; Ephesians 1:12.
[11] McKnight, "L1," 21:07.

rather a subversion in which Christ is crowned and enthroned, and the called are conformed to His image.[12]

This subversive tactical interplay between hierarchy, authority, and power characterizes Paul's gospel praxis and animated much of Grimké's EEH activism, consciously or subconsciously, as he echoed Paul's hermeneutic and heart.[13] An analysis of this undercurrent, as we will soon observe in a *re-viewing* [emphasis added] of Romans 13:1 and Philemon, prompts reflection on the role of the epistles in challenging and reshaping established power structures.[14] Through this epistolary

---

[12] Ibid., 41:50. McKnight says, "The irony of the strong and weak in Rome is that they both claimed privilege. The weak claimed their covenant heritage as privilege, while the strong claimed higher status in the city of Rome. We can add a significantly important element to our understandings of weak and strong. If the food is the unclean food of the Pagan temple . . . if there is an ethnic reality to the weak and strong, there is also a status issue." See also Karl Kautsky, *The Dictatorship of the Proletariat*, trans. H. J. Stenning (London: Forgotten Books, 2018; originally published 1918), 12–24, passim.

[13] Ibid., 15:55. McKnight gives an expanded treatment of lament including the interpersonal and intercultural interplay that informed the ethic of the early Roman house churches.

[14] Philip La Grange du Toit, "Paul, Empire and Eschatology," *HTS Teologiese Studies/Theological Studies* 77, no. 4 (2021): 1–10, https://doi.org/10.4102/hts.v77i4.6904. In a helpful appraisal of common Pauline interpretative approaches, du Toit writes, "In the traditional, so-called 'Lutheran' approach to Paul, his gospel message is understood in terms of justification by faith in Christ over against justification based on works, which would have been part of his Judaean heritage. In the so-called New Perspective on Paul, Paul's embeddedness in his Judaean heritage has been reappreciated, explaining his gospel not to be against his Judaean past but rather in continuation with it (e.g. Dunn 1983; Sanders 1977). By reading Paul through the lens of his relationship to the Roman Empire, the assumption of the separation between religion and politics is questioned. In this approach, the Roman Empire is understood in terms of the interwovenness of religious and political elements, which was especially evident in the cultic divinisation and veneration of emperors. Because the gentiles were subjects of the Roman Empire and comprised the bulk of Paul's audiences, his letters are read through the lens of his relationship to empire rather than through his relationship to his Judaean heritage."

lens, we probe the broader implications of Paul's prophetic praxis and its present-day relevance to the indicative character of the gospel.[15]

Unmasking the Subversive Echoes of Paul's "Homiletic"

Concerning Paul's rhetoric and "homiletic," Duane Litfin notes, " Paul's . . . [preaching of] the message of the cross, while not antirational, is calculated to subvert."[16] Crisler further observes that subtle layers of meaning and intention often lie beneath the surface in biblical interpretation. He cautions, however, that unraveling the text's less apparent dimensions of thought is no slight journey.[17] With these observations in tow, we analyze our texts to examine plausible contextual armaments of hierarchical subversion.[18] The unmasking of these texts ultimately leads us beyond conventional interpretations to consider what Neil Elliott describes as a subversive "propaganda" epistolary narrative.[19] In framing the "subversive echoes" of Paul's

---

[15] Crisler, "Interview 1."

[16] Duane Litfin, *Paul's Theology of Preaching: The Apostle's Challenge to the Art of Persuasion in Ancient Corinth* (Downers Grove, IL: IVP Academic, 2015), 337. Litfin's larger argument surrounds Paul's use (or lack thereof) of rhetoric. However, his observation concerning his rhetorical interactions with the culture's "idolatrous tendencies" is a weighty consideration of sociological interaction or activism.

[17] Channing L. Crisler, "Interview 2," interviewed by Eric J. Freeman, June 22, 2023.

[18] Neil Elliott, *The Arrogance of Nations: Reading Romans in the Shadow of Empire* (Minneapolis: Fortress Press, 2018), 62. Elliot asserts, "Romans does offer a political declaration of war, and we can recognize in it a critique of the claims of imperial propaganda, if we attend carefully to the sorts of oblique references and implied contrasts to which the considerations in chapter one point us. The letter is not a treatise on how wicked human beings can be saved; to the contrary, as we shall see, it begins by driving a rhetorical wedge between the justice of God and the false claims of mortals who pretend at justice but deserve God's wrath instead."

[19] Ibid.

homiletic, we agree with Keener, who, quoting Elliot, argues that Paul was, in fact, subversive in his epistles.[20]

As a final reflection, there are recognized constraints associated with this exercise—the most obvious of which is a limited sample. But, given our aim to create a space for an analysis of Paul's gospel interactions with his day's sociological and cultural realities, especially within the church, they are compelling enough to frame the subversive nature of the gospel's indicatives.[21] We defer to NT scholarship to resolve the plausibility of a "hidden criticism." As Heilig notes:

> The need for such an assessment is . . . demonstrated by [J. Albert] Harrill's telling remark: "If Paul wrote coded and ambiguous speech in order to avoid detection, how can modern readers detect his 'real' message in Romans? After all, it's supposedly hidden! [Clearly], this rhetorical question is absurd: How could anyone try to decode messages of the Nazis in the Second World War? After all, they were coded!"[22]

Subversive echoes, much like the coded language often used in marginalized communities, present an inherent challenge for "decoding."[23] Though not a precise parallel, this complexity may partly

---

[20] Keener, "Romans," 19:51; Crisler, "Interview 5." Up to this point in our study, "echoes" has referred to textual or thematic connections within scripture or scriptural actors. Here, however, in alignment with Keener's and Crisler's work, our use of "subversive echoes" expands to include cultural cues, language, or references repurposed to underscore the lordship and redemptive work of Jesus Christ—particularly His triumph over sin, death, Satan, and the fear of divine wrath, with broader implications for society.

[21] For extended considerations and debates on Paul's "sociological and cultural realities," see Francis Watson, *Paul, Judaism and the Gentiles: A Sociological Approach* (Cambridge: Cambridge University Press, 1986), 1, 38–48, *passim*.

[22] Heilig, *Hidden*, 23.

[23] Geneva Smitherman, *Word from the Mother: Language and African Americans*, 1st ed. (London: Routledge, 2021), xii–xiii.

explain why Grimké's EEH appears enigmatic and has been largely overlooked in certain circles. Nevertheless, we agree with Heilig's suggestion that this phenomenon is plausible.

Defining a Subversive Homiletic

Understanding subversion in a homiletics context is foundational to this study. Referencing Cleophus J. LaRue's work regarding "communal interpretive strategies" and genre in his seminal text *The Heart of Black Preaching*, we define a subversive homiletic as the intentional and tactical use of religious discourse within oral or written communications to challenge, question, and disrupt unrighteous or unjust social constructs.[24] It embraces a nuanced approach in which seemingly conventional teachings embed subtextual messages that prompt critical reflection, engender social transformation, and provoke a reframing of prevailing authorities.[25]

A subversive homiletic denotes how the Apostle Paul and subsequent gospel echoers like Grimké, through the gospel announcement, employ a rhetorical approach that subverts traditional hierarchical paradigms.[26] Through linguistic devices, paradoxes, and countercultural messages, a homiletic emerges through which Paul advances a subtextual discourse to upend existing hierarchies and advocate for a radical socio-ethical praxis.[27] On the whole, preaching the gospel, framed as the announced death and resurrection of Jesus

---

[24] LaRue, *Heart*, 34–40. For an expanded explanation read this section of LaRue.

[25] McKnight, *Reading*, 57. Note McKnight's second approach to reading Romans 13:1–7.

[26] Jonathan T. Pennington, *Reading the Gospels Wisely: A Narrative and Theological Introduction* (Grand Rapids, MI: Baker Academic, 2012), 3. Pennington refers to the Gospel as an "announcement." See also, LaRue, *Heart*, 77–93.

[27] Weima, *Paul*, 2–7.

Christ, is inherently subversive and emancipatory, respectively, to and from the fractured agencies of this world.[28]

The Element of Hierarchy in Subversion

The concept of hierarchy concerning subversion is another central element in exploiting the Pauline ethic and praxis in Romans 13:1 and Philemon. Throughout the epistles, the hierarchical aspects of citizenship, ethnicity, religious orders, and particularly, the imperial cult and household codes become potent tools through which subversion operates.[29,30] These hierarchical constructs contextualize the subtle notes of challenge and a reimagination of orders that align with the remarkably distinct ethical and spiritual indicatives of the gospel.[31]

To expound further, hierarchical subversion entails an intricate interplay between apparently endorsing prevailing social constructs and concomitantly introducing subtextual cues (subversive echoes) that disrupt and challenge these norms.[32] Paul's hierarchical ethic in

---

[28] Crisler, "Interview 3." See also Litfin, *Preaching*, 337.

[29] Porter and Westfall, "Caesar," 93. For an extended explanation, read Porter and Westfall's framing of the emperor cult and the Priene Calendar Inscriptions of 9 BCE to understand Paul's possible subversive engagement with the prominent hierarchical constructs of the day.

[30] Cain Hope Felder, *Stony the Road We Trod: African American Biblical Interpretation* (Minneapolis: Fortress Press, 1991), 232–46. Lewis uses familial language to refer to prevailing social construct of household codes.

[31] McKnight, *Reading*, 10–11.

[32] Marcin Kowalski, "The Lion Against the Eagle: A Critical Appraisal of the Anti-Imperial Reading of Paul," *Collectanea Theologica* 93, no. 2 (2023): 57, https://doi.org/10.21697/ct.2023.93.2.03. Author's Note: This author is inclined to agree with Kowalski's advocacy for a *careful* (emphasis added) application of empire criticism to Paul, which can tender a better understanding of the New Testament background and message of Paul. Kowalski notes that although Paul does not fight with the Empire, the Good News he preached and the communities he founded possess an anti-imperial potential. Therefore, he suggests that empire criticism should not be ignored but critically assessed for its methodology and premises. Kowalski also cautions that contemporary ideologies can strongly inform empire criticism

Romans 13:1 and Philemon, seemingly advocating for submission and obedience, becomes a conduit for subversive discourse as these writings deftly introduce notions of justice, equality, and empathy that invite readers to question and reconsider the legitimacy of prevailing power structures.[33] This *subversive maneuvering* (my emphasis) of hierarchy enables Paul to advocate for change without overtly contradicting the social fabric of his time. We observe similar maneuvers, which we will unpack in the next chapter, in Grimké's EEH and activism as he navigated Jim Crow and the rampant lynchings of his day.

Ultimately, the hierarchical motif contributes to the complexion of Paul's socio-ethic praxis, and thoughtful analysis can reveal how one might leverage a subversive homiletic to provoke introspection, foster critical engagement, and instigate activism.[34]

Hierarchy, Authority, and Power in the Pauline Epistles

The intersection of hierarchy, authority, and power is the heartbeat of this exploration. These interconnected themes permeate Paul's epistles, reflecting the politico-cultural ambiance of the early Christian community and the unique dynamics of human relationships.[35] More pointedly, hierarchy, the explicit or implicit political arrangement of authorities and powers, was a prominent construct in Paul's day and the backdrop against which his ethical

---

and overlook the complexity of Paul's thought and the historical context in which he wrote.

[33] Karl Barth, *The Epistle to the Romans*, trans. Edwyn C. Hoskyns, 6th ed. (London: Oxford University Press, 1933), 477–92. See Barth's dialectic on the dangers of "Legitimism" versus "Revolution" for potential insight into the sensitive nature of Paul's balancing act in his subversive homiletic. This author does not fully concur with Barth's end, but the juxtaposition is helpful.

[34] McKnight, *Reading*, 185–87. Read McKnight's concluding thoughts on the "weak" and "strong."

[35] McKnight, "L1," 20:10–21:56.

teachings advanced.[36] Closely examining linguistic nuances, rhetorical techniques, and historical context unveils how Paul's hierarchical ethic served as a vehicle for subversive discourse. For Paul, his hierarchical ethic was the gospel of Jesus Christ; in Romans and Philemon, he explicitly demonstrates this by addressing the defects of hierarchical politics, prompting hearers (mainly Christians) to reconsider the ethical implications of their personal, political, and cultural praxis.[37]

Analyzing hierarchy, authority, and power reveals the sophistication of Paul's homiletical approach. His nuanced engagement with societal structures often subverts conventional norms, particularly as these align with the influence of sin, death, Satan, and the fear of divine wrath—forces that shape both societal and individual behaviors. Grimké aligns fully with this view of Paul's work, writing, "The seriousness of the work in which he engaged the apostle Paul fully realized. It was the work of saving men, of turning them from darkness to light, and from Satan to God."[38] Notice Grimké's language, which moves from the terrestrial ("darkness to light") to the cosmic ("Satan to God"), suggesting his awareness of both the sensate or physical and spiritual dimensions of a fallen humanity. Understanding the triadic effect of these themes and their role in shaping epistolary engagement makes apprehending the subversive echoes and homiletic within Romans 13:1 and Philemon more accessible.[39]

---

[36] N. T. Wright, "Paul's Gospel and Caesar's Empire," in *Paul and Politics: Ekklesia, Israel, Imperium, Interpretation. Essays in Honor of Krister Stendahl*, ed. R. A. Horsley (Harrisville, PA: TP, 2000), 161.

[37] Ibid., 164. Read Wright's section on "God's Justice Revealed in the Gospel: Romans."

[38] Grimké, *Works III*, 560.

[39] Jeremy Punt, "Paul the Jew, Power of Evil and Rome," *Scripture* 117 (2018): 8–9, https://doi.org/10.7833/117-1-1389. Punt writes, "History shows how the exertion of dominating power was met in the past by resistance. In the first century, too, resistance sprung up from anger and resentment and took various forms, only occasionally open revolt. In its negotiation of Empire, the Pauline letters, too show resistance against contemporary, Roman-aligned symbols of domination. The letters' stance is ambivalent, not unlike such

The Epistle to the Romans and Philemon: Context, Themes, and Agendas

Situating the contextual and thematic interplay of the historical dynamics embedded in Paul's epistles is important to identifying subversive echoes.[40] By navigating the involvement of these elements within the texts, we disinter a striking understanding of the intricate transactions between hierarchical dynamics, ethical imperatives or indicatives,[41] and the subversive essence that underpins Paul's gospel message. Accordingly, examining these epistles through the literary lens of genre—and how Paul employs it as a device to convey his messages—is a vital key in unraveling the interpretive mazes that shroud his hierarchical ethic and praxis.[42]

Beyond context and themes, historical interpretative agendas are another factor in walking the exegetical labyrinth of Paul's epistles. From the early Patristic era to the Reformation, each generation has brought its contextualized hermeneutical lens to bear on Paul's words, revealing and sometimes complicating how his texts were understood, expressed, and embodied. Arguably, all streams of the Christian tradition encounter the pronounced effects of these interpretive

---

negotiations in other hegemonic contexts. A choice between pro-Empire or anti-Empire readings is insufficient to make sense of the letters and inappropriate to both the literature and socio-historical context. Crude oppositional models which entertain only support or subversion are inadequate. The alternative to avoiding this impossible choice is, however, not 'a perspective which reads political history according to a different script' (Barclay, 2011:386)—a more plausible alternative approach is not to divorce politics from religion but rather to explore their intersections in the first century."

[40] Weima, *Paul*, 2.

[41] Stanley E. Porter, "Wittgenstein's Classes of Utterances and Pauline Ethical Texts," *Journal of the Evangelical Theological Society* 32, no. 1 (March 1989): 85–87.

[42] Weima, *Paul*, 3.

agendas. Porter, in defining the contextual dimensions of hermeneutics, posits:

> There are many different explanations as to what might be transpiring in the act of human understanding, e.g., sociological, psychological, biological, chemical, neurological. Some of these have met with more success than others. There are also many different hermeneutical descriptions, many of which do not agree with one another or with the more scientific explanations. One of the unique claims of hermeneutics is that it goes beyond the biological, psychological, etc., because it looks at what makes all of them possible.[43]

In other words, context inherently shapes every method of interpretation and has limitations that require the illumination of the Holy Spirit. Or, as Grimké, true to form, attested, the "presence and power of the Holy Spirit."[44] Therefore, acknowledging and accounting for genre-informed nuances and the limitations of historical interpretative strategies is a key to clarifying Paul's hierarchical ethic and praxis. We address the latter in the following two sections.

Historical and Cultural Context of Early Christianity

Early Christianity's historical and cultural context provides a crucial backdrop for understanding the nuances of Paul's epistles to the Romans and Philemon. When the apostle wrote these letters, the fledgling Christian community was situated within the complex sociocultural amalgam of the Greco-Roman world.[45] The movement existed as a minority group amidst diverse religious beliefs, social

---

[43] Stanley E. Porter and Jason C. Robinson, *Hermeneutics: An Introduction to Interpretive Theory* (Grand Rapids, MI: Eerdmans, 2011), 2.

[44] Grimké, *Works IIII*, 276.

[45] Keener, "Romans," 36:30. The language employed in this section relies heavily on notes from Keener's introductory lecture on the book of Romans.

norms, and hierarchical power structures. Hierarchical distinctions between what McKnight refers to as the strong and the weak stood pronounced.[46]

In the case of Paul's letter to the Romans, the context is particularly weighty. It was written during the mid-50s CE, when Rome was a sprawling metropolis that epitomized both the grandeur of imperial power and the sociological disparities of the time.[47] Diversity characterized the early Christian community in Rome.[48] This diverse composition exposed believers to varying cultural backgrounds and religious practices, resulting in a dynamic interplay of ideas and beliefs.[49] Paul's epistle to the Romans was penned against this backdrop as he addressed theological and ethical questions within a culture marked by internal and external religious animosities, social inequalities, and the pervasive authority of the Roman Empire.[50]

Similarly, the early Christian context holds consequential implications in the letter to Philemon. The epistle is a personal appeal to Philemon, a prominent member of the Christian community, regarding the treatment of Onesimus, a runaway slave.[51] As slavery was an entrenched institution in the ancient world, a careful reading of Philemon divulges its complex dynamics of hierarchy, power, and social relationships.[52] Lloyd A. Lewis's appraisal of the "Philemon–Paul–Onesimus Triangle" in Felder's compendium demonstrates how the cultural backdrop of the Greco-Roman society, characterized by distinct social classes and power differentials, profoundly influenced Paul's approach and language in addressing the matter at hand; and,

---

[46] McKnight, *Reading*, 25–33.

[47] Keener, "Romans," 54:16.

[48] McKnight, *Reading*, 24.

[49] Keener, "Romans," 20:15.

[50] Ibid., 37:50.

[51] Felder, *Stony*, 233.

[52] Crisler, *Romans*, 319–33. The subsection Romans 3:24 and the Echo of Απολύτρωση betrays just how entrenched the constructs of slavery were in the Greco-Roman milieu.

inferentially, how Paul confronts the pervasive defects of authority, freedom, and ethical responsibility within the context of the Christian community.[53]

Contextual Agendas in Early Christianity

Noting the potential of contextual agendas in early Christianity is another definitive element for unraveling the multifaceted layers of hierarchical lenses that shaped the theological and ethical landscape of the time. As Peter Oakes emphasizes in his work *Reading Romans in Pompeii*,[54] early Christian communities did not exist in isolation but were deeply enmeshed within the sociocultural milieux of their surroundings.[55] Oakes underscores that these communities engaged with the prevalent cultural narratives and social structures, influencing their hermeneutic and praxis.[56] Diverse hierarchical agendas that imbued early Christian thought and practice elevated the dynamics of this interaction between faith, context, and application.

Furthermore, early interactions with Paul's epistles were not abstract exercises, but they were inextricably linked to the material environment surrounding them.[57] Here, Oakes is functional again in highlighting the interconnectedness between the urban setting of Pompeii and the interpretive lenses through which the epistles,

---

[53] Felder, *Stony*, 232–46.

[54] Peter Oakes, *Reading Romans in Pompeii: Paul's Letter at Ground Level* (Minneapolis: Fortress Press, 2009), Kindle edition.

[55] Ibid., Location 1555.

[56] Ibid., Location 1158. Concerning practical implications of contextual agendas, Oakes writes, "We will now turn to a passage that deals with issues of social dynamics, Romans 12, and consider how the points raised by the text would relate to our model house church. This could be thought of as an exercise in considering the likely early reception of the letter. However, since the model is designed to represent hearers expected by Paul, the exercise could also be seen as a way of raising possibilities for what he intended in terms of practical application of what he was writing."

[57] Porter and Westfall, "Caesar," 93. See commentary on the widespread use of terms that divinized the Caesars.

especially Romans, were written and received by early Christians.[58] He argues that the presence of inscriptions and visual cues in Pompeii shaped the conceptual framework of the community, leading to specific interpretive agendas in their engagement with Paul's letters.[59] We find similar arguments from Porter, whom we visited earlier in this treatment.[60] This contextual perspective demonstrates the complexity of Paul's audience and emphasizes the role of localized agendas in determining Paul's epistolary approach.

Textual Analysis and Interpretation: A Synopsis

Negotiating the subtextual intricacies of Romans 13:1 and Philemon requires careful attention to the contextually informed hierarchical elements in Paul's epistolary discourse. In Romans, the apostle subversively undergirds his tactical utilization of scriptural precedent and calls for *civic obedience* [my emphasis] with ultimate allegiance to the authority of God and the lordship of Jesus Christ—not Caesar.[61] Meanwhile, Philemon reveals Paul's artful skill in letter writing, encouraging Philemon to transcend hierarchical norms through the socially disruptive indicatives of Christ's gospel.[62]

Romans 13:1: Unveiling Subversive Dimensions

Many interpret the thirteenth chapter of Paul's letter to the Romans as perplexing in ethical discourse and theological analysis, especially when discussing the relationship between Christians and governing authorities.[63] However, a closer study explicates this tension

---

[58] Oakes, *Pompeii*, Locations 624–90. Oakes estimates that most of the urban land was owned by 2.5% of the population.

[59] Ibid., Location 694.

[60] Porter and Westfall, "Caesar," 91.

[61] Wright, "Empire," 165.

[62] Weima, *Paul*, 205.

[63] Judy Diehl, "Empire and Epistles: Anti-Roman Rhetoric in the New Testament Epistles," *Currents in Biblical Research* 10, no. 2 (2012): 231.

and uncovers subversive dimensions that confront conventional notions of authority.

Wright notes that Romans 13:1 represents a provocative and enigmatic text.[64] He suggests that a thorough textual analysis and interpretation is necessary to unveil its subversive potential. Admittedly, this endeavor lacks sufficient space for the treatment inferred by Wright. However, we provide the following synopsis, relinquishing a deeper dive into the ongoing conversations on this matter to NT scholarship.

The opening verses of Romans 13 establish the foundation for Paul's interaction with governing authorities.[65] His proclamation in Verse 1, which details the emphasis of this pursuit, "Let every person be subject to the governing authorities. For there is no authority except from God, and those that exist have been instituted by God," inaugurates a paradoxical hierarchical maze.[66] This seemingly straightforward injunction frames Paul's dissonant gesture to interact civic compliance with ultimate allegiance to God. Significantly, the phrase "from God" instigates contemplation on divine sovereignty[67]—does Paul emphasize God's ordination of all authorities, or does he covertly challenge the authority claimed by the Roman Empire? Or does he do both?

We assert that the historical backdrop of Roman imperial power provides further insight into Paul's subversive intent. Porter explains how the imperial cult demanded unwavering loyalty, placing Christians' fidelity to God in tension.[68] Within this framework, Paul's call to "be

---

[64] N. T. Wright. *Paul for Everyone, Romans: Part Two* (Louisville, KY: Westminster John Knox Press, 2004), 85–87. Reader's note: Wright says, "Paul is anxious, precisely because he believes that Jesus is the true Lord of the world, that his followers should not pick unnecessary quarrels with the lesser lords. They are indeed a revolutionary community, but if they go for the normal type of violent revolution they will just be playing the empire back at its own game."

[65] Du Toit, "Paul," 4.

[66] Diehl, "Empire," 231–32, 248. See also Romans 13:1 ESV.

[67] Wright, *Paul*, 165.

[68] Porter and Westfall, "Caesar," 91, 96–97.

subject" [69] assumes subversive undertones—a tacit acceptance of Roman authority while quietly questioning the empire's self-declared divinity.[70] This subversive undercurrent resonates with the broader theme of Christ's sovereignty over all powers,[71] mirroring Paul's assertion in Colossians 1:16 ESV that "by him all things were created, in heaven and on earth, visible and invisible, whether thrones or dominions or rulers or authorities."

Contextually, Romans 12:21 sheds a helpful light on the subversion within Romans 13.[72] Karl Barth underscores the connection, emphasizing that Paul's exhortation to overcome evil with

---

[69] Du Toit, "Paul," 5. Contextual note: "Regarding the question [of] whether Paul advances the notion of unqualified obedience to the state, Cranfield and Moo draw attention to the fact that Paul in verse 1 uses the word 'submission' (ὑποτάσσω), which has to be differentiated from the idea of obedience as such. Jewett goes further and argues that ὑποτάσσω can have the notion of 'to submit voluntarily' (cf. 1 Cor 16:6) on the basis of the possibility that ὑποτασσέσθω in verse 1 and ὑποτάσσεσθαι in verse 5 are in the middle voice. But more importantly, Moo argues that the idea of submission involves 'to recognize one's subordinate place in a hierarchy' and interprets this passage as denoting 'God's providential ordering of human history.' In Moo's understanding, obedience to the government is thus not absolute, and it should be evaluated in light of the gospel."

[70] Porter and Westfall, "Caesar," 96. Porter and Westfall write, "Paul turns this formulation on its head by specifying what it is that distinguishes Jesus Christ as the 'good news' for humanity. Paul's statement indicates that God designated Christ Jesus as the son of God in power on the basis of the spirit of holiness as evidenced in the resurrection from the dead, and that as a result Jesus Christ is [ultimately] our Lord."

[71] Ibid., 98. Though where Porter and Westfall take their argument is not precisely the course of this exercise, the following observation is insightful: "I believe that in the light of how Paul opens his letter to the Romans, what Paul is saying in Rom 13:1–7 is consistent with his epistolary opening. The letter to the Romans is set within a context in which there is only one true Lord, Jesus Christ."

[72] Oakes, *Pompeii*, Locations 2009–41. Reader's note: This section relates primarily to the Barthian hermeneutical construct. However, for broader historical context, Oakes's thoughtful engagement with Romans 12–15 is instructive.

good, immediately preceding the discourse on authority, frames the latter as an embodiment of subversive love and righteousness.[73] Barth's commentary illuminates how Paul's ethical appeal in Romans 12:21 sets the stage for his subversive engagement with authority in the subsequent chapter. While tempering the temptation for a revolution that fights evil with evil (in the Barthian ethic, no mortal man is qualified to fight evil due to his own evil), Barth presents "revolution" in the person and Lordship of Jesus Christ.[74]

Furthermore, McKnight's hermeneutic of reading Romans backward lends additional credence to the text's subversive potential. McKnight invites readers to consider Romans in reverse, allowing the themes and motifs to reveal themselves in a fresh light. Applying McKnight's suggestion to Romans 13:1 involves lifting the text in the context of how various members in a typical Pompeii household might have heard the instructions.[75] When juxtaposed against the more significant Romanic hierarchical theme of the weak and strong, a sophisticated subversive dance begins to appear between Paul and the recipients of his letter.[76]

Paul's *propositio* [emphasis added] in Romans 1:16–17 also provides a fascinating perspective on his theology and approach to subversion. He boldly declares, "For I am not ashamed of the gospel, for it is the power of God for salvation to everyone who believes, to the Jew first and also to the Greek. For in it the righteousness of God is revealed from faith for faith, as it is written, 'The righteous shall live by faith.'"[77] This proclamation is crucial in Paul's subversive homiletic and praxis as it challenges the Roman imperial ideology of power and

---

[73] Barth, *Romans*, 484.

[74] Ibid., 482. Barth argues, "[Paul] really means that Revolution which is the impossible possibility. He means forgiveness of sins and resurrection of the dead. He means Jesus Christ."

[75] McKnight, "L1," 47:31. Note: McKnight borrows this descriptive from Oakes.

[76] Ibid., 4:26.

[77] Romans 1:16–17 ESV.

authority. The phrase "the righteousness of God" points to God's divine action, undermining the Roman claim to righteousness through military might and governance. Instead, Paul presents the gospel as the true source of salvation and divine righteousness. He subtly contests the Roman socio-political structure by elevating faith in Christ over and against submission to the Roman authorities.

Additionally, Paul's reference to the OT prophet Habakkuk in Romans 1:17, alongside his allusion to the Hebrew poetry of the Psalms, provides a broader frame of reference informed by his encounter with Christ and a renewed reading of the scriptures.[78] His framework, therefore, is not confined to Imperial Rome but rather encompasses a cosmic and eternal vision of salvation history, positioning the gospel as the culmination of God's redemptive plan for all creation—a concept especially provocative in a context where Caesar claimed divine cosmic authority.[79] This duality portrays a Pauline praxis echoed in Grimké's EEH. One might argue that much of the oppression experienced under Jim Crow and segregation was justified by propagators who claimed a self-ascribed, higher authority.[80]

---

[78] Cf. Habakkuk 2:4; Psalm 98.

[79] Diehl, "Empire," 222; Craig R. Koester, *Revelation and the End of All Things*, 2nd ed. (Grand Rapids, MI: Wm. B. Eerdmans Publishing Co., 2018), 89; Porter and Westfall, "Paul Confronts Caesar," 92, 94, 96–98.

[80] George Fitzhugh, *Cannibals All! Or, Slaves Without Masters* (Richmond: A. Morris, 1857); Benjamin M. Palmer, *The South: Her Peril and Her Duty* (New Orleans: J.O. Nixon, 1860); Josiah Priest, *Bible Defense of Slavery: And Origin Fortunes, and History of the Negro Race* (Glasgow, KY: Rev. W. S. Brown, 1851). These works propagate a notion of a divinely sanctioned racial and social hierarchy, positioning particular groups as inherently superior, with enslavement justified as necessary for societal stability. Such interpretations parallel ancient ideological justifications for subordination, distorting biblical texts to imply divine approval for slavery. Cf. Romans 1:25, a passage with which Grimké would have been well acquainted, in which Paul critiques those who "exchanged the truth about God for a lie, and worshiped and served the creature rather than the Creator"—a reminder of human tendencies to elevate themselves or societal structures to a godlike status.

We witness a contemporary expression of this in Grimké's sermon on Psalm 27:14, "God, and Prayer as Factors in the Struggle," which we will fully examine in the next chapter. In a manner similar to Paul, Grimké engages this psalm of lament to confront worldly and cosmic forces of evil with the hope of the gospel. He preaches:

> If the Devil was on the throne of the universe, there would be no such ground of rejoicing; no such hope could possibly exist. But he is not on the throne. It is true he is called the "God of this world," and at times would seem to be all-powerful in it, but it is only apparent. There is but one supreme power in the universe; and to that power one day every knee is to bow, and every tongue confess. There has been no abdication on the part of God. Because wrong goes on, it doesn't mean that everything has been turned over to the evil one; that wrongs are never to be righted. No, there is a Just One, who never slumbers nor sleeps, and who is not indifferent to what is going on. He will one day "make requisition for blood." Isaiah tells us that "righteousness is the girdle of his loins, and faithfulness the girdle of his reins."[81]

He continues:

> Thank God, I say, this lawless, murderous, Negro-hating spirit that is running riot in the South, that unblushingly flaunts its shame in the face of the civilized world, while it may murder Negroes and despoil them of their civil and political rights, cannot prevent them from lifting their eyes to heaven, or breathing a prayer; nor can it shut the ears of heaven to their cries. It may shut the ears of a cowardly pulpit, and a prejudiced church, but there its power stops. It cannot block the way of approach to the Holy of Holies. God has opened the way, and no man can shut it; all the powers of darkness cannot do it. Into that august presence the

[81] Grimké, *Works III*, 275–76.

> Negro may come, black though he may be, ignorant though he may be, poor though he may be, with the same assurance of acceptance as the whitest, the most cultivated, the most wealthy.[82]

He closes with:

> I believe in the reality of prayer. I believe in the power of prayer. I believe that our cause can be helped by prayer. This doesn't mean that we are to do nothing but pray, that we are to fold our arms and expect God to fight our battles for us; nor does it mean that we are not to stand up for our rights, that we are not to agitate and protest against wrong—the agitation must go on; the demand which we are making for equal recognition of our rights, civil and political, under the Constitution, must never be relinquished—what it means is, that in the midst of the conflict, while we are doing all we can, while we are seeking to make the most of ourselves and of our opportunities, we are at the same time to lay fast hold of the Almighty, to keep ourselves and our wants ever before Him, and to look to Him for help in every time of need. 'Wait on the Lord,' is the exhortation;[83]

This integrated sentiment appreciably reflects Paul's approach, proclaiming a hope that inherently challenges visible and invisible structures of oppression and calls believers to lament, repent, and recognize Christ's sovereign reign over all creation, with His ultimate victory over the inimical forces of sin, death, Satan, and the fear of God's wrath.[84]

With this in mind, we continue Paul's *propositio*, noting that the striking relationship between Romans 1:16–17 and Romans 13:1

[82] Ibid., 280.

[83] Ibid., 289.

[84] Crisler, "Interview 5." Crisler emphasized the significance of considering Paul's cosmic vision, a perspective that informs the interpretative approach of this section.

becomes evident as Paul addresses the issue of submission to governing authorities. As detailed earlier, at first glance, the injunction in Romans 13:1 seems to advocate for compliance with the Roman Empire. However, a deeper layer of meaning unfolds when viewed within the context of Paul's subversive praxis. He establishes the gospel as the source of divine righteousness, thus creating a pragmatic theological tension between God's authority and Rome's authority. Moreover, he introduces a radical notion of divine sovereignty over human power structures by asserting that God, through the lordship of Jesus Christ, institutes and oversees all authorities. This premier claim of the Pauline gospel praxis and homiletic subverts the Roman claim of imperial divinity and challenges the exclusive legitimacy of Roman authorities. Paul's call for submission to authorities is thus not a passive endorsement of Roman rule but a tactical move to encourage obedience within a larger framework of divine authority that undermines imperial claims.

Furthermore, Paul's subversive homiletic can be understood in light of his use of rhetorical devices to convey his message. The literary structure of his letter plays a crucial role in creating telling connections between various sections. For instance, the meticulous progression of thought from Romans 1:16–17 to Romans 13:1, when closely examined, is revealing—with Paul employing chiasm and inclusio patterns as he echoes the ancient Hebrew prophets and poets.[85] These structures subtly, and sometimes not so subtly, draw attention to the center of the argument, reinforcing the discordant link between the

---

[85] Adele Berlin, *The Dynamics of Biblical Parallelism*, revised and expanded ed. (Grand Rapids, MI: Eerdmans, 2008), 33, 183, 226, 242. See also Kenneth J. Langley, *How to Preach the Psalms* (Dallas: Fontes Press, 2021), 62, 63–66. Berlin and Langley identify chiasms and inclusios as common practices in ancient Hebrew writings, with which Paul would have been most familiar. The use of parallelisms by Hebrew poets and prophets is a nuanced and debated topic in OT scholarship. However, for the scope of this work, it is sufficient to note that these patterns would have been readily referenced by Paul, a well-trained Pharisaic Hebrew.

power of the gospel and submission to Roman authorities. Paul's intent becomes increasingly evident through this careful arrangement of ideas, where his theological assertion about divine righteousness amplifies his resistance to the oppressive Roman regime.

A final and perhaps most striking consideration in Romans 13 is Paul's undeniably positive and respectful tone toward governing authorities, whom he describes as "servants" or "ministers" of God.[86] However, the tension created by this reverent tone may not have been unsettling to Paul's earliest readers, nor to Grimké, given their unique societal contexts. For Paul's audience, who lived under a Roman system with limited autonomy, such an approach would underscore the sovereignty of God over even the highest earthly powers. Similarly, Grimké's context of navigating a society shaped by entrenched racial hierarchy may have lent itself to strategically interpreting Romans 13 with an emphasis on God's authority over all governing systems, regardless of human failings.[87]

---

[86] Cf. Romans 13:4.

[87] Porter and Westfall, "Caesar," 100. More could be explored on this matter, particularly with respect to public discourse within marginalized or oppressed communities. Balancing Paul's positive yet subtly critical portrayal of governing authorities reveals deeper nuances in his rhetoric. Porter observes, "Paul gives reasons why obedience to just authorities should occur. One is that there is no legitimate authority except as that authority is put in place by God. This is what makes sense of Romans 13:3. Rulers, Paul says, are not a cause of fear for those who do good works, but for evil. But it is only just authorities and rulers about whom one can say this. The only way not to have fear of authority and to be able to count on receiving praise from them is if they are just and honorable. Only a just authority can be a minister of God for good purpose. No corrupt authority can guarantee that if one does evil there will be punishment, or that punishment will not be given to those who do good." Porter's framing suggests that Paul's positive tone could serve as a rhetorical strategy, disarming accusations while embedding a higher allegiance to God's kingdom. Furthermore, Paul's counsel for Christians to respect authority may encourage the Roman Christians to navigate a tense political environment peaceably, yet without compromising their commitment to Christ's lordship. While this exceeds the scope of our current research, it

In conclusion, our synopsis of Romans 13:1 unveils its subversive potential against the larger backdrop of the letter's content and context. By examining Paul's strategic rhetoric, historical context, and intertextuality, we discover a multilayered approach confronting the prevailing notions of authority and power as it advocates a gospel-centric activism. Or, to put it another way, Romans 13:1, borrowing from the interpretive strategies and tactical observations of LaRue, McKnight, Porter, and others, becomes a fulcrum for constructing a subversive hierarchical ethic rooted in the gospel's indicatives, thereby unveiling a patterned Pauline praxis that holds allegiance to the gospel announcement while concomitantly operating an activist ethic that embodies its subversive yet emancipatory essence in confronting systemic oppression.

Philemon: Unveiling A Subversive Gospel

The epistle to Philemon, despite overt themes of hierarchy and authority, has in many circles become an exegetical stepchild relegated to the utility of providing links to justify the inclusion of Colossians within the Pauline homologoumena.[88] This ironic observation exceeds our scope but suggests a premise for future investigation. In response, we contend that Paul's letter to Philemon is more than a supporting cast to his corpus; it is at the core of understanding his developed hierarchical ethic and subsequent praxis.[89] We further insist that this

---

opens avenues for future studies on rhetorical strategies within oppressed communities.

[88] Felder, *Stony*, 233.

[89] Diehl, "Empire," 251–52. Citing Richard J. Cassidy, Diehl argues, "Historically, then, Paul's circumstances changed between the writing of Romans and his communication to Philemon, as did his perspectives concerning the Roman imperial system. Dating Philemon after Romans, after Paul had experienced the full force of Roman custody, ill health, a dependence upon friends and fellow workers, hope for release, and battles within the judicial system, the small letter of Philemon takes on a sense of anti-imperial rhetoric that is not found in Romans 13."

short letter provides sensible contextual insight for negotiating power dynamics, social relationships, and the implications of the gospel's indicatives.

The Philemon letter provides a succinct platform for investigating the subversive dimensions of the gospel in Paul's hierarchical ethic and praxis. As Weima notes, its narrative intricacies illuminate Paul's strategic use of rhetoric to subvert conventional notions of authority, relationships, and social hierarchies. He writes, "[Philemon] contains many instances where Paul has deftly adapted and cleverly used various epistolary conventions and literary forms to persuade Philemon to obey God's will in the highly sensitive matter of his slave Onesimus."[90] Weima's keen observation unveils how Philemon offers a thoughtful framing of subversion and its usefulness in actualizing the emancipatory indicatives of the gospel of Jesus Christ.

The epistolary structure of Philemon is the canvas for its subversive intent. As a first matter of order, Paul addresses the recipient, Philemon, and subsequently (and not coincidentally so) salutes Apphia, Archippus, and the church that meets in their house. His appeal intentionally includes a broader audience, escalating a private matter to a communal concern.[91] Weima notes that Paul's deliberate inclusion of the community magnifies the subversive impact of his request for Onesimus's emancipation.[92] This tactic destabilizes the traditional power dynamics between "master" and "slave," as the collective audience witnesses Philemon's ethical response to Paul's gospel-driven insistence.[93]

---

[90] Weima, *Paul*, 205.

[91] Felder, *Stony*, 242. Cf. Philemon 1–2.

[92] Weima, *Paul*, 211.

[93] Ibid. Reader's note: Citing Douglas Moo, Weima reminds readers that "[The] strategy of making the letter's request a public matter should not be viewed as a sneaky and questionable tactic of Paul but ought to be viewed in the context of the corporate nature of the early church, in which no matter was purely 'private' but rather involved indirectly, if not directly, one's relationship with fellow brothers and sisters within the new family of God."

The following verses further stage Paul's approach. He greets Philemon, praising his love and faith, but strategically employs the phrase, "I appeal to you for my child Onesimus, whose father I became in my imprisonment." [94] This subtextual allusion to fatherhood challenges the conventional master–slave relationship, positioning Paul as a spiritual father to both Philemon and Onesimus.[95] Wright argues that this effectually makes them sibling equals, urging Philemon to accept Onesimus as if he were the apostle himself.[96] Such a subversion echoes Galatians 3:28, in which Paul asserts the obliteration of social hierarchies in Christ.[97]

Moreover, Paul's use of persuasion through reciprocity betrays a subversive strategy. He expresses his desire to keep Onesimus as a helper, acknowledging his recent runaway past as unhelpful but envisioning him as "useful to you and to me."[98] Lewis writes:

> Paul's language in verse 11 includes the well-discussed pun on the runaway's name. Our interest, however, needs to be on why

---

[94] Philemon 5–10 ESV.

[95] Felder, *Stony*, 244. Lewis writes, "We might note that Paul in his own writings rarely refers to himself as a "father" to fellow Christians, and reserves that title for times when he is speaking to those whom he has converted to Christianity (1 Corinthians 4:15) or for particularly sharp issues of ecclesial conflict."

[96] N. T. Wright, *Paul and the Faithfulness of God* (Minneapolis: Fortress Press, 2013), 19–20. Wright posits the following, "Paul sets up the climax by expressing in the strongest and most evocative terms his own personal unity with both Philemon and Onesimus. Philemon is his beloved fellow worker (verse 1), the one whose faith, love, and refreshing ministry have cheered Paul in prison (verses 5-7). Onesimus, meanwhile, is Paul's child, begotten in prison (verse 10), Paul's own very heart (verse 12), and a beloved brother (verse 16). Very well: the two of them are joined, in Paul, and this is how the *κοινωνία τῆς πίστεως*, the 'partnership of faith,' is to be powerfully effective."

[97] Ibid., 238–39.

[98] Ibid., 244–45. Read Lewis's discussion on Onesimus' conversion and the meaning of his name for context. Cf. Philemon 11.

> Onesimus was once useless, but now is useful. Surely Paul could not be speaking of the usefulness/uselessness of Onesimus as a slave. Otherwise, we would have to read the latter half of verse 11 as a sign that conversion's greatest effect on Onesimus was the power for greater diligence in his chores, and that out of his conversion he had ended up with two slavemasters [*sic*] instead of one. Verse 12 provides stronger clues for solving this riddle. Onesimus was now being sent to Philemon to stand as the representative of Paul.[99]

One cannot help but notice the hierarchical disruption in Lewis's assertion. Paul's engagement with Philemon introduces a new "family dynamic."[100] This new family dynamic embodies the heart of the subversive nature of the gospel's effect on the early church community.

Interestingly, McKnight's "reading Romans backward" methodology sheds light on the socially disruptive rays of the text. When viewed backward, the epistle culminates in Paul's final instructions to "prepare a guest room for me"—a request that subtly, or not so subtly, encourages Philemon's interpretation and response to the earlier elements of the letter.[101] This structural tactic aligns with Paul's overarching intent to reframe relationships within the community of believers, destabilizing the hierarchical norm.[102]

Paul's palpable subversion surfaces as he pens this haunting plea for Onesimus: "If he has wronged you at all, or owes you anything, charge that to my account."[103] The subtext of Paul's appeal, as Crisler

---

[99] Ibid.

[100] Ibid., 245. Lewis observes, "I see in Paul's almost dizzying display of family language even Paul struggling with the fact that the gospel that subverts the fundamental distinction between Jew and Gentiles would not long leave the issue of slavery alone."

[101] Crisler, "Interview 2." Crisler notes the tension of an impending visit from Paul. Cf. Philemon 22.

[102] Felder, *Stony*, 233–34.

[103] Philemon 18–19 ESV.

notes, frames Paul as the satisfier of Onesimus's debt, echoing Christ's redemptive act, eliminating the demarcations of the slave-to-master dynamic, and redefining power and authority through the reverberations of Christ's selfless sacrifice.[104]

In conclusion, this synopsis of Philemon showcases its subversive tenor. Through examination of structure, rhetorical tactics, and interconnectedness with broader Pauline and Christological themes, Philemon proves a masterful treatise, challenging conventional societal constructs and inviting an honest and pragmatic embodiment of the gospel's indicatives.

Synthesizing the Praxis

Hypothesizing a subversive Pauline praxis and homiletic through an epistolary analysis of the apostle Paul's tactics in Romans 13:1 and Philemon, we have witnessed how Paul deftly interacted with societal norms and power dynamics by infusing his letters with messages that intersect and maneuver hierarchical structures. A synthesis of our findings presents a nuanced harmonization, as modeled by Paul, between activism and the gospel of Jesus Christ—intimating no actual distinction between the two but rather portraying the former as an extension of the latter. This tension becomes evident through four prominent Pauline tactics: (1) the use of scriptural precedent and intertextuality, (2) the modeled sacrifice of Christ, (3) his appeal to familial unity in the body of Christ, and (4) a call to embody the indicatives of the Gospel actively in opposition to unrighteous ruling authorities. As we piece together these threads, a holistic picture emerges, portraying a Pauline homiletic and hierarchical subversion that catalyzes an emancipatory, gospel-embodied activism.[105] Paul's

---

[104] Crisler, "Interview 2."

[105] Reader's note: The formula prescribed in this sentence suggests a Pauline pattern that Bebbington observes much later, though not directly so, in his quadrilateral of evangelical priorities—biblicism, crucicentrism, conversionism, and activism. See Bebbington, *Evangelicalism*, 2–4, passim.

structured (and tactical) approach echoed that of the Hebrew prophets and poets with whom he was well-acquainted, stamping a pattern that still reverberates throughout the NT church. We now consider an example of Pauline praxis and its priorities by examining Grimké's sermon, "God, and Prayer as Factors in the Struggle."[106]

---

[106] Grimké, *Works I*, 274–90.

CHAPTER 5

THE GRIMKÉ ECHO: COURAGEOUS EMANCIPATORY ECHOES OF A HEBREW POET

Extending the Pauline prophetic praxis detailed in Chapter 4 as a descriptive–comparative backdrop to Grimké's poetic homiletic, we now consider the Pauline patterned echoes of Grimké and their activist resonance with the penitential laments of the OT poets in his sermon on Psalm 27, "God, and Prayer as Factors in the Struggle."[1] This transition from Paul's epistolary form to Hebrew poetry underscores how Grimké's use of the psalms aligns with his commitment to an EEH, positioning the gospel as both a message of personal salvation and a force for societal transformation. Exploring Psalm 27 in Grimké's homiletic emphasizes how the penitential and lamentative nature of Hebrew poetry connects the gospel's spiritual and ethical dimensions with its subversive call for justice.[2] But first, before analyzing Grimké's sermon and its distinct emancipatory echoes and evangelical priorities, we must explain the unique dynamics of Hebrew poetry in the scriptures and its relevance to the end or aim of gospel echoes.

In describing Hebrew poetry and its ultimate end, noted OT scholar Bryan Cribb shares an anecdote of how he persuaded his

---

[1] Grimké, *Works I*, 274–90.

[2] Paul consistently echoes the Psalms in his pastoral epistles and, in two epistles, he directly admonishes others to do the same (Ephesians 5:19; Colossians 3:16). Cf. Romans 3:10-18 (quoting Psalms 14:1-3, 53:1-3, 5:9, 10:7, 36:1), Romans 4:6-8 (quoting Psalm 32:1-2), Romans 8:36 (quoting Psalm 44:22), Romans 10:18 (quoting Psalm 19:4), Romans 15:11 (quoting Psalm 117:1), 1 Corinthians 10:26 (quoting Psalm 24:1), Hebrews 1:5-13 (quoting Psalms 2:7, 110:1, 45:6-7), Ephesians 4:8 (quoting Psalm 68:18), and 1 Corinthians 15:25-27 (quoting Psalms 110:1 and 8:6).

newlywed wife to drive instead of fly to their honeymoon destination in Plymouth, Massachusetts. Among several stops, their twenty-hour journey included a visit to Princeton Theological Seminary in hopes of breathing the hallowed air of luminaries such as Jonathan Edwards, Hodge, Warfield, and our subject, Grimké.

Upon their arrival, the campus bustled with activity due to a visit from Jerry Seinfeld, which Cribb admits was initially disappointing. (He had hoped for a more scholarly focus.) Nevertheless, discovering one of Seinfeld's Porsches parked nearby piqued his curiosity, as he straightway asked his newly minted wife to take a picture of him with the vehicle. Memorializing the moment, Cribb confesses that he was not simply interested in showing the car's superior aesthetic but, more importantly, in eliciting a *response* [my emphasis] from his colleagues and friends back home—"You are the coolest college professor ever!"

Cribb closes the tale by comparing his aim in taking and sharing the "celebrity car selfie" to the purpose of the ancient Hebrew poets in the Bible. He asserts that they did not write primarily for the beauty of prose or language but to provoke a response in the affective domain—a surrendered "amen" of heart and head, embodied through a responsive activism in the reader.[3] We advance our argument with this framing to establish a canvas for Grimké's historic courageous sermon.

Overview of the Penitential Psalms

The five books of Hebrew poetry are Job, Psalms, Proverbs, Ecclesiastes, and Song of Songs. Each offers practical wisdom, striking poetry, and probing proverbs.[4] Their themes, as the ancient poetic language expert Michael E. Travers highlighted concerning the psalms, resonate deeply with those who recognize their shortcomings and yearn

---

[3] Bryan Cribb and Channing Crisler, *The Bible Toolbox* (Nashville: B&H Academic, 2019), 243–45. See Green, *Dialectic*, 3; Chapter 1, note 12.
[4] Ibid, 245.

for spiritual renewal.[5] In this instance, however, we will focus on the poetic and activist (or pietistic) elements of the Penitential Psalms and Psalm 27.[6]

Acknowledging that the particularity of this discourse constrains our exploration, we expect that our synopsis of the Penitential Psalms, as C. H. Spurgeon declared, will provide "boundless profit and ever-growing pleasure" in detailing the essential elements of Hebrew poetry.[7] This foundation is crucial for understanding the echoed gospel of the Pauline praxis and Grimké's EEH. Additionally, the following sections may strike us as pedantic, discursive, or even repetitive, but they will, in due course, prove necessary for evaluating Grimké's hermeneutic on Psalm 27.

The Seven Penitential Psalms

The classification of the Penitential Psalms, traditionally attributed to early Church Fathers like Augustine, identifies seven psalms associated with themes of repentance and confession.[8] This system has been integral to Jewish and Christian liturgical practices, particularly during periods of personal and communal repentance. These psalms boast thematic elements such as confession of sin, expression of sorrow, plea for mercy, and trust in divine justice.

Psalm 6. The sixth psalm is a plea for God's mercy and healing. Feeling the weight of divine displeasure, the psalmist cries out for relief

---

[5] Michael E. Travers, "Severe Delight: The Paradox of Praise in Confession of Sin," in *The Psalms: Language for All Seasons of the Soul*, ed. Andrew Schmutzer and David Howard (Chicago: Moody, 2013), passim.

[6] The author asserts that Grimké's allegiance to a pious lifestyle was bedrock to his insistent activism. In other words, for Grimké, piety was the embodiment of the gospel's indicatives.

[7] Charles Haddon Spurgeon, *The Treasury of David*, vols. 1–6 (London: Marshall Brothers, n.d.), 1:v. Note: The larger connections and inferences drawn, herein, are informed by Cribb's work in Chapter 6 of *The Bible Toolbox*.

[8] Alfred G. Mortimer, *Notes on the Seven Penitential Psalms, Chiefly from Patristic Sources* (London: Joseph Master & Co., 1889), preface.

from physical and emotional distress, capturing the deep anguish of someone who acknowledges his need for God's compassionate intervention. This psalm exemplifies the confession of sin and plea for mercy, as indicated in the key verse, "O Lord, do not rebuke me in Your anger, Nor chasten me in Your wrath."[9]

Psalm 32. The thirty-second psalm celebrates the joy of receiving God's forgiveness. It contrasts the burden of unconfessed sin with the relief and blessedness of confession and pardon. The psalmist reflects on the power of God's grace, actively encouraging others to seek God's forgiveness. This psalm features the themes of confession of sin and the resulting joy of forgiveness, encapsulated by the key verse, "How blessed is he whose transgression is forgiven, Whose sin is covered!"[10]

Psalm 38. The thirty-eighth psalm is a lament over personal sin and its toll on the psalmist's body and spirit. This psalm describes the physical and mental anguish accompanying a sense of guilt and estrangement from God. The psalmist appeals to God's mercy, expressing an earnest awareness of personal failings. The themes of sorrow for sin and a plea for mercy are evident in the verse, "O Lord, rebuke me not in Your wrath, And chasten me not in Your burning anger."[11]

Psalm 51. The fifty-first psalm is a prayer of repentance, traditionally associated with David's contrition after his sin with Bathsheba. The psalmist asks for a clean heart and a renewed spirit, emphasizing God's steadfast love and abundant mercy. It is one of the most personal and moving confessions in the Psalms, illustrating the themes of deep remorse and a heartfelt plea for forgiveness. The key verse of the psalm captures these sentiments, "Be gracious to me, O

---

[9] Psalm 6:1 (New American Standard Bible 1995) Note: All scriptural quotations are NASB95, unless otherwise stated or directly quoted from a cited source.

[10] Psalm 32:1.

[11] Psalm 38:1.

God, according to Your lovingkindness; According to the greatness of Your compassion blot out my transgressions."[12]

Psalm 102. The one-hundred-and-second psalm is a cry for help during intense distress. The psalmist describes his affliction and pleads for God's attention and intervention. This psalm captures the desolation of feeling abandoned but still turning to God with hope for restoration. The themes of expressing sorrow and seeking divine intervention are evident in the verse, "Hear my prayer, O Lord! And let my cry for help come to You."[13]

Psalm 130. The one-hundred-and-thirtieth psalm calls for God's mercy from the depths of despair. The psalmist yearns for divine forgiveness, waiting and hoping in the Lord. This psalm portrays the transition from despair to hope as the psalmist places trust in God's redeeming love. The themes of a plea for mercy and trust in divine justice are highlighted in the verse, "Out of the depths I have cried to You, O Lord."[14]

Psalm 143. Last, the one-hundred-and-forty-third psalm is a supplication for God's faithfulness amidst severe trials. The psalmist asks for guidance and deliverance from enemies, affirming trust in God's righteousness and faithfulness. This psalm combines lament, a plea for mercy, and a strong declaration of faith, as seen in the verse, "Hear my prayer, O Lord, Give ear to my supplications!"[15]

Throughout history, believers have used these seven psalms, known for their themes of repentance and emotive pleas for divine mercy, to guide their personal and communal devotion. Interpretative echoes and gospel pleas, from Paul to Grimké, draw on their relevance and emotional depth. As we move to the next section, we explore how various historical and liturgical contexts have shaped the understanding, preaching, and use of these psalms, and how Grimké

---

[12] Psalm 51:1.
[13] Psalm 102:1.
[14] Psalm 130:1.
[15] Psalm 143:1.

framed Psalm 27 as an *eighth Penitential Psalm* [emphasis added], calling the nation to repent for the corporate sin of racial prejudice.

An Echoic History of Interpretation and Activism

The Penitential Psalms feature prominently throughout history in Jewish and Christian traditions—postured as activist texts for personal reflection, repentance, and communal penance. These psalms are significant in Jewish and Christian liturgical practices, most notably during personal and communal repentance (Teshuvah).[16] In Jewish tradition, they are recited during the High Holy Days and other penitential seasons, provoking worshippers to spiritual reflection and action.[17] In Christianity, the Penitential Psalms have been integral to liturgy since the early church.[18] Augustine and the Fathers frequently referenced these psalms in their sermons and writings to inspire communal acts of repentance and heightened personal devotion.[19]

The richness of the Penitential Psalms lies in their terse structure.[20] Unlike poetry dependent on rhyme or meter, Hebrew poetry's reliance on parallelism—a rhythm of ideas rather than sounds—allows it to translate effectively into all languages. This literary technique, involving paired lines that complement or contrast each other, enhances the emotional and spiritual impact of the text without reliance on the linguistically constrained rhetorical elements often deployed in Western discourse.[21] For instance, the chiastic structures in Psalm 51 punctuate the central plea for a pure heart, underscoring the psalmist's deep desire for inner transformation.

---

[16] Shmuel Yosef Agnon, *Days of Awe* (New York: Schocken Books, 1965; originally published in 1948), 24–25. Agnon writes, "Therefore let every man regret his sins, great or small, and do Teshuvah. And let no man be lazy and say, 'I will have time,' lest, God forbid, the hour slip [away]."

[17] Ibid.

[18] Langley, *How to Preach the Psalms*, 132.

[19] Mortimer, *Notes on the Seven Penitential Psalms*, preface.

[20] Cribb and Crisler, *Bible Toolbox*, 254.

[21] Berlin, *Dynamics*, 230–38.

Similarly, the parallelisms in Psalm 6 reinforce the intensity of the plea for mercy and healing, making the psalmist's desperation palpable. The providence in this structure ensures that the subtextual themes of repentance and divine forgiveness are accessible and resonant across different cultures and epochs.[22]

As a final note, Psalm 27, though not traditionally classified among the Penitential Psalms, contains elements of trust and lament, which supports Grimké's inferred penitential hermeneutical application. The psalmist's declaration of confidence in God's protection and plea for deliverance amidst adversaries resonate with the penitential themes of seeking God's mercy and expressing trust in His justice. We revisit this observation's pragmatic and homiletical worthiness later.

Jewish Traditions. The so-called Penitential Psalms historically play a vital role in Jewish tradition. Adherents have faithfully recited them during designated periods of personal reflection, repentance, and communal penance for generations. These psalms are uniquely significant during the High Holy Days, including Rosh Hashanah and Yom Kippur, and during the month of Elul, which precedes these holidays.[23] This period is known as a time for spiritual introspection and seeking forgiveness. Interestingly, Psalm 27, which we later lift as our sermonic illustration, is also recited during Elul, emphasizing themes of trust in God's protection and deliverance, which align with the penitential spirit.[24]

Early Christian Traditions. Likewise, among Christians, the Penitential Psalms have been integral to liturgical practices since the early church. These psalms are recited during Lent and other penitential seasons, guiding the faithful to express remorse for their sins and seek God's mercy.[25] Early Church Fathers, including Augustine,

---

[22] Cribb and Crisler, *Bible Toolbox*, 252.

[23] Agnon, *Days of Awe*, viii, 16–26.

[24] Matthew Berkowitz, "A Psalm of Repentance," *JTS*, August 28, 2004/5764, accessed July 11, 2024, https://www.jtsa.edu/torah/a-psalm-for-repentance.

[25] Langley, *How to Preach the Psalms*, 144.

frequently referenced these psalms in their sermons and writings.[26] Augustine's extensive commentary on the Psalms highlights their importance in the believer's life, emphasizing themes of confession, sorrow for sin, and divine mercy. His influence helped to cement the Penitential Psalms' role in Christian worship and their use in daily prayers and communal penitential services.[27]

Medieval Traditions. The Medieval church continued this tradition, with the Penitential Psalms recited during periods of plague, war, and other calamities as supplication and intercession.[28] Monastic communities, in particular, incorporated these psalms into their daily prayers, using them as a personal and communal repentance tool.[29] The repetition of these psalms, as in times past for Jewish and Christian communities, brought comfort and spiritual renewal, reinforcing the corporate themes of penitence, mercy, forgiveness, and trust in divine justice.

The musical and artistic influences of the Penitential Psalms were particularly arresting during the Renaissance and Baroque periods. Composers such as Orlande de Lassus and Giovanni Pierluigi da Palestrina created intricate polyphonic settings for these texts to enhance their emotional and spiritual impact.[30] These musical

---

[26] Mortimer, *Notes on the Seven Penitential Psalms*, passim.

[27] Ibid, 5. Reader's note: It is important to acknowledge that many OT scholars do not find Augustine's exegetical work on the Psalms fully satisfactory, but few can argue against its pragmatic and pastoral effects. Mortimer writes, "I think it is S. Augustine, who beautifully puts it thus, 'The needle of fear must go before the thread of love.' The needle punctures the place where the thread is to enter, the needle is drawn out, the thread remains, and holds the work together; so in penitence, fear punctures the hard heart, and gives us the Grace of Compunction, and love follows and by contrition completes the work, and binds the soul to God forever."

[28] John D. Witvliet, *The Biblical Psalms in Christian Worship: A Brief Introduction and Guide to Resources* (Grand Rapids, MI: Eerdmans, 2007), 149–50.

[29] Ibid, 153–54.

[30] James Haar, "Orlande de Lassus," in *The New Grove High Renaissance Masters: Josquin, Palestrina, Lassus, Byrd, Victoria*, ed. Stanley Sadie (New York:

compositions were used in liturgical settings to actuate a sense of reverence and introspection during penitential seasons. For example, the *Miserere* (Psalm 51) by Gregorio Allegri is perhaps one of the most famous settings. It is known for its hauntingly beautiful melody and use during Tenebrae services in the Sistine Chapel.[31]

In addition to musical compositions, the Penitential Psalms have inspired various forms of visual art.[32] Artists have depicted scenes of repentance and divine mercy, drawing from the imagery and themes found in these psalms. These artworks served as visual aids for meditation and reflection, reinforcing the messages conveyed through the psalms. The integration of these psalms into both music and art reflects their deep resonance within the cultural and spiritual life of faith communities.

Puritanical and Reformed Traditions. While the Penitential Psalms might seem to align well with the piety of the Puritans and the Reformed tradition, Clare Costley King'oo observes a notable underemphasis on them within these traditions. Although the Book of Common Prayer, the central liturgical text of the Church of England first issued under Edward VI in 1549, prescribed the reading of the entire Psalter once per month, it did not specifically refer to the Penitential Psalms as a distinct group. King'oo further reports that in the Reformed Tudor church, the seven Penitential Psalms were typically encountered individually as part of the sequential recitation of all 150 psalms during Matins and Evensong. This recitation

---

W. W. Norton & Company, 1984), 157–227; Lewis Lockwood and Jesse Ann Owens, "Giovanni Pierluigi da Palestrina," in *The New Grove High Renaissance Masters: Josquin, Palestrina, Lassus, Byrd, Victoria*, ed. Stanley Sadie (New York: W. W. Norton & Company, 1984), 93–153.

[31] Graham O'Reilly, '*Allegri's Miserere' in the Sistine Chapel* (New York: Oxford University Press, 2020), 1–4.

[32] Clare L. Costley, "David, Bathsheba, and the Penitential Psalms," *Renaissance Quarterly* 57, no. 4 (Winter 2004): 1244–71, published online by Cambridge University Press, November 20, 2018, accessed July 29, 2024, https://www.jstor.org/stable/4143695.

followed the nonchronological order of the Book of Psalms rather than highlighting the Penitential Psalms as a collective unit. [33]

Despite the penitential psalms' historical role as instructive texts for repentance, humility, and seeking God's mercy, according to King'oo, their prominence in Puritanical and Reformed traditions is less pronounced than might be expected. Though King'oo represents only one well-researched and respected perspective on this matter, the observed de-emphasis perhaps suggests a theological perspective beyond the purview of this study and hints at complexities in how repentance, particularly its communal aspects, was understood and practiced within these traditions.[34] Nevertheless, the broader Reformed emphasis on scripture as the authoritative guide remains pertinent to this exercise and is crucial for understanding the role of Psalms, including the Penitential Psalms, as divinely inspired instructions for the church, gospel preaching, and activism.

The Reformed Tradition and the Apostle Paul. Grasping the influence of the Apostle Paul's theological emphases and ethos upon Puritanical and Reformed doctrine is foundational to exploring the interpretive and, in turn, homiletical praxis of these traditions. Though many accuse Paul of misunderstanding or deliberately distorting the "Jewish view of Law and Salvation," Krister Stendahl points out that "for the Jew, the Law did not require a static or pedantic perfectionism but supposed a covenant relationship in which there was room for forgiveness and repentance and where God applied the Measure of Grace."[35] Paul covenantally draws on the OT throughout his epistles,

---

[33] Clare Costley King'oo, *Miserere Mei: The Penitential Psalms in Late Medieval and Early Modern England*, Reformations: Medieval and Early Modern (Notre Dame, IN: University of Notre Dame Press, 2012), 157–86. For more nuanced evaluation of this topic, read Chapter 5, "Parody and Piety."

[34] Tise, *Proslavery*, 112–98. The overwhelming majority of the extant examples of pro-slavery sermons from 1701–1840 were found amongst Presbyterian and Reformed Baptist clergy. See Tables 5.1–6.23.

[35] Krister Stendahl, "The Apostle Paul and the Introspective Conscience of the West," *Harvard Theological Review* 56, no. 3 (July 1963): 201.

including the Penitential Psalms, both textually and thematically. His pastoral notes access—for Jew and Gentile, weak and strong, bond and free, offended and offender—covenant themes of repentance, God's mercy, justification, trust in divine justice, and the transformative power of divine grace, paralleling specifically, and not coincidentally, the Penitential Psalms' focus.[36] Such a focus is not startling. Paul, a well-educated first-century Jewish thinker, would undoubtedly have been saturated in the tradition of reciting and singing the Psalms, deeply embedding their themes and language into his theological framework.[37]

Consider, for instance, Romans 3:1–20, in which Paul underscores human sinfulness, echoing themes of contrition and the necessity of seeking God's forgiveness from Psalm 51.[38] Similarly, in 2 Corinthians 7:10, Paul states, "For the sorrow that is according to the will of God produces a repentance without regret, leading to salvation, but the sorrow of the world produces death," reflecting Psalm 32:5, which emphasizes the transformative power of confession and God's forgiveness: "I acknowledged my sin to You, And my iniquity I did not hide; I said, 'I will confess my transgressions to the LORD'; And You forgave the guilt of my sin" and Psalm 27:9, "Hide not your face from me. Turn not your servant away in anger, O you who have been my help. Cast me not off; forsake me not, O God of my salvation!" Additionally, in 1 Timothy 1:15, Paul writes, "It is a trustworthy statement, deserving full acceptance, that Christ Jesus came into the world to save sinners, among whom I am foremost of all," mirroring

---

[36] Mortimer, *Notes on the Seven Penitential Psalms*, 64. Mortimer reasons that Paul echoes David from the fourth penitential psalm in 1 Corinthians 8:12, reflecting David's confession that, even though he was king, his sin against his neighbor was nonetheless a direct sin against God. This sin could only be reconciled with God through acknowledgment and reconciliation with that neighbor as a covenantal co-equal of God's creation.

[37] Hays, *Letters*, 2. It is also important to note that our use of the term echo originates with Hays who makes a distinction between echoes and allusions. He uses the term echo in a less technical sense, and we will do the same.

[38] Ibid, 48.

the deep contrition and plea for mercy found in Psalm 51:1–2: "Be gracious to me, O God, according to Your lovingkindness; According to the greatness of Your compassion blot out my transgressions. Wash me thoroughly from my iniquity and cleanse me from my sin." Finally, though not classically identified as a Penitential Psalm, in 2 Corinthians 4:16, Paul echoes the penitential elements of Psalm 27:14 with, "Therefore we do not lose heart, but though our outer man is decaying, yet our inner man is being renewed day by day," reflecting the psalmist's exhortation, "Wait for the LORD; Be strong and let your heart take courage; Yes, wait for the LORD."

The intertextuality observed above, among several other examples throughout the Pauline corpus, reinforces the significance of the OT corpus, including the Penitential Psalms and Psalm 27, within these traditions, as Paul's teachings profoundly shape Reformed theology.[39] While this enterprise provides a circumscribed treatment of Paul's OT echoes of the Penitential Psalms and their elements, much more evidence supports this course of study and may prove fruitful for future research.

The Reformed Tradition and Grimké. Princeton Theological Seminary has perpetuated the Reformed tradition through its rigorous academic and spiritual formation of clergy for centuries. The seminary's historically attested adherence to Reformed principles underscores the prominence of scripture and the Pauline tradition in nurturing a deep, reflective spirituality among its students and

---

[39] Ibid, 6. Here, Hays keenly observes that "Through much of the history of Christian theology and biblical interpretation, Paul's innovative readings of Scripture posed no problem because Christians heard the Old Testament through the translating headset of a Pauline hermeneutic: what Scripture really meant was whatever Paul (and other New Testament writers) said it meant. Historical criticism, however, has restored a proper sense of Scripture's identity as a separate voice (more properly, a chorus of separate voices, though Paul would not have so understood it) and thus afforded us the possibility of discerning how Paul plays the *rebound of Scripture's voice* [my emphasis] off his own experience and confession."

faculty.[40] Grimké, who committedly appropriated his evangelical Reformed convictions to operate a social justice apparatus in his ministry for half a century, is a textbook example of this. According to Ferry, Grimké's engagement with the scriptures, and notably the psalms, which we demonstrate in the following sections, reflected his commitment to the Reformed ideals of rigorous biblical scholarship and personal piety, intertwined with a scriptural mandate for nonpartial civility (social justice) and the upliftment of African Americans.[41,42]

Grimké's reliance on the scriptures, and certainly, the psalms, was his signature, as he mobilized their themes of repentance and divine mercy at both a national and a local level to confront his racially segregated denomination and to challenge the moral temperature of his predominantly African American congregation—or, to borrow from McKnight, he examined their Christoformity, or lack thereof, as he invoked penitential notes and a call for communal repentance and social activism.[43] He urged his listeners to seek God's forgiveness while striving for righteousness and justice in a post-reconstruction Jim Crow tyranny.[44] This duality betrays Grimké's chiastic blend of Reformed

---

[40] Ferry, "Puritan." 2–3.

[41] Ferry, "Puritan," 2–3.

[42] Note: For a biblical basis of Grimké's ethos of social justice and impartial civility among professed Christians, see Galatians 3:27–28. According to Ferry, this defined the orthodoxy of Grimké's social ethic. Additionally, the author contends that the phrase "social justice" connotes more of a status than a mandate, whereas "social activism" better reflects the demands of an embodied gospel ethic.

[43] Francis James Grimké, *Works of Francis James Grimké*, vol. 1 (Washington, DC: Associated, 1942), 3–4. See also McKnight, "L1," 15:29.

[44] Calloway, "Rhetorical," 8. Grimké was shaped to a significant measure by the ethos of his famous white abolitionist aunts, Sarah and Angelina Grimké. In a personal note to Frank and his older brother, Archibald, dated April 6, 1868, his Aunt Angelina wrote the following, "let us pray God as he gradually removes by death the *petty tyrants* [emphasis added] of the South, that He will raise up a generation of true and loving ones from the ranks of the oppressed who will labor as fearlessly for the great Christian doctrine of liberty, Equality

piety and prophetic activism. It demonstrates how the penitential elements of the psalms were a powerful gospel tool for spiritual renewal and social critique in the African American religious experience.

Preaching Psalm 27 and its Penitential Elements. As noted earlier in the chapter, though Psalm 27 is not classically identified as penitential, people have historically recited it during the Jewish Season of Repentance, particularly in Elul. This period, leading to the High Holy Days of Rosh Hashanah and Yom Kippur, invites intense spiritual reflection and repentance. For an extended time, Jews worldwide engage in personal introspection, seeking forgiveness from God and reconciliation with others.[45] Psalm 27, with its themes of trust and lamentation, is also of priority in this season, as it captures the dual aspects of seeking divine protection and acknowledging human frailty.[46]

The themes of Psalm 27 are multifaceted, encompassing trust in God, lamentation over adversities, repentance, and praise. The psalm opens with a powerful declaration of confidence in God's protection: "The Lord is my light and my salvation; whom shall I fear?"[47] This trust is juxtaposed with the psalmist's acknowledgment of adversaries and the trials faced, which brings a tone of lamentation. As the psalm progresses, it moves towards a plea for God's continued presence and deliverance, encapsulating the essence of repentance. The psalmist's desire to "dwell in the house of the Lord" reflects a longing for divine communion and sanctuary, culminating in expressions of praise for God's faithfulness.[48]

Richard M. Davidson, a noted Adventist theologian, provides a compelling interpretation of Psalm 27. He describes the psalm as

---

and Fraternity of all races as the Slave-holder has labor'd and lived—fought and died for Slavery. Will you my young friends pledge yourselves to God—not to me, to this holy work."

[45] Agnon, *Days of Awe*, viii, 16–26.

[46] Berkowitz, "A Psalm of Repentance," passim.

[47] Psalm 27:1.

[48] Psalm 27:4.

encapsulating a "spiral of repentance and ever-heightening joy."[49] According to Davidson, the psalmist's journey in Psalm 27 is not a linear path but a dynamic process in which moments of repentance lead to a more enraptured joy and assurance in God's presence.[50] This interpretation highlights the power of repentance, where acknowledging one's sins and seeking God's mercy results in spiritual renewal and increased trust in God.

Davidson also emphasizes the integration of penitence and praise within sanctuary worship.[51] In Psalm 27:6, the psalmist speaks of offering sacrifices with shouts of joy and singing praises to the Lord—note the intimations of activism in the psalmist's sacrificial response. The blend of penitential practices with joyful worship underscores a holistic approach to the expressions of the human spirit found throughout the Psalms.[52] This integration is crucial for Davidson as it reflects a balanced piety in which penitence is not an end but a pathway to deeper communion with God and community and an active embodiment of His joy and peace.

The historical and thematic elements of Psalm 27 reveal its significant role in individual and communal worship. Its recitation during Elul serves as a preparation for the High Holy Days, helping gathered worshippers to focus on their reliance upon God and their corporate need for His guidance and forgiveness.[53] The psalm's

---

[49] Richard M. Davidson, "A Song for the Sanctuary: Celebrating Its Goodness, Its Truth, Its Beauty," *Adventist Review*, July 2, 1992, 706.
[50] Ibid.
[51] Ibid, 704.
[52] Ibid, 706.
[53] Alan Cooper and Elaine Ravich, "Psalm 27: The Days of Awe," *Jewish Theological Seminary*, last modified August 25, 2012, accessed July 12, 2024, https://www.jtsa.edu/torah/psalm-27-the-days-of-awe/. "The custom of reciting Psalm 27 during the penitential season, variously understood to entail the period from Rosh Hodesh Elul through Yom Kippur, Hoshanah Rabbah, or Shemini Atzeret, is codified in Mishnah Berurah, *siman* 581: 'In our region it is customary to recite [Psalm 27] followed by kaddish at the conclusion of

emphasis on trust amidst adversity and its calls for repentance and expressions of praise make it a compelling text for personal and social activism.

Against the backdrop of the Penitential Psalms, Psalm 27 offers a unique perspective, with themes that align closely with those of confession, seeking mercy, and trusting in divine justice. Though not the primary thrust of this body of work, the psalm's structure and poetic elements, exemplified in its employ of Hebrew parallelisms and figures of speech, enhance its emotional and spiritual impact. In the next section, we excogitate themes and principles for preaching the penitential elements of a psalm as we prepare to analyze Grimké's historic turn-of-the-century sermon on Psalm 27, "God and Prayer as Factors in the Struggle."[54]

Themes and Principles: Preaching the Penitential Elements of a Psalm

Preaching the psalms offers a consequential opportunity for gospel preaching that leads congregations through personal and communal seasons of repentance, confession, reconciliation, and seeking God's divine mercy. Augustine constructively suggested, "If the psalm prays, you pray; if it laments, you lament; if it exults, you rejoice; if it hopes, you hope; if it fears, you fear. Everything written here is a mirror for us."[55] In his commentary on the psalms, Calvin described them as "an anatomy of all the parts of the soul."[56] Most significantly, the apostle Paul encourages believers in Ephesus and Colossae, saying, "[Speak] to one another with psalms" and "the word of Christ dwell in

---

the morning and evening services every day from Rosh Hodesh Elul until Yom Kippur; we customarily recite it until Shemini Atzeret.'"

[54] Grimké, *Works I*, 274–90.

[55] Augustine, *Expositions of the Psalms 1–32*, III/15, introduction by Michael Fiedrowicz, translation and notes by Maria Boulding, OSB, ed. John E. Rotelle, OSA (Hyde Park, NY: New City Press, 2000), 30[2].3.1.

[56] John Calvin, *Commentary on the Book of Psalms*, trans. James Anderson (Grand Rapids, MI: Christian Classics Ethereal Library, n.d.), Preface.

you richly in all wisdom, teaching and admonishing one another in psalms."[57] To wit, these adages expose the depth and breadth of the psalms (even more exactingly so with the Penitential Psalms) and advance principled clues on hermeneutical approaches to engaging and preaching their gospel.[58] See Table 1 in Appendix II for a thematic rubric on interpreting and preaching the penitential elements of a psalm. [59]

Synopsis Overview

Preaching the Penitential Psalms offers rich opportunities to guide congregations through a structured five-fold thematic rubric: (1) divine presence, (2) contemporary relevance, (3) the power of prayer, (4) hope and perseverance, and (5) communal experience. This practical framework is a taxonomy for preaching the penitential elements of a psalm, and it is a subset of Bebbington's Evangelical priority of Biblicism referenced in prior chapters. As Augustine, Calvin, and others highlight, when preached effectively, the psalms motivate and comfort believers, providentially guiding them toward a deeper relationship with God and a fuller experience and expression of His grace. We now crystallize these principles through Grimké's sermonic witness.

---

[57] Ephesians 5:19 ESV; Colossians 3:16 ESV. Also, Cf. Romans 3:10–18 (quoting Psalms 14:1–3, 53:1–3, 5:9, 10:7, 36:1), Romans 4:6–8 (quoting Psalm 32:1–2), Romans 8:36 (quoting Psalm 44:22), Romans 10:18 (quoting Psalm 19:4), Romans 15:11 (quoting Psalm 117:1), 1 Corinthians 10:26 (quoting Psalm 24:1), Hebrews 1:5–13 (quoting Psalms 2:7, 110:1, 45:6–7), Ephesians 4:8 (quoting Psalm 68:18), 1 Corinthians 15:25–27 (quoting Psalms 110:1 and 8:6).

[58] Cribb and Crisler, *Bible Toolbox*, 273. Cribb argues that "Psalms . . . clearly fits into salvation history. In fact, due to the book's thousand-year composition history—covering virtually all the history found in the OT—the psalms do speak of most of the essential salvation historical themes and events."

[59] Author's note: This rubric prescribed in Appendix II was inspired by the author's study of Hebrew poetry with OT scholar Bryan Cribb.

Poetic Gospel Echoes: A Sermonic Witness

Grimké's sermon on Psalm 27:14, delivered December 11, 1900, is a telling witness to the power of biblical reliance in activist gospel preaching. This sermon was the final lesson in a series preached by Grimké following a period of intense racial upheaval at the turn of the twentieth century. During this time, the United States witnessed a rapid increase in lynchings—a violent manifestation of "racism" and oppression.[60]

Additionally, anti-Negro views found expression in the publication of Charles Carroll's *The Negro Beast, or In the Image of God* in 1900.[61] Ferry notes how "[Carroll's] bizarre interpretation of scripture, [which] aimed to 'prove' that African Americans were soulless beasts devoid of moral ability," further fueled racial hatred and justified violent discrimination.[62] Carrol's book was wildly popular, especially among white Christians, and it further entrenched racist ideologies.[63] Grimké, in turn, leveraged his national platform to respond with a biting series of sermons. His response was unapologetically biblical and carried all the notes of an ancient Hebrew prophet and poet.

Built on the scriptural foundation of Psalm 27:14, the titles and dates of the sermons in Grimké's series were: "Discouragements: Hostility of the Press Silence and Cowardice of the Pulpit" delivered on November 20, 1900; "Sources from Which No Help May Be Expected,—The General Government, Political Parties" delivered on November 27, 1900; "Signs of a Brighter Future" delivered on December 4, 1900; and "God and Prayer as Factors in the Struggle"

---

[60] Ferry, "Puritan," 233. Ferry writes, "Negroes found themselves the local target for the *racism* [my emphasis] which underlay the concept of the 'white man's burden.'"

[61] Charles Carroll, *The Negro Beast, or In the Image of God* (St. Louis, MO: American Book and Bible House, 1900).

[62] Ferry, "Puritan," 234.

[63] Calloway, "Rhetorical," 63.

delivered on December 11, 1900.[64] In his culminating preachment, Grimké, the prized student of Princeton Theological Seminary's Charles Hodge, masterfully integrates themes of divine presence, contemporary relevance, the power of prayer, hope, and perseverance, and the importance of community and collective experience.

An analysis of the sermon's treatment of the penitential elements of Psalm 27 is in Table 2 of Appendix II.

Additional Consideration

Allowing for the previously discussed Pauline pattern of OT textual and thematic echoes in Chapter 2, Grimké's sermon on Psalm 27:14 structurally echoed the chiastic literary elements, along with several other devices of the penitential psalmist, to reinforce the cyclical and activist nature of repentance and divine assurance, and to amplify the poetic rhythm defined by Richardson as a "spiral of repentance and ever-heightening joy."[65] A review of his sermonic movements amplifies the point. First, Grimké opened his sermon with a strong affirmation of God's existence and support: "The first ground of hope to which our attention is here directed is in the fact that God is." He then moved through a series of lamentations and prayers, addressing inter and intra-communal struggles.[66] This chiastic structure was resolved later

---

[64] Ibid., 120–21.

[65] Note: All sermon quotes in Table 2 of Appendix II, and in the Additional Consideration subsection, are pulled from the copy-typed manuscript, "God and Prayer as Factors in the Struggle," in the body of this work. Cited quotes are emphasized in the body of the manuscript for clarity and reference purposes. Figure 3, reference Ernst Wendland, "Text Analysis and Genre of Jonah (Part 2)," *JETS* 39/3 (September 1996) 376–77. The homiletical application of chiastic structure can "serve to illustrate the importance of certain deliberate alterations to basic generic patterns as a means of augmenting the artistic appeal and rhetorical impact of the discourse. In the hands of the Hebrew composers . . . literary structure was never a straitjacket but was always flexible tool whereby subdued as well as powerful communicative effects could be achieved when the need arose."

[66] Calloway, "Rhetorical," 144.

in the sermon when he reiterated the importance of hope, bringing the focus back to the actuating power (activism) of God's presence with the sermonic denouement,

> May God make us such men and women: and to this work may we, one and all, dedicate ourselves today. Whatever we can do, as individuals, as families, as churches, to lift ourselves, and this race with which we are identified, to higher levels, let us do it, and do it with our might.
>
> "O small beginnings, ye are great and strong, Based on a faithful heart and weariless brain." And these we must have, — "the faithful heart, and the weariless brain," if we are to "build the future fair, and conquer wrong."[67]

This sermonic close, resonating tightly with the exhortative nature of Psalm 27:14, culminates a cyclical framework that encapsulates (inclusio) a thematic journey from hope to despair and back to divine assurance, homiletically echoing the poetic structures of a Hebrew poet.[68]

Within the body of the sermon, Grimké employs a chiastic arrangement of themes such as lament, prayer, divine assurance, and communal solidarity. For instance, he discusses the lament over racial oppression, follows it with the power of prayer, centers his message on God's unwavering justice, revisits the importance of praying for the oppressors, and concludes with a reaffirmation of hope and faith. This A–B–C–B'–A' structure emphasizes the central theme of God's justice (C) and reflects the upward trajectory of Richardson's "spiral." By moving from lament (A) to prayer (B), then to divine assurance (C), and back to prayer (B') and renewed hope and activism (A'), Grimké punctuates the transformative process of repentance and the deepening

---

[67] See the underlined bold text in the manuscript.

[68] See the linguistic analysis of Psalm 27 in Appendix II, Table 3.

of faith. This chiastic approach highlights the interplay between human struggle and divine intervention, betraying the emancipatory emotionalism of the psalmist and illustrating how each cycle of repentance leads to greater resilience, resolve, and joy.[69]

Conclusion

In summary, Grimké's sermon on Psalm 27:14 exemplifies the homiletical echoes of a Hebrew poet, calling both a nation and his community to repentance and hope in the gospel of Jesus Christ. By highlighting divine presence and assurance, relating the psalm to contemporary struggles, incorporating prayer, encouraging hope and perseverance, and focusing on community and collective experience, Grimké provides a powerful and inspiring message that resonates deeply with his congregation. His sermon offers spiritual guidance and serves as a call to action, urging his listeners to rely on their faith and unity in their fight for justice and equality.

This chapter further demonstrates that Grimké's EEH draws upon Paul's harmonious focus on the spiritual and social dimensions of faith. Just as Paul leveraged his writings to foster individual transformation and communal reconciliation, Grimké undertakes a similar approach, using Psalm 27 to inspire inner renewal and a resilient stand against hierarchical inequalities, particularly within the church. In the same way that Paul, in Acts 16:35–40, refuses a quiet

---

[69] Here, we discern echoes of Trudie Kibbe Reed's research on the transformative and emancipatory power of conversational learning spaces, as seen through the lens of "Paul on the Road to Damascus: A Significant Emotional Experience." Just as Paul's encounter led to a radical transformation of identity and mission, all preaching, being inherently conversational, holds the potential for such transformative moments. When responsibly conducted, this discourse ultimately leads to the emancipatory witness of the gospel, expressed through lives that are redeemed and reconciled with one another. See Trudie Kibbe Reed, *The Caring Community: A Journey into the Spiritual Domain of Transformative Leadership*, ed. Claudette McFadden (Bloomington, IN: iUniverse, 2010), 47–51.

dismissal after unjust treatment, demanding instead a public acknowledgment of his rights as a citizen, Grimké insists on the full recognition of African American citizenship within the church and society.[70] This alignment with Pauline priorities in Grimké's homiletic further illustrates how Grimké's EEH channels Hebrew poetic traditions and captures the socially charged nature of Paul's gospel praxis. See the manuscript in Appendix III.

[70] Note: Strikingly, Paul makes a request to be escorted out of the city in Acts 16:35-40, where he and Silas, despite being Roman citizens, were unjustly beaten and imprisoned without a trial in Philippi. When the magistrates order their release, Paul refuses to leave quietly, insisting that the officials escort them out, publicly acknowledging their wrongful treatment. Paul says to the officers, "They beat us publicly without a trial, even though we are Roman citizens, and threw us into prison. And now do they want to get rid of us quietly? No! Let them come themselves and escort us out" (Acts 16:37 NIV). This public escort was a powerful statement, vindicating their rights and affirming their dignity as Roman citizens.

CHAPTER 6

THE ECHO CONTINUED: TOWARD AN EVANGELICAL EMANCIPATORY HOMILETIC

This chapter marks a turning point in the journey of this study: from analysis to synthesis. Here, we begin constructing a homiletic-specific framework for understanding *echoes*—as previously defined—as a theological and rhetorical device in gospel preaching. This concept of echo, rooted in scripture and shaped by context, provides a pathway toward a biblically grounded and culturally responsive theology of proclamation.

Through the lens of Francis James Grimké's Evangelical Emancipatory Homiletic (EEH), we explore how gospel preaching functions not only as a declaration of doctrinal truth but also as a catalytic response to social injustice. Echoes, in this tradition, do more than recall biblical language—they extend the ethical and prophetic implications of the gospel into lived reality. Drawing from Grimké's journals, particularly those curated by Carter G. Woodson in 1942, we construct a vision of preaching that fuses evangelical orthodoxy with Spirit-led public witness.

The central aim of this chapter is to offer a fresh theological perspective on evangelical activism, framed through Bebbington's Quadrilateral—*biblicism*, *crucicentrism*, *conversionism*, and *activism*. It is the fourth dimension, activism, that becomes most visible in Grimké's homiletic—not as political posturing or isolated protest, but as a sustained, pneumatologically empowered expression of faith in action. For Grimké, true gospel proclamation issues not just in assent, but in embodiment—an enduring "amen" lived out in public life.

This homiletic posture parallels the *call-and-response* tradition found in African American preaching. Yet for Grimké, the "response" extended beyond the sanctuary. It shaped how believers engaged injustice, advocated for dignity, and bore witness to the redemptive work of Christ in society. This chapter thus moves us toward a constructive vision of Evangelical Emancipatory Homiletics—a gospel preaching tradition that refuses to separate spiritual transformation from social responsibility.[1]

Overview

> *For, "Everyone who calls on the name of the Lord shall be saved." But how are they to call on one in whom they have not believed? And how are they to believe in one of whom they have never heard? And how are they to hear without someone to proclaim him? And how are they to proclaim him unless they are sent? As it is written, "How beautiful are the feet of those who bring good news!"*[2]

---

[1] Reed, *Caring Community*, 68. Reed, the highly regarded former president of Bethune–Cookman University, writes, "In spite of America's racial divide, [Mary McLeod] Bethune spoke the language of [incarnational] identification. She connected with others because, first and foremost, she saw all people as members of the human family. . . . When she spoke, she touched hearts and opened doors of hope because hers was the language of the [emancipating] bridge builder." See also Green, *Dialectic*, 3. Green writes, "Celebrations of the Constitution and the Bill of Rights continue, but day after day their complex affirmations dwindle into slogans. . . . Young and old alike find it hard to shape authentic expressions of hopes and ideals. Lacking embeddedness in memories and histories they have made their own, people feel as if they are rootless subjectivities. . . . And yet, those of us committed to education are committed not only to effecting continuities but to preparing the ground for what is to come." Appending the latter, this body of work asserts that the artful and committed presentation of the gospel (homiletics) is a heart and head transformational emancipatory instrument empowering its hearers to activism over and against the world's hostilities.

[2] Cf. Joel 2:32 NRSV; Isaiah 52:7 NRSV. Paul echoes the Hebrew prophets in verses thirteen and fifteen, respectively, "Then everyone who calls on the name of the Lord shall be saved; for in Mount Zion and in Jerusalem there shall be those who escape, as the Lord has said, and among the survivors shall be those whom the Lord calls." "How beautiful upon the mountains are the feet of the messenger who announces peace, who brings good news, who announces salvation, who says to Zion, 'Your God reigns.'"

Romans 10:13–15 NRSV

The apostle [Paul] tells us, "The world by wisdom knew not God,'" and, therefore, any attempt to win men to Christ by appealing to their intellects, is a fool's project. Men are not won in that way. The old way, and the Bible way, of winning men is by the simple presentation of the truth of God, in dependence upon the Holy Spirit to make the truth effectual . . .

Francis James Grimké[3]

There is no shortage of literature on the "what is" and "how to" of preaching. However, a comprehensive theology of preaching must be contextualized: "Into what" and "to whom" are we preaching? And "to what end?" This treatise asserts that a substantial preaching praxis requires a comprehensive *theology of context* [my emphasis] without compromising content. Furthermore, we argue that the EEH predicates a contextually engaged sensitivity to the hearer's ear and heart. Preaching must be relatable. Even more, gospel preaching is not simply an announcement but an invitation or proposal to engage and act. Much like the marriage proposal, it requires a response—and that response renders an activism between the participants and beyond. Moreover, the term "homiletics," derived from the Greek ὁμιλητικός (homiletikos) and rooted in ὁμιλέω (homileo), meaning "to associate with" or "to converse," underscores the relational and dialogical dimensions inherent in gospel preaching. This dialogical nature reflects its early Christian usage, as seen in Paul's missionary interactions and exhortations to the churches, where the proclaimed word was not merely a declaration but an invitation to engage and respond.[4] This

---

[3] Grimké, *Meditations*, 20.

[4] Cf. Acts 17:2–4; 1 Corinthians 9:22–23 for examples of relational and dialogical preaching. See Henry George Liddell and Robert Scott, *A Greek-English Lexicon*, 9th ed., rev. by Henry Stuart Jones and Roderick McKenzie (Oxford: Clarendon Press, 1996), 1229; and Karl Barth, *Homiletics*, trans.

phenomenon aligns with Cribb's description in Chapter 5, where he compares the Hebrew poets' purpose to his own aim of provoking a response—an affective 'amen' that inspires reflection and action.

Objective

Our objective is rooted in three rudimentary claims distilled from Grimké's homiletic: 1. We preach because the gospel must be heard. 2. We preach with conviction and hope that the gospel message heard might be gladly received. 3. We preach knowing the gospel message demands a response—acceptance or rejection, action or inaction.

This chapter seeks to articulate a homiletic framework that emphasizes the reciprocal dynamic of proclamation and response, illustrating how gospel preaching inherently echoes through both the preacher and the hearer.

Moreover, the act of preaching and responding is a necessary dynamic of gospel preaching characterized in this exercise as echoing for two chief reasons: 1. because the preacher carries and repeats (echoes) a message not his or her own; 2. because its proclaimer and recipients, through the redemptive and emancipatory interactions of the gospel, respond with (or echo) an amen—in assent and act.[5]

Defining "Echoes" in Preaching

As observed in previous chapters, careful examination of NT writings reveals a pronounced presence of OT scriptural references. These episodes of intertextual engagement are literary operatives, generally, but not always technically, referred to as echoes.[6] The

---

Geoffrey W. Bromiley and Donald E. Daniels (Louisville: Westminster John Knox Press, 1991), 24.

[5] See Diagram at the end of the chapter.

[6] Hays, *Gospels*, 2–10. A detailed treatment of the criticism and various voices that characterize literary echoes is beyond the purview of a preaching treatise. Because the objective of this exercise is to establish biblical precedence for scripturally based proclamation (we argue that the earliest preachers of the

execution of these echoes extends beyond repeating or reciting (mimicking) the Hebrew Bible or simply reinterpreting the ancient text; more principally, it suggests an underlying ethos of how the earliest preachers of the gospel of Jesus Christ understood, lived, and proclaimed their faith.[7]

Understanding these patterned and patented scriptural echoes, as modeled by Jesus, the Apostle Paul, and others within the NT writ, is foundational in developing a homiletic or preaching theology that is biblical and contextually relevant. Borrowing from Alcántara, we ultimately assert that all constructive gospel preaching relevant to the day's issues requires a scriptural foundation.[8] Or, as Grimké argued, "Our duty is to preach what the Bible teaches, its ideals, principles, great truths concerning God and man, sin, and righteousness, never mind what others may think or say."[9]

To summarize, echoes are principled patterns deeply embedded and embodied within the ethos and theology of the Christian church tradition—gospel preaching by default illustrates this. In short, all gospel preaching is an echo.

Echoes: An Activist Pneumatological Phenomena

Since the inception of the beloved community we call the church, a resilient record of dialogue and communal discourse has shaped her identity. In the 1931 polemic, *Jesus Came Preaching*, George Buttrick identified the heartbeat of this community conversation as preaching.[10]

---

gospel of Jesus Christ ordinarily and reflexively used OT scripture to support their claims), the term echo in this body operates as an umbrella term to capture what Hays "approximates" as "scriptural citations, allusions, and echoes." For clues to further investigation, see Porter, "Use of the Old Testament," 79–96, and Porter, "Further Comments," 98–110.

[7] Hays, *Gospels*, 1–3. Note Hays's commentary on Luther's "figural reading" of the gospels.

[8] Alcántara, *Preaching*, 81.

[9] Grimké, *Meditations*, 110.

[10] George A. Buttrick, *Jesus Came Preaching* (New York: Scribner, 1931).

Reflecting upon Buttrick's work and building upon the example of Christ and His Great Commission, one cannot help but contemplate the leading role of proclamation in the church's life. But how does this act engage the community? How is the community invited to engage in the act? What is the expected community response to the act or conversation we call preaching? And who is the activator of these interactions?

We offer three final working definitions before extending a summary treatment. The term discernment (used in a practical sense in the following sections) refers to the Spirit-enabled ability to identify, analyze, and engage the personhood of a community of listeners.[11] Second, the word audience does not strictly follow a technical definition; it generally refers to any community gathered or positioned to hear the preached gospel at a specific moment. The expression activism relates to what is typically deemed call-and-response in certain faith traditions, though implicitly operated through a pneumatological lens to extend beyond the immediate preached moment in this analysis.[12,13]

The Gospel Echo Heard: Contextuality in Discerning the Hearers' Ear

> *I have become all things to all people, that I might by all means save some. I do it all for the sake of the gospel, so that I may share in its blessings.*
>
> 1 Corinthians 9:23 NRSV

---

[11] James Forbes, *The Holy Spirit & Preaching* (Nashville: Abingdon Press, 1989), 81. Forbes comments, "The Spirit . . . acts as a kind of cosigner of our 'epistles of encouragement,' by helping us to reach the hearts and minds of the people."

[12] John Neuhaus, *Freedom for Ministry* (Grand Rapids, MI: Eerdmans, 1979), 175.

[13] C. F. Stewart, *Soul Survivors: An African American Spirituality* (Louisville, TN: Westminster John Knox Press, 1997), 65.

Whether popular or not, it is our duty to declare the whole counsel of God. Only thus will our skirts be clean and our title to be called ambassadors of God be fully vindicated. No cowardly minister who is afraid to declare the whole word of God lest he give offense, or interfere with his popularity, has any right in any Christian pulpit.

Francis James Grimké[14]

Preaching Must Be Culturally Aware. Walter Lippman, the Pulitzer Prize-winning twentieth-century American journalist and political commentator, quipped, "The music is nothing if the audience is deaf."[15] Lippman's repartee is a fitting reflection as we consider that throughout the church's history, preaching has occurred invariably within the complexities of culture. As such, cultural sensitivity is an inextricable aspect of the preaching exercise. Without such sensitivities, one cannot consistently preach the gospel message with efficacy. LaRue avers, "The . . . sermon at its best arises out of the totality of the people's existence."[16] Hence, praying for discernment of the cultural distinctives of a gathered community is of the highest order.

Alcántara notes that the preached gospel, though universal in its implications, historically "incarnates itself as a localized word in the language and culture of time and space."[17] If preaching is, in fact, incarnational, then incarnational preaching, by definition, facilitates contextual engagement. In other words, the preached word must engage in a way that is contextually accessible. This incarnational dynamic is powerfully echoed in the Johannine proclamation that "the Word became flesh and lived among us," reminding us that gospel

[14] Grimké, *Works III*, 580–81.

[15] Walter Lippmann, *A Preface to Morals* (New York: Routledge, 2017), 324, originally published 1929.

[16] LaRue, *Heart*, 19.

[17] Alcántara, *Preaching*, 89–90.

proclamation must also dwell meaningfully within the cultural realities of its audience.[18]

Preaching Must Be Personally Relatable. Rebecca West, the famed British author and literary critic, is noted to have said, "Any authentic work of art must start an argument between the artist and his audience." [19] Her literary prowess provides insight into the interpersonal aspects of preaching. Like the writer, the preacher's words must elicit engagement. The distinction, however, for the preacher is the extended nature of the dialogue over time in real-time. Or, put another way, the conversation's echoic quality. One must not underestimate this quality, as it pointedly positions the preached word as a dynamic interpersonal and intrapersonal dialectic tradition. To punctuate the point, it fosters intimate conversation between the pulpit and the pew over time, resulting in more than a scant aggregation of listeners but personally and corporately engaged participants whose hearts and lives are transformed, emancipated, and mobilized to action.[20]

Preaching Must Be Communally Engaged. In a general sense, we have covered aspects of communal engagement in the last two points. However, there is a contextual distinctiveness that we have not yet visited. For clarity, we will refer to this distinctive as *contextual corporate tendencies* [my emphasis]. Larue observed that every community throughout history has a collective narrative that informs how it hears and engages the gospel message. He argued that engagement, informed by the various "categories of life experiences,"

---

[18] Cf. John 1:14 NRSV. The author contends that the gospel writers' incarnational language here is more cultural than personal, echoing the OT Tabernacle Narrative. See John C. Meagher, "John 1:14 and the New Temple," *Journal of Biblical Literature* 88, no. 1 (1969): 57–68, https://doi.org/10.2307/3262833; Gary A. Anderson, *That I May Dwell Among Them* (Grand Rapids, MI: Eerdmans, 2023), preface.

[19] Rebecca West, *The Court and the Castle: Some Treatments of a Recurrent Theme* (New Haven, CT: Yale University Press, 1957), 5.

[20] Forbes, *Holy Spirit*, 20.

attunes the ear to a unique corporate hermeneutic known as a "communal interpretive strategy."[21] Note that LaRue's observation is not isolated. In many ways, it is an OT echo, as we see what Cribb similarly describes as providential structural "strategies" in the writings of the Hebrew poets.[22]

The tendency of communities to embrace an interpretive strategy or lens through which they receive messages presents contextual opportunities and challenges. The opportunities mainly reside in the ability to engage in dialogue with a significant aggregation of listeners through the employment of a singular message or method. Conversely, the danger is a presumed or assumed monolith. Careful consideration of these factors must always remain at the forefront of the preacher's thinking because faithfully and consistently discerning the communal ear is inconceivable without the guidance of the Holy Spirit and a life of prayer.

Nevertheless, with these dynamics in tension, understanding the contextual corporate tendencies of a particular community by the leading of the Holy Spirit is a keen instrument in discerning the ear and, subsequently, the heart of the listening audience. Grimké said it this wise, "When the Holy Spirit is upon you, the truth grips you in a way that it doesn't at other times, and the truth as uttered by you at such times, grips others in a way different from the ordinary preaching of the word."[23]

The Gospel Echo Received: Discerning and Engaging the Hearers' Heart

> *These Jews were more receptive than those in Thessalonica, for they welcomed the message very eagerly and examined the scriptures every day to see whether these things were so.*
>
> Acts 17:11 NRSV

---

[21] LaRue, *Heart*, 34–39.

[22] Cribb and Crisler, *Bible Toolbox*, 252.

[23] Grimké. *Meditations*, 2–3.

> *We need educated ministers, yes; we need men who know what is going on in the world about them, yes; but the great need is for men who believe firmly in the Scriptures as the word of God, and who faithfully preach the truth therein contained, in dependence upon the Holy Spirit to give efficacy to the truth, and not upon their training, their education, their ability to construct arguments in defence [sic] of the truth.*
>
> Francis James Grimké[24]

The Engaged Preacher. Conventional wisdom affirms that healthy conversations are foundational to building strong relationships. But what constitutes a truly "healthy conversation" in the context of preaching?[25] Peter Sanlon, in his article *Depth and Weight: Augustine's Sermon Illustrations,* highlights Augustine's use of vivid illustrations to draw listeners into meaningful dialogue with the scriptural depth of his sermons. Sanlon's insight underscores a vital principle: the preacher must labor to bring the "weight of man's heart" into communion with the "depth of scripture."[26] When this happens, a transformative and emancipatory dialogue unfolds, producing a harvest of surrendered hearts and minds.

Augustine's approach offers an additional lesson: his commitment to understanding his audience. By exegeting both scripture and the lived realities of his hearers, Augustine exemplified a pastoral heart attuned to the "weight" of their burdens. Similarly, Broadus, centuries later, emphasized the preacher's responsibility to address the "restless hearers of the present day." [27] Such sensitivity requires spiritual

---

[24] Grimké, *Works III,* 191.

[25] See the commentary in the body of this chapter associated with footnote 4 for context regarding the dialogical, or "conversational," nature of preaching.

[26] Sanlon, "Depth," 61–76.

[27] John A. Broadus, *On the Preparation and Delivery of Sermons* (Auckland: Titus Books, 2014), Kindle edition, Location 3672.

discernment, prayerful dependence on the Holy Spirit, and diligent preparation.

The Engaged Hearer. Preaching, when lived out well, is more than a monologue—it initiates a dialogue that becomes a doorway to the heart. This sacred conversation, empowered by the Holy Spirit, enables the preacher to connect deeply with the hearer and inspire commitment and action. As communication expert Eric W. Rothenbuhler notes, "Communication . . . [is] essential for the growth and maintenance of attachments to and involvement in the community."[28]

When hearers are drawn into this sacred dialogue, preaching transforms into a communal act, uniting pulpit and pew in a shared purpose. Greg Heisler describes this dynamic as the illuminating work of the Holy Spirit, which activates and compels hearers toward an active, tangible response.[29] Once engaged, the hearer's participation reflexively demands not only assent but also action. Over time, this echoed response not only forms the enduring foundation of the church's life and mission but also reflects the rock upon which Christ declared His church would stand.[30]

The Gospel Echo Response: Let the Church Say Amen

> *For all the promises of God find their Yes in him. That is why it is through him that we utter our Amen to God for his glory.*
>
> 2 Corinthians 1:20 ESV

> *A great deal of discussion is going on . . . about Christianity, what it is, what it requires . . . but what is most important . . . is living it. However much we may be talking and writing about it, if we are not*

[28] Eric W. Rothenbuhler et al., "Communication, Community Attachment, and Involvement," *J&MC Quarterly* 73, no. 2 (Summer 1996): 446.
[29] Greg Heisler, *Spirit-Led Preaching: The Holy Spirit's Role in Sermon Preparation and Delivery* (Nashville: B&H Academic, 2007), 41–57.
[30] Cf. Matthew 16:15–18.

> *living it, it will have but little influence. Words are cheap . . . a Christianity that is lived, in its simplicity and power, is what is most sorely needed everywhere.*
>
> Francis James Grimké[31]

The Means. What shall we say of the gospel's means? Aquinas argued that the "new law" or gospel of reconciliation requires the "faithful to be *instructed* (emphasis added) . . . both by word and writing . . . as to what they should believe and as to what they should do."[32] As in any human dynamic, a course of instruction requires dialogue. Admittedly, the dialogue can be highly contextual, but it must nevertheless be present because the inspired activism of dialogue necessarily characterizes the outcome or end of the preached word. In short, preaching demands an articulation and, in turn, a response in word, heart, and act.

Another note of emphasis, holding to Aquinas's instructor/instruction illustration, is the urgency of preaching never being sought for the sake of mere feedback. When a teacher instructs their student, the student's feedback is not the end. It serves more as a needful milepost toward the end. In like manner, the community and preacher's activism definitively navigates the journey toward the end, which is not the goal itself but the necessary means.

Safeguarding the Means. Grimké, betraying his evangelical and activist bent, writes:

> [We must] get hold of [this] great idea or truth and have it vitalized in our lives, that is, to so come under its influence as to be controlled by it, is of the greatest importance. Take the great truth which underlies the Gospel,—the truth as to the atoning

---

[31] Grimké, *Works* III, 103–104.

[32] Thomas Aquinas, *Summa Theologica, Pars Prima Secundae,* eBook #17897 (Salt Lake City: Project Gutenberg Literary Archive Foundation, 2006), qn 106.

> sacrifice of Jesus Christ. The Bible teaches us that by his suffering and death, an atonement was made for the sin of the world, for your sin and mine, for all the sinful race of Adam. It is a stupendous fact, this dying of Jesus Christ for the sins of the world; and ought to have certain definite effects upon us.[33]

In this brief reflection, detailing the heart of Grimké's EEH, we discern the four core principles of gospel preaching: a reliance on the authority of scripture (biblicism), the work of Christ and the cross (crucicentrism), the regenerative work of grace (conversionism), and an outward working of the indicatives of the gospel (activism).[34] The gospel proclaimed requires these priorities—if it is to echo the preaching of the apostle Paul, the fathers of the church, and the many traditioned exemplars of gospel preaching. Outside these priorities, gospel preaching is for naught.

The End. The gospel, by its very nature, has an end. To what end is the gospel preached? In his letter to the Roman church, Paul asserted that the gospel is "the power of God for salvation to everyone who has faith." [35] Therefore, the gospel's end is humanity's salvation and communal reconciliation with the God of all creation and one another. With this in view, responsible preaching of the gospel is never gratuitous. It is a matter of life and death.

Moreover, the gospel's central character is the life, death, resurrection, and imminent return of Jesus Christ. Contextuality, method, and means must never displace the Christ-centered focus of the preaching exercise. To do so is to lose its end. Note the following deliberation of Bryan Chapell: "balanced preaching inevitably points

---

[33] Grimké, *Works III*, 55.

[34] Bebbington, *Evangelicalism*, 2–4. See Diagrams 1 and 2 in the Schedule of Diagrams.

[35] Romans 1:16 NRSV.

both preacher and parishioner to the work of Christ as the only proper center of a sermon."[36] Grimké further asserts:

> The function of the pulpit is not to entertain, to amuse, to satisfy an idle curiosity: it is to instruct, to inspire, to fire the heart and mind, to implant within us noble desires and ambitions, and, above all, to keep ever before men the one supreme figure in history, the Lord Jesus Christ, and to beget within them a passion for him, and for a Christly life.[37]

Herein belies the heart of the beautiful grace of preaching in the body of Christ.

The Ultimate Amen. If the gospel is transformative, it must affect its agents. What is the evidence of the gospel's effect? At the 2014 Clamp Preaching Lectures, Robert Smith offered that the impact of gospel preaching is apparent when its hearer "attains, adapts, and models its doctrinal truths through the power of the Holy Spirit."[38] Smith's approach is helpful as it frames a construct for describing the ultimate amen of gospel preaching. His sensitivity also points to a final observation concerning the homiletical exercise and our subsequent concern of activism: preaching is pastoral. This point is notable because, historically, the emphasis often falls on the prophetic and instructional dimensions of preaching but not necessarily the pastoral. In his seminal text on pastoral leadership, Michael Quick writes, "Jesus did not spend his three years' ministry writing a leadership manual but initiating

---

[36] Bryan Chapell, *Christ-Centered Preaching: Redeeming the Expository Sermon*, 2nd ed. (Grand Rapids, MI: Baker Academic, 2005), 34.

[37] Grimké, *Meditations*, v–vi.

[38] Robert Smith, Jr., "Clamp Preaching Lectures 2014, Part 1," Clamp Divinity School, accessed October 10, 2022, https://youtube.com/playlist?list=PLWAWCkW7P-ezi6bui45FJE7uMRY0BeXmW.

disciples into full-blooded Kingdom living."[39] In other words, Jesus' witness was not simply instructional with the hopes of activism but pastoral with a mandate to act. We observe a similar ethos in the Pauline letters.[40] Grimké echoes this pastoral sensitivity, as well, emphasizing that the power and worth of gospel preaching lie not in its rhetorical finesse but in its reliance on the Holy Spirit to transform lives:

> The preaching of the apostles consisted very largely of the simple story of Jesus and his love, culminating in his death upon the cross, his resurrection and ascension, calling attention particularly to the purpose for which he came, and the meaning of his suffering and death, and depending for the effect of their words not upon anything in themselves but upon the presence and power of the Holy Spirit. . . . A discourse, however learned, eloquent, or rhetorically correct in construction is valuable only so far as it is used by the Holy Spirit, and the measure of its worth will depend upon how far it actually helps in bringing men to Christ or in building them up in faith and holiness, in Christian character.[41]

In summary, Gospel preaching requires the gentle yet courageous work of the pastor's heart, longing to engage the parishioner innovatively and tangibly in the most incredible conversation in the history of humanity.[42] It is, without reservation, a high call to a

---

[39] Michael J. Quicke, *360-Degree Leadership* (Grand Rapids, MI: Baker Books, 2006), 64.

[40] Hays, *Letters*, x. Hays observes, "Paul's letters are the earliest writings in the New Testament. Although this fact is somewhat obscured by the conventional arrangement of the New Testament canon, these letters were all sent as pastoral communications to particular churches long before the earliest of the canonical Gospels had been composed."

[41] Grimké, *Meditations*, 5.

[42] Scott Cormode, "Innovation that Honors Tradition: The Meaning of Christian Innovation," *Journal of Religious Leadership* 14, no. 2 (Fall 2015):

remarkable assignment to proclaim the King and his Kingdom contextually and pastorally.

Conclusion: Theology of an Evangelical Emancipatory Homiletic

In the seventy-eighth Psalm, the psalmist observes that David shepherded the children of Israel with an "upright heart" and "skillful hand."[43] One does not typically think of David as a pastor or preacher. However, scriptures intimate a pastoral or priestly dimension to his leadership worthy of emulation. David (foreshadowing the iterative pastoral and homiletical ethos of Paul and generations of preachers to follow) ostensibly understood his audience and consistently did the careful and pastoral work of engaging an entire nation to effect change. Today's preachers must be of the same heart. We must skillfully steward and shepherd the preaching of the gospel. When done with an upright heart and skillful hand, preaching provokes parishioners to the ultimate amen: lives transformed to show forth the glory of God actively.[44]

In conclusion, gospel preaching is an emancipatory activist phenomenon, with respect to message and messenger, for two reasons: 1. the message, though offensive and subversive to a world divided in hostilities, is paradoxically emancipatory;[45] Grimké writes, reflecting on his own fallen nature, "The record, such as it is, imperfect as it is, must stand. To be entrusted with the gospel of the grace of God for a lost world, is not only a great honor, but carries with it also the greatest responsibility."[46] 2. its bearers communicate the message with authority exampled through their activist and Spirit-led embodiment of the

---

99–102. Note: Cormode's outline of the parameters for Christian innovation is helpful in defining creativity in evangelical homiletics.

[43] Psalm 78:72 NRSV.

[44] Cf. Romans 15:6; 2 Corinthians 1:20; Philippians 1:11; Ephesians 1:12.

[45] Cf. 2 Corinthians 2:15–16; Galatians 5:1; 1 Corinthians 1:18; Romans 1:16.

[46] Grimké, *Works III*, 589.

emancipatory power of the gospel.[47] Grimké asserts, "It is a great thing, in preaching, to have a message and to be able to give it in demonstration of the Spirit and of power. It is the only way the gospel message should ever be given, and it is the only way to give it effectively."[48]

Simply stated, the preacher is a vessel and an object of the good news. In a sense, the preacher, in personhood, is an echoing echo. Herein lies the essence of gospel preaching. And in the words of William H. Pipes, the African American historian of "old-time negro preaching," Let the church "Say Amen!"[49]

---

[47] Cf. 1 Corinthians 2:4–5; 2 Corinthians 3:6; Ephesian 6:19–20; Romans 15:18–19.

[48] Grimké, *Works III*, 598.

[49] William H. Pipes, *Say Amen, Brother! Old-Time Negro Preaching: A Study in African American Frustration* (Detroit: Wayne State University Press, 1951), xvii.

CHAPTER 7

PREACHING THAT TRANSFORMS: KEY INSIGHTS AND THE WAY FORWARD

This work has explored how Grimké's interpretation and embodiment of the Pauline tradition serve as a model for evangelical preachers addressing ethnic prejudice. This study proposes that Grimké's ministry, beyond merely echoing gospel principles, uniquely adapted and embodied the redemptive work of Christ, and addressed with scriptural integrity the divisive issue of ethnic prejudice in a post-Civil War America. The findings highlight the core components that position Grimké's EEH as a model of socially engaged evangelicalism.

Furthermore, the research shows that Grimké's unique life experiences—his journey from enslavement to theological training—shaped his approach to gospel preaching. Informed by his grounding in evangelical doctrine and the social intimations of Paul's gospel, Grimké's homiletical approach evolved into a socially conscious gospel preaching model characterized by the following principles:

1. **Integration of Spiritual Salvation and Social Reconciliation**: For Grimké, the gospel was indivisible from Christ's redemptive work on a personal and societal level. He saw social reconciliation and personal salvation, particularly among believers, as twin imperatives, confronting inimical forces such as sin, death, and prejudice that undermine both personal and communal flourishing.
2. **Proclamation of Righteousness and Justice as Gospel Indicatives**: Grimké's sermons emphasized just relationships within the Christian community, framing the gospel's call for reconciliation as a model of unity and communal restoration. His homiletic advocated for the active pursuit of justice, inspired by a reformed

view of the cross's significance for personal salvation and societal impact.

Key Reflections

Grimké's life and ministry underscore how his EEH harmonizes personal faith with social engagement. The following findings outline the essential components of his distinctive, Pauline-resonant homiletic.

Gospel Preaching as Holistic Transformation

Grimké's homiletic, grounded in evangelical priorities, provides a model of gospel preaching that emphasizes personal and societal transformation. This dual-focus approach reinforces the gospel's power to reach every dimension of life—spiritual and communal.

1. **Evangelical Commitment**: Rooted in the principles of biblicism, crucicentrism, conversionism, and activism, Grimké upheld an evangelical preaching model that affirmed scripture as the ultimate authority. His discourse consistently pointed to the centrality of Christ's crucifixion and resurrection, emphasizing conversion and the transformative journey that should follow a confession of faith. Through this model, Grimké upheld the gospel as a foundation of personal faith and a call to engage actively in societal healing and justice, positioning activism as an organic gospel indicative.

2. **Whole-Person Transformation**: Grimké's preaching urged a holistic, "whole-person" response to the gospel. His sermons emphasized *Christoformity*—a life molded after Christ's character—whereby personal transformation becomes visibly manifest in actions that uphold justice and mercy. His call for a full surrender to the gospel's effects reflected his belief that true gospel acceptance should overflow into character and conduct that confronts social wrongs as an aspect of righteous

living. For Grimké, the gospel's work was incomplete if it failed to incite inward transformation and outward reconciliation.

Conversionism and Activism as Gospel Indicatives

Grimké's conception of gospel-embodied activism emerges from his conviction that social action and personal transformation are inseparable aspects of the Christian faith. These indicatives of the gospel—*conversionism* and *activism*—are communicated through the word of God (*Biblicism*) and demonstrated through the atonement of Christ (*Crucicentrism*), grounding both in the theological foundation of the gospel. *Biblicism* emphasizes that the revealed word informs the gospel's call, while *Crucicentrism* underscores the redemptive power of the cross. Together, these *predicates* make *conversionism* and *activism* both possible and imperative to a life encountered and emancipated through the gospel.[1]

1. **Gospel-inspired Conversionism and Activism**: Grimké regarded conversionism and activism as direct outcomes of gospel engagement. Conversionism reflects the transformation of the heart through faith in Christ, leading to personal salvation, while activism embodies the practical outworking of that transformation in confronting systemic sin and societal injustice. This form of "practical piety" reflects Paul's message of reconciliation in Christ and underscores that activism is not optional but intrinsic to the gospel's call to confront sin in all its forms, including prejudice and systemic oppression. Just as Paul's letters championed social harmony among believers, Grimké's ministry sought a wider reconciliation, addressing ethnic hostilities and inequalities as fundamental gospel indicatives.

---

[1] See Diagram 2 in the Schedule of Diagrams for a visual representation of the relationship between gospel predicates and indicatives.

2. **Public Engagement**: Grimké emphasized that Christian principles demand active involvement in the public square, particularly in addressing urgent issues such as racial violence and discrimination. He viewed true Christianity as Spirit-led contextual awareness and identification with the suffering of others, bearing witness to human dignity and equality. Grounded in *Biblicism* and *Crucicentrism*, Grimké's approach to public engagement modeled a bold, faithful response to the gospel's call for justice and communal well-being. This construct demonstrates that gospel indicatives are deeply rooted in the predicates of the gospel—*Biblicism* and *Crucicentrism*—extending their redemptive power into personal and social dimensions.

The Preacher as a Conduit of Personal and Social Change

Grimké's conception of the preacher as a transformative agent reflected a synthesis of personal integrity and social responsibility, positioning the preacher as both a messenger of divine truth and a model of gospel-embodied activism.

1. **Role as God's Messenger**: Grimké's understanding of his role as preacher was deeply Pauline, grounded in his belief that a preacher's authority stems from their role as an echo of God's message. For Grimké, preaching involved a solemn responsibility to deliver the unaltered "whole counsel of God," as he described it, which included calling out social injustices within the community of believers. His alignment with Pauline authority meant his sermons emphasized the transformative and emancipatory power of Scripture, positioning the preacher as one who not only proclaims but embodies divine truth in both personal integrity and public witness.

2. **Personal Integrity and Social Responsibility**: Grimké maintained that effective preaching required the preacher's own life to mirror the gospel's transformative call. He viewed moral integrity as essential for proclaiming a message of justice and reconciliation. This meant that the preacher's own life and conduct needed to embody the values of Christ's teachings, making the preacher's personal walk an integral part of their public ministry. In Grimké's framework, social responsibility was not merely an adjunct to the preacher's role but a core component, as he believed that a true evangelical message called believers to seek justice, confront prejudice, and act as agents of reconciliation both within and outside the church.

Teasing Out the Distinctions

The unique contours of Grimké's EEH and the influence of his personal biography reveal nuanced distinctions that shape his approach to gospel-embodied activism. These distinctions highlight the foundational elements that formed Grimké's homiletical praxis—his redemption through Christ, his Reformed education, and his deep fluency in scripture—while considering how these elements interacted with his lived experiences to frame his EEH. Additionally, comparing Grimké's context to Paul's brings further clarity to Grimké's homiletic and missional outlook.

1. **Foundation of Redemption through Christ vs. Socio-Cultural Framework**
   Grimké's redemption through Jesus Christ, rather than his personal experiences, formed the core of his EEH. His biography, while essential in framing his ministry, was not its source. Grimké saw himself first and foremost as a redeemed follower of Christ, and this redemptive identity fueled his commitment to social justice within a gospel-embodied framework. His writings reflect this, as he notes that true

activism flows from a life changed by Christ, rather than from social or political motivations. This documented distinction affirms that his work in racial and social justice was inseparably sourced from his embodiment of the gospel.

2. **Reformed Education as a Theological Foundation vs. Social Experience**
   Grimké's education and theological convictions shaped his understanding of doctrine, particularly regarding grace, sin, and redemption, in a way that transcended personal background. His Reformed training provided a theological framework through which he viewed the gospel's power over both personal sin and systemic injustices. Rather than allowing social experiences to be the primary interpreter of scripture, Grimké's theological training guided his reading of the Bible and informed his social actions. This distinction emphasizes that Grimké's response to social injustice was rooted in a conviction that the gospel itself addresses individual and corporate sin, aligning his homiletic with a biblically grounded perspective that was contextually framed by his biography.

3. **Fluency in Scripture vs. Personal Cultural Identity**
   Grimké's fluency in scripture, especially the Pauline epistles, shaped the substance of his sermons and social critiques. His reflexive reliance on scripture empowered him to echo Pauline themes in his preaching, as he brought the gospel's redemptive message to bear on issues of racial inequality and societal sin. While Grimké's cultural identity undoubtedly shaped the urgency and specificity of his message, it was his understanding of the biblical text that formed its essence. Thus, his EEH categorically relied on the bible's authority and its transformative and emancipatory power, underscoring that

the gospel itself, rather than cultural identity, was the ultimate foundation for his advocacy and ministry.

4. **Cultural Context of Grimké's Preaching vs. Paul's Context** Grimké's audience operated within a predominantly Protestant, self-identified Christian nation, while Paul ministered in a largely pagan, non-Christian world. This contextual difference shaped their respective homiletical priorities. Grimké focused on reformation within a religiously aligned culture, addressing a Christian society that professed belief yet failed to authentically embody the gospel. In contrast, Paul's mission involved introducing the gospel to an uninitiated audience, laying a foundational understanding of faith. More pointedly, Grimké's preaching demanded action from a society entrenched in hypocrisy, challenging the church to confront its failures and live out the gospel's indicatives more fully. By comparison, Paul's task was to proclaim the gospel where it was previously unknown, fostering initial belief and community formation. This juxtaposition underscores the distinct challenges each faced: Paul sought to establish the gospel's presence, while Grimké sought to hold a professing Christian society accountable to its claims.

By contrasting these distinctions, this analysis illustrates that Grimké's homiletic was built on a theological foundation grounded in redemption, Reformed education, and biblical fluency. His personal biography framed his ministry's context and urgency, but it was his commitment to Christ and scripture that formed the perennial core of his message. These distinctions provide a nuanced understanding of Grimké's EEH as biblically rooted and contextually responsive. (Refer to Diagram 3 in the Schedule of Diagrams for further illustration.)

Summary of Research Contributions: Closing the Gap

This research frames an evangelical homiletic that harmonizes biblical theology and social activism. It examines how textual truth intersects with the realities of time and culture, providing a framework for addressing contemporary challenges. Grounded in the preaching and activism of Grimké and his EEH, the study advocates for a gospel-embodied homiletic that confronts personal and corporate sin. The study has identified and addressed four key research gaps:

1. **Theoretical Gap**: The intersection of biblical theology and social activism lacks robust theoretical frameworks in homiletics, particularly within the evangelical tradition, as it pertains to ethnic prejudice. By introducing the "Pauline–Grimkéan" model, this study establishes a grounded framework for understanding how gospel indicatives can inform and sustain a comprehensive praxis of activism. This model highlights Grimké's integration and embodiment of the gospel's ethical indicatives with a commitment to social reform, showing that theological understanding can and should be a catalyst for personal and collective action against systemic sin, including ethnic prejudice.

2. **Practical Knowledge Gap**: This research closes a gap in practical application by providing actionable strategies for gospel-driven responses to societal injustices, including corporate sins such as racial prejudice, especially among fellow believers. Drawing from Grimké's approach, this study illustrates how a homiletic grounded in gospel indicatives addresses societal ills in a manner that resonates with believers and the broader community. By framing activism as an inherent outgrowth of evangelical convictions, this model equips preachers to address complex social issues with theological integrity and practical effectiveness.

3. **Archival Preservation Gap**: To support ongoing research, this treatise preserves and analyzes Grimké's sermons, offering a primary source archive for understanding how evangelical faith can inform social engagement. The study provides seven pivotal sermons in Appendix IV, titled *Prominent Notes of an Evangelical Activist: Three Decades of Preaching*, which will aid future scholarship in exploring how Grimké's sermons addressed issues of prejudice, systemic sin, and social responsibility. Most importantly, this archival contribution supports the historical context of evangelical social activism.

4. **Pedagogical Process Gap**: By examining Grimké's homiletic, this study establishes a model for integrating faith and activism into homiletics education. The model presented emphasizes gospel preaching as a comprehensive, emancipatory tool fully capable of freeing hearts from the oppression of sin, death, Satan, and the fear of God's wrath—confronting societal ills and the inimical forces from which they derive, especially among fellow believers. Inspired by Grimké's commitment to activism, rooted in an authentic heart transformation through Christ's redemptive work, this framework encourages educators to approach ministerial training as a head-and-heart endeavor grounded in a gospel-embodied perspective. It envisions Spirit-led, emancipatory learning spaces that address ethnic and societal injustices, thereby equipping future preachers to confront contemporary issues through the full embodiment of the gospel and its indicatives. To aid in teaching these concepts, a diagram of Grimké's EEH is provided at the end of this chapter, along with a suggested pedagogical process detailed below.

A Taxonomy for Teaching EEH:

a. **Introduce Social Activism as a Gospel Indicative**: Begin by defining "indicative" in the evangelical context, explaining that Grimké's model sees activism not as optional but as a visible sign of a transformed heart. Use scriptural examples to illustrate how true faith leads to actions that confront social hostilities, especially among fellow believers.

b. **Emphasize "Head-and-Heart" Ministry Development:** Teach students to harmonize intellectual and spiritual growth by studying the biblical foundation for activism alongside the gospel's transformative witness in their personal lives. This approach fosters a conversion-centered embodiment of the gospel's indicatives, integrating personal faith and public witness organically.

c. **Encourage Contextual Awareness and Historical Memory:** Use Grimké's historical context as a case study to show how past injustices inform present responsibilities in pastoral preaching, as modeled by Grimké's embodiment of Paul's hermeneutic and heart. Encourage students to integrate historical knowledge, particularly regarding social and ethnic issues, into their ministry practices as appropriate for their context.

d. **Cultivate Spirit-Led Learning Spaces:** Establish a learning environment that encourages honest dialogue about the social implications of a life transformed by the gospel. This environment should include key features of Grimké's homiletic, such as prayer, reflective exercises, and open discussions on how to practically embody the gospel amid today's societal challenges.

e. **Utilize Visual Aids and Practical Exercises:** Present Grimké's EEH diagram and guide students in practical exercises, such as developing a sermon outline that addresses a current social issue. This hands-on approach reinforces the holistic, socially engaged gospel witness that Grimké exemplified. See Diagram 1 in the Schedule of Diagrams.

Grounding the Theoretical Framework

The theoretical framework supporting this research is grounded in Grimké's practical application of biblical theology in response to the evangelical, Reformed tradition. By drawing on interpretive practices from Paul to Grimké, the framework positions gospel preaching as biblically faithful, contextually aware, and transformative in the lives of individuals and society.

1. **Biblical Theology as Foundation**: Grimké's commitment to the authority of scripture emphasized that gospel preaching should address all forms of sin, from individual failings to broader issues like ethnic prejudice. His approach demonstrates that gospel preaching can directly address societal and corporate sins and the inimical forces that drive them without compromising doctrinal integrity.

2. **Gospel Proclamation and Social Activism**: This framework proposes that gospel preaching is inherently transformative, with social activism as an extension of the gospel's "ultimate amen" or response. Grimké's model encourages preachers to embody a gospel activism that is biblically grounded and contextually aware.

Directions for Future Research

While this treatise provides a detailed exploration of Grimké's EEH, several areas remain ripe for further investigation, offering opportunities to deepen our understanding of Grimké's life, theology, and homiletical practice.

1. **Grimké and the Social Gospel Movement**: Explore Grimké's apparent silence regarding Walter Rauschenbusch's Social Gospel movement, as noted by Ferry, and assess the theological or practical reasons behind this lack of engagement.

2. **Grimké and the Pauline Corpus**: Investigate why Grimké interpreted and embodied Paul's writings differently from many of his Reformed contemporaries, particularly in relation to social and racial issues.

3. **Pathos and Affective Rhetoric**: Examine the role of pathos in Grimké's rhetoric and its impact on the affective domain of his audience, offering insights into his persuasive and emotive preaching style.

4. **Paul's vs. Grimké's Audiences**: Compare the distinctions between Paul's secular audience and Grimké's predominantly professing Christian audience, highlighting how these apparent contextual differences shaped their respective homiletical strategies.

5. **Grimké's Lamentative Turn**: Analyze the lamentative shift in Grimké's journaling in his later years, particularly after the loss of his wife, Charlotte. This could provide guidance for spiritual formation in pastors navigating difficult seasons in ministry.

6. **Grimké's Influences**: Revive the legacies of the preachers Grimké admired and mentioned throughout his corpus, exploring how these figures shaped his theology and homiletic.

7. **Manuscripts vs. Preached Sermons**: Explore transcribed versions or recordings of Grimké's sermons (if available) and compare them with his existing sermon manuscripts. This comparative study could uncover valuable theoretical and practical insights into the dynamics between written preparation and the realities of preaching delivery, shedding light on the interplay between structure, spontaneity, and audience engagement in homiletics.

Implications for Homiletics: Blind Spots and the Way Forward

Grimké's EEH model presents a holistic, gospel-embodied approach that addresses personal salvation, societal renewal, and the inimical forces that drive the hostilities of the world. His example offers a balanced method for confronting various social issues across the scope of evangelical preaching today. However, this tension between personal piety and public justice is not unique to evangelicalism; it resonates across most American pulpits, irrespective of denominational background. From conservative to mainline streams, many churches face similar challenges when harmonizing gospel proclamation with comprehensive social engagement.

1. **Holistic Engagement with Social Issues**: Grimké's EEH advocates a balanced approach to addressing social issues. In today's context, evangelical preaching often emphasizes certain issues—like the sanctity of life—while other areas, such as racial justice or immigration, may receive less focus. This trend is evident in broader American pulpits as well, where sermons may tackle some societal concerns head-on but remain

cautious on others, often aligning with perceived congregational preferences. As Grimké's model demonstrates, the church's witness is strengthened by consistency in addressing both personal and corporate sins, just as Paul called for communal unity and personal holiness.[2] Through this dual lens, preaching remains faithful to the full implications of the gospel, meeting the needs of all groups while embodying the wholeness of Christ's love and justice.

2. **Gospel Integrity Through Consistency in Advocacy**: One of the great challenges across denominations is maintaining consistency in advocating for justice. While some pulpits may prioritize individual salvation, others emphasize justice-related themes like social equity, often neglecting other gospel indicatives. Grimké's EEH encourages a consistency that doesn't draw selective boundaries around gospel values, pointing out that real gospel integrity requires a commitment to address all manifestations of injustice—whether advocating for the unborn, racial minorities, or marginalized immigrants. This approach aligns with Paul's teaching on the equal worth of every individual as a bearer of God's image.[3] American pulpits that strive to bridge these gaps exemplify the gospel's universal call to love and transformation, resonating with believers and non-believers alike.

3. **Educational Integration of EEH Principles**: Grimké's model offers actionable insights for homiletics education across denominations, equipping preachers to address a wide range of critical issues through a gospel-embodied lens. By emphasizing both the spiritual and social dimensions of the gospel, his approach can be integrated into homiletics

---

[2] Cf. Romans 12:1-2; 1 Corinthians 12:12-27.

[3] Cf. 1 Corinthians 9:19-23.

curricula as an extension of the earlier taxonomy in several ways:

a. *Case Study-Based Learning*: Grimké's sermons, though they most likely would need to be abbreviated for today's standards, can serve as case studies for analyzing how he addressed issues like racial prejudice, injustice, and the sanctity of human life through a gospel-embodied framework. Students can evaluate how he structured his sermons to confront societal challenges without compromising gospel integrity, gaining concrete examples for constructing sermons that balance depth, compassion, and biblical and theological faithfulness.

b. *Integrative Sermon Development Exercises:* Homiletics and preaching programs could incorporate Grimké's EEH model into sermon-building exercises, encouraging students to address multiple facets of the Christian experience (e.g., justice, personal transformation, and social ethics) within a single homily or preachment. This approach equips students to engage with issues like the sanctity of life, racial reconciliation, and poverty while maintaining textual integrity and a gospel-embodied focus.

c. *Cross-Denominational Application:* Grimké's approach provides a framework for addressing shared challenges across denominational lines, emphasizing the unifying power of gospel-embodied preaching. His focus on gospel indicatives offers a model for engaging diverse social issues—such as immigration, justice for marginalized communities, and ethical integrity—through shared Christian commitments. By examining Grimké's framework, students can develop a vision for preaching that fosters theological unity and addresses pressing societal concerns, while remaining anchored in the gospel's transformative and emancipatory power.

d. *Emphasis on Personal Integrity and Cultural Awareness:* Grimké's life reflects a harmony between personal convictions and public advocacy, a balance that homiletics education can emphasize to future preachers. Drawing on Grimké's example, programs can teach the importance of cultural awareness and personal integrity in ministry, preparing students to thoughtfully address the unique challenges of their congregations and communities.

Through these instructional methods, homiletics programs can integrate Grimké's EEH model to help future preachers address complex societal and personal issues with theological rigor and pastoral sensitivity. This integration cultivates a generation of preachers capable of engaging pressing topics with the transformative and emancipatory power of the gospel at the forefront of their ministry.

Final Thoughts

Grimké's Evangelical Emancipatory Homiletic (EEH), much like Paul's ministry, offers a balanced approach to the challenging yet essential task of gospel preaching, harmonizing personal transformation with contextual awareness and social activism. As American pulpits grapple with similar tensions across traditions, Grimké's model provides a gospel-embodied framework for addressing corporate sins by fully embodying the transformative and redemptive power of the gospel.

This study reaffirms the relevance of Grimké's EEH as a transformative framework for contemporary preaching. By embodying the social indicatives of the gospel proclamation, Grimké demonstrates that the gospel's call extends beyond individual salvation to include community reconciliation and justice, especially among fellow believers. His life and preaching exemplify a holistic gospel that empowers preachers to engage the moral and social challenges of their time as a demonstration of doctrinal integrity and biblical fidelity.

Grimké's approach also provides a compelling pathway for homiletics education, offering practical insights for equipping future preachers. By examining case studies of Grimké's sermons, engaging in sermon-building exercises, and fostering Spirit-led learning spaces, students can learn to address complex societal issues with a biblically grounded and contextually relevant perspective. These educational practices underscore the need to harmonize theological rigor, cultural awareness, and personal integrity in ministry preparation.

Grimké's reflections in his later years offer a fitting summary of his vision for effective gospel preaching. As an aged octogenarian, he wrote:

> It is a great thing, in preaching, to have a message, and to be able to give it in demonstration of the Spirit and of power. It is the only way that the gospel message should ever be given, and is the only way to give it effectively. In order to do this there must be [contextually framed] care in preparing the message, and care in seeking the enduement of the Holy Spirit in giving it. It is not a matter of chance. Preaching effectively requires careful preparation in both of these directions.[4]

These words encapsulate the heart of Grimké's EEH: a gospel-embodied proclamation that is both theologically faithful and socially sensitive. His legacy not only serves as a model for preachers but also calls them to embrace the full breadth of the gospel's transformative and emancipatory power by courageously addressing personal and communal renewal in an increasingly divided world.

---

[4] Grimké, *Works III*, 598–99.

SCHEDULE OF DIAGRAMS

Evangelical Emancipatory Homiletics[1]

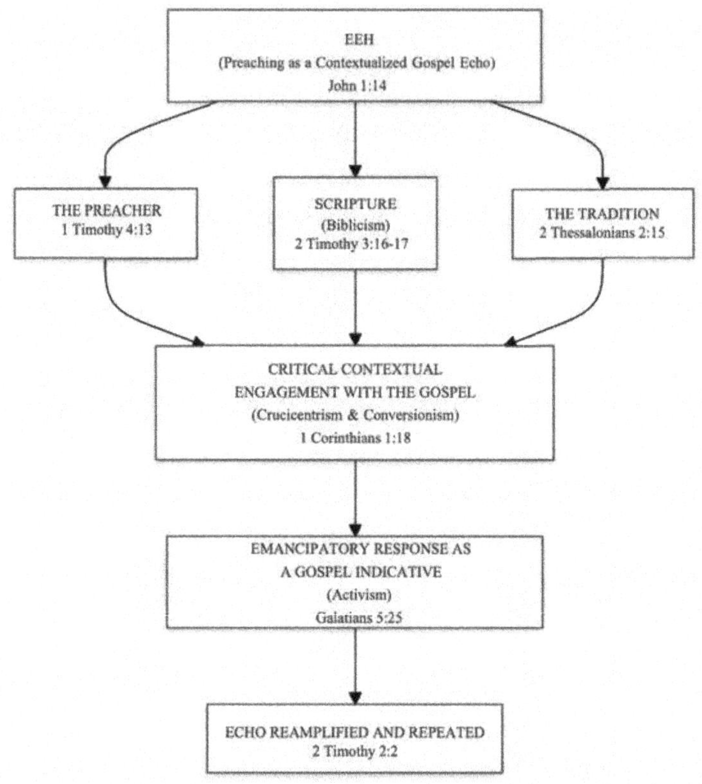

Diagram 1

[1] Pedagogical note: Green and Reed's work on emancipatory learning emphasizes the creation of learning environments that challenge oppressive structures and foster critical reflection. This approach views education as a tool for personal and social transformation, where learners engage in questioning power dynamics and pursue liberation through awareness and action. Reed, in particular, highlights the importance of conversational learning spaces that encourage dialogue and transformative leadership. These

The Evangelical Priorities of Gospel Preaching

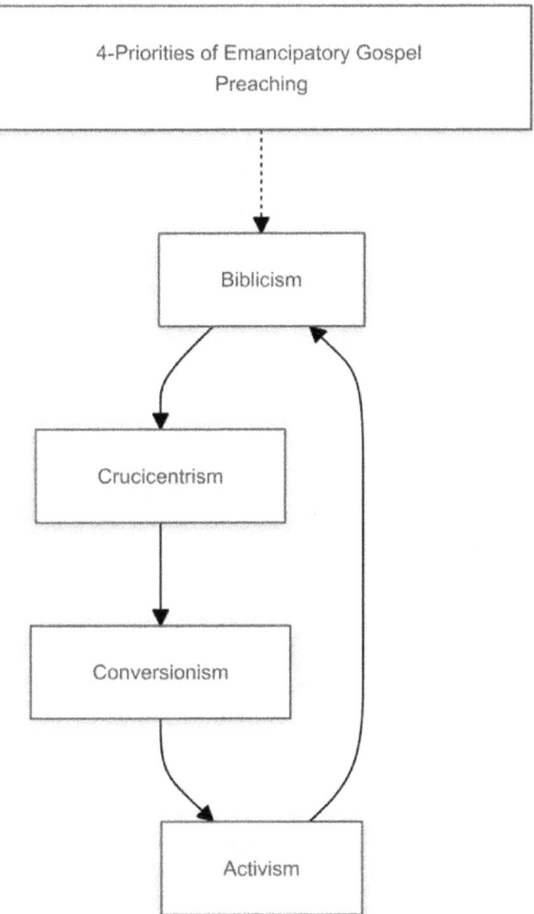

Diagram 2

---

principles resonate with an EEH, which seeks to propagate the gospel to its "ultimate amen"—transforming hearts and, thereby lives, to actively reflect the glory of God.

Cultural Contexts of Paul and Grimké's Ministries

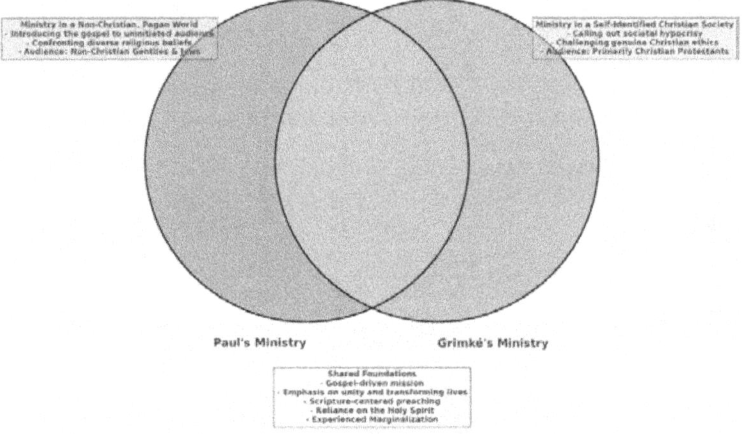

Diagram 3

APPENDIX I

Table 1. Textual Echoes—Jesus	
Matthew 4:4	During the temptation in the wilderness, Jesus responds to Satan by quoting Deuteronomy 8:3, saying, "It is written, 'Man shall not live by bread alone, but by every word that comes from the mouth of God.'"
Matthew 4:7	Again, in the wilderness, Jesus counters another temptation by citing Deuteronomy 6:16, "Again it is written, 'You shall not put the Lord your God to the test.'"
Matthew 4:10	To rebuff Satan's final temptation, Jesus quotes from Deuteronomy 6:13–15, stating, "For it is written, 'You shall worship the Lord your God and him only shall you serve.'"
Matthew 21:42	Jesus quotes Psalm 118:22–23 when discussing His rejection by the religious leaders, saying, "The stone that the builders rejected has become the cornerstone; this was the Lord's doing, and it is marvelous in our eyes."
Luke 4:18–19	In the synagogue at Nazareth, Jesus reads from Isaiah 61:1–2, proclaiming His anointed mission to "proclaim good news to the poor . . . proclaim liberty to the captives and recovering of sight to the blind, to set at liberty those who are oppressed."
Matthew 22:44	During a dispute with the Pharisees, Jesus cites Psalm 110:1 to question the Messiah's lineage, "The Lord said to my Lord, 'Sit at my right hand, until I put your enemies under your feet.'"
Matthew 12:3–4	When His disciples are accused of breaking Sabbath laws, Jesus refers to 1 Samuel 21:1–6, recounting how David ate the Bread of the Presence.

Mark 7:6–7	Jesus rebukes the Pharisees' hypocrisy by quoting Isaiah 29:13, "This people honors me with their lips, but their heart is far from me; in vain do they worship me, teaching as doctrines the commandments of men."
Matthew 15:8–9	Similarly, He critiques shallow worship by citing the same passage from Isaiah to highlight the disconnect between true worship and human traditions.
John 6:45	Teaching about divine instruction and belief in Him, Jesus references Isaiah 54:13, "It is written in the Prophets, 'And they will all be taught by God.'"
Matthew 11:10	Discussing John the Baptist, Jesus refers to Malachi 3:1, "This is he of whom it is written, 'Behold, I send my messenger before your face, who will prepare your way before you.'"
Luke 19:46	While cleansing the temple, He cites Isaiah 56:7 and Jeremiah 7:11, combining, "My house shall be a house of prayer, but you have made it a den of robbers."
Matthew 24:15	Speaking of the end times, Jesus references Daniel 9:27, "So when you see the abomination of desolation spoken of by the prophet Daniel, standing in the holy place (let the reader understand)."
Matthew 27:46; Mark 15:34	On the cross, Jesus cries out Psalm 22:1, "My God, my God, why have you forsaken me?"
Luke 4:4	Responding to the devil about turning stone to bread, Jesus cites Deuteronomy 8:3 to underline the importance of spiritual nourishment from God's words.
John 10:34	Jesus uses Psalm 82:6 to defend His claim of divinity, stating, "Is it not written in your Law, 'I said, you are gods'?"
Luke 20:17	Jesus challenges the Pharisees with Psalm 118:22, asking about the rejected stone becoming the cornerstone.

Mark 12:29–30	He affirms the Shema from Deuteronomy 6:4–5, emphasizing the foundational Jewish confession of the oneness of God and the commandment to love God wholly.
Matthew 22:32	In discussing the resurrection with the Sadducees, Jesus cites Exodus 3:6, "I am the God of Abraham, the God of Isaac, and the God of Jacob."
Luke 22:37	Jesus identifies with Isaiah 53:12, stating, "For I tell you that this scripture must be fulfilled in me: 'And he was numbered with the transgressors.'"

Table 2. Thematic Echoes—Jesus	
Matthew 5:17–20	In the Sermon on the Mount, Jesus emphasizes that He came not to abolish the Law or the Prophets but to fulfill them, embodying the deeper spiritual intents of the Mosaic law.
John 8:58	By declaring, "Before Abraham was, I am," Jesus subtly echoes Exodus 3:14, aligning Himself with the eternal "I AM" identity of God.
Matthew 5:43–44	Jesus extends the OT command to love one's neighbor (Leviticus 19:18) and counters it with the call to love one's enemies, embodying the prophetic teachings of love and forgiveness.
Luke 10:30–37	The parable of the Good Samaritan embodies the Levitical command to love one's neighbor by expanding its boundaries to include enemies and strangers, echoing the universal scope of God's mercy.
Matthew 5:38–42	Jesus recontextualizes the law of retaliation (Exodus 21:24) by advocating non-retaliation and peaceful resistance, exemplifying the prophetic ideals of peace and mercy.
Matthew 20:28	By stating that the Son of Man came to serve and give His life as a ransom, Jesus embodies the servant imagery of Isaiah 53, showcasing a messianic identity centered on sacrifice.
John 10:11	Identifying Himself as the "good shepherd," Jesus adopts imagery from Psalm 23 and Ezekiel 34, demonstrating His protective and providential role.
Matthew 9:13	Quoting Hosea 6:6, "I desire mercy, and not sacrifice," Jesus emphasizes His mission to call sinners, not the righteous, reflecting God's priority on inward righteousness over ritual compliance.

Luke 4:25–27	Jesus references the stories of Elijah and Elisha ministering to Gentiles (from 1 Kings and 2 Kings), using them to illustrate His ministry's outreach beyond Israel.
Matthew 2:15	His life itself echoes Hosea 11:1, "Out of Egypt I called my son," as described in Matthew's Gospel, underscoring Jesus as the fulfillment of Israel's story.
Matthew 5:21–22	Jesus deepens the commandment against murder to address even anger and insult, reflecting the spiritual depth of the law.
Matthew 5:27–28	He extends the commandment against adultery to even lustful thoughts, demonstrating the comprehensive moral vision of the law.
Luke 13:34	Jesus expresses His lament over Jerusalem with imagery reminiscent of a hen gathering her chicks (Psalm 91:4), embodying God's protective love.
Matthew 12:6	He claims that "something greater than the temple is here," positioning Himself as the new locus of God's presence, echoing themes from 1 Kings 8.
Matthew 12:40	Jesus uses the story of Jonah as a sign of His resurrection, embedding the narrative of Jonah's three days in the fish as a prophetic sign of His own three days in the tomb.
John 15:1	Declaring Himself the true vine, Jesus takes up imagery from Isaiah 5:1–7, positioning Himself as the fulfillment and true source of life and nourishment.
Luke 4:21	In proclaiming "Today this scripture has been fulfilled in your hearing," Jesus declares His mission as the embodiment of Isaiah's prophecy (Isaiah 61:1–2).
John 2:19–21	Discussing His body as the temple, Jesus invokes the destruction and raising of the temple, echoing prophetic themes about the restoration of God's house.

Matthew 5:14–16	Calling His followers the light of the world, Jesus embodies the prophetic call of Israel to be a light to the nations (Isaiah 42:6).
Matthew 11:28–30	Offering rest for the weary, Jesus fulfills the prophetic imagery of comfort and rest promised in scriptures like Jeremiah 31:25.

Table 3. Textual Echoes—Paul	
Romans 1:17	Paul cites Habakkuk 2:4, "The righteous shall live by faith," to underpin his central argument on justification by faith.
1 Corinthians 15:45	Paul refers to Genesis 2:7 in discussing the resurrection, stating, "The first man Adam became a living being;" he then contrasts this with Christ, "the last Adam, a life-giving spirit."
Galatians 3:13	Citing Deuteronomy 21:23, Paul explains Christ's redemptive work: "Cursed is everyone who is hanged on a tree."
2 Corinthians 6:2	He invokes Isaiah 49:8 to emphasize the immediacy of salvation: "In a favorable time I listened to you, and in a day of salvation I have helped you."
Romans 4:7–8	Paul quotes Psalm 32:1–2 to discuss the blessedness of the man to whom God counts righteousness apart from works.
Romans 10:5	Paul references Leviticus 18:5 when discussing the righteousness based on the law: "The person who does the commandments shall live by them."
Galatians 4:27	He cites Isaiah 54:1 to encourage the Galatians, using the imagery of the barren woman who breaks forth in joy.
Romans 11:26–27	Drawing from Isaiah 59:20–21, Paul speaks of the future redemption of Israel: "The Deliverer will come from Zion, he will banish ungodliness from Jacob."
Ephesians 6:2–3	Paul quotes the Fifth Commandment with a promise from Exodus 20:12, "Honor your father and mother."
Romans 9:33	He cites Isaiah 28:16 and Isaiah 8:14 about Jesus as the cornerstone and a stone of stumbling.

Romans 3:10–18	Paul strings together various Psalms and Isaiah to paint a picture of human unrighteousness.
1 Corinthians 9:9	Paul quotes Deuteronomy 25:4, "Do not muzzle an ox when it treads out the grain," applying it to the rights of apostles.
Romans 15:9	He references 2 Samuel 22:50 and Psalm 18:49, showing that Christ's ministry confirms God's promises to the patriarchs.
Galatians 3:10	Citing Deuteronomy 27:26, Paul discusses the curse of the law: "Cursed be everyone who does not abide by all things written in the Book of the Law, and do them."
Romans 12:19	Paul quotes Deuteronomy 32:35, "Vengeance is mine, I will repay, says the Lord," to teach on Christian conduct.
1 Corinthians 1:19	He uses Isaiah 29:14 to explain the futility of human wisdom against God's wisdom: "I will destroy the wisdom of the wise."
Romans 10:15	Citing Isaiah 52:7, Paul describes the beauty of those who preach the good news.
1 Corinthians 10:26	Paul quotes Psalm 24:1 to affirm God's sovereignty over creation: "For 'the earth is the Lord's, and the fullness thereof.'"
Romans 4:3	He refers to Genesis 15:6, "Abraham believed God, and it was counted to him as righteousness."
Galatians 3:16	Paul discusses the promises made to Abraham and his "offspring," citing Genesis 12:7, Genesis 13:15, and Genesis 24:7, interpreting "offspring" as Christ.

Table 4. Thematic Echoes—Paul	
Romans 5:14	Paul presents Adam as a type of Christ, an embodiment that draws from Genesis to illustrate Jesus' role in redemption.
Romans 6:4	Through baptism, believers are buried and raised with Christ, echoing the death and resurrection narratives and applying them to spiritual renewal.
1 Corinthians 5:7	Paul invokes the Passover lamb imagery from Exodus, applying it to Christ: "For Christ, our Passover lamb, has been sacrificed."
Ephesians 5:31–32	He uses the Genesis account of marriage to reveal the profound mystery of Christ and the church, embodying the union described in Genesis 2:24.
2 Corinthians 3:3	Paul contrasts the stone tablets of the Mosaic covenant with the "tablets of human hearts," a spiritual embodiment of the new covenant.
Galatians 3:29	If believers are Christ's, then they are Abraham's offspring, heirs according to promise, embodying the spiritual lineage and inheritance promised in Genesis.
Ephesians 2:14–16	Christ as our peace who breaks down the dividing wall, embodying the prophetic visions of peace and unity.
Romans 8:22–23	Creation groaning and believers groaning inwardly echo the OT themes of creation longing for redemption.
Philippians 2:7–8	Christ's incarnation is described using the language of *kenosis* (emptying oneself), echoing servant themes from Isaiah.
1 Corinthians 10:4	Christ as the spiritual Rock that followed the Israelites, embodying the divine sustenance provided in the wilderness.

Romans 7:4	Believers belong to Him who was raised from the dead, that we might bear fruit for God, echoing the life-giving power of resurrection.
2 Corinthians 5:17	In Christ, one is a new creation; old things have passed away, embodying themes of renewal and restoration.
Ephesians 6:17	The sword of the Spirit, which is the word of God, embodies the active and defensive aspects of God's word as seen in the Psalms.
Galatians 2:20	Living by faith in the Son of God echoes the trust and reliance depicted in the lives of OT saints.
Romans 9:25–26	Citing Hosea, Paul discusses Gentiles becoming God's people, embodying the prophetic expansion of God's family.
Ephesians 3:6	Gentiles are co-heirs, members of the same body, and partakers of the promise in Christ Jesus through the gospel, embodying the unity and fulfillment of God's promises.
1 Thessalonians 4:16–17	The imagery of the Lord's descent and the call to meet Him in the air embodies prophetic and apocalyptic visions found in Daniel.
Romans 13:8–10	Loving others fulfills the law, embodying the commandments' essence found throughout the Torah.
Philippians 3:9	Being found in Christ, not having a righteousness of one's own from the law, but one through faith in Christ, embodies the prophetic critique of superficial righteousness.
Romans 15:12	Paul references Isaiah to illustrate the inclusion of the Gentiles, embodying the prophetic vision of a restored and inclusive kingdom.

Table 5. Textual Echoes—Other NT Examples	
Hebrews 8:5	The author quotes Exodus 25:40 regarding Moses making the tabernacle according to the pattern shown on the mountain, illustrating Christ's more perfect priestly ministry.
James 2:23	James cites Genesis 15:6, affirming that Abraham's faith was counted to him as righteousness, establishing the principle that faith produces works.
1 Peter 2:6	Peter quotes Isaiah 28:16, emphasizing Jesus as the cornerstone and the foundation of the believer's faith.
Hebrews 1:5	The writer references Psalm 2:7 and 2 Samuel 7:14 to assert Jesus' superior status as the Son of God compared to the angels.
Jude 1:14–15	Jude cites Enoch's prophecy, which, while extracanonical, was revered in Jewish tradition, to warn against ungodly individuals.
1 Peter 2:22	Peter quotes Isaiah 53:9 to describe Christ's sinless behavior as an example for believers.
James 4:6	James references Proverbs 3:34, which speaks of God opposing the proud but giving grace to the humble.
Hebrews 10:30	The author cites Deuteronomy 32:35–36 to discuss God's judgment and vindication of His people.
2 Peter 1:17	Peter refers to the transfiguration account, echoing the divine voice from heaven found in Psalm 2:7 and linking it to Jesus' divine sonship.
Hebrews 4:4	The writer quotes Genesis 2:2 about God resting on the seventh day, using it as a basis for the promise of rest for God's people.
James 2:11	James refers to the commandment from Exodus 20:14 and Deuteronomy 5:18, forbidding adultery, to illustrate the indivisibility of the law.
Revelation 2:27	John cites Psalm 2:9, portraying Jesus' rule with a rod of iron as fulfillment of messianic prophecy.

1 Peter 1:16	Peter quotes Leviticus 11:44, "Be holy, for I am holy," calling Christians to a life of holiness.
Hebrews 12:5–6	The author recalls Proverbs 3:11–12, encouraging believers to endure hardship as discipline from a loving God.
2 Peter 3:8	Peter recalls Psalm 90:4, explaining that to God "a day is like a thousand years," to describe God's view of time.
James 5:11	James mentions Job as an example of patience and suffering, drawing from the narrative of Job's life.
Revelation 1:7	John alludes to Daniel 7:13, describing the Son of Man coming with the clouds of heaven.
1 Peter 4:18	Peter quotes Proverbs 11:31, "If the righteous are scarcely saved, what will become of the ungodly and the sinner?"
Jude 9	Jude references the archangel Michael disputing with the devil over Moses' body, drawing from Jewish tradition.
Hebrews 13:5	The author quotes Deuteronomy 31:6, "I will never leave you nor forsake you," to assure believers of God's constant presence.

Table 6. Thematic Echoes—Other NT Examples	
Hebrews 9:9–14	The rituals of the Old Covenant are seen as symbols for the time then present, prefiguring Christ's sacrificial work.
1 Peter 3:20–21	Peter uses Noah's ark as a typology for baptism, which now saves believers, not by removing dirt from the body but as an appeal to God for a good conscience.
Revelation 5:5–6	John portrays Jesus as both the Lion of the tribe of Judah and the slain Lamb, fusing prophetic and sacrificial imagery.
Hebrews 7:1–3	Melchizedek is presented as a type of Christ, embodying principles of priesthood that transcend Levitical norms.
James 1:17	Describing God as the Father of lights, James draws on the creation imagery to emphasize God's unchanging nature.
1 Peter 2:24	Peter refers to Isaiah 53:5, describing Christ bearing our sins in His body on the tree, highlighting the healing brought by His wounds.
Revelation 12:1–5	The woman clothed with the sun, with the moon under her feet, embodies Israel and the church, reflecting struggles and triumph.
Hebrews 3:7–11	The writer recontextualizes Psalm 95:7–11 to warn Christian believers about hardening their hearts as Israel did in the wilderness.
James 3:6	Describing the tongue as a fire, James evokes imagery from Proverbs and Psalms about the destructive power of speech.
2 Peter 2:22	Peter draws from Proverbs 26:11 to illustrate the folly of returning to sinful behavior, using the vivid images of a dog returning to its vomit and a washed pig returning to mud.

1 John 2:8–10	John discusses walking in the light, a thematic echo of Psalm 119:105, in which God's word is a lamp to the feet and a light to the path.
Revelation 21:1–4	The vision of a new heaven and new earth embodies Isaiah 65:17–25's prophetic imagery, signaling ultimate renewal and divine habitation among people.
Hebrews 10:20	The new and living way opened through the curtain, Jesus' flesh, echoes the temple veil's symbolism, signifying direct access to God's presence.
James 1:21	The implanted word, which can save souls, evokes Deuteronomic themes of the life-giving law.
1 Peter 1:24–25	Peter embodies Isaiah 40:6–8 by comparing human mortality to grass and God's eternal word to everlasting life.
Revelation 1:12–16	John's vision of Christ among the lampstands uses Daniel's "son of man" imagery to depict Christ's eternal priesthood and kingship.
Hebrews 4:12	The word of God is living and active, sharper than any two-edged sword, embodying themes from the Wisdom literature about the discerning power of God's word.
1 John 3:11–12	Referencing the story of Cain and Abel, John teaches the foundational Christian ethic of love over hatred, echoing Genesis 4's narrative.
2 Peter 1:19	Peter speaks of the prophetic word as a light shining in a dark place, reflecting Psalm 119's imagery and reinforcing the guidance of scripture until Christ's return.
Jude 12	Jude uses natural imagery like hidden reefs, waterless clouds, and fruitless trees to describe deceitful individuals, drawing on OT prophetic metaphors to warn the church.

APPENDIX II

TABLES CHAPTER FIVE

TABLE 1. *Five-Fold Principles for Preaching Penitential Psalms*

PRINCIPLE	DESCRIPTION
Highlight Divine Presence and Assurance	*The Penitential Psalms echo God's reassuring presence during times of deep distress and repentance. They resonate with divine support amidst the psalmist's acknowledgment of sin and guilt, offering a constant reminder of God's unwavering presence. Psalm 6 beautifully captures this assurance:* ***"O Lord, rebuke me not in your anger, nor discipline me in your wrath. Be gracious to me, O Lord, for I am languishing; heal me, O Lord, for my bones are troubled"*** *(Psalm 6:1–2).*
Relate the Psalm to Contemporary Struggles	*The Penitential Psalms resonate powerfully with contemporary struggles, bridging the ancient and modern worlds. Psalm 38, for instance, vividly depicts the physical and emotional toll of personal sin:* ***"There is no soundness in my flesh because of your indignation; there is no health in my bones because of my sin"*** *(Psalm 38:3). This raw portrayal of the impact of sin can be paralleled with today's struggles of guilt, shame, and the consequences of one's actions.*
Incorporate Prayer as a Central Element	*Prayer is the Penitential Psalms' heartbeat, serving as a direct conduit between the psalmist and God. Psalm 51 exemplifies this deeply personal communication:* ***"Have mercy on me, O God, according to your steadfast love;***

	according to your abundant mercy blot out my transgressions. Wash me thoroughly from my iniquity, and cleanse me from my sin!" *(Psalm 51:1–2). This psalm's fervent plea for forgiveness and purification showcases the power of prayer in seeking divine mercy.*
Encourage Hope and Perseverance	*Although the Penitential Psalms often begin with sorrow and repentance, they frequently transition to a place of hope and trust in God's deliverance. Psalm 130 is a strong example of this journey from despair to hope:* ***"Out of the depths I cry to you, O Lord! O Lord, hear my voice! Let your ears be attentive to the voice of my pleas for mercy . . . I wait for the Lord, my soul waits, and in his word I hope"*** *(Psalm 130:1–2, 5).*
Focus on Community and Collective Experience	*The Penitential Psalms often encapsulate individual repentance, communal lament, and the collective seeking of God's mercy. Psalm 102 is an important example of this communal cry for help:* ***"Hear my prayer, O Lord; let my cry come to you! Do not hide your face from me in the day of my distress! Incline your ear to me; answer me speedily in the day when I call!"*** *(Psalm 102:1–2). This psalm captures the shared experience of suffering and the collective plea for divine intervention.*

TABLE 2. *Analysis: Five-Fold Principles for Preaching Penitential Psalms*[1]

PRINCIPLE	ANALYSIS
Highlight Divine Presence and Assurance	*Grimké emphasizes God's presence and support during times of distress and repentance, a key element of preaching the Penitential Psalms. He reminds his congregation of the omnipotent presence of God, stating,* ***"The first ground of hope to which our attention is here directed is in the fact that God is. The being of God is asserted. There is a God, the psalmist says."*** *This assurance that God is ever-present and all-powerful provides comfort and strength to the oppressed, reinforcing the belief that God will ultimately deliver justice and peace.*
Relate the Psalm to Contemporary Struggles	*Grimké skillfully relates the themes of Psalm 27 to the contemporary struggles of his congregation, particularly the racial oppression and injustices they faced. He draws parallels between the psalmist's adversities and the experiences of African Americans during the post-Reconstruction era, stating,* ***"Yes, God is. This universe is not the result of blind, unconscious forces; back of all that we see is a great intelligence. . . . It will help us to weather the storms that are before us and nerve us for the conflicts that await us in our efforts to rise and in our struggles for recognition against a bitter, Negro-hating spirit of caste."*** *By connecting the Psalm to their lived experiences, Grimké makes the scripture relevant and impactful.*

[1] For the quotes referenced within the table, see the shaded and italicized bold text in the sermon manuscripts.

Incorporate Prayer as a Central Element	*Prayer is central to Grimké's sermon, highlighting its importance in repentance and seeking God's help. He emphasizes the power of prayer, citing numerous biblical examples and urging his congregation to embrace prayer in their struggles:* ***"Prayer is a power. It is a mighty power. It is one of the mightiest forces in the universe."*** *Grimké's insistence on the necessity of prayer for personal and communal upliftment demonstrates the transformative potential of sincere supplication to God.*
Encourage Hope and Perseverance	*While acknowledging the harsh realities faced by his congregation, Grimké instills hope and perseverance by reminding them of God's justice and deliverance. He draws on the psalmist's confidence in God's protection and encourages his listeners to maintain their faith:* ***"Because God reigns, there is hope for the oppressed, for the downtrodden, for all upon whose necks the iron heel of oppression rests. There need be no fear as to the ultimate result, as to the final issue."*** *This message of enduring hope amidst trials is crucial for sustaining the congregation's spirit and determination.*
Focus on Community and Collective Experience	*Grimké addresses the communal aspects of repentance and the collective seeking of God's mercy, fostering a sense of solidarity and shared resilience among his congregants. He underscores the importance of praying for both themselves and those who oppress them, urging,* ***"We must not forget to pray also for those who are oppressing us, who have their heels upon our necks. . . . Pray that God would have mercy upon them; that he would open their blind eyes, that he would show them the error of their ways."*** *This call for collective prayer and forgiveness highlights their struggle's communal nature and unity's power in seeking divine intervention.*

TABLE 3. *Linguistic Analysis of Psalm 27*

Verse	Parallelism Types	Figures of Speech	Text	God and Prayer in the "Struggle"
1	LQR SC SX SCP	MET METN INC METN MET SYN Parallelism	A1 The Lord is my *light* and my *salvation*; B1 Whom shall I fear? The Lord is the *defense* B2 of *my life*; A2 Whom shall I dread?	**I. A Testimony of God-Confidence in the "Struggle" (*SX A1*)** • Confidence in God's Presence
2	LN SCP LCE	HYB HYC SYN REP HEN	When evildoers came upon me to *devour my flesh*, My adversaries and my enemies, they stumbled and fell.	• Confidence in God's Protection
3	LN SC LQ SCP LCE (implied)	REP HYB PER Parallelism	Though a host encamp against me, My heart will not fear; Though war arise against me, In *spite of* this I shall be confident.	• Confidence in God's Power
4	LP LN LQ SC	Parallelism REP METN METN	One thing **I have asked** from the Lord, that **I shall seek:** That **I may dwell** in the *house of the Lord* all the days of my life, **To behold** the beauty of the Lord And **to meditate** in His *temple*.	**II. A Testimony of Prayer in the "Struggle" (*SX B1*)** • A Prayer for God's Presence
5	LQ LN	Parallelism MET REP HYC	For in the day of trouble **He will** conceal me in His tabernacle; In the secret place of His tent **He will** hide me; **He will** lift me *up on a rock*.	• A Prayer for God's Protection
6		I PER	And now *my head* will be lifted up above *my enemies*	• A Prayer *of Praise* for God's Power

Psalm 27 II

	LN RC	REP Parallelism	around me, And **I will** offer in His tent sacrifices with shouts of joy; ***I will*** *sing*, yes, ***I will*** *sing* praises to the Lord.	
7	LN (Sub SX A1) LQ	ANP	Hear, O Lord, when I cry with my voice, And *be gracious to me* and answer me.	**III. A Cry for God in the "Struggle" (*SX C*)** • A Cry for Help
8	LN (Sub SX B1) LQ	ANM METN	*When You said, "Seek My face,"* my heart said to You, "Your face, O Lord, I shall seek."	• A Cry of Repentance
9	RC LN (Sub SX C1) LCE LQ	ANM ANP HEN	Do not *hide Your face* from me, Do not turn Your servant away *in anger*; You have been my help; Do not abandon me nor forsake me, O God of my salvation!	• A Cry for Acceptance
10	SA (Sub SX C2)	HYB I ANM	For my father and my mother have forsaken me, But the Lord will *take me up.*	**IV. A Hope in God in the "Struggle" (*SX B2*)** • A Hope for Acceptance
11	LN (Sub SX B2) LQ LEC LP	METN METN	Teach me Your *way*, O Lord, And lead me in a level *path* Because of my foes.	• A Hope for Restoration

Psalm 27 III

12	RE LN (Sub SX A2) LQ LEC LP	PER	Do not deliver me over to the desire of my adversaries, For false witnesses have risen against me, And such as breathe out violence.	• A Hope for deliverance
13	LQ LN LEC LP		*I would have despaired* unless I had believed that I would see the goodness of the Lord In the land of the living.	
14	SX	INC REP HEN	*Wait for the Lord;* a1 b1 Be strong and let your heart take courage; b2 Yes, *wait for the Lord.* a2	**V. A Confidence in God through the "Struggle" (*SX A2*)**

APPENDIX III

MANUSCRIPT: GOD, AND PRAYER AS FACTORS IN THE STRUGGLE

God and Prayer as Factors in the Struggle

Wait on the Lord; be of good courage, and He shall strengthen thine heart.
— Psalm 27:14
December 11, 1900

In my discourse of last Sabbath, I pointed out five reasons why I was hopeful of a brighter future for us in this land; namely, the growth of manhood in the Negro, the growing sense in him of what he is entitled to, and his determination to stand up for his rights; the fact that he is making progress in wealth and education; the certainty that right is ultimately to triumph; the presence of the religion of Jesus Christ in this land, and its power to conquer all prejudices, to break down all walls of separation, and to weld together into one great brotherhood men of all races; and the fact that both in the North and in the South there are white men and women who do not believe in the treatment which is accorded to us, and who are in sympathy with us in the fight which we are making.

There are two other grounds of hope to which I desire to direct attention this morning in closing, and they are the ones pointed out in the words of our text—"Wait on the Lord; be of good courage, and He shall strengthen thine heart; wait, I say, on the Lord." In the revised version it reads, "Wait on the Lord: be strong, and let thine heart take courage; yea, wait thou on the Lord."

The first ground of hope to which our attention is here directed is in the fact that God is. ***The being of God is asserted. There is a God, the psalmist says.*** He calls him Jehovah, the God of Abraham, of Isaac, and of Jacob; the God to whom Moses referred when he said to the children of Israel, with the Red Sea before them and the advancing hosts of the Egyptians behind them, "Stand still and see the salvation of the Lord." ***Yes, God is. This universe is not the result of blind, unconscious forces; back of all that we see is a great intelligence.*** That intelligence we call God; that is the great Being to whom the psalmist here refers, to whom he directs attention. God! How important is the thought. Let us get hold of it: let the idea sink deep into our hearts. ***It will help us to weather the storms that are before us and nerve us for the conflicts that await us in our efforts to rise and in our struggles for recognition against a bitter, Negro-hating spirit of caste.*** It was this thought — the thought of God — that brought hope back to the almost despairing soul of Frederick Douglass, many years ago, during one of the darkest periods of the anti-slavery struggle. You remember the story. It was a great meeting: Mr. Douglass was speaking in the most despairing tone. Everything was against us, apparently: there was hardly a ray of light to illumine the darkness as he looked out into the future. He was going on in this dismal strain when he was interrupted by Sojourner Truth, who said, "Is God dead, Frederick?" That shot a ray of light into his soul, and revived his drooping spirits. God! It is impossible to project that great thought into the mind of man, in any emergency or crisis in his life, without bracing him up, without giving him something to lean upon. It was the prop that Sojourner Truth laid hold upon, and that sustained her during all that long and painful and discouraging struggle through which she passed in the death-grapple with slavery. And it will sustain us, if we will lay hold of it, in the equally momentous struggle through which we are passing.

Higher than man, than all mundane influences, than principalities, and powers, and might, and dominion, than even the mightiest names of earth is a great Being, without beginning of days or end of years, who knows all things, who has all power and who is infinite in justice. This great Being is on the throne of the universe; he holds the scepter of universal empire. ***Because God reigns, there is hope for the oppressed, for the down-trodden, for all upon whose necks the***

iron heel of oppression rests. There need be no fear as to the ultimate result, as to the final issue. Hence the language of the psalmist, "The Lord reigneth." The very thought thrills him, and he calls upon the whole earth to rejoice. "The Lord reigneth; let the earth rejoice; let the multitude of isles be glad. Clouds and darkness are around about him: righteousness and judgment are the foundation of his throne." In that fact he sees ultimately the righting of all wrongs, the breaking of all yokes, and the oppressed going free. If the Devil was on the throne of the universe, there would be no such ground of rejoicing; no such hope could possibly exist. But he is not on the throne. It is true he is called the "God of this world," and at times would seem to be all-powerful in it, but it is only apparent. There is but one supreme power in the universe; and to that power one day every knee is to bow, and every tongue confess. There has been no abdication on the part of God. Because wrong goes on, it doesn't mean that everything has been turned over to the evil one; that wrongs are never to be righted. No, there is a Just One, who never slumbers nor sleeps, and who is not indifferent to what is going on. He will one day "make requisition for blood." Isaiah tells us that "righteousness is the girdle of his loins, and faithfulness the girdle of his reins."

The thought in the mind of the psalmist, as expressed in the words of the text, is—Keep that great Being in mind; don't lose sight of him—of the fact that he is, and what he is. And the promise is, "He shall strengthen thine heart," he will hold you up, will keep you from becoming utterly cast down; will put new life and energy and hope in you; will bring you out more than conqueror. Isaiah expresses the same thought in the fortieth chapter of his prophecy. "Hast thou not known, hast thou not heard, that the everlasting God, the Lord, the Creator of the ends of the earth, fainteth not, neither is weary? There is no searching of his understanding. He giveth power to the faint; and to them that have no might he increaseth strength. Even the youths shall faint and be weary, and the young men shall utterly fall: but they that wait upon the Lord shall renew their strength; they shall mount up with wings as eagles; they shall run, and not be weary; and they shall walk, and not faint."

Take away this idea of God; banish the thought of such a being, and the outlook would indeed be dismal. But it cannot be done: everywhere it meets us. In external nature we see traces of his footsteps. "The heavens declare his glory, and the firmament sheweth his handiwork," and in the inner world, in the deeper recesses of our own natures, we see in the still small voice of conscience a witness to his existence. Yes, God is, and because he is, there is hope for the oppressed Negro in this land. The Lord of all the earth will see that right is done.

> Careless seems the great Avenger; history's pages but record
> One death grapple in the darkness 'twixt old systems and the Word;
> Truth forever on the scaffold, Wrong forever on the throne,—
> Yet that scaffold sways the future, and behind the dim unknown,
> Standeth God within the shadow, keeping watch above his own.

The second ground of hope—understanding by the expression, "Wait on the Lord," the formal presentation of our case to him with a view to his interposition—is to be found in the efficacy of prayer. ***Prayer is a power. It is a mighty power. It is one of the mightiest forces in the universe.*** It is Tennyson who says,

> More things are wrought by prayer
> than this world dreams of.

And a greater than Tennyson has said, "In nothing be anxious; but in everything, by prayer and supplication, with thanksgiving, let your requests be made known unto God. And the peace of God, which passeth all understanding shall guard your hearts and your thoughts in Jesus Christ." The Bible is full of illustrations of the power of prayer. When God appeared unto Moses in the burning bush, he said to him, "I have surely seen the afflictions of my people which are in Egypt, and have heard their cry by reason of their taskmakers." What was that cry? It was the cry to high heaven that went up from his suffering people. And God says, "I have heard their cry, and am come down to deliver them." In the time of Hezekiah, Sennacherib, king of Assyria, we are told, sent Rabshakeh with a great army to Jerusalem, to besiege it. The record is, "Then Rabshakeh stood, and cried with a loud voice in the Jews' language and spake, saying, Hear ye the word of the great king of Assyria. Thus saith the king, Let not Hezekiah deceive you; for he shall not be able to deliver you out of his hand; neither let Hezekiah make you trust in the Lord, saying, The Lord will surely deliver us, and this city shall not be given into the hand of the king of Assyria. Hearken not unto Hezekiah: for thus saith the king of Assyria, Make your peace with me, and come out to me; and eat ye every one of his vine, and every one of his fig tree, and drink ye every one the waters of his own cistern; until I come and take you away to a land like your own land, a land of corn and wine, a land of bread and vineyards, a land of oil olive, and of honey, that ye may live, and not die: and hearken not unto Hezekiah, when he persuadeth you, saying, The Lord will deliver us. Hath any of the gods of the nations ever delivered his land out of the hand of the king of Assyria? Where are the gods of Hamath, and of Arpad? Where are the gods of Sepharvaim, of Hena, and Ivah? Have they delivered Samaria out of my hand? Who are they among all the gods of the countries, that have delivered their country out of my hand, that the Lord should deliver Jerusalem out of my hand?" But we are told that Hezekiah went into the house of the Lord and prayed: and what a prayer it was, "O Lord, the God of Israel, that sitteth upon the cherubim, thou art the God, even thou alone, of all the kingdoms of the earth; thou hast made heaven and earth. Incline thine ear, O Lord, and hear; open thine eyes, O Lord, and see; and hear the words of Sennacherib, wherewith he hath sent him to reproach the living God. Of a truth, O Lord, the kings of Assyria have laid waste the nations and their lands, and have cast their gods into the fire: for they were no gods, but the work of men's hands, wood and stone; therefore they have destroyed them. Now, therefore, O Lord, our God, save thou us, I beseech thee, out of his hand, that all the kingdoms of the earth may know that thou art the Lord God, even thou only." And you remember what the result was: the prophet Isaiah was instructed to say to the king that his request would be granted:—"Thus saith the Lord, the God of Israel, Whereas thou hast prayed to me against Sennacherib, king of Assyria, I have heard thee." So when the angel of the Lord appeared to Zacharias, the declaration was, "Fear not, Zacharias: because thy supplication is heard, and thy wife, Elizabeth, shall bear thee a son." And did not Jesus himself say, "Ask, and it shall be given unto you?" And in James 5:17, 18, is it not recorded:—"Elias was a man of like passions with us, and he prayed fervently that it might not rain: and it rained not on the earth for three years and six months. And he prayed again; and the heavens gave rain, and the earth brought forth her fruit."

There is nothing clearer in the Word of God than the fact that there is power in prayer, that, through it, effects may be produced, that definite results may be accomplished. This power may be made to play an important part in the great struggle through which we are passing in this country. It played a most important part, I believe, in the struggle out of bondage into freedom. We speak of the labors of Garrison and Sumner and Phillips, and the whole host of anti-slavery agitators; we speak of the Emancipation Proclamation, and of the clash of arms, as agents in bringing about the final result: and they were most important agents,—too much cannot be said in praise of all that was done, of the magnificent fight that was made by our soldiers in the face of rebel bullets, and by the reformers on the bloodless fields of thought and sentiment,—of the moral heroism and physical courage that were displayed. But the poor slave himself, I believe, had a part in that struggle second to none; it was the part which he played on his knees. In the rude cabins of the South, in lonely places, in the seclusion of the forest, in the darkness of the night the voice of the slave was heard in piteous appeals to heaven. When they were hoeing in the cotton field, when the crack of the overseer's whip was sounding in their ears, when their backs were smarting under the lash of the hard taskmaster, when they stood upon the auction block, when families were broken up,—

the father going in one direction, the mother in another, and the children in still another,—there went up from their bleeding hearts the cry to heaven, "How long, O Lord, how long?" Every day, every night, almost every hour in the day, the cry of their bleeding hearts was poured into the ear of heaven. And I believe, as mighty as were the other influences, there was none more potential than this. Prayer was their only weapon at that time, and how mightily did they wield it. And we know with what result. The answer came at last, and they went out from under the yoke of bondage, free men and free women; went out, after wrestling earnestly in prayer with God for deliverance. The God, who said to Moses, "I have seen the affliction of My people in Egypt, and have heard their cry, and am come down to deliver them," came down in answer to the prayers that went up from the rude cabins of the South, from the cane-brakes and the rice fields, and the cotton patches, and brought deliverance. And this same power is available today. Lawless ruffians may keep the Negro away from the polls by shotguns; and by unrighteous laws and intimidation may shut him out of first-class cars, but there is no power by which all the combined forces of evil in the South can keep him from approaching the throne of grace. Here is one thing, thank God, that this Negro-hating spirit cannot do,—it cannot prevent him from praying.

What is prayer?

Prayer is the soul's sincere desire,
Uttered or unexpressed;
The motion of a hidden fire,
That trembles in the breast.
Prayer is the burden of a sigh,
The falling of a tear,
The upward glancing of an eye,
When none but God is near.

Thank God, I say, this lawless, murderous, Negro-hating spirit that is running riot in the South, that unblushingly flaunts its shame in the face of the civilized world, while it may murder Negroes and despoil them of their civil and political rights, cannot prevent them from lifting their eyes to heaven, or breathing a prayer; nor can it shut the ears of heaven to their cries. It may shut the ears of a cowardly pulpit, and a prejudiced church, but there its power stops. It cannot block the way of approach to the Holy of Holies. God has opened the way, and no man can shut it: all the powers of darkness cannot do it. Into that august presence the Negro may come, black though he may be, ignorant though he may be, poor though he may be, with the same assurance of acceptance as the whitest; the most cultivated, the most wealthy.

What use shall we make of this power? Shall we allow it to remain dormant, unused? Shall we not avail ourselves of this privilege? Shall we not begin, in earnest, to ask God to take a hand in this struggle in which we are engaged? It is a suggestion that is well worthy of our most serious consideration. In addition to what we are already doing, we should add this power of prayer; should make our troubles more a subject of prayer than we do. Some seven years ago this thought was brought to our attention, as some of you will remember. The idea originated, I believe, with Peter H. Clark, and after consultation, an address was issued "To the Colored People of the United States and Their Friends," calling upon them to set apart a day for special prayer. After setting forth the sad condition of our people, the unjust discriminations against us, the brutal manner in which we are treated in the South, and the seeming inability or indisposition of those in authority to protect us, it closes in these words:

> To whom, then, can we turn, save to the Lord God; to him who has the power to enlighten and soften men's hearts; to him, who brought Israel out of bondage with many signs and wonders; to him, who recently in the history of our country caused the wrath of man to praise him, and forced from the unwilling hand of Abraham Lincoln the Emancipation Proclamation. Let us turn to him:—

> We therefore request you to set aside the thirty-first day of May next as a day of humiliation, fasting, and prayer. Let the more devout fast faithfully. Let all pray. Let the farmer leave his plough, the mechanic his bench, the business man his shop, let the schoolmaster secure for himself and pupils a vacation, let those employed as household servants get leave of absence.
>
> Let us meet in our places of worship, and there, led by our ministers, devoutly pray to Almighty God: First, That if it is our fault that the hearts of our fellow countrymen are so cruelly turned against us, He will show us the evil, and give us the wisdom to remove it. Second: That our white fellow citizens may be made to see that the only security for the continuance of Republican institutions is found in the observance of law by all, however powerful, and by the extension of its protection to all, however weak; that he will make them see that in permitting these lynchings they are sowing a wind which will grow a whirlwind in the time of their children.
>
> Finally, that they will remember our lately enslaved condition, that they will not forget our centuries of toil without requital upon the fields of their fathers, and that instead of visiting us with proscription and murder, they will be patient with our shortcomings and encourage us to rise to that level of intelligence and virtue which marks the character of a good citizen.

This address was signed by Peter H. Clark, Frederick Douglass, Bishops Daniel A. Payne, Benjamin T. Tanner, and A. W. Wayman, Booker T. Washington, J. C. Price, Albion W. Tourgee, T. Thomas Fortune, W. S. Scarborough, Frances E. Harper, George T. Downing, John M. Langston, and many other representative men and women. It was printed, I believe, in all of the colored newspapers throughout the country, and was very generally observed. Hundreds and thousands of our people met in their respective places of worship, and gave themselves up to prayer. It attracted very wide attention: it was noticed in many of the leading journals of the country. In an editorial in the

New York Evangelist, of June 2, the editor, in commenting upon it, said, "The fact that the colored people of the United States spent Tuesday of this week as a day of fasting and prayer to Almighty God, that he would deliver their race from persecution and injustice, and grant them the free enjoyment of life, liberty, the pursuit of happiness and full protection in their persons, homes, and in the exercise of all legal rights and privileges in every part of the American Union, is one that may well give Christians pause. It is a solemn thing when seven millions of souls, however poor and humble they may be, carry their appeal from man's injustice to the bar of the Almighty. It is a serious matter for a nation when any body of people, however, few, betake themselves not to revolt, but to prayer."

This is a line of attack upon our enemies that we cannot afford to lose sight of. I do most earnestly wish, therefore, that the suggestion which was made in the address which was issued nearly seven years ago might be revived. And, that in addition to the setting apart a day annually for prayer in our churches, all believers might be urged to bring the matter to the attention of God, also in their private devotions. Praying only once a year won't do; praying in public and by the ministers only won't do; there must be constant prayer, every day, and by all of God's people. In the church, in our Endeavor meetings, in our Sabbath school gatherings, at the family altar, and in the secret chamber, on weekdays and Sabbath days, by clergy and laity,—the whole religious strength of the race ought to be brought to bear upon the subject, the cry that goes up to heaven ought to be the cry of a united people, of all who believe in God and in the power of prayer.

What are we to pray for? For self-effacement, political or otherwise? No. For a cowardly and unmanly spirit of submission to outrage, without entering a protest? No. For quiet acquiescence in the desire to keep us poor and ignorant, mere hewers of wood and drawers of water, to make of us a mere servile race? No, emphatically no! What are we to pray for, then? (1). That God would help us by His grace to be true men and women; that He would put deep down into our souls a divine unrest, a holy ambition to be something, and to make something of ourselves; that He would kindle in our heart of hearts a desire for the things that are true, and just, and pure, and lovely, and of good report; that he would help us all to come in the unity of the faith and of the knowledge of the Son of God, unto a perfect man, unto the measure of the stature of the fullness of Christ. What we need is development along every line that makes for righteousness, for a better, purer, nobler manhood and womanhood. It is our duty to pray to God to help us, to put his great, strong arm under us while we struggle up the steep and difficult ascent "on stepping stones of our dead selves to higher things."

We have faults, of course, and very serious ones; this no one has ever denied. It would be strange if we had not, after two hundred and fifty years of slavery, an institution which attached no importance whatever to virtue, and which ignored entirely the family idea. The very purpose of slavery was to make the Negro a mere beast of burden, to degrade him to the level of the brute. That anything was left in him, upon which to rear the superstructure of a self-respecting manhood and womanhood, is the marvel.

The white race itself is not free from faults. It has had more than a thousand years of culture and civilization behind it, and yet it has faults and very serious ones. If I were disposed to draw an indictment against it, I think I could draw a very strong one, one that would not be very flattering to its pride. I think the faults of the Negro, measured by the divine standard, are not a whit worse than those of the whites. In many respects their sins are the same. The Negro is said to be licentious; well, so are the whites. Are all white men paragons of virtue? Where did all the mulattoes in the South come from? Were the old masters forced by their black slaves to part with their virtue, or was the reverse true? Were the slaves the aggressors, or the masters? And today, the South, that holds up its hands in holy horror at the thought of miscegenation, thinks nothing of the illicit intercourse between white men and colored women. In the last Constitutional Convention of South Carolina, Section 34 of the new Constitution reads as follows: "The marriage of a white person with a Negro or with a mulatto, or person who shall have one-eighth or more of Negro blood, shall be unlawful and void." To this section, the Hon. Robert Smalls proposed an amendment, adding after the word "void," in the second line, the words, "and any white person who lives and cohabits with a Negro, mulatto, or person who shall have one-eighth or more of Negro blood, shall be disqualified from holding any office of emolument or trust in this State, and the offspring of any such living or cohabiting shall bear the name of the father, and shall be entitled to inherit and acquire property the same as if they were legitimate."

In support of this amendment, Mr. Smalls said, among other things: "This entire matter, sir, has no right in the Constitution of the State. If your women are as pure as you stated, and I have reason to believe that they are, they can be trusted; then why the necessity of this being placed in the Constitution? Can you not trust yourselves? Is it because these wrongs that have been perpetrated here since the formation of the government, make you feel that you cannot be trusted? When I say you, I mean the white men of the entire State. I fear not; hence I trust the amendment will be adopted. These wrongs have been done, and are still being done. They are not done by colored men; they are done by white men. If a Negro should improperly approach a white woman, his body would be hanging on the nearest tree, filled with airholes, before daylight next morning, and perhaps, properly so. If the same rule applied on the other side, and white men who insulted or debauched Negro women were treated likewise, this convention would have to be adjourned sine die for lack of a quorum." At this point he was called to order by some member on the floor, to which he made this reply: "The gentleman called me to order, stating that I had reflected on the convention. I do not wish to reflect on the convention, but do say, that if he has clean hands, he will keep his seat, because I do mean to reflect on any man who objects to the intermarriage of a Negro or a mulatto woman with a white man, and is not willing to prohibit the cohabitation, which is the root and branch of the evil. Stop this evil, and there will be no occasion for your intermarriage law." And yet, in the face of this pointed speech, incredible as it may seem, the amendment was defeated: every white man voting against it. That proves conclusively of course, that licentiousness is a sin peculiar to the Negro, that white men are never guilty of violating the Seventh Commandment.

Another charge made against the Negro is that he will steal: that is also a sin peculiar to the race. White men never steal, of course. Who are all these absconding bank cashiers and other trusted officials that I read of from time to time in the newspapers? Are they white men or colored men? Who are the men who adulterate our food products, who run up prices by forming iniquitous combinations of various kinds, and in this way, by overcharging, rob the consumers of millions of dollars? Are they white men or colored men? The only difference that I can see between the two races is, that the one steals on a small scale, the other on a large scale,—the one takes a few dollars, or a few dollars' worth, the other takes hundreds and thousands of dollars. The one kind of stealing is regarded, I know, as more respectable than the other, but it is stealing all the same. It is safe to conclude that stealing is as much a peculiarity of one race as the other.

One of the things that I have never been able to understand, is the lofty, self-complacent air with which the white man deals with the faults and imperfections of the Negro. It is always on the assumption that he is all right, and that the Negro is all wrong. It never seems to occur to him that he has any faults at all; if he happens to be guilty of the same offense, it becomes very much less heinous in him. A violation of the Seventh Commandment makes the Negro a low brute; the white man, especially if it happens to be with a woman not of his own race, still remains a gentleman, is guilty only of a little indiscretion. Who ever heard, in all the Southland, with its boasted civilization, and its hypocritical cant about the fear of contamination with an inferior race, of a white man being ostracized, shut out from respectable society, because of his known intimacy with a woman of another color? That kind of thing, according to the moral standard in vogue there, is either not regarded as a sin, or is winked at.

The white man seems to be surprised that the Negro is not perfect, that he is not a paragon of all the virtues; he is constantly abusing him, applying all kinds of vile epithets to him, because he is no better than he is. Of course, he isn't perfect. It is unreasonable to expect him to be perfect. You can't perfect a race in a single generation: and nobody knows that better than the white man himself; and he of all men ought to be the last one to upbraid him. Yes, the Negro has faults, but that is no reason why he should be shot down like a dog, why his rights, civil and political, should be trampled in the dust, why he should be treated in the brutal and inhuman manner in which he has been treated in the South. You can't make a better man by that kind of treatment. If you think he needs reforming, if you want to improve his condition, you have got to use other methods, you have got to come to him in a different spirit. You can't play the part of the bully, the ruffian, and hope to have any influence with him for good; you can't put your foot on his neck, deny his manhood, treat him as an inferior, as fit only to be a servant, and hope to have him profit by anything that you may say to him. He may be helped, he needs help, but you have got to clear out of his way the bloody murders that throw themselves athwart his pathway, you have got to set him a better example. If the white man wants to help the Negro to be a better man, he must begin to be a better man himself, to stop all of his meanness. After that bloody, murderous, treasonable assault at Wilmington upon law and order and the most sacred rights of man, it was one of the paragons of the pulpit in that city, even our great Doctor Hoge, who said: "Now having cast out Negro leaders, let us prove to the Negroes that we are really their true friends. We must look more closely after their industrial life, and by precept and example must teach them the gospel of Christ as a religion, not of emotion, but of life and conduct." Is there any wonder that the Negro is no better than he is with such examples before him, with such beautiful exponents of Christianity for his guide? Men holding themselves up as examples, who the day before had dyed their hands in their brothers' blood.

But to return from this digression,—in laying hold of this mighty instrument of prayer in relation to ourselves, let us not forget that we have shortcomings, that we are not by any means all that we ought to be, and that God can help us to overcome the evil that is in us, to break the fetters of sin that bind us, and make us freemen indeed. The individual who lays hold of God in the struggle upward against his lower nature, is sure to succeed. And so with a race; when it begins reaching out after God in earnest prayer for strength to overcome its besetting sins, it is sure to prevail. Pray? Yes, let us pray, pray without ceasing, that God would not only help us to build ourselves up in the great and positive elements that go to make up a true manhood and womanhood, but also that he would help us with his own great might to resist with all the energy of our natures the things which stand in the way of our progress, which tend to drag us down. Prayer can help us in this struggle,—let us lay hold of it. Let us make the most of it. But (2) in praying we must not stop with self, ***we must not forget to pray also for those who are oppressing us, who have their heels upon our necks***, and whose cry is "this is a white man's government." Jesus himself says, "Pray for them which despitefully use and persecute you." An elder in the Mormon church was once reminded that it was his duty to pray for his enemies: he said, "I do pray for them, I pray that God would damn them and send them down to hell." That is what we would naturally be inclined to do; that is what doubtless many of us have often done; but that is not the kind of prayer that I am talking about: It never can be right for us to pray such a prayer. We are to ***pray that God would have mercy upon them; that he would open their blind eyes, that he would show them the error of their ways,*** that he would quicken their dead consciences, and soften their hard hearts, and lead them to conform to principles of right, of justice and humanity. Prayer can do wonders in this respect. You remember how Esau felt towards Jacob: he hated him with perfect hatred, he had murder in his heart: he would have killed him had he met him at the time. And even after the lapse of twenty years, the old feeling was still there. When he heard of his return, he started to meet him with a strong band of armed men.

Poor Jacob was terrified, and fell upon his knees in earnest prayer to God for deliverance. "And Jacob said, O God of my father Abraham, and God of my father Isaac, the Lord which said unto me, Return into thy country, and to thy kindred, and I will deal well with thee, I am not worthy of the least of all thy mercies, and of all the truth which thou hast showed to thy servant, for with my staff I passed over this Jordan, and now I am become two bands. Deliver me I pray thee from the hand of my brother Esau; for I fear him, lest he will come and smite me, and the mother with the children." And with what result we all know. The record is, "And Jacob lifted up his eyes and looked, and behold Esau came, and with him four hundred men." And what? There was a conflict, and Jacob and his whole family were annihilated? Not at all. "And Esau ran to meet him, and embraced him, and fell on his neck and kissed him, and they wept." All the old grudge, the old bitterness and hatred, were taken out of him, and love,—beautiful, tender, sympathetic love,—took its place. A mighty transformation was wrought in answer to prayer. The two brothers, long estranged, were again brought together on terms of friendship: we see them in each other's arms, weeping on each other's necks. And in this there is a hint for us as a people in our relations with the Southern whites. We can do in our imperiled condition among them, just what Jacob did in the dire emergency which confronted him,—betake ourselves to prayer: and the same God who interposed to soften the heart of Esau will also interpose in our behalf.

How are we to pray? In what spirit are we to pray? We are to pray,—whether for ourselves or for the Southern whites,—if we are to succeed, in the same humble, earnest, persistent, and loving spirit that Jacob did. He came to God in the attitude of a humble suppliant, in the consciousness of his own weakness and imperfections. "I am not worthy of the least of all thy mercies," is the opening sentence of his appeal. It was not in the spirit of self-righteousness, but of humble penitence that he came: so must we.

He came to God in a spirit of deep earnestness. His whole soul cried unto God for deliverance from his brother Esau. It came up from great depths of his nature, and expressed a need that was most keenly felt by him: so it must be with us.

He came to God in the spirit of resolute determination to get what he wanted. All night he wrestled with God in prayer. And as the day began to dawn, the angel said, "Let me go, Jacob;" but his reply was, "I will not let thee go till thou bless me." And he did not let him go until he had the assurance that he had prevailed; so must we. If we are not in earnest, dead in earnest, are not animated by a spirit that will not take nay as an answer, we cannot, will not succeed.

He came to God in the spirit of love: there is no evidence of any bitterness or hatred on his part towards his brother. This was the spirit exhibited by the Lord Jesus Christ upon the cross when He prayed, "Father, forgive them,"—his murderers, the men who had nailed Him to the cross, and who were looking on with fiendish delight as his life was ebbing away; and the spirit that was exhibited by Stephen, while he was being stoned to death, when he said: "Lord, lay not this sin to their charge." And this is the spirit in which we must come to God. It is not an easy thing to do, I admit. When we think of all that we have suffered and are still suffering in the South,—of the hundreds and thousands of our people who have been shot down, murdered in cold blood, and of all the other villainous acts that have been perpetrated upon us, with a view of humiliating us, of crushing the manhood out of us, it is very difficult not to feel some bitterness, not to be full of hate. But if we are to have any influence with God, in this matter, we have got to get rid of that feeling. God will not answer our prayers, if we come in any such spirit. And, therefore, I am especially anxious that this element of prayer should enter into the great problem which we are seeking to solve in this country, for our own sakes, as well as for the sake of the whites. It will do them good to have us pray for them, and it will do us good to pray for them, since it will have the effect, if we enter into it with the purpose and determination of succeeding, of rooting out of our hearts that bitterness, which these awful outrages which are constantly occurring in the South tend to engender. It will be a good thing for us as a race, if we can get into an attitude of prayer, and keep in that attitude. It will put us in touch with God, and keep us in touch with Him. And then, the gates of hell will not be able to prevail against us.

I believe in the reality of prayer. I believe in the power of prayer. I believe that our cause can be helped by prayer. This doesn't mean that we are to do nothing but pray, that we are to fold our arms and expect God to fight our battles for us: nor does it mean that we are not to stand up for our rights, that we are not to agitate, and protest against wrong,—the agitation must go on; the demand which we are making for equal recognition of our rights, civil and political, under the Constitution, must never be relinquished,—what it means is, that in the midst of the conflict, while we are doing all we can, while we are seeking to make the most of ourselves and of our opportunities, we are at the same time to lay fast hold of the Almighty, to keep ourselves and our wants ever before Him, and to look to him for help in every time of need. "Wait on the Lord," is the exhortation; look to Him for strength, for courage, for wisdom to guide, to direct: in a word, don't attempt to lift this great weight that is pressing upon you, and holding you down, in this country, in your own strength; don't attempt to fight your battles alone, with human instruments alone; link yourself with God, take Him into your confidence; look to Him, rely upon Him.

With this wonderful thought before us,—the thought that in this struggle through which we are passing in this country, it is possible to have the Almighty associated with us,—together with the encouraging signs to which our attention was directed on last Sabbath, if I am asked, What of the night, for the Negro race in this country? I say, unhesitatingly, Well. There is a future here for us; in this land there are better things in store for us.

Out of the dark the circling sphere
Is rounding onward to the light;
We see not yet the full day here,
But we do see the paling light;

And Hope, that lights her fadeless fires,
And Faith, that shines, a heavenly will,
And Love, that courage re-inspires,—
These stars have been above us still.
O sentinels whose tread we heard
Through long hours, when we could not see,
Pause now; exchange with cheer the word,—
The unchanging watchword, Liberty.
Look backward, how much has been won!
Look round, how much is yet to win!
The watchers of the night are done;
The watchers of the day begin.
O Thou, whose mighty patience holds
The night and day alike in view,
Thy will our dearest hope enfolds:
O keep us steadfast, patient, true.

I have had a three-fold object in preaching these sermons: (1). To let the white people know that we are conscious of what our rights are, and that we mean to have them. (2). The hope of helping to awaken the sleeping conscience of the American people to the wrongs that we are suffering. And (3) to inspire those of our own people, who may be disposed to become despondent, with hope and with renewed determination to keep up the struggle.

I thank you for the patience with which you have listened to me during these weeks: and trust that all of us realize, as we have never done before, the seriousness of the task that is before us. The uplifting of a race, with all the tremendous odds against us in this land, is no child's play. It requires work, hard work; true and brave hearts:—

Men of faith, and not of faction,
Men of lofty aim in action,
Strong and stalwart ones;
Men whom highest hope inspires,
Men whom purest honor fires,
Men who trample self beneath them,
Men who never fail their brothers,
True, however false are others.

May God make us such men and women: and to this work may we, one and all, dedicate ourselves today. Whatever we can do, as individuals, as families, as churches, to lift ourselves, and this race with which we are identified, to higher levels, let us do it, and do it with our might.

"O small beginnings, ye are great and strong, Based on a faithful heart and weariless brain." And these we must have,—"the faithful heart, and the weariless brain," if we are to "build the future fair, and conquer wrong."[1]

[1] Grimké, *Works I*, 274–90.

APPENDIX IV

HISTORICAL ARCHIVE: SERMON'S OF FRANCIS JAMES GRIMKÉ

Prominent Notes of an Evangelical Activist: Three Decades of Activist Preaching

Grimké's theological conservatism was evident in his commitment to biblical authority and the person and work of Christ. However, his commitment did not prevent him from engaging in social activism; rather, it propelled him into it.

A Thirty-Year Survey: Socially Charged Sermons of an Evangelical Activist

What sets Grimké apart as a gospel preacher is his ability to harmonize the threads of biblicism, crucicentrism, conversionism, and activism into a cohesive and compelling narrative that calls for both personal and societal transformation. He emphasized the need for the regeneration of individual hearts, but he also insisted that true conversion must manifest in a commitment to social justice. For Grimké, the cross of Christ was not just a symbol of personal salvation, but also a powerful indictment against all forms of oppression and injustice. His sermons often challenged his congregation and the broader church to examine their own complicity in the systems of racial injustice and to take concrete action to address these wrongs. In this way, Grimké's preaching was both deeply spiritual and unapologetically political, reflecting his belief that the gospel demanded nothing less.

The titles and dates, in and of themselves, are telling:

- The Afro-American Pulpit in Relation to Race Elevation, *1892.*
- Frederick Douglass, *March 10, 1898.*

- Its Causes: A Low State of Civilization and Race Hatred, *June 4, 1899.*
- Its Causes: The Crimes of the Negro, *June 18, 1899.*
- The Remedy for the Present Strained Relations between the Races in the South, *June 25, 1899.*
- Sources from Which No Help May be Expected—The General Government, Political Parties, *November 27, 1900.*
- Signs of a Brighter Future, *December 4, 1900.*
- God, and Prayer as Factors in the Struggle, *December 11, 1900.*
- The Roosevelt–Washington Episode, or Race Prejudice, *October 27, 1901.*
- A Resemblance and a Contrast between the American Negro and the Children of Israel in Egypt, *October 12, 1902.*
- God and the Race Problem, *May 3, 1903.*
- Things of Paramount Importance in the Development of the Negro Race, *March 29, 1903.*
- The Negro and His Citizenship, *1905.*
- The Atlanta Riot, *October 7, 1906.*
- Discouragements, Hostility of the Press, Silence and Cowardice of the Pulpit, *November 20, 1909.*
- Equality of Rights for All Citizens, Black and White, Alike, *March 27, 1909.*
- Thanks to Mr. Andrew Carnegie on Behalf of the Trustees of Howard University, *April 25, 1910.*
- Christianity and Race Prejudice, *May 29, 1910* and *June 5, 1910.*
- The Paramount Importance of Character, or Character, the True Standard by which to Estimate Individuals and Races, *October 27, 1911.*
- Fifty Years of Freedom, with Matters of Importance to both the White and Colored People of the United States, *October 26, 1913.*

- Excerpts from a Thanksgiving Sermon and Two Letters Addressed to Woodrow Wilson, *November 26, 1914.*
- Evangelism and Institutes of Evangelism, *1916.*
- Lincoln University Alone of Negro Institutions Shuts Colored Men Out of Its Trustee Board and Out of Its Professorships, *March, 1916.*
- Anniversary Address on the Occasion of the Seventy-Fifth Anniversary of the Fifteenth Street Presbyterian Church, Washington, DC, *November 19, 1916.*
- "Billy" Sunday's Campaign in Washington, DC, *March, 1918.*
- Victory for the Allies and the United States a Ground of Rejoicing, of Thanksgiving, *November 24, 1918.*
- A Special Christmas Message in View of Present World Conditions, *December 22, 1918.*
- Address of Welcome Given at a Reception Tendered to the Men Who Have Returned from the Battlefront, *April 24, 1919.*
- The Race Problem—Two Suggestions as to Its Solution, *1919.*
- The Race Problem as It Respects the Colored People and the Christian Church in the Light of the Developments of the Last Year, *November 27, 1919.*
- The National Association for the Advancement of Colored People, Its Value—Its Aims—Its Claims, *April 24, 1921.*

This brief linear survey of Grimké's socially charged sermons that garnered national attention from the pulpit to the public square not only reveals his profound impact on both church and society, but also sets the stage for a deeper exploration of the common themes and notes that define his work.

Grimké, the Evangelical Activist: Common Notes in the Corpus

We now aim to capture the theological and social evolution of Grimké over a span of several decades. These sermons, delivered between 1899 and 1919, reveal the depth of Grimké's commitment to the principles of Christianity as he navigated the turbulent waters of racial prejudice, social reform, and the role of the church in upholding the teachings of Christ in an America grappling with its racial conscience.

As Grimké confronted the racial crises of his time—ranging from the Atlanta riots to the systemic injustices perpetuated by a largely silent church—he wielded his pulpit as a platform for advocacy, demanding that Christian faith be measured not just by personal piety, but also by its capacity to challenge and transform the societal norms that perpetuated inequality and oppression.

Seven Pivotal Sermons: Two Decades of Activist Preaching

Sermon 1—The Remedy for the Present Strained Relations Between the Races in the South

In this sermon, delivered June 25, 1899, Grimké addresses the ongoing racial tensions in the South and advocates for a return to Christian principles as the solution to these problems. He emphasizes the importance of education, moral uplift, and the application of biblical teachings as the key to resolving racial conflicts. Grimké argues in this sermon, "The church is in a position to wield a tremendous influence in this matter, if it will only arouse itself to a sense of its responsibilities, and will have the courage to do what it knows to be right." This sermon highlights the centrality of Christian teachings in addressing social issues and calls for a moral and spiritual transformation of society, starting with the church.[1]

Sermon 2—A Resemblance and a Contrast between the American Negro and the Children of Israel in Egypt

This sermon, delivered October 12, 1902, draws parallels between the experiences of African Americans and the Children of

---

[1] Quotes are sourced in the relevant sermons. Full manuscripts are included in the appendix.

Israel in Egypt, highlighting the similarities in their struggles for freedom and justice. Grimké emphasizes the importance of perseverance and faith in the face of adversity, arguing that African Americans, like the Children of Israel, must contend earnestly for their rights. He argues that, just as the children of Israel were called upon to stand firm and fight for their freedom, so too must the American Negro be steadfast in his pursuit of the rights guaranteed under the Constitution. The sermon serves as a call to action, urging African Americans to remain vigilant in their fight for justice and equality.

Sermon 3—God and the Race Problem

This sermon, delivered on May 3, 1903, addresses the persistent racial injustices faced by African Americans, urging his audience to find solace and strength in their faith in God. He emphasizes that despite the growing hostility and challenges, African Americans must rely on God as their refuge and strength, drawing from the biblical assurance that God is an ever-present help in times of trouble. Grimké calls for a collective spiritual renewal and steadfastness, reminding his listeners that their ultimate victory over oppression lies in their unwavering trust in God's guidance and justice. Through this sermon, he reinforces the importance of maintaining dignity, moral integrity, and a deep spiritual connection as the foundation for overcoming racial adversity.

Sermon 4—The Atlanta Riot

In this sermon, delivered October 7, 1906, Grimké addresses the violent race riots that occurred in Atlanta, condemning the brutality and injustice of the attacks on African Americans. He critiques the societal structures that allow such violence to occur and calls for a collective awakening to the injustices faced by black Americans. Grimké warns that the Atlanta Riot is a stark reminder of the deep-seated racial hatred that continues to plague the nation. He then persuasively lifts it as a call to all men of good conscience to stand up against this evil and demand justice for the oppressed. This sermon emphasizes the need for societal change and the importance of addressing the root causes of racial violence.

Sermon 5—The Paramount Importance of Character, or Character, the True Standard by which to Estimate Individuals and Races

This sermon, delivered October 27, 1911, emphasizes the importance of character as the true measure of an individual or race. Grimké argues that moral integrity and uprightness should be the standards by which people are judged, rather than race or social status. He asserts that "God is no respecter of persons;" it is a character that counts with Him, and the same should be true for Christians. The sermon calls for a rejection of racial prejudice and an embrace of the biblical principle of judging others based on their moral character.

Sermon 6—Evangelism and Institutes of Evangelism

In this sermon, delivered in 1916, Grimké critiques the superficial nature of much of the evangelism practiced in America, particularly among white Christians. He argues that true evangelism should lead to a genuine transformation of character and a commitment to justice, rather than simply a nominal acceptance of Christian beliefs. Grimké laments, "Away with all this hypocrisy! Let us get down to bedrock, to fundamentals, to essential principles of Christianity. Let us have an evangelism . . . that will keep off evangelistic committees . . . men who are so unchristian as to be influenced by this wicked and contemptible spirit of race prejudice." This sermon emphasizes the need for an authentic application of Christian teachings in the lives of believers, particularly those serving in church leadership.

Sermon 7—The Race Problem as it Respects the Colored People and the Christian Church, in the Light of the Developments of the Last Year

Delivered on November 27, 1919, in the aftermath of World War I, this sermon reflects on the continued racial struggles faced by African

Americans despite the supposed advances in democracy. Grimké highlights the persistence of lynchings, growing racial prejudice, and the failure of the government to protect black citizens. He notes the increasing awareness among African Americans of their constitutional rights and emphasizes the necessity of self-defense in the face of unrelenting violence. Grimké critiques the Christian church for its failure to address racial injustices, arguing, the "so-called Christian church" had failed utterly in its mission to bring about the kingdom of God on earth, so long as it remained silent on the question of race prejudice. This sermon reflects Grimké's growing frustration with the lack of progress in racial justice and the church's complicity in maintaining the status quo.

Summary

These sermons, delivered across different periods and contexts, reflect Grimké's evolving approach to addressing the racial issues of his time. The earlier sermons, such as *The Remedy for the Present Strained Relations* and *A Resemblance and a Contrast between the American Negro and the Children of Israel in Egypt,* are deeply rooted in biblical teachings and emphasize the need for a moral and spiritual transformation guided by Christian principles. Grimké's belief in the power of the Gospel to bring about societal change is evident when he states, "Only the power of the Gospel can change the hearts of men and lead them to live together in peace."

In contrast, the later sermons, particularly *The Race Problem as it Respects the Colored People and the Christian Church, in the Light of the Developments of the Last Year,* reflect a growing frustration with the lack of progress in racial justice and the church's complicity in maintaining the status quo. Grimké emphasizes the need for activism and self-defense in the face of continued racial violence, urging African Americans to take a more active role in defending their rights. He critiques the Christian church for failing to live up to its ideals, essentially asserting that the church had failed to live out the gospel it preached, and that until it did, there would be no true peace in the land.

Across all these sermons, Grimké's unwavering commitment to justice and his belief in the power of Christian teachings to bring about meaningful social change remain central. His voice, resolute and prophetic, calls upon his listeners to align their lives with the true principles of the Gospel, urging them to confront and dismantle the racial injustices that plague society. Grimké's sermons are not just rhetorical; they are a call to embody the transformative power of Christian faith in the pursuit of justice, urging a moral reckoning that requires more than passive belief—it demands active, faithful engagement.

To preserve the depth and nuance of Grimké's preaching, full transcripts of the sermons are herein included. On that wise, a great debt is owed to Woodson for cataloging Grimké's manuscripts and journals more than four score years ago. Only minor editorial adjustments, for clarity's sake, have been made. Intentionally brief footnote annotations are included in each manuscript to highlight Grimke's EEH. These transcripts are vital for preserving the work of a voice whose contributions, particularly in the realm of preaching, have not been extensively studied.

In summary, Grimké's textual and thematic accents hint at echoes of patterns found in Pauline epistles. His sermons, intentionally or otherwise, betray a deep resonance with Paul's teachings, whose writings are foundational to Grimké's evangelical and Reformed heritage.

Sermon 1

The Remedy for the Present Strained Relations Between the Races in the South[2]

[2] Grimké, *Works I*, 317–33. Delivered June 25, 1899.

Then they cried with a loud voice, and stopped their ears, and ran upon him with one accord, and cast him out of the city, and stoned him.
—Acts 7:57

In my last discourse, after calling attention to the awful possibilities that lie wrapped up in a continuance of the present condition of things in the South, and of the duty of all who are interested in the welfare of our common country, and of the progress of the kingdom of righteousness in the earth, to do whatever they can to avert the impending danger, two questions were asked:

1. Is there any remedy for the present condition of things?
2. If so, what is the remedy?

These are the questions which I desire to take up and discuss this morning.

I. Is There Any Remedy?

I believe there is. The present strained condition between the races in the South is not, I believe, an incurable one. There is nothing in the nature of the Southern white man as such, or in the nature of the Negro as such, which renders it impossible for them to live together in harmony, and in mutual respect for each other. These two races have lived together harmoniously in the past, and they may in the future. There is every reason to believe they will under proper influences, and after sufficient time has elapsed for the passions to subside, and for reason and conscience to assert themselves. Already, as a matter of fact, there are Southern white men—men who were cradled in the lap of slavery and who fought for the Lost Cause—who have come, in the process of development, to where they find no difficulty in thus mingling with their black fellow citizens and neighbors.

I remember some years ago reading a very interesting letter from a missionary of the Southern Presbyterian Church who was laboring in Brazil. He spoke particularly of the fact that he was raised in the

South, where he had been taught to look down upon colored people as inferiors and to treat them as such, but that since his stay in Brazil, a great change had come over him in this respect, so much so that he hardly knew himself. "The questions that perplex us in the South," he said, "never rise to trouble us here." And, if I may be permitted to speak from personal experience, I can truthfully say that one of the few white men that I have had close personal contact with during my life, and who was as free from colorphobia as any white man I ever saw, was a Southern man. And the same may also be said of some of the most refined and cultivated Southern white women, whom I have had the pleasure of meeting. These, and other examples that might be adduced, show what the possibilities are, what may take place under favorable conditions.

II. What is the Remedy?

How is this change to be brought about? How are the present discordant elements to be harmonized? Out of this chaos of conflicting passions and interests, how are we to get order, beauty, harmony?

From a careful study of the situation, it is evident that certain things must occur if there is to be a change for the better:

1. The grade of civilization in the South must be raised.
2. The white man must modify his views of the Negro, or the Negro must modify his views of himself, i.e., must be willing to give up his ideas and accept the white man's ideas as to what he shall be and do, or as to what his social, civil, and political status shall be.
3. This element of hate in the white man must be eliminated.
4. The Negro must be elevated; the general plane upon which he lives must be raised.

Let us look at these several elements for a moment:

1. **Raising the Plane of Civilization in the South**: That there is room, and very great room for improvement in this respect will hardly be called into question by anyone acquainted with the facts. In every direction, the evidences of a low grade of civilization are apparent, and these are multiplying rather than diminishing. Neither will it be doubted that an improvement in this respect will be helpful in dealing with the race problem. As the grade of civilization goes up, the brutal instincts of our nature will become more and more subdued—the tendency, so widely prevalent in the South, to resort to brute force in the settlement of wrongs or supposed wrongs, will assert itself less and less, and there will grow up a greater respect for law and order.

2. **The Southern White Man's Views of the Negro**: Before asking any man to change or modify his views on any matter, we ought first to satisfy ourselves as to the character of his views—are they right views, or are they wrong views? If they are right, if they have reason and common sense and justice on their side, we have no right to ask him to change them; if they are not right, however, we may ask him to change or modify them, yea, it is our duty to do so. To the character of the Southern white man's view of the Negro, I desire therefore in this connection to direct attention.

   The Southern white man thinks that the Negro belongs to an inferior race, an inferiority not based upon circumstances, but inherent, inborn; in other words, that God created him inferior, and that in virtue of that inferiority, it is his duty to treat him as an inferior. The meaning of this, if I understand it correctly, is that the rules which obtain between one white man and another white man in their relations and dealings with each other, are not the rules which ought to obtain when the white man comes to deal with the colored man. A difference ought to be made, and that difference is due to the fact that the one is superior, and the other is inferior. That the underlying conception of the relation which the white race sustains to the black race, as here expressed, is untenable, is without foundation in fact, is evident from the Word of God. As we are living in a land where there are 135,000 ministers, 187,000 churches, and over 26,000,000 communicants in these churches; a land where there are 1,305,000 Sabbath school teachers, and 10,000,000 Sabbath school scholars; where there are more than 50,000 societies of Christian Endeavor and upwards of 3,500,000 members of such societies, we may assume that the Bible will have some weight in determining this question.

1. According to this book, which we receive as the inspired word of God, and the only infallible rule of faith and practice, God "hath made of one blood all nations of men," or as it is rendered in the Revised Version, "and made of one every nation of men." And this agrees with the statement in Genesis as to the origin of the race: "And God said, Let us make man in our image, after our likeness; and let them have dominion over the fish of the sea, and over the fowls of the air, and over the cattle, and over all the earth, and over every creeping thing that creepeth upon the earth. And God created man in his own image, in the image of God created he him; male and female created he them."

   The man thus created was Adam; and "for him God made a help-meet. He caused a deep sleep to fall upon him; and took one of his ribs and closed up the flesh instead thereof; and the rib which the Lord God had taken from the man he made a woman and brought her unto the man. And the man said, this is now bone of my bones, flesh of my flesh; she shall be called woman, because she was taken out of the man." In the third chapter and twentieth verse, we have also this record: "And the man called his wife's name Eve; because she was the mother of all living."

   Whatever views may be entertained as to the existence of a Pre-Adamite race, the record in Genesis, seventh, eighth, ninth, and tenth makes it perfectly plain that no such race at present exists upon the earth. For in Genesis 7:23 it is recorded: "And every living thing was destroyed which was upon the face of the ground, both man, and cattle, and creeping things, and fowls of heaven; and they were destroyed from the earth; and Noah only was left, and they that were with him in the ark." The sixth verse of the same chapter tells us who were with him: "And Noah went in, and his sons, and his wife, and his sons' wives with him, into the ark." According to the first statement, all who existed on the earth prior to the flood descended from Adam and Eve, all were created in the image of God. There isn't a hint or suggestion, or anything that could in any way be twisted into even so much as the semblance of an argument in support of the belief that some races were created superior to others, in the sense in which that term is used by the Southern whites in dealing with the race question. According to the second statement, all races now upon the earth have descended from the family of Noah; and since the Negro exists, he must therefore have also come from that family. If the Bible is to be accepted as authority, the equality of the Negro race in the great human family, with all other races, is thus put beyond all cavil or doubt. From the same parent stock as all the other races he has come. When the flood subsided and Noah and his three sons and their families came out of the ark, we have a miniature picture of the whole human race—you were there and I was there, the white man was there—the Southern white man and the Northern white man; we were all there, white and black alike; and we were there not as superiors and inferiors, but on terms of perfect equality, as members of the same family, having the same common rights and privileges.

2. According to this Book, which we receive as the inspired word of God, the moral standard which it reveals as the rule of life is the same for all races of men. The Ten

Commandments, the Sermon on the Mount, the great principles enunciated in the thirteenth chapter of First Corinthians are binding alike upon all races. The moral standard isn't one thing for the white race and another thing for the black race; it is the same for both. *Thou shalt not kill. Thou shalt not commit adultery. Thou shalt not bear false witness. Thou shalt not covet. Honor thy father and thy mother*—all are binding upon all men of all races. So far as the moral law is concerned, in its application, as revealed in the word of God, there isn't a single thing which favors in any way this idea of one race being created inferior to another. If such a thing existed, we would naturally expect to find the difference recognized in the standard of life prescribed for each, but no such difference is found. Since both are required to conform to the same standard, it is unphilosophical to assume such a difference. The Southern white man cannot consistently hold the Negro to the same moral standard as he does himself, and at the same time affirm his natural inferiority.

3. In the plan of salvation which this Book reveals, and which we receive as the inspired Word of God, no such difference is recognized. All men of all races stand upon precisely the same footing. All are invited. All are equally welcomed. The conditions imposed are the same for all. The same gospel is to be preached to all. All nations, the apostles were directed to go and disciple. And in the kingdom which the Lord Jesus Christ has set up in this world we are distinctly told, "There is neither Greek, nor Jew, barbarian, Scythian, bond, nor free." "There is one body, and one Spirit, even as ye are all called in one hope of your calling; one Lord, one faith, one baptism, one God and Father of all, who is above all, and through all, and in you all."

The Southern white man thinks that the rules which obtain in the relations of white men with white men are not the rules which ought to obtain in the relations of white men with black men. This Book, which is God's Book, however, recognizes no such distinction. It says, "*Thou shalt love the Lord thy God with all thy heart, and with all thy soul, and with all thy mind. This is the first and great commandment. And the second is like unto it— Thou shalt love thy neighbor as thyself. On these two commandments hang all the law and the prophets.*" And to the question, "*And who is my neighbor?*" the Lord Jesus answered by relating the parable of the Good Samaritan, which was intended particularly to show the spirit that should bind all men together, of whatever race or nationality. The neighbor that we are to love as ourselves is not the member of our own family, or nation, or race only; but any and everybody, of whatever race or nation—whether white, or black, or red, or brown, makes no difference. And the same is required by the rule laid down by Jesus in the Sermon on the Mount: "*Whatsoever ye would that men should do to you, do ye even so to them.*" It doesn't say white men are to treat white men as they would like to be treated, or that black men are to treat black men as they would like to be treated, but man as man in his relations with his fellow-men is to be governed by this rule.

The Southern white man thinks the Negro ought not to enjoy the same civil and political rights as white men enjoy. The result is, in traveling on railroads, he is not only put off to himself, but is forced to accept for the same fare much inferior accommodations to those which are accorded to white passengers. And, in hotel accommodations and restaurant service along the route of travel, no provision whatever is made for him. He must carry something to eat with him, or else he must endure the pangs of hunger until he reaches his journey's end. Hence also, the bull-dozing and other methods of intimidation that have been resorted to to keep him from the polls, and the various constitutional amendments that have been enacted to deprive him of the suffrage. Such a view is obviously, however, inconsistent with the spirit of the Declaration of Independence, is in direct violation of the provisions of the Constitution, and is contrary to the genius of republican or democratic institutions. In the Declaration of Independence it is asserted: "*We hold these truths to be self-evident, that all men are created equal; that they are endowed by their Creator with certain inalienable rights; that among these are life, liberty and the pursuit of happiness; that to secure these rights, governments are instituted among men, deriving their just powers from the consent of the governed.*" Article XIV of the Constitution declares: "*All persons born or naturalized in the United States and subject to the jurisdiction thereof are citizens of the United States and of the State wherein they reside.*" Article XV declares: "*The right of citizens of the United States to vote shall not be denied or abridged by the United States, or by any State, on account of race, color or previous condition of servitude.*" There are no rights guaranteed to white men under the Constitution that are not equally guaranteed to the colored man. All citizens, whether white or black, stand upon the same footing, are entitled to equal consideration. Distinction among citizens in rights, in privileges is the very thing which the democratic idea of government, which has had such a wonderful growth within the century, is intended to combat. From these and other considerations that might be adduced, it is evident that the Southern white man's view of the Negro is wrong. It is contrary to the Word of God; and it is contrary to the expressed provisions and declarations of the Constitution. The Negro is not by nature inferior, as he thinks; nor is he unworthy of being treated as other men are treated. He has a good heart and, if he is encouraged, will measure up to his responsibilities and opportunities just as other men.

3. **As to the Negro Modifying His Views of Himself**: What are his views of himself?

    1. He believes that he is a man; that the same God who created the white man created him; that in Genesis when it is said, "*in the image of God created he him, male and female created he them,*" he was included in that statement; and that whatever of dignity, therefore, there is that attaches to man as man, as a being created in the image of God, attaches to him.

    2. He believes that he is entitled to be treated as a man—humanely, civilly, with the ordinary consideration which one human being owes to another.

    3. He believes that he has the same right to live here as the white man has; that this is just as much his home as it is the white man's home. This is the only home that he has ever known. He has been here as long as the white man has been here. He has labored as hard for it as the white man has labored.

    4. He believes that he is an American citizen, and that as such he is entitled to enjoy the same rights and privileges as other citizens of the Republic.

    5. He believes that to the measure of his character and capacity the same opportunities ought to be afforded him of making an honest living and of improving himself as are afforded to other men.

Is he right or wrong in these assumptions? Are these things true of him, or are they not? Is he a man? Is he entitled to be treated as a man? Is this his home as much as it is the home of the white man? Is he an American citizen, and is he entitled to all the rights and privileges that are enjoyed by other citizens? Ought he to be free as other men are free, to make a place for himself in the struggle of life, conditioned only by his character and capacity? If these questions are answered in the affirmative, as they must be by every candid, right-thinking person, then it is not only unreasonable to expect the Negro to modify his views of himself, or to recede from his present position; it would be wrong to ask him to do so. He could not take any other position than the one he has taken and maintain his own self-respect or the respect of others.

4. **As to Eliminating this Element of Hate from the Breast of the White Man for the Negro**: Race hatred, whether by white men for black men or black men for white men, is wrong. It is an evil, an unqualified and unmitigated evil, that ought to be eradicated as soon as possible. It is bound to work injury to both races. No good can possibly come from it. Unless it can be removed, very little progress can be made toward the amicable settlement of this grave question, toward a better understanding between the races. That a change here is desirable will be readily admitted.

5. **As to the Moral Elevation of the Negro**: That there is need, and very great need, in this direction, the Negro himself frankly admits. He not only realizes that there is great room for improvement, but, to his credit, let it be said he has not been indifferent to the opportunities that have been afforded him for self-improvement. The moral elevation of the Negro is important not only for the Negro, but also for the white man. If these two races are to live side by side, neither can be indifferent to the moral status of the other. It is to the interest of the white man to have this black race elevated. Character is what the black man needs, and character is what the white man needs; and when you have developed the right kind of character in each, one great step will have been taken toward the solution of this race problem.

Reverting now to the question with which we began, namely, what is the remedy for the present condition of things in the South? How is a change for the better to be brought about? I answer, it is to be largely through education—social, political, moral, religious. There is need for light, for knowledge, for careful instruction, line upon line and precept upon precept, here a little and there a little. It is by the plain, simple, earnest, faithful presentation of the truth that we can hope to permanently dislodge error and so make it possible for the right to triumph. The prayer of the psalmist was: "*O send out thy light and thy truth.*" And that is what is needed today—light, truth—if these two races are ever to be lifted to where they can look each other in the face and feel toward each other as one human being should feel toward another human being, as one brother man should feel toward another brother man. A campaign of education, wisely, intelligently, fearlessly conducted, is what is needed.

Concerning this education, I observe:

1. **That It Is to Be Partly Destructive and Partly Constructive**: In the soil of the South certain ideas were planted more than two centuries ago, and they have been growing during all these years. These ideas grew out of the institution of slavery. Under such a system, very naturally, the Negro came to be regarded in a certain light, and to be treated in a certain way. He was scarcely looked upon as a human being. He was regarded as a mere beast of burden, a chattel, a piece of property, a thing to be bought and sold, with no rights which white men were bound to respect. That condition of things lasted for nearly two hundred and fifty years. During all that time the Negro had no voice in anything; he was not even permitted to say what disposition should be made of himself. In 1865, however, slavery was abolished, and the Negro became a free man, and later an American citizen, clothed with the sacred right of the ballot. In view of this change, it is evident that the old ideas which the masters had of the Negro as a slave are entirely out of place in the new order of things. These old ideas, therefore, must be uprooted and ideas in harmony with the new order of things must be implanted. The Negro, e.g., is not a mere beast of burden; he is a man, a human being, belonging to

> the same category as the white man. The Southern white man needs to be educated into a recognition of this fact, into the habit of thinking of the Negro as a human being, and not as some lower form of existence that puts him beyond the ordinary civilities of life. During the anti-slavery agitation in this country one of the things upon which special emphasis was laid in the beginning of that struggle was the fact that the Negro was a man. As the abolitionists went from place to place they kept saying to the people: The Negro is a man. The Negro is a man. The Negro is a man. And as that fact sank into their hearts, as they came to realize that the Negro was a human being just as they were, they came to see the iniquity of the slave system, and threw their influence against it. And so, in this work of education in the South, the same thing must be done. The humanity of the Negro must be held up and emphasized. Over and over again that thought must be presented. Everywhere that gospel must be proclaimed. You remember Whittier's noble lines in "The Branded Hand":

In the lone and long night-watches, sky above and wave below,
Thou didst learn a higher wisdom than the babbling schoolmen know;
God's stars and silence taught thee, as His angels only can,
That the one, sole, sacred thing beneath the scope of heaven is Man.
That he who treads profanely on the scrolls of law and creed,
In the depth of God's great goodness may find mercy in his need;
But woe to him who crushes the Soul with chain and rod,
And herds with lower natures the awful form of God.

And that is just what the Southern white man has been doing to the Negro, and the lesson which he needs to learn is, that the Negro is not to be herded "*with lower natures*," that he is a man, and must be recognized as such.

Again, the Negro is no longer a slave: he is a free man and an American citizen. As a free man and an American citizen there are certain rights that belong to him that the Southern white man must be educated to recognize and respect. He may not want to do it; he may find it difficult to bring himself to do it,—he will find it difficult to do, but since it is the right thing to do, it ought to be done. And the sooner the effort is made to mold public sentiment in accordance with what is right, the better it will be. The whole trend of education in the South should be towards bringing that section to conform its notions to the new order of things which has been brought about by freedom and which is required by the genius of our institutions.

Again, we are living under a republican form of government,—a government "of the people, by the people, for the people." The Southern white man needs to be educated to understand that the term "people," means not the white people only, but the black people as well, that all are included, without distinction of race or color. "This is a white man's government," is the shibboleth of Southern Democracy. That sentiment is widely prevalent in the South. And its meaning is that the same condition of things which existed during slavery shall be perpetuated under freedom. The aim is to make the Negro a political nonentity, to eliminate him entirely from politics. But the Negro can not be justly eliminated from politics under a republican form of government. To do so would be unrepublican. And therefore that sentiment cannot be allowed to stand: it must be changed. The Southern white man must be so educated that he will come to recognize the justness of the Negro's claim to equal recognition under the Constitution. The Negro is here, and he is here to stay: and to stay not as the civil and political inferior of the white man, but as his equal under the laws. And sooner or later that fact must be accepted, not in one section of the country,—in the North and not in the South,—but in every section of it. The right of the Negro as an American citizen must be recognized; and we must begin everywhere, but especially in the South, to educate public sentiment with that end in view. The education of which I am speaking, you will perceive, is not education in the ordinary sense of the term, in the knowledge of books, as carried on in the schools,—in the common schools, in the academies, colleges and universities, but education in the knowledge of the rights of man and respect for those rights; in the knowledge of the great principles underlying democratic institutions, as enunciated in the Declaration of Independence and in the Constitution, and in respect for those principles.

What are some of these rights and principles? The right to life, liberty and the pursuit of happiness; freedom of speech; freedom of the press; the right of petition; the right to a speedy and public trial by an impartial jury; the right not to be deprived of life, liberty, or property without due process of law; the right to the equal protection of the law; the right not to be discriminated against in the franchise on account of race, color, or previous condition of servitude. These are principles that ought to be dear to every true American, and they are principles that lie at the very foundation of democratic institutions. They are principles, however, that are but slightly regarded in the Southern section of our country. There is no freedom of speech there, no freedom of the press. Even white men, Northern white men or Southern white men, are not allowed to express sentiments not in keeping with Southern pro-slavery ideas. The man who does it does it at his peril. The reason why R. R. Tolbert of South Carolina is today an exile from his home is because he dared to differ with his neighbors. The intolerance of the South is one of its most characteristic features. There is no equal protection of the law, there is no impartial trial by jury. There may be for white men, but so far as the Negro is concerned, it is never thought of. There is scarcely a single principle that goes to make up a government of the people, by the people, for the people, that is not ruthlessly trampled underfoot in the South. There is great and pressing need therefore for the most earnest and aggressive educational work in that section along the lines that I have indicated. And the importance of the work lies, not only in its effects upon the South, but upon the whole country. You cannot trample upon democratic principles in one section of the country without feeling its injurious effects in every other part of it. The whole nation, therefore, is interested in this work of educating the South in respect for the rights of man, and for the great principles of democracy.

I. **That This Work of Education Is to Be Mainly Carried on by Ministers of the Gospel, by Editors, and Teachers**: They can do more than any other class of people to create a healthy public sentiment in favor of justice and humanity. To the ministers, especially, we have a right to look. They are God's representatives, called and commissioned to be the teachers of mankind, in all matters affecting character and life. The book which they are to expound is the Bible, the word of God, which the apostle tells us is "*profitable for doctrine, for reproof, for correction, for instruction in righteousness, that the man of God may be perfect, thoroughly furnished unto all good works.*" The men who fill the pulpits in the South know as well as they know that they exist, that the manner in which the Negro is treated there is not in harmony with the letter or spirit of that Word. It is their duty, therefore, to bring the teaching of that Word to bear upon present conditions, however unpopular it may be to do so. The gospel that teaches the fatherhood of God, the brotherhood of man, the spirit of sympathy, of love, of the strong bearing the infirmities of the weak, of the more fortunate coming to the help of the less fortunate, cannot be faithfully preached in the South without being blessed of God. It may not be popular at first, but it is bound sooner or later to triumph, if persisted in. God has promised that his word shall not return unto him void. I have the greatest faith in the efficacy of God's truth to win its way and bear down all opposition, if it is faithfully presented.

The press can also do much in this campaign of education. If the men who are at the head of the daily and weekly journals will use the opportunity which they have of inculcating right principles, of keeping before the people the great ideas underlying democratic institutions, of insisting upon law and order, and respect for the rights of others—for the humblest as well as the greatest—a new order of things will very soon set in.

The teacher can also aid very materially in this work, the teachers in the common schools as well as the higher schools of learning. In the higher schools of learning, where the leaders are being trained, what a splendid opportunity is afforded to a wise teacher who is anxious to correct false impressions, and to set things in their true light, as they ought to exist under our form of government, and under our

Christian civilization, to make his influence felt. And in the common schools the teacher can also be of very great service in helping to remove this bitter race feeling. If they have come to see and feel rightly themselves, they will have an influence over the children committed to their care. In the New England states, very much has been done through the schools to inculcate in the children sentiments of kindness to dumb animals. There has been a wonderful change in these states in this respect. And in the South, if the teachers would set themselves to work, a similar change could be wrought in the sentiments of the white child for the colored child. If the teachers themselves spoke respectfully of colored people, if the tendency on the part of white children to apply opprobrious epithets to colored children and to colored people in general was rebuked by the teacher, it would have its effect, and would hasten the coming of better times. The union of these forces—the working together of preacher, and teacher, and editor towards a reconstructed South founded upon sentiments of justice and humanity for all—white and black alike, is what is needed, and what must come sooner or later, if our present troubles are ever to end, if peace and harmony are to prevail.

II. **That the Place for This Work to Begin Is in the Church, i.e., Among the Professed Followers of Christ**: If there is any class of persons anywhere that we have a right to expect to act upon Christian principles, to treat a fellow being as he ought to be treated, to accord to him all his rights, it is those who make up the Christian Church. Christ's own words are, "*Ye are the light of the world. A city set on a hill cannot be hid. Neither do men light a candle and put it under a bushel, but on a candlestick; and it giveth light unto all that are in the house. Let your light so shine before men that they may see your good works, and glorify your Father which is in heaven.*" The church, therefore, is the place to begin this work.

Let the ministers, and elders, and deacons, and members, those who have come out from the world, and have taken upon themselves the name of Jesus, first get right themselves on this subject; let them accord to the Negro his rights as a citizen; let them treat him as he ought to be treated, as a man and brother, as is required by God's most holy law, which they profess to believe and to follow, and it will not be difficult to get those on the outside to fall into line. The church is in a position to wield a tremendous influence in this matter, if it will only arouse itself to a sense of its responsibilities, and will have the courage to do what it knows to be right. It ought to lead in this matter. Its members ought to set the example to those who make no profession. The time has come, when Christian men and women in the South should cease to consult their prejudices, to be influenced by the sentiments about them, and should look to God's Word, to the example of Jesus Christ, and the great principles which he enunciated and for which his kingdom stands, for light, for guidance in dealing with this race problem. If Christianity is worth anything, it ought to be able to adjust these differences; it is able to adjust them if the principles underlying it are followed. Here is the church's opportunity of demonstrating the power of Christianity to deal with the most difficult social problem. It was Bishop Haygood, I believe, who once said, "In the light of the Ten Commandments and the Sermon on the Mount, this race problem may be solved." And it may be, but in order to do this the Ten Commandments, and the Sermon on the Mount, must have back of them a living church—a church made up of men and women who are willing to take them up, and put them into their hearts, and live them out, regardless of whether they accord with the sentiments about them or not. The question, for the church, is not as to whether it is a popular thing to treat the Negro as a man, as a human being, as a brother; as to whether it accords with tradition, with custom, with public sentiment, but is it right? Is it as he ought to be treated? Is it as Jesus Christ would treat him if he were acting in our stead?[3] "Back to Christ," is the cry of certain theologians today,—and that is where the church needs to get in dealing with this race problem—back to the spirit of Christ, back to the great principles which he enunciated for the government of man—back to the fatherhood of God, to the brotherhood of man; back to loving our neighbor as ourselves, to doing by others as we would have them do by us. These are the great principles upon which the church ought to stand, and the spirit in which it ought to address itself to every problem, whether it be the Negro problem, or any other problem. In that spirit, it is bound to conquer. There are no difficulties that it may not overcome. If things do not get better in the South, the church will be largely responsible for it. It will be because it fails to do its duty—to lift up a standard for the people, to let its light shine.

Along with this should also be coupled strenuous efforts to improve the system of public education, both as to the quality of the teaching force, and the length of the school term for both races; and also to multiply and encourage all agencies, such as temperance societies, associations for the promotion of good citizenship, etc., that will tend to strengthen what is good, and to counteract what is evil in the community.

---

[3] Grimké's exhortation for the church to lead in racial justice embodies his EEH by rooting moral action in *Biblicism* and *Crucicentrism*—calling Christians to God's Word and Christ's example to subvert and overcome social prejudices. His emphasis on transformative influence reflects *Conversionism* and echoes Pauline praxis in Romans 12:2, urging believers to "not be conformed to this world" but to be renewed in mind, embodying and thereby proving God's will. By admonishing Christians to follow Christ's way "regardless of public sentiment," Grimké preaches an *Activism* that challenges the church to sustain a redemptive, culturally subversive witness over and against the inimical forces of the world's hostilities, especially among believers.

A campaign of education, wisely, intelligently, lovingly conducted along the lines indicated, and by the forces enumerated will do much towards bringing about a better condition of things in the South, toward adjusting race differences.

Wonders can be accomplished if we will only make up our minds to go steadily forward as God gives us the light, and with but one thought before us—the thought of pleasing him, of doing what is right. Those who are to work among the whites, and those who are to work among the colored should each come to the task with a due sense of the importance, the transcendent importance of the work, and with an earnest desire to succeed. These strifes and dissensions must cease; these race feuds must die out—but not by the sacrifice of a single principle, not by trampling upon the rights of anyone; but by each race doing what is right, by the triumph of law and order, and Christian principles—the principles of the Decalogue and the Sermon on the Mount. I have faith in those great principles, and faith in their ultimate triumph. The task is not an easy one, however; nor can it be accomplished in a day, or a week, or a month, or a year, or a decade of years; nor will it be accomplished without hardships, sufferings, discouragements. Bryant evidently foresaw all this when he penned his noble poem entitled *The Battlefield.*

Once this soft turf, this rivulet's sands,
Were trampled by a hurrying crowd,
And fiery hearts and armed hands
Encountered in the battle-cloud.
Ah never shall the land forget
How gushed the life-blood of her brave—
Gushed, warm with hope and courage yet,
Upon the soil they fought to save.
Now all is calm, and fresh, and still,
Alone the chirp of flitting bird,
And talk of children on the hill,

And bell of wandering kine are heard.
No solemn host goes trailing by,
The black mouthed gun and staggering wain;
Men start not at the battle-cry,
Oh, be it never heard again.
Soon rested those who fought; but thou
Who minglest in the harder strife
For truths which men receive not now,
Thy warfare only ends with life.
A friendless warfare, lingering long
Through weary day and weary year.
A wild and many-weaponed throng
Hang on thy front, and flank, and rear.
Yet nerve thy spirit to the proof,
And blench not at thy chosen lot.
The timid good may stand aloof,
The sage may frown,—yet faint thou not.
Nor heed the shaft too surely cast,
The foul and hissing bolt of scorn;
For with thy side shall dwell, at last,
The victory of endurance born.
Truth, crushed to earth, shall rise again;
The eternal years of God are hers;
But Error, wounded, writhes in pain,
And dies among his worshippers.
Yea, though thou lie upon the dust,
When they who helped thee flee in fear,
Die full of hope and manly trust,
Like those who fell in battle here.
Another hand thy sword shall wield,
Another hand the standard wave,
Till from the trumpet's mouth is pealed
The blast of triumph o'er thy grave.

It is well for us, It is well for all who enter upon the work of uprooting old ideas and replacing them by new ones to remember this and to carry with us into this work of education upon which we have entered the magnificent thought, the inspiring hope here expressed. It will be all right by and by. Only let us be faithful; let the good work go on; let us keep the ideal before us and work steadily towards it; and though we may not live to see the realization of our hopes, those who follow us will.

Slow are the steps of Freedom, but her feet
Turn never backward; hers no bloody glare;
Her light is calm, and innocent, and sweet,
And where it enters there is no despair.

I do not despair. This Negro problem will be solved; and when it is ultimately solved, the Negro will have all of his rights. There will be none to molest him or make him afraid; there will be no disposition to molest or make him afraid. The stars and stripes will mean equal protection to all citizens, in the enjoyment of every right, whether at home or abroad. The principles of the Declaration of Independence will be no longer glittering generalities, mere empty sentiments, but realities, living, vitalizing forces in the life of the nation; America will be no longer, in name only, as we lyingly and hypocritically sing today, "*The land of the free, and the home of the brave*," but in reality. It will then be the land of the free. Its citizens, white and black alike, will be free, in the enjoyment of life, liberty, and the pursuit of happiness in every section of it. It will then be the home of the brave. Its prejudices will have been conquered, and right will have been enthroned in the hearts of the people.

Sermon 2

A Resemblance and a Contrast between the American Negro and the Children of Israel in Egypt, or the Duty of the Negro to Contend Earnestly for His Rights Guaranteed under the Constitution[4]

And he said unto his people, Behold, the people of the children of Israel are more and mightier than we: Come, let us deal wisely with them; lest they multiply, and it come to pass, that, when there falleth out any war, they also join themselves unto our enemies, and fight against us, and get them up out of the land.
—Exodus 1:9–10

In this record, there is a contrast suggested between our people in this country and the children of Israel in Egypt, and also a resemblance to which I desire, for the moments that I shall occupy, to call attention.

1. **The children of Israel went down into Egypt of their own accord.** Ten of the sons of Jacob first went down to buy corn, owing to a very severe famine that was raging in their own country, and in all the surrounding countries. This journey was again repeated some time afterwards, at which time they were joined by Benjamin—the man in charge of affairs having made that a condition of their seeing his face. It was during this second visit that Joseph was made known to his brethren, through whom an earnest invitation was sent to his father, Jacob, and all the members of the family to come and stay in the land, with the promise that all of their wants would be supplied. It was in response to this invitation that the family packed up everything which they had and went down into Egypt. They went down from choice; it was a voluntary thing on their part. They were not forced against their will.

---

[4] Works, *Grimké*, 347–64. Delivered October 12, 1902, in Connection with the Encampment of the Grand Army of the Republic in Washington, DC.

The opposite of this was true in the case of the coming of our forefathers to this country. It was not a voluntary act on their part. They were seized by slave hunters and against their will forced from the land of their birth. Left to themselves they never would have sought these shores.

2. **The children of Israel were few in number when they went down into Egypt.** There were only about seventy-odd souls in all. During their sojourn, however, they greatly multiplied; so much so that at the time of the Exodus, 1491 BC, according to the census that was taken under the divine direction, there were 603,550 men over twenty years of age who were able to go to war. No mention is made of the male members of the population under twenty, nor of the old men who were unfit for active military service; nor of the women and female children. The whole number must have been between two and three million. Assuming that Jacob went down in the year 1706 BC, and that the Exodus was in 1491 BC, this increase came about in a little over two centuries.

   The same fact is noticeable in reference to our people in this country. The first installment came in 1619, and the importation of slaves was prohibited in 1808. According to the census for 1790, we numbered then 752,208. Fifty years afterwards, the number had increased to 2,873,648. In 1890, the number had gone up to 7,470,040, while the last census shows our present number to be 8,840,789. This is a very remarkable showing, when we remember the large mortality of the race, and the fact that the increase has been purely a natural one, without any accessions through immigration. It shows that we are a very prolific race, and that there is no danger of our dying out.

3. **The Egyptians were alarmed at the rapid increase of the children of Israel**, and sought in one way or another to diminish their number, or to arrest their increase. The first method was to work them to death, to kill them off by hard labor, and by cruel treatment. This method failed, however;

instead of decreasing, they went on steadily increasing, becoming more and more numerous. Then another method was resorted to—the midwives were directed to strangle the male children to death at birth. This also failed. And a third and last method was devised: a decree was issued compelling parents to expose their own children to death. Under this decree, Moses, the great lawgiver, would have perished had he not been providentially rescued by Pharaoh's daughter from an untimely death.

The rapid increase of our people in this country has also been a source of disquiet, if not of positive alarm, to the white element of the population. In 1889, when the census showed an increase of over 22 percent, you will remember what an excitement it created, and what absurd predictions were made as to the possibility of the country being overrun by Negroes. In 1890, when the percentage was cut down owing to inaccuracies in the census of 1890, what a sense of relief was felt by the whites. The rapid increase of the colored population of this country is no more welcomed or relished by the white American than the rapid increase of the Jewish population was by the Egyptians. There has been no concerted action on the part of the whites to cut down our numbers, as was done in Egypt; the process of destruction, however, has gone on all the same. In the Southern section of our country, especially, the hand of violence has been laid upon our people, and hundreds and thousands of them have, in this way, been sent to untimely graves. The convict lease system has also had its influence in diminishing our numbers. Whether this was its intention originally or not, I am not prepared to say, but the fact is, it has had that effect. Through the convict camps, the exodus from this world to the next has been amazingly frequent. The avarice, the cupidity of the white man, as illustrated in the grinding conditions imposed upon the colored farmer, under the crop lease system, has also done much to increase the hardships of life for us and to shorten our days.

4. **The Egyptians were afraid that the children of Israel would get up and leave the land**: and this, they didn't want them to do. They wanted them to remain, not because they loved them, or because of any special interest which they felt in them as such; but from purely selfish considerations. They were valuable as laborers. From the narrative we learn that they worked in the fields, made bricks, and built treasure cities for Pharaoh. It was a great thing to have at their disposal a population of this kind, who could be pressed into service whenever they were needed. In those oriental monarchies, when great public works, like the building of the pyramids, were carried on by the State, and when it required an enormous number of workmen, it was of the utmost importance to the State to have constantly at hand the means of supplying this want. And this they found in the rapidly increasing Jewish population, and accordingly, were not disposed to tolerate for a moment the idea of their departure. How strongly they felt on this matter is evident from the reply which Pharaoh made to the demand of Moses, "Thus saith the Lord, the God of Israel, Let My people go that they may hold a feast unto me in the wilderness." And Pharaoh said, "Who is the Lord, that I should hearken unto His voice to let Israel go? I know not the Lord, and moreover I will not let Israel go." The same is also evident from the fact that it was not until the land had been visited by ten great plagues, ending with the death of the firstborn, that they were willing to let them go.

When the children of Israel first went down into Egypt, it was with no intention of remaining there permanently. It was intended to be only a temporary sojourn, during the continuance of the famine, which drove them there. Nor was it in accordance with the divine plan that they should remain permanently, as is evident from the record, in forty-six of Genesis: "And God spake unto Israel in the vision of the night, and said, 'Jacob, Jacob.' And he said, 'Here am I.' And he said, 'I am God, the God of thy fathers: fear not to go down into Egypt, for I will there make of thee a great nation:

I will go down with thee into Egypt, and I will surely bring thee up again.'" And you will also remember what God said to Abraham, in response to the question, "Whereby shall I know that I shall inherit it," that is, the land of Canaan. "Know of a surety that thy seed shall be a stranger in a land that is not theirs, and shall serve them; and they shall afflict them four hundred years; and also that nation, whom they shall serve, will I judge: and afterwards they shall come out with great substance."

Now, in both of these respects, things seem to be somewhat different with us in this country. If we may judge from the representations in the newspapers and magazines, which are made from time to time, it would appear that the white Americans would be very glad to have our people arise and get out of the land. We hear a great deal about schemes for deporting the Negro, and in certain sections of the South, and even in certain parts of Illinois, the attempt has been made to forcibly drive him out. While I do not apprehend that there will ever be any general movement to get rid of us, to forcibly deport us from the country, nevertheless, I do not believe that there would be any regrets or tears shed on the part of the whites if such a thing should occur. I think the great majority would be glad to get rid of us. With the Negro out of the country, what a love feast there would be between the North and the South; how they would rush into each other's arms, and fondly embrace each other, and rejoice over the fact that at last the great barrier which has stood between them for so many years had been removed. With the Negro out of the country, what a bright prospect there would be of building up a respectable White Republican Party in the South; so we are told by some Republican fools, who lose sight of the fact that the glory of the Republican Party does not depend upon its getting rid of the Negro, but on the contrary, whatever of glory there is attached to it has come from its connection with the Negro. Why is it called the grand old party? What is it that has given it its pre-eminence; that has rendered it immortal; that has covered it with imperishable glory? Is it not the noble stand which it took for human rights; the magnificent fight which it made against slavery and rebellion, out of which came the great amendments to the Constitution, the Thirteenth, Fourteenth, and Fifteenth? It was the enactment of these great amendments that has given it its chief claim to distinction, and that will ever constitute its crowning glory. Yes, even the Republican party, I believe, would be glad to see us go. In two Southern States already, two Republican conventions have declined to receive or admit colored delegates. If some Moses should rise up today, as of old, and say to this nation, as was said to Pharaoh, "Let my people go," it would not be necessary to send any plagues in order to have the demand enforced. I believe from every part of the land—North, South, East, and West, there would be but one voice, and that would be, Let them go.

The children of Israel wanted to go, while the Egyptians didn't want them to go. The reverse of that, I believe, is true in our case in this land. The white Americans would be glad to have us go, but there is no desire or disposition on our part to go. So far as I have been able to ascertain the sentiments of our people, it is our purpose to remain here. We have never known any other home, and don't expect, as a people, ever to know any other. Here and there an individual may go, but the masses of our people will remain where we are. Things are not exactly as we would like to have them; no, they are very far from being so, or from what we hope some time they will be, but bad as they are, we are nevertheless disposed to remain where we are. Besides, it would be cowardly to run away. Wherever we go, we will have to struggle. Life is real, life is earnest everywhere. And since we are in the struggle here, we had just as well fight it out here as anywhere else. And that is what we are going to do. We are not going to retreat a single inch. We are not going to expatriate ourselves, out of deference to a Negro-hating public sentiment.

It was the divine plan that Israel's stay in Egypt should be only temporary; God's purpose was ultimately to lead them back to the land of Canaan, from which they had come. And it has been intimated, from certain quarters, that that is to be true of us; that God has providentially permitted us to be brought to this land, in order that we might be trained for future usefulness in the land of our forefathers. This is the view that has been taken by some white men, and also by some colored men. It may be so; but I confess, so far, I have not been able to discover any evidences of such a purpose. In the case of the Jews, the record showed what the purposes of God were in regard to that people; but we have no such revelation touching ourselves. God spoke to Abraham, and God spoke to Jacob, and showed them what was to be; but where are the Abrahams and Jacobs among us to whom He has spoken? There are those who are ready to speculate, but speculation amounts to nothing. What the divine purposes are touching this race, no one knows. And therefore, in the absence of any definite and positive information, we will assume that this purpose is that we remain just where we are. Until we have very clear evidence to the contrary, we are not likely to take any steps to go elsewhere.

5. **The Egyptians were afraid that the children of Israel, in case of war with a foreign power, would join their enemies and fight against them.** And well might they have feared. In the first place, the whole world at that time was in a state of war. It was might that made right. Wars of conquest were constantly going on. One nation or state felt perfectly justified in making war against another if it was deemed to its interest to do so. As a matter of fact, there was always liability of an invasion from some foreign power. This was a possibility, which Egypt, as well as every other country, had to take into consideration, and to provide against. At any moment, the enemy might be seen approaching; at any moment their safety might be imperiled.

In the second place, with this possibility staring them in the face, their treatment of the Jews, in case of an invasion, would very naturally have led them to feel that the sympathy of the Jews would be with the invaders instead of with them. The reason assigned in the narrative, however, for this fear is, lest through such an alliance with a foreign power, they succeed in getting out of the land. This shows conclusively that the Jews evidently wanted to get out of the land and had possibly intimated that. The Egyptians didn't want them to go; and yet, strange to say, instead of setting themselves to work to make it so pleasant and agreeable for them that they would not want to go, the very opposite policy is pursued—the policy of oppression, of injustice, of violence. Instead of seeking to win them by acts of kindness, they inaugurated a reign of terror; sought to intimidate them, to crush out of them every spark of manhood, to reduce them to the level of dumb, driven cattle. What a strange thing human nature is; how short-sighted, how blind, how utterly stupid men often are, and men from whom we might naturally expect better things. If the Jews were to remain in Egypt, as the Egyptians desired to have them do, wasn't it a great deal better to have their love than their hatred, their friendship than their enmity? And even if they were going out, was it not better to have their goodwill than their ill-will? For it was just possible that some time in the future, they might need the help even of the descendants of Jacob, little and insignificant as they were at that time in their estimation. It was the day of small things with them; but there was no telling what the future might bring forth. As a matter of fact, we know that they did become a great and powerful nation.

It is just possible that the absurd and ruinous policy pursued by the Egyptians was due also to a sense of race superiority, and the assumption that if they were in any way civil, if they treated the Jews with the common courtesies that one human being owes to another, it might create within them a desire for social equality. It is possible that the fear of being overrun by an inferior race may also have fired their imagination, blinding their vision, and blunting their moral sensibilities. Whatever the reason may have been, the fact remains that the policy inaugurated by them was an utterly heartless and brutal one; and this policy they continued to pursue until it was reversed by the divine interposition, until God's righteous indignation was excited, and the angel of death was sent forth and smote the firstborn throughout the land, and overthrew the tyrants in the Red Sea. It is only a matter of time when all such oppressors the world over will meet a similar fate. God is not dead—nor is He an indifferent onlooker at what is going on in this world. One day He will make requisition for blood; He will call the oppressors to account. Justice may sleep, but it never dies. The individual, race, or nation which does wrong, which sets at defiance God's great law, especially God's great law of love, of brotherhood, will be sure, sooner or later, to pay the penalty. We reap as we sow. With what measure we mete, it shall be measured to us again.

The absurdity of pursuing such a policy is evident from the disastrous consequences which followed. The voice of lamentation that was heard throughout the land of Egypt, the pall of death that hung over every home, and the appalling catastrophe at the Red Sea, which was the culmination of a series of terrible judgments, all came out of it. It was a policy which brought upon them only wretchedness and misery from which they did not derive a single advantage, or reap a single benefit.

The policy pursued by them not only did not benefit them, but did not in the least interfere with the divine purposes concerning the Jews. In spite of their policy of oppression, of injustice, of bitter hatred, God led the children of Israel out all the same, and safely conducted them to the Promised Land. The race that puts its trust in God, and is willing to be led by God, is safe. The heathen may rage and the people imagine a vain thing, but they will be powerless to stay its progress.[5] They may worry and vex it for a while, but they will not be able to do it any permanent injury, or seriously to interfere with its development, with its onward and upward march. The race that puts its trust in God has always, under all circumstances, more for it than against it. There is never therefore any reason for fear, or for becoming discouraged as long as it maintains its grip upon the Almighty, as long as its attitude is one of simple child-like trust and dependence.

This is not the point, however, that I had in view in referring to this aspect of the subject, which we are considering under this fifth general head. We were speaking under this head of the fear entertained by the Egyptians of the children of Israel joining their enemies, in case of an invasion, and fighting against them. And what I want to say, in this connection, is that there is no just ground for any such fear in regard to our people in this country. Whatever else may be said of the black man, the charge of disloyalty cannot be truthfully made against him. From the very beginning, he has been loyal to the flag, and has always been willing to lay down his life in its defense. In the War of the Revolution; in the War of 1812; in the Mexican War; in the great Civil War; and in the War with Spain, he stood side by side with other citizens of the Republic facing the enemy; and in all of our national cemeteries may be found evidences of his patriotism and valor. It is only necessary to mention Milliken's Bend, Port

---

[5] In this excerpt, Grimké's EEH emerges through an explicit reliance on scripture, reflecting *Biblicism* as he invokes Psalm 2 ("The heathen may rage") to illuminate divine justice against oppression and to reinforce the gospel's message of judgment and deliverance. His encouragement for trust in God's sovereignty emphasizes *Conversionism*, as faith in divine purposes shapes moral resolve. Grimké's use of Exodus as a model for liberation aligns with *Activism*, urging his audience toward perseverance in liberation and social justice. Lastly, the *Crucicentric* feature is evident in the assurance of God's ultimate power over oppression, positioning struggle as part of God's redemptive history. This message echoes Pauline praxis in passages like Romans 8:31, affirming, "If God is for us, who can be against us?" by encouraging trust in divine support as a bulwark against injustice.

Hudson, Fort Wagner, Olustee, during the great Civil War, and San Juan Hill, during the Spanish War, as evidences of his valor and patriotism. Joseph T. Wilson, who was himself a gallant soldier in the 54th Massachusetts, has written a book, entitled, *The Black Phalanx,* in which he traces the history of the Negro soldiers of the United States, from the earliest period through the great war of the Rebellion. It is a glorious record, and one that puts the patriotism of the Negro beyond all question. Whenever the call of danger has been sounded, he has always been ready to respond, to bare his bosom to the bullets of the enemy.

This is all the more remarkable when we remember what his treatment has been in this country. Buffeted, spit upon, his most sacred rights trampled upon, without redress, discriminated against in hotels, restaurants, in common carriers, deprived of his political rights, shot down by lawless ruffians, every possible indignity heaped upon him, while the State and Nation look on, the one justifying the outrages, or at least doing nothing to prevent them, and the other protesting its inability to protect its own citizens from violence and injustice. Such treatment is not calculated to inspire one's patriotism, to kindle one's love for a government that permits such injustice and oppression to go on without, at least, the attempt to check them. And yet, in spite of these monstrous wrongs that have gone on and are still going on, unrestrained by State or Federal authority, the record of the Negro for patriotism will compare with any other class of citizens. He has been just as constant, just as unswerving in his devotion to the Republic as the most favored class. Oppressed, down-trodden, discriminated against, denied even the common civilities of life, and yet, in the hour of danger, always ready to stretch forth his strong black arm in defense of the Nation. How to explain this, I do not know, nor is it necessary. It is with the fact alone that I am concerned. There it is, and it is true of no other element of the population. There is no other class of citizens, which, if treated as we have been and are still being treated, would evince any such patriotism, would show any such willingness to lay down their lives at the nation's call, as we have. The fear of the Egyptians cannot therefore be the fear of the white citizens of this country. The Negro has never shown any disposition to fight against the Republic, or to ally himself with a foreign foe. His sympathies have always been with the stars and stripes.

In our city, we are now having what is known as the annual encampment of the Grand Army of the Republic. This army is an organization made up of the surviving veterans of the great Civil War. It is called the Grand Army. Mr. Gladstone used to be called the Grand Old Man, because he summed up in himself many great qualities. He was a matchless orator, a profound thinker, a great scholar, a man of encyclopedic information. The Republican Party is sometimes called the Grand Old Party, and the name is not inappropriately applied to it. There are many things connected with its history that justify that title. It has done some grand things, and it has had associated with it some of the bravest, truest, noblest, and brainiest men that this country has produced—men who were not afraid to do right; who felt, as Lowell has expressed it:

Though we break our fathers' promise,
we have nobler duties first;
The traitor to Humanity is the traitor
most accursed;
Man is more than Constitutions; better
rot beneath the sod,
Than be true to Church and State while
we are doubly false to God.

A party with such men, as it had in it years ago, may well be called "The Grand Old Party." I take the term *grand* to apply to the old party—the party as it used to be, not to the party as it is today, with its petty little program of a white Republican Party in the South; the elimination of Negro office-holders in the South, out of deference to white southern sentiment; white supremacy in the Philippines and Puerto Rico; and the undue prominence that is given to material things; while it is indifferent to the rights of its citizens of color—caring more for dollars and cents, for material prosperity, than for righteousness, for simple, even-handed justice, which alone exalts a nation. It used to be the Grand Old Party. It is no longer such. There isn't a single thing about it, either in what it is at present doing or in its purposes with reference to the future, to which the term *grand* can be truthfully applied. It has lost its fine sense of righteousness. It no longer gives evidence of those higher instincts, those nobler sentiments, that make nations and parties truly great. It grovels in the dust. Its aims and purposes are of the earth earthy. It is in the interest of commerce and trade and material development that it is bending its energies and taxing its resources—forgetful of the fact that it is true of a nation as of an individual, that its real true life does not consist in the abundance of the good things which it possesseth. Lowell, in his *Ode on France*, after describing the overthrow of the French tyrant during the great revolution, gives utterance to these significant words:

What though
The yellow blood of trade meanwhile
should pour
Along its arteries a shrunken flow,
And the idle canvas droop around the
shore?
These do not make a state,
nor keep it great;
I think God made
The earth for man, not trade;
And where each humblest human creature
Can stand, no more suspicious or afraid
Erect and kingly in his right of nature,
To heaven and earth knit with harmonious ties,—
Where I behold the exaltation

Of manhood glowing in those eyes
That had been dark for ages,
Or only lit with bestial loves and rages,
There I behold a Nation;
The France which lies
Between the Pyrenees and the Rhine
Is the least part of France;
I see her rather in the soul whose shine
Burns through the craftsman's grimy countenance,
In the energy divine
Of toil's enfranchised glance.

Unfortunately, neither Republicans nor Democrats in this country seem to recognize the great fact enunciated in these lines, but it is true nevertheless; and no party is entitled to the designation *grand* which does not accept it and act in the light of it.

It is not of the Republican party that I started to speak, however, but of the Grand Army of the Republic. The term *grand*, as applied to this army, is a fitting tribute to the great services which it has rendered to the Republic. It was this army, the remnant of which is in our city today, that saved the life of the Republic; that put down rebellion; and that gave efficacy to Lincoln's great Proclamation of Emancipation. Had he not had this army behind him, his proclamation would have been unavailing. An army that has to its credit these great achievements may well be called *grand*. It is the Grand Army of the Republic. There have been other armies of the Republic—the army of the Revolution, the army of 1812, the army of the war with Mexico, and the Spanish–American War—but the Army of the Republic, both as to numbers and as to the importance of its achievements, is the Army that put down the great Rebellion, and with it the accursed system of slavery, which was like a millstone about the neck of both races. All honor to these brave men. Too much cannot be said in praise of their valor and patriotism. As the years go by, as their numbers decrease, as one by one they go to join their comrades on the other side, the more and more should we honor those who still remain among us. I am glad of this annual encampment; glad of the parade connected with it; glad to look into the faces, and to have others look into the faces of the brave men who stood by their guns, and stood watch over the nation when Rebellion sought to dissolve the Union and to rivet more firmly the fetters upon four million bondmen. And I am especially glad to know that in these parades of the veterans who saved the Nation, are to be found not only white men, but black men as well. I hope that these representatives of our race will always attend these annual gatherings, even though it may entail some sacrifice on their part to do so. It is a splendid object lesson to the whole nation; and it is a fitting rebuke to those recreant white Americans who say, "This is a white man's country." If it is a white man's country, what are these black heroes doing in these annual parades? If it is a white man's country, why is it that in all our national cemeteries are the graves of Negroes? Why is it that in every war since the beginning of the Republic, on sea and land, the blood of the Negro has spurted in its behalf? Why is it that on the pension roll of the nation today are widows and orphans and battle-scarred heroes of this race? If this is a white man's country, why are Negroes ever called upon to take up arms in its defense? I am glad of these annual encampments, I say, and glad of the share which we have in them. Let every Negro veteran who can, always make it a point to be present at these gatherings, and always get into the ranks and march with the procession, in order that the multitudes who gather from all parts of the country may look on and take knowledge of the fact that the Negro is a man, and that he can do a man's part, and that he may be relied upon to do his part as a citizen of the Republic. It is a grand object lesson, I say, to the nation, to see these colored men in line under such circumstances. And so far as we are concerned, we should never by our absence, permit that lesson to be lost.

In thinking of this Grand Army of the Republic, I am painfully reminded of the fact that though the War of the Rebellion is over and has been over for more than thirty-five years; and though the great amendments to the Constitution have been enacted, making us freemen and citizens, and giving us the right of the ballot, we have not yet been put in possession of these rights. We are still discriminated against, and treated as if we had no rights which white men were bound to respect. And I have called attention to this condition of things, in this connection, to remind us of the fact that though the Civil War is over, the battle for our rights in this country is not yet over. The great amendments are a part of the law of the land, but the same treasonable and Negro-hating spirit that sought to perpetuate our bondage, and to keep us in a state of hopeless inferiority, is still endeavoring to accomplish its purpose by seeking to nullify them. There is a spirit abroad in this land which is determined that we shall never be accorded the rights of American citizens. And that spirit you have got to meet, and I have got to meet, and we have all got to meet. And it is from these old battle-scarred survivors of the Civil War, that we may learn how to meet it—with courage, with invincible determination; with the earnest purpose never to surrender. Be assured that these wrongs from which we are suffering, will never be righted if we sit idly by and take no interest in the matter. If we are indifferent, even those who might be disposed to assist us will also become indifferent. We must show the proper appreciation, the proper interest ourselves. We must agitate, and agitate, and agitate, and go on agitating. By and by, our very importunity will make itself felt. The people in the midst of whom we are living, if not from a sense of justice, or right, of fair play, will on the principle of the unjust judge, who cared neither for God nor man, but who said, "I will right the widow's wrong, lest by her continual coming she weary me," be constrained to right our wrongs.

In the struggle which we are making in this country for the recognition of our rights as men and citizens, there is another thing which I want to say. There is little or nothing to be expected from those members of our race, whether in politics or out of it, who value their little petty personal interests above the interests of their race; whose first and last and only thought is, *What is there in the struggle for me, what can I get out of it?* And who, when they have gotten their little out of it, are perfectly willing to sacrifice the race, to turn it over to the tender mercies of its enemies; to stand by and see it despoiled of its rights without one word of protest. It is not from such men that anything is to be expected. It is rather from the men who are willing to make sacrifices, and to suffer, if need be, for principle; who cannot be satisfied, and cannot permit themselves to be silent in the presence of wrong, in order to ingratiate themselves into the favor of the dominant race, or that they might hold on to some petty office or position. If we are to succeed; if we are to make the proper kind of a fight in this country for our rights, we have got to develop a class of men who cannot be won over by a few offices, or by being patted on the shoulder; men who, like John the Baptist, are willing to be clothed in camel's hair, and to subsist on locusts and wild honey—to wear the coarsest clothing, and be content with the plainest food, in order that they might be free to follow the dictates of their own conscience that they might be unhampered in the fight which they are making for their rights, and for the rights of their race. The men whose policy is to look out for self first, and to concern themselves about the race only so far as professing interest in it may be a help to them in working out their selfish ends and purposes, are men that are unworthy of our confidence. The men that we should honor, and that we may safely follow, are those who are willing to lose themselves, to subordinate their selfish interests in order that the race may find itself, may come into the full enjoyment of all its rights. That was the spirit exhibited by Garrison, though he was battling for the rights, not of white men, but of black men.

In a small chamber, friendless and unseen,
Toiled o'er his types one poor, unlearned young man;
The place was dark, unfurnitured, and mean;
Yet there the freedom of a race began.
Help came but slowly; surely no man yet
Put lever to the heavy world with less.

What a picture is that! We can see it all! The dingy little room, dark, unfurnitured, and mean; and we can understand how difficult it must have been for him to keep soul and body together; and yet he was willing to endure all, to suffer all, for the sake of the cause to which he had dedicated his life. That was a white man suffering for black men! What ought not black men to be willing to suffer, to endure, for themselves? If we are to succeed, I say, in the struggle through which we are passing, we have got to develop within the race itself more of the spirit which Garrison possessed—the willingness to be found, if necessary, in a small chamber, dark, unfurnitured and mean, and to be friendless, in the struggle which we are making for the new emancipation from the fetters of caste prejudice, and from the injustice and oppression to which we are at present subjected. We are still dragging the chain; and we will go on dragging it until the race itself wakes up and sets itself earnestly to work to break it. We are not sufficiently in earnest; we are too easily lulled to sleep; we are too easily satisfied; we are not sufficiently impressed with the gravity of the situation—with the true inwardness of the motive which is leading our enemies on, enemies within the race as well as without it, in the assaults which they are making upon our rights. Edwin Markham, in a little poem, entitled *Thoughts for Independence Day,* asks the question:

What need we, then, to guard and keep us whole?
What do we need to prop the State?

And the answer which he makes among others is:

We need the Cromwell fire to make us feel
The public honor or the public trust
To be a thing as sacred and august
As some white altar where the angels kneel.

And that is what we need, "The Cromwell fire," to make us feel that the rights guaranteed to us under the Constitution, are

as sacred and august
As some white altar where the angels kneel.

If we felt that way, we would not lightly surrender these rights, as too many are disposed to do.

At this Grand Army Encampment, when the issues of the great Civil War are brought vividly before us, it is a good time to look into each other's faces; to give each other the pass-word; and to pledge ourselves anew to stand by our colors. Mr. Webster, in his eulogy on Adams and Jefferson, represents John Adams as saying, on the question of independence, "Sink, or swim; live, or die; survive, or perish, I give my hand and heart to this vote." And in the same spirit, let us say today, "Sink, or swim; live, or die, survive, or perish," we pledge our hands and hearts to each other, never to give up the struggle. Stanley is represented, while in Africa, as saying, "Nothing except the Bible gave me such comfort and inspiration as these lines from Browning:

What on earth had I to do
With the slothful with the mawkish, the unmanly?
Being—who?
One who never turned his back, but marched breast forward,
Never doubted clouds would break,
Never dreamed, though right were worsted, wrong would triumph,
Held, we fall to rise, are baffled to fight better,
Sleep to wake."

And that is what we must do, "March breast forward;" that is the kind of men that we must be—the kind of men that we must seek more and more to develop among us—men of courage, of faith, of steady purpose, of uncompromising fidelity to principle. Douglass was a man of that type. A majestic figure! A leader, who never turned his back; and who never compromised his race; a leader, who was always true; and who, down to the very last, stood panoplied in its defense. It is the Douglass-type of leaders that we want—leaders who respect themselves, and to whom the interests of their race are above price. Long may the memory of this illustrious man linger with us, to stimulate our ambition; to arouse our slumbering energies; and to put within us the earnest purpose to continue the fight for equal civil and political rights in this land which we have helped to develop and to save.

At the battle of Copenhagen, 1801, Nelson was vice-admiral, and led the attack against the Danish fleet. By accident, one-fourth of the fleet was unable to participate, and the battle was very destructive. Admiral Parker, a conservative and aged officer, seeing how little progress was made after three hours' conflict, signaled the fleet to discontinue the engagement. That signal was No. 39. Nelson continued to walk the deck, without appearing to notice the signal. "Shall I repeat it?" said the lieutenant. "No; acknowledge it." He turned to the Captain: "You know, Forley, I have only one eye. I can't see it," putting his glass to his blind eye. "Nail my signal for close action to the mast," cried Nelson. That was his order to continue the fight. And the fight was continued, and the battle was won. And so, when signals come to us, as they have come and are coming, from within the race, as well as from without it, bidding us give up the struggle; telling us to cease to agitate, to protest, to stand up for our rights; telling us not to trouble ourselves; that it doesn't do any good; that we had better let things go, which means, go the way our enemies want them to go; that all this agitation tends only to make things worse, to engender hard feelings—to all such signals, let us, like the intrepid Nelson, turn our blind eye towards them; let us not see them; and go right on fighting the battles of the race. If we are true to ourselves and to God, the victory will be ours. It may be slow in coming, but come it will. Nothing is to be gained by withdrawing from the contest. Our duty is to remain firm; to plant ourselves squarely and uncompromisingly upon the rights guaranteed to us under the Constitution, and to hold our ground. No backward step should be our motto.

Today is the day of battle,
The brunt is hard to bear;
Stand back, all ye who falter,
Make room for those who dare.

Thank God there have always been among us men of this stamp; men who have realized the necessity of fighting, and who have been willing to go forward, regardless of personal consequences—brave men, true men, unselfish men.

Let us hope that the number of those who falter, who are disposed to stand back, to meekly surrender their rights, may be steadily on the decrease; and that the number of those who dare, who are resolved to go forward, to stand firmly for the right, may go on steadily increasing, until there shall not be left one lukewarm, indifferent, half-hearted, non-self-respecting member of the race; until all shall be aroused, and shall be equally interested in a cause that ought to be dearer to us than life itself.

Let us be men; and let us stand up for our rights as men, and as American citizens.

Be strong!
It matters not how deep entrenched the wrong,
How hard the battle goes, the day, how long.
Faint not, Fight on! To-morrow comes the song.

Sermon 3

God and the Race Problem[6]

God is our refuge and strength, a very present help in trouble. Therefore will we not fear, though the earth do change, and though the mountains be shaken into the heart of the seas; though the waters thereof roar and be troubled, though the mountains tremble with the swelling thereof.
—Psalm 46:1

The following circular has been sent out, a copy of which reached me last week:

> *Recommendation to the Negroes of America for a day of prayer and humiliation to God.*
>
> *God bless our enemies, and guard and guide our friends, and help us in the discharge of our several duties to His glory and the best interest of our fellow men.*
>
> *In view of the fact that the American Negro is the bone of contention in the United States, and the American press does not give the Negro's side of the contention to the reading public, so that the Negro is placed in a very bad light before the civilized world, thus causing him to lose friends and multiply enemies.*
>
> *Therefore, we, the Colored Ministers' Baptist Conference of Greater New York and vicinity, in conjunction with the Afro-American Cosmopolitan Non-Denominational Preachers' Meeting of Greater New York and vicinity, make the following recommendation in the*

---

[6] Grimké, *Works I*, 364–78. Delivered May 3, 1903, on the day set apart as a day of fasting, prayer, and humiliation for the colored people throughout the United States.

> *name of God, and in behalf of our people: To the faithful and prayerful God-fearing Negroes of the United States:*
>
> *Brethren—We are confronting a crisis in our life as citizens unlike any other former trial through which we have passed—a crisis full of deadly menace to all that freemen hold dearest—our friends are dying, or becoming indifferent—our enemies, emboldened by our apparent helplessness, are seeking to deprive us of all the sacred guarantees of the Constitution of the United States, which are so dear to us, and mean so much to every American citizen—that we, therefore, herein designate the First Lord's Day in May, 1903, as a day of fasting and prayer; and that every Negro who can will read the fourth chapter of Esther, and that every Negro minister of all denominations throughout the United States preach a special sermon, calling the schools, colleges, organizations, and the people's attention to our need of God's help and God's attention to our helplessness.*

It is in compliance with this request that I shall attempt to say a few words this morning with reference to ourselves, as a people in this country. In the circular just read in our hearing we are reminded of several things:

1. **That there is a God.** This is involved in the idea of a day of prayer. Prayer is the offering up of our desires to whom? To God. God is, therefore, and that fact we must not forget. It is of the utmost importance for us as a people to remember that God is. The consciousness of that great fact will be a help to us in many ways in our efforts to work out our salvation in this land.

2. **We are reminded of the fact we stand in need of guidance;** that we are not sufficient of ourselves. We have not all the wisdom that we need, and it is important that we recognize that fact; it will have a stimulating effect upon us; it will keep us in a receptive attitude. We need light, information, knowledge—and the more of it the better.

3. **We are reminded of the fact that we have enemies.** And so we have—many and bitter ones. The feeling of hostility against us seems to be steadily on the increase. David, in the Third Psalm, breaks out in these words: "Lord, how are they increased that trouble me! Many are they that rise up against me." And the same is true of us as a people in this country—the number of our enemies is steadily on the increase, or, at least, seems to be steadily increasing. In every direction the forces seem to be marshalling themselves against us. Not only in the South, but in the North as well there seems to be a growing disposition to limit the aspiration of the Negro, to keep him in an inferior position, to deny him the rights and the privileges that are accorded to white men. The lines are more tightly drawn now than ever before. There are many things that are transpiring to indicate this growing hostility. Only last month the Board of Education in New York City voted to eliminate or to exclude "Uncle Tom's Cabin" from the school libraries. The alleged ground for this action was that it had served its mission, as if a book like "Uncle Tom's Cabin," that breathes the loftiest sentiments of Christianity, that inculcates sympathy for the weak, the downtrodden, the oppressed, and that rebukes injustice, tyranny, inhumanity to man, could ever have served its mission, in the sense of being no longer necessary. Slavery is gone, it is true, but the spirit of it still remains, the same purpose and determination to keep the Negro down still persists, and never was more active, more alive than it is today; and "Uncle Tom's Cabin" stands in just as absolute antagonism to this surviving spirit of slavery as to the institution of slavery itself. If the teachings that pervade this book were carried out; if the great principles therein inculcated were recognized and acted upon, all the fetters that a narrow race prejudice is still seeking to rivet upon the Negro would be broken just as effectually as the manacles that bound him physically were broken. And this is the reason why it has been excluded; not because it has served its mission, but because it is still crying aloud, in terms as eloquent as it ever did, against the barbarism of slavery—against the barbarism of the surviving

spirit of slavery, which still pursues the Negro, and is still determined that he shall not have a man's chance in the race of life. Back of the vote which said "this book shall no longer be allowed to circulate through our schools" is this feeling of hostility, of unfriendliness to the Negro. It was done in deference to Southern sentiment, which is a Negro-hating sentiment, and a sentiment that is rapidly pervading the whole country. It was done not in the interest of the Negro—not in order to make the way easier for him—but to retard his progress, to make it more and more difficult for him to go forward by removing out of the way this friendly influence. Think of the splendid service which this book has rendered to freedom in this land; and of what it is still doing to educate public sentiment in the right direction; and then think of a great Board of Education ruling it out on the ground that it had served its mission; that what it has to say is no longer of any importance. Of course, what it has to say is no longer of any importance. It never was of any importance to the enemies of the Negro. If they had had their way it never would, at any time, have had any circulation. It must go not because it has fulfilled its mission, but because it takes the part of the Negro, because it is a plea for his better treatment, and because it exposes the inhumanity of the white man and the barbarism of a system that the South still holds to be divine. If it had been "The Leopard's Spots" or some other vile publication that seeks to hold the Negro up to ridicule and contempt, to belittle him in the eyes of others, to deepen and intensify the feeling against him, the probabilities are no movement would have been made in the Board of Education for its removal. That is the kind of books that the enemies of the race want to give the widest circulation. A few years ago, when Thomas's infamous book was published, which painted the Negro as a moral leper, as utterly given over to sensuality and vice, as little raised above the brute, everything was done to call attention to it. It was put into all the libraries; it was to be found on the shelves of all booksellers; it was taken up and reviewed by all the papers and magazines. The whole country—North, South, East, and West—became aware of the fact that such a book had been published. Recently another book has been published entitled "The Souls of Black Folk," by Dr. W. E. B. Du Bois, which, in my judgment, is one of the most remarkable contributions that has yet been made on the Negro question. It is written by a man of trained intellect, of the broadest culture; by a man who knows how to write, and who knows thoroughly the subject of which he is writing; by a man who believes in higher education for the Negro, who believes that the Negro is a man, that he has the same desires and aspirations as other men, and that he is entitled to the same rights and privileges and opportunities as other men. And it is in this spirit that he writes; it is for these things that he contends. I wonder if that book will be put at once in all of the libraries; whether it will be found on the shelves of all booksellers; whether the papers and magazines of the country will contain extended reviews of it; whether any special effort will be made to call attention to it—to the fact that a book of commanding ability, asserting in a manly way the claims of the Negro as a man, has been published? It is almost impossible to conceive of such a thing, for the reverse has always been the case. The press and the country have never had much patience with the manly assertion of the Negro for equality of rights and privileges; have never had much patience with the higher aspirations of Negroes. The things that they have ever stood ready to magnify have been those to his discredit, not to his credit. It is the Negro who does not want very much, who does not claim very much for his race; who thinks that an industrial education is quite sufficient; who thinks that the ballot is immaterial, that civil rights may be dispensed with—the Negro who is willing to accept less than the treatment that is due to a man, that it delights to notice and hold up. So much so that when the press begins to praise a Negro you may put it down, in nine cases out of ten, he is a traitor to his race; is playing into the hands of the men who believe that the Negro is an inferior being, and that as such he has a place and ought to be kept in his place; in nine cases out of ten he will be found to be an unmanly Negro, a Negro who is deficient in self-respect. I do not expect, therefore, to find any extended or laudatory notices of Dr. Du Bois and his masterly presentation of our cause in his recent publication, in the daily or weekly press. Dr. Du Bois will be classed hereafter among the bad or dangerous Negroes, and perhaps he may be asked to leave the South.

The action of the Board of Education in New York is only one of the many straws that indicate the direction in which public sentiment is moving. There are many others.

In the same city a little while ago a great meeting was held in the interest of one of our educational institutions. It was presided over by ex-President Cleveland, who made a speech which was greatly lauded by the newspapers. Mr. Cleveland has never been suspected, heretofore, so far as I know, of having any sympathy whatever with the South in its outrageous treatment of the Negro. He said as much as that in his speech in the interest of a similar educational work in Philadelphia a short while ago; but in the New York speech, the tone is entirely changed. There he appears rather as an apologist for the South. "I do not know," he says, "how it may be with other northern friends of the Negro, but I have faith in the honor and sincerity of the respectable white people of the South in their relations with the Negro and his improvement and well-being. They do not believe in social equality of the race and make no false pretense in regard to it. That this does not grow out of hatred of the Negro is very plain. It seems to me there is abundant behavior among the southern whites toward the Negro, to make us doubt the justice of charging this denial of social equality to prejudice, as we usually understand the word. Perhaps it is born out of something so much deeper and more imperious as to amount to racial instinct. Whatever it is, let us remember that it has condoned the Negro's share in the humiliation and spoliation of the white men of the South during the saturnalia of reconstruction days and has allowed a kindly feeling for the

Negro to survive the time when the South was deluged by a perilous flood of indiscriminate, unintelligent, and blighting Negro suffrage. Whatever it is, let us try to be tolerant and considerate of the feelings and even prejudice racial instinct of our white fellow-countrymen of the South, who, in the solution of the Negro problem, must, amid their own surroundings, bear the heat of the day and stagger under the weight of the white man's burden." Even Mr. Cleveland has come to feel that the North should be considerate of the South, should be tolerant of the South; that the South, practically, should be left to deal with the Negro problem as it sees fit.

In the same city another event of similar import has also taken place within the last month. A committee of the Union League, one of the most powerful political organizations in the country, recommended to the league the importance of taking up the matter of cutting down southern representation, based upon the disfranchisement of nearly the entire Negro population of the South, and urging upon Congress the duty of carrying out the provisions of the Constitution which make such a reduction imperative. The proposition precipitated a lively discussion, and was finally defeated through the influence of Mr. Robert C. Ogden. Mr. Ogden is a northern man, the president of the board of trustees of Hampton Institute, and has always been regarded as a man who believed in equality of rights for all men in this country, black and white alike. But even Mr. Ogden, good man as he is, has now come to feel that it is better to allow the Negro to be despoiled of his political rights and the Constitution to be openly violated; better to permit the South to do a wrong and then to profit by its wrongdoing than to excite its displeasure. Even Mr. Ogden has come to feel that the South must be propitiated, even though it be at the expense of the Negro, even though it involves a wrong to the Negro. The feeling is, after all, these are only Negroes. What difference does it make whether they get their rights or not? It is more important for us white men of the North to stand in with our southern white brethren than to be troubling ourselves about the rights of black folk. If we let the South have its way, it will be a great deal pleasanter for us. When we go South we will be received with open arms; the southern papers will speak well of us, will make much of us. And you know we have always felt our inferiority to the southern people, and to have them pat us on the shoulder, to say pleasant things to us and about us is too great a boon for us to forego simply because of these black people, who belong to another race anyhow. It is true, we profess to be Christians, and if Jesus were here He would doubtless feel very different in regard to these black people, who are also God's children, as well as we are; but He isn't here. And while, in his absence, it is our duty to represent Him, nevertheless it isn't expedient for us to do so. If we do, the southern people won't be pleased with us, and so, rather than lose their favor, we will do what they want us to do, rather than what Christ would have us do. And so, men like Mr. Ogden and scores of others are going over to the southern view of things, are content to allow the South to have its way.

One other incident I want to call attention to. It occurred in our own city, and recently. It was the marriage of a colored man and a white woman. The fact was announced through the papers, and the name of the minister who performed the ceremony was given. No sooner did the fact become known than the minister became alarmed, and hastened through the press to say that he didn't know the man was colored; that he was such a nice, respectable-looking man that he supposed he was white, and that had he known that he was colored he would not have married them. Why would he not have married them? Is there anything in the laws of the District of Columbia against such a marriage? No. Is there anything in the Bible against intermarriage of the races? No. Is there anything in the religion of Jesus Christ which forbids such a union? No. Why then should a minister of Christ say, "I would have refused to marry them?" Why? Either because he is himself infected with the virus of race prejudice, or because he is a moral coward; because he is afraid of the Negro-hating sentiment that is prevalent in this community—afraid that it might lead people to leave his church, or give him the cold shoulder. And he is a northern man and is the successor of Byron Sunderland—of Byron Sunderland, the man who years ago in this city, when the Negro had few friends, and when Frederick Douglass, our own great Douglass, found it difficult to get a place in which to speak, threw his church open and made the great orator welcome, though he knew that he would be severely criticized for it. Imagine Byron Sunderland saying, "Had I known that he was a colored man I would not have married them." Imagine Jesus Christ, whom this man professes to represent, making such an ignoble speech, such an inglorious surrender of principle, through cowardice. It only shows the drift of sentiment; it is only another illustration of the truth that we have enemies, and that they are increasing. If this man were charged with being an enemy to the race, he would doubtless deny it. He thinks, perhaps, he is a friend, and may be able to persuade himself that he is, but he could never persuade me that he is. I regard no man as a friend, I care not what his profession may be, or how many good things he may say patronizingly of the Negro, or how much money he may give for Negro education, if, by word or act, he denies the essential equality of the Negro as a man, if he looks upon him and treats him as an inferior being, belonging to a lower order of creation; if he thinks that a Negro ought to be satisfied with less than a white man is satisfied with; that there are things that white men may aspire to that Negroes have no right to aspire to. I care not, I say what he may think of himself or what others may think of him, I class him among the enemies of the race, among those who are seeking, consciously or unconsciously, to break down in the Negro that which is most essential to his true manhood—his self-respect. Look upon a man as an inferior, treat him as an inferior, encourage others to treat him as an inferior, and it doesn't make any difference how much you may do for him under the guise of philanthropy, you can never repair the injury that you do him. If you want to help him; if you are really his friend, you will treat him in a way to stimulate his self-respect, to encourage every manly aspiration within him.

That is just the thing, however, which the great majority of even the so-called friends of the Negro do not want to stimulate within him. It isn't the manly Negro, it isn't the self-respecting Negro, it isn't the Negro who feels, and rightly feels, I am a man, and wants to be treated as a man, that the country is anxious to develop. Those are the Negroes that are labeled in the South "undesirable": the Negroes, they say, that think they are just as good as white men, and who put bad notions in the heads of other Negroes. Even our so-called friends are not over-anxious, I say, to develop a very large crop of that type of Negro. It is the Negro who accepts the doctrine of his supposed inferiority, and who is content to be treated as an inferior—the Negro humbly and gratefully accepts any recognition which the superior race may see fit to bestow upon him—never losing sight of the fact, however, that he has his place and that he must keep in it. In other words, it's the Negro who believes in self-effacement, or who pretends to believe in it, that our enemies delight in and that even our friends prefer to have dealings with. That is the kind of Negro who never gives any trouble. He is never an agitator; he never has any complaints or grievances. You may kick him and cuff him about: you may take away his right to vote; you may prescribe Jim Crow cars for him—it's all the same—he is satisfied; he is not disposed to make any trouble. Our enemies, and even our friends, may rejoice in the production and in the multiplication of that type of a Negro, but the race, thank God, never has and never will. That is the kind of Negro that the race utterly despises. I don't care what kind of education may be prescribed for the Negro, whether by friend or foe, if it does not recognize the fact that he is a man, and not a man minus something, and doesn't deal with him as a man, it will fail. Education which sacrifices the manhood of a race, the self-respect of a race, is not the education which the Negro, or any race of men, wants. If it is to be helpful in the highest and best sense of the term, it must recognize the fact, and address itself to the fact, that the Negro is every whit a man, created in the image of God, just as truly as the white man, and endowed with the same faculties and capacities, the same desires and aspirations. I get utterly tired of hearing men classed as friends of the Negro, or who class themselves as his friends, who at heart regard him as an inferior being, and who show by their treatment of him and by the course which they may outline for him that that is their estimate of him. The first requisite to a true friendship for the Negro is the recognition of the fact that he is a man, and that he is entitled to be treated as other men are treated. The man who doesn't believe that, and who isn't willing to act on that assumption, cannot, in the nature of the case, be to him a friend in the true sense of the term, and it is sheer nonsense to speak of him as such. As long as white men feel and act on the theory that the Negro is not to be placed in the same category as themselves, is not to be accorded the same rights as themselves, they may want to help him, but they cannot, in that which is most essential—in strengthening, in developing his manhood. What the Negro expects and demands from his friends is treatment that will conserve and not destroy his self-respect.

Returning now to the circular, we are reminded in it, in the fourth place, that our friends are dying out. The reference here is to the men and women who stood by us in the dark days of slavery and the period immediately succeeding the war. A nobler band of men and women the world has never seen. These old battle-scarred heroes are rapidly disappearing—only here and there one remains. Our friends are not only dying out in the sense of passing from the stage of action, but also in the sense of losing interest. Many have waxed cold; many have gone entirely over to the enemy. They have come under the withering and benumbing touch of the subtle, pernicious, and pervasive influence of the South.

5. **We are reminded also of the fact that "we are confronting a crisis in our life, as citizens, unlike any other former trial through which we have passed—a crisis full of deadly menace to all that freemen hold dearest."** And this is also true. The enemy seems to be unusually active just now, and to be having very largely his own way. There never was a time when the peril to our rights as citizens seemed more real or more threatening than at present.

6. **We are reminded also of the fact that there is on our part need of humbling ourselves before God.** This is to be to us a day of humiliation as well as a day of prayer—a day of confession of our shortcomings. The implication is that we are not all that we ought to be; that too often we do the things that we ought not to do and leave undone the things that we ought to do. This, I think, none of us will deny. And our attention is called to this fact in connection with this day, in the hope of stimulating us all to more strenuous efforts at self-improvement, in the hope of impressing us all more deeply than ever with the necessity of setting ourselves resolutely against all forms of evil and of seeking earnestly to appropriate and assimilate all that is good. It is well for us, as a race, to keep our eyes upon ourselves; to hold ourselves to a strict account. Only as we do this can we hope to profit by past mistakes and blunders; can we hope to keep ourselves in line with what is highest and best.

And now, in view of all that has been said,—in view of our present condition and environment in this country, it is evident that if we are to succeed, we must not only be alive, wide awake, ourselves, but we must have help, and help that is more than human. And in the text which we are considering, such a source of help is pointed out to us. The words are, "God is our refuge and strength, a very present help in trouble. Therefore will we not fear, though the earth do change, and though the mountains be shaken in the heart of the seas: though the waters thereof roar and be troubled, though the mountains tremble with the swelling thereof." If as a people, we would only make that language ours; if that was really the sentiment of our hearts; if God was to us, what He is represented here as being, we would have no need to fear anything, nor anybody,—the gates of hell could not prevail against us. And this is the thought that I want to dwell on just for a moment, in closing. The text calls attention, first, to the fact that God is. It assumes the existence of God. It affirms His being and reality.

Second, it declares that He is a refuge. What is a refuge? It is a strong tower, into which those who are being pursued, those who are in danger, may run and find safety. God is such a strong tower, for the oppressed, for the downtrodden, for the poor, the weak, the friendless.

Third, it declares that God is a source of strength. The psalmist says, God is our strength, i.e., through him they were enabled to do what they could not do otherwise. They were strong, because their dependence was upon God, because they looked to him in every time of need; they were strong because they had linked themselves to Him.

Fourth, it declares that where God is thus accepted, where he becomes the refuge and strength of an individual or a race, there is never any need for alarm, never mind how unfavorable, how unpropitious the circumstances may appear. "Therefore will we not fear, though the earth do change, and though the mountains be shaken into the heart of the seas; though the waters therefore roar and be troubled, though the mountains tremble with the swelling thereof." What we need, therefore, as a people, is to stay ourselves on God, is to make Him our refuge and strength. And yet this, I am afraid, is just what we are not doing. In too many cases we are growing up ourselves, and we are allowing our children to grow up, with little or no thought of God. He isn't in our thoughts, and He isn't in their thoughts. The life which we are living, and the life which we are training them to live, is a life with God left out of it, or so nearly left out of it as to practically amount to the same thing.[7] This

[7] In this excerpt, Grimké's EEH is betrayed through four embodied expressions: *Biblicism* is present in Grimké's focus on divine refuge and strength as he draws from Psalm 46 to ground the congregation in scriptural

is to be greatly deplored. And the plea which I want to make here this morning, not only to the fathers and mothers, but also to the young men and women, and even the children, is, that we centre [*sic*] our thoughts upon God, that we take Him into our lives and give Him the place of empire there, not only for our own sake, as individuals, but because as a race, it is the surest way to solve this difficult and perplexing problem with which we are grappling in this country. If we will be true to God: if we will do what He wants us to do; if we will make His word a lamp to our feet and a light to our path, He will discomfit our enemies and give us the victory. "Oh that there were such a heart in them, that they would fear me, and keep all my commandments always, that it might be well with them, and with their children forever." That is what God said of the children of Israel. And what He was willing to do for them, He will do for us if we trust Him, if we delight ourselves in Him, if we will serve Him with the whole heart.

On this day of humiliation and prayer, let us remember, therefore, that there is help for us in God if we will let Him help us if we will put ourselves where He can help us. The heathen may rage, the people may imagine a vain thing; the kings of the earth may set themselves and the rulers take counsel together against us, but if God is our strength and refuge, if it is His will that we are delighting to do, their counsel will come to naught, it will avail nothing. "Touch not mine anointed," is what God says. We are told that He rebuked kings for their sake. Let us see to it, then, that we are His anointed: that His mark is upon us. In this way, we, who are members of this race, can do more to help it than in any other way: in this way, we

---

assurance. *Conversionism* is implicit in his call for communal realignment toward God-centered living. *Activism* emerges as he exhorts the community to uphold their faith collectively, challenging believers to renew their public and private dedication to God. Lastly, *Crucicentrism* is reflected in his conviction that enduring trials requires Christ-centered resilience, positioning the cross as central to understanding both personal and social deliverance. This call echoes Pauline praxis in Ephesians 6:10, where Paul urges believers to "be strong in the Lord and in the strength of His might," encouraging faith that is actively grounded in God's sustaining power.

can call to our aid a power that is invincible, that is more than a match for our enemies. And vice versa, if we want to injure this race, if we want to make it more and more difficult for it to succeed, all we have to do is to shut God out of our hearts, is to go the way that He doesn't want us to go, and to train our children to do the same.

I have been speaking of enemies of the race, on the other side of the line, but there are enemies also within the race itself. And who are these enemies? I am not referring now to those members of the race who play into the hands of the enemies on the outside, giving them aid and succor by their cowardly acquiescence, for personal ends, in the treatment that is accorded to their race, in the low estimate that is put upon it. It is not of such traitors that I am speaking. It is of an entirely different class of enemies, and who are they? They are the fathers and mothers, who live themselves and who train their children to live without God; they are the men and women, whether old or young, who are indifferent to religion, who think they can get along without God. Such men and women are among the very worst enemies that we have. What hope is there for us as a race, in this land, surrounded as we are by so many hostile and powerful forces, if we drift away from God? There is none whatever. This I believe with all my heart; and just in proportion, as this fact roots and grounds itself in the consciousness of the race, will we be strong. With God on our side we have nothing to fear; but God is on the side of the man or the race only who is on His side. The important thing for us, therefore, is to get on God's side and to stay on His side. And this is the thought, which this day is intended particularly to emphasize. It is a solemn call to the whole race to turn to God, and to turn to God with full purpose and determination to serve Him, and Him only. That is the path of safety; the path that leads to victory; the path that is sure to bring peace, prosperity, happiness.

If we fail in the struggle; if we are driven to the wall; if our enemies get the better of us, it will be our own fault. It will be because we haven't made God our refuge and strength, because we haven't been seeking first His kingdom. Joshua, in his farewell address to the people, you will remember, said, "And, behold, this day I am going the way of all the earth: and ye know in all your hearts and in all your souls, that not one thing hath failed of all the good things which Jehovah your God spake concerning you; all are come to pass unto you, not one thing hath failed thereof." God is a covenant-keeping God. His words endure to a thousand generations. What He says may be relied upon with absolute assurance. And, therefore, although we are living in troublous times, although the waters are roaring about us, and the mountains are shaking in the heart of the sea; although everything seems to portend evil, we need have no fear, if we are anchored in God. He is a sure defense; He is an ever-present help in trouble. In the psalm from which our text is taken, there runs all through it a note of triumph, and it is because underneath it is the consciousness of the abiding presence of God.

There is a river, the streams whereof make glad the city of God,
The holy place of the tabernacles of the Most High.
God is in the midst of her; she shall not be moved:
God will help her, and that right early.
The nations raged, the kingdoms were moved:
He uttered His voice, the earth melted.
Jehovah of hosts is with us;
The God of Jacob is our refuge.
Come, behold the works of Jehovah,
What desolations he hath made in the earth.
He maketh wars to cease unto the end of the earth;
He breaketh the bow, and cutteth the spear in sunder;
He burneth the chariots in the fire.
Be still, and know that I am God:
I will be exalted among the nations,
I will be exalted in the earth.
Jehovah of hosts is with us;
The God of Jacob is our refuge.

And this same God will be our God, if we will accept Him, if we will surrender ourselves to His guidance and direction; if we will make Him our pillar of cloud, by day, and our pillar of fire by night. "I will be exalted among the nations," is what God says here: and, if we will exalt Him in our hearts, in our lives, He will exalt us. He will break the bow, and cut the spear in sunder, and burn up the chariots of our enemies. The God of Jacob is a mighty God. His power is infinite. You remember Luther's grand old hymn:

A mighty fortress is our God,
A bulwark never failing;
Our Helper He amid the flood
Of mortal ills prevailing:
For still our ancient foe
Doth seek to work us woe;
His craft and power are great,
And, armed with cruel hate,
On earth is not his equal.

Did we in our own strength confide,
Our striving would be losing;
Were not the right man on our side,
The man of God's own choosing:
Dost ask who that may be?
Christ Jesus, it is He;
Lord Sabaoth His Name
From age to age the same,
And He must win the battle.

And though this world, with devils filled
Should threaten to undo us;
We will not fear, for God hath willed
His truth to triumph through us:
The prince of darkness grim,—
We tremble not for him
His rage we can endure,
For lo, his doom is sure,
One little word shall fell him.

O, let us as a people never forget this. And whether our earthly friends be few or many, let us remember that the one friend without which we cannot succeed—the one friend that is more important for us to have than all the others, is God. If He is for us, it matters not who is against us, what weapons may be raised against us; it matters not if the South succeeds, for the time being, in winning the whole North over to its way of thinking, we will be taken care of all the same, we will get our rights all the same. The unholy alliance cannot, will not last. To God, therefore, let us turn our thoughts, and the thoughts of our children more and more. With Him as our refuge and strength, we need have no fear.

Sermon 4

The Atlanta Riot[8]

Of the Jews five times received I forty stripes save one. Thrice was I beaten with rods, once I was stoned, thrice I suffered shipwreck, a night and a day I have been in the deep; in journeyings often, in perils of rivers, in perils of robbers, in perils from my countrymen, in perils from the Gentiles, in perils in the city, in perils in the wilderness, in perils in the sea, in perils among false brethren.
—2 Corinthians 11:24–26

The apostle Paul, in these words, sets forth the condition in which he found himself almost constantly. The term which he uses to describe this condition is the word *peril.* He tells us that he was in constant peril; that he was beset by dangers on all sides. The sources of the danger of which he speaks, as set forth here, are four-fold:

1. From natural causes. He was in perils of rivers; he was in perils in the sea.
2. From the criminally inclined. He was in perils of robbers.
3. From his own countrymen; from the men of his own race, the men with whom he was identified by blood.
4. From the Gentiles, from those who were not Jews.

The apostle was a traveling missionary; and so was constantly on the go. Sometimes in these missionary tours, he had to travel by water; and so was exposed to all the dangers of the sea—to storms and tempests. One of these terrible storms, in which the ship was lost, his traveling companion, Luke, has left a description of for us in the *Acts of the Apostles.*

Sometimes in his travels, he had to journey along lonely passes and over barren mountain wastes, infested by robbers and other desperate

---

[8] Grimké, *Works I,* 406–18. Delivered October 7, 1906.

characters: and so was liable to be treated as the man on his way from Jericho was, who was waylaid, robbed, and beaten almost to death.

Sometimes in the discharge of his duties, as the ambassador of the Lord Jesus Christ, he ran up against the prejudices of his own countrymen. The course which he was pursuing, and which he felt that he must pursue in obedience to the dictates of his own conscience and the expressed command of Jesus Christ, whom he once persecuted, but in whose service he had now enlisted for life, excited in his countrymen the most violent opposition. They were ready to kill him at the first opportunity, as they tried to do when he last visited Jerusalem. You remember that turbulent scene, as Luke describes it in *Acts, 21*st *chapter*: *"And all the city was moved, and the people ran together; and they laid hold on Paul, and dragged him out of the temple. And as they were seeking to kill him, tidings came to the chief captain of the band that all Jerusalem was in confusion."* A little farther on in the description of what took place, we have also this record: *And they gave him audience unto this word; and they lifted up their voices and said, Away with such a fellow from the earth: for it is not fit that he should live.*

Among the Gentiles, he also found himself beset by dangers. At Philippi, he and Silas were seized, cast into prison, and beaten with many stripes. At Ephesus, a riot was precipitated, during which the apostle had to conceal himself from the violence of the mob.

In view of the record which has come down to us, we can readily understand what the apostle means when he speaks of being in perils. He was in constant danger, bodily danger; liable at any time to be violently assaulted; to be maimed, or beaten to death. Whether he was on land or sea, in the city, or in the country, it was all the same. The same conditions surrounded him. Whichever way he went, whichever way he looked, the ghastly visage of danger stared him in the face. He was encompassed by perils.

And what was true of the apostle Paul is true today of our race in this country, especially in the southern section of it. We are in constant peril; no one is safe for a moment. We are liable at any time to be shot down, to be brutally murdered. Character, intelligence, wealth, count for nothing. The most intelligent, the most respectable, the most industrious, the most law-abiding are in just as great danger as the most ignorant, the most vicious, the most indolent, the most lawless. Sometimes the more progress that is made, the higher the type represented, the greater the peril. The feeling among certain elements of southern society, among the poor whites—the lower classes—is more pronounced, is more virulent in its opposition to the well-to-do, the self-respecting, the aggressive elements of the colored race than against the shiftless, non-progressive, self-satisfied, who are content to remain just as they are, who are without hope, without aspiration, without ambition. They are more tolerant of the one type, than of the other; they will take more from the one than they will from the other; they are not so easily offended by the one as by the other. And the reason for this is two-fold:

1. It is the result of envy, born of hatred. It hurts this class of whites to see the Negro prospering. They don't want him to succeed; they don't want him to get along. Somehow, they seem to feel that it detracts from them: that if this higher class of Negroes were out of the way, it would be better for them. The unprogressive Negro, the Negro that is content with present conditions, they are not concerned about, they have nothing to fear from that class; but it is the rising Negro, the Negro that is forging to the front; who sees a future before him, and who is alive, wide-awake to the possibilities of the future—that he looks with especial disfavor upon; and the reason for this is because he sees in that type of Negro a rival, a competitor in the struggle of life. And, in regarding him as a competitor, he is not mistaken. He is the type of Negro that he will have to reckon with in the fierce battle of life. He is in the struggle, and he is there to win. He is bound to get his share of the plums. The hatred, the opposition of this class of whites is not going to dampen his ardor or discourage him in the least. He has begun to forge ahead, and he is going to continue to forge ahead. You can't stop the progress of a people; you can't keep

a people from rising by hating them, by exhibiting toward them an envious and malicious spirit, if they themselves are in earnest: if they themselves are determined to go forward; if their minds are firmly made up to succeed. And this I believe is true of our race,—if not of all,—of a sufficient number, at least, to guarantee the result. *Onward!* is our watchword; and more and more is that thought taking possession of the masses of our people; more and more are we waking up to the thought that we have got to work out our own destiny in this country. And out of that thought or conviction is coming more and more activity from within the race. As long as we feel that we must depend upon others; as long as we feel that we must look to others and not to ourselves, there will be more or less stagnation within the race. It is only as we come to feel, and to feel deep down in the bottom of our hearts that we *"must sink or swim; live or die; survive or perish,"* through our own exertions, that the latent powers within the race itself will be awakened, and the forces necessary to lift it, to carry it forward, be generated. It is only as the race becomes self-reliant that it will grow strong; that it will become self-respecting; and that it will, command respect from others. And because the race is becoming more and more self-reliant; because the evidences are multiplying every year of greater activity from within, we have nothing to fear from the envious and malicious spirit of the lower classes of whites in the South, in keeping us from rising, from taking an honorable place in the procession of those who are moving forward, in the onward march of progress.

2. Another reason why a certain class of whites in the South, why, I may say, a very large proportion of the southern whites, are less tolerant of the aggressive, progressive, intelligent, thrifty, well-to-do Negro, than of the other class, is because it is the intelligent, progressive Negro who gives the lie to their theory of the Negro's inferiority. *God made the Negro inferior,* they say, *God made him to be a servant; to be a beast of burden; a hewer of wood and a drawer of water.* Some have gone so far as to deny his humanity, as to declare that

he hasn't a soul. And while they are proclaiming his inferiority, while they are believing, or pretending to believe in his inferiority, right in their midst, all about them, the Negro is demonstrating his capacity, by proofs as strong as words of holy writ, to take his place alongside his detractors in all the avenues of life, where he has had the opportunity. This hopelessly inferior race, this lowest type of humanity, if he be really human, strange to say, is found doing, and doing just as well, what the highest type is doing. In business, in scholarship, in all the higher activities he has been tried, not a great many, perhaps, but a sufficient number to determine the capacity of the race. He is succeeding in business; in the professions; he is measuring up to the requirements of all the great universities of the land; and in the field of athletics, where discipline and nerve, and the highest skill of a certain kind are necessary, he is not a whit behind his white competitor. I do not believe in prizefighting and yet I was gratified the other day to read what referee George Siler had to say about Gans, the colored champion: *"It is generally conceded,"* he said, *"that Booker T. Washington has done much good and will do much for the colored race for its uplifting, its education, for making its members citizens in a true sense of the word; but with all that, in the entire course of his life work he never did one-tenth to place the black man in the front rank as a gentleman than has been done by Joe Gans. He has shown forbearance; he has shown courtesy; and in the ring on Monday, he displayed chivalry which is not unworthy of being classed with the superlative notions of the gentlemen of the middle ages who wore spring suits of boiler plate and tilted at everything in sight for the defense of some fair lady. He failed to take advantage of technicalities; he aided his fallen foe and was assaulted even while his glove still maintained his friendly grasp on that of his adversary. He fought a good fight when crippled, and although fouled more than once, refrained from taking the advantage which the rules gave him."*

In the *Boston Sunday Post* is also this statement: *"The victory of Gans brings up an interesting question. Is not the Negro a greater fighter than the white man? There are certainly good grounds for coming to that conclusion when one recalls the name of Peter Jackson, the Australian heavy-weight, the only fighter whom John Sullivan ever feared; George Dixon, whose equal has not yet been found among the bantam and featherweights; Joe Walcott, who still stands pre-eminent as the welterweight champion; and now Joe Gans, the lightweight champion without a peer. There are four champions in four classes, and they were almost contemporaries. Add to that great quartette a few of the present near champions—Jack Johnson, the cleverest of all big men; Young Peter Jackson, Sam Langford, and others, and then remember that all the white champions are steadfastly refusing to box with Negroes. It looks as if the black man had something on the white man in the ring."*

Wherever the Negro has been fairly tested, he has made an honorable record for himself; has demonstrated his capacity to do what other races have done. All over the southland are unmistakable evidences of his progress; unmistakable evidences of his capacity to do what other men have done. And yet, in spite of the record which he is making, the daily, hourly proof that he is offering of his ability to succeed, the old theory of his inferiority is still maintained, is still insisted upon; is still accepted as true. Instead of revising their theory in view of the facts, instead of rejoicing in the ever-growing evidence of the black man's progress and aiding in every possible way to hasten his development, the fact that he is forging to the front seems only to intensify the feeling against him. And one reason for this, as I have already said, is because it gives the lie to the white man's theory. It is worse than puerile to talk about the inferiority of the Negro in view of what he has done, is still doing, and of the promise which he gives of still larger things in the future. Every man who has given the matter any thought, who has taken the pains to inform himself, to get hold of the facts, knows that the Negro is going forward, that he is making progress, commendable progress, along many lines. And in no part of the country is there greater evidence of this fact than in the southern section of our country. And yet there isn't a member of this race in all that southland who isn't in daily peril, who may not at any moment be violently assaulted, who has any rights which white men are bound to respect. To have a dark face is to become a target for abuse, for insult; is to give every white man the right to maltreat you, to kick and cuff you, and spit upon you. And if you resent it, if you dare to protest, to intimate that you have some rights that you would like to have them respect, the mob spirit is instantly evoked, and your brains are knocked out, or you are shot to death or burned at the stake. That is the condition of things all over the South. There is no part of it, no section of it, however remote, of which this is not true. Everywhere the black man is beset by perils. He doesn't know what a day may bring forth; he doesn't know what day he may be shot down, or some member of his family, or some friend or acquaintance murdered. We have just had an exhibition, a most shocking exhibition of the constant peril in which this race is forced to live, in the unprovoked, brutal, and dastardly assaults that were made upon members of it in Atlanta, Ga. Assaults not upon the guilty, not upon the criminal classes, but upon all Negroes indiscriminately. The country was horrified; the whole civilized world stood aghast; and yet what took place in Atlanta may take place in any southern city at any time; the spirit that pervaded Atlanta—the murderous, blood-thirsty, Negro-hating spirit—is the spirit that pervades the entire South; it needs only the occasion to call it forth. Paul was in peril of rivers, in peril of robbers, in peril of his own countrymen, in peril of the Gentiles—the Negro in the South is in peril of the white man. And it isn't an imaginary, it is a real peril, as the actual daily experiences of this race all over the South will testify. This is one reason why so many are getting away from the South. We are inclined to blame them, at times, but dare we under the circumstances? If we were situated as they are, what would we do? What would any man do who felt that he could not surrender his manhood, and yet who was unwilling to sacrifice his life, to expose himself to the bullets of white assassins and murderers?

Now, I know what will be said, what is being said: "*The Negro has brought all this on himself; he has induced this condition of things; this peril that surrounds him is of his own making.*" It is a lie! The Negro race is not responsible for this condition of things. This is what John Temple Graves and others of his ilk have said in reference to the Atlanta massacre. Several assaults, it is alleged, were made on white women by Negroes, four or five in one week. Grant it. In what sense were the colored people of Atlanta responsible for those assaults? Were they parties to them? Did they know the assailants? Did they know that these assaults were to be made? Was it with their knowledge, with their approval? Did they connive at them? Did they give aid and succor to the assailants? No! Not even such whited sepulchers as John Temple Graves, Hoke Smith, and Clark Howell, who did everything in their power to fan the flames of race hatred, believed anything of the kind. The Negroes of Atlanta, as a class, had no more responsibility for those assaults than the whites as a class had. The fact that the assailants were black furnished no justification or excuse for assailing the other members of the race who had nothing to do with them, and no knowledge of them. It is only a subterfuge, a lying device, behind which to hide their hatred of all Negroes. According to their own statement, the probabilities are that of all those who were brutally murdered, not one guilty person suffered. They were all innocent, so far as we know, and so far as those who murdered them knew. The guilt or innocence of the victims played no part in the bloody tragedy. It was race hatred pure and simple. One Negro answered as well as another the demand of the mob.

Now, I am not blaming white men; I am not blaming men of any race for being concerned about the protection of their women from assaults by brutes of any kind, be they white or black; I am not blaming white men for feeling indignant, wrought up, for being stirred to the very depths of their being, in view of such assaults. They would be less than men if they did not feel strongly about the matter. Such assaults cannot be too severely condemned; they are unspeakably infamous; and ought to be put down with a strong hand. I am not blaming white men for rising up and saying, *"This thing must stop."* But I am blaming them—

1. Because their concern is only for the protection of white women, while they care nothing about the protection of black women. It isn't the virtue of womanhood that they are anxious to protect, but of white womanhood. Black women might be assaulted every day in the year without giving them the slightest concern; without exciting in them the least indignation. The poor black woman's virtue counts for nothing with them.

2. I am blaming them for taking the law into their own hands. Criminal assault is an offense for which the State has provided an adequate penalty. And the State alone is charged with the enforcement of the law. Great criminals and small criminals alike are to be tried by the properly constituted authority, and if found guilty, punished. It is not the province of any man, or set of men, who feel aggrieved, to take the law into their own hands. In the case of assaults, as in the case of all other crimes, the law must be allowed to take its course. Those charged with enforcing it must be upheld. Everybody else must keep their hands off. Over against private revenge, against the individual attempting to right his own wrongs, stands this great idea of government.

3. I am blaming them for not discriminating between those who commit assaults upon white women and those who do not. Four or five assaults were made in and about Atlanta in one week, we are told, and therefore, Negroes indiscriminately must be shot down; Negroes indiscriminately were shot down. If the assailants

> themselves had been apprehended, the mob would have had no right to touch a hair of their heads—that was the function of the civil authorities—but when it attempts to deal with innocent men and women, to hunt them down like wild beasts with murderous intent, simply because of their race identity with the assailants, how much more to be condemned is such conduct.

I regret to say there is a disposition, and a growing disposition, on the part of a great many white people, North as well as South, to blame the Negro race because of its criminal class. I, as a member of that race, utterly repudiate any responsibility for Negro criminals. What have I to do with the criminal Negro? What have you to do with him? What have hundreds and thousands and millions of our people all over the country to do with him except to extend him a helping hand in trying to reform him, to lift him up, to make him a better man? But the fact that he is a criminal, what right has that to affect my standing in this community as an upright, straightforward, honorable citizen? What right has it to affect your standing in this community? What right has it to affect the standing of the same class of colored citizens in other communities? Because there are criminals among us, is that a reason why we should be classed as criminals? Why we should be treated as criminals? As an individual, I claim the right to be judged by what I am; not by what somebody else is. This is the right which every white man claims, the right which is accorded to white men; why not to black men? Why should one criminal Negro, or a dozen, or a hundred, or a thousand of them, make all Negroes criminal? Why is the Negro race to be judged by its criminal class, and the white race not? The standing of no white man, or set of white men, is affected in any community by the fact that there are white criminals in that community. It is only where people of color are concerned that that rule is applied. I for one protest against it. It is wrong; totally, absolutely wrong. It has no foundation in reason, common sense, or justice. I am no criminal; and I do

> not belong to a criminal race; and I will never rest content under any such aspersion. I utterly repudiate the imputation: I repudiate it for myself; I repudiate it for you, who are here; I repudiate it for all the self-respecting people of color all over this country. So far as the criminal Negro is concerned, it is the duty of the State to deal with him as with other criminals of other races. So far as the Negro who is not a criminal is concerned—the Negro who is trying to make something of himself—it is the duty of the State, it is the duty of society, it is the duty of the community where he lives to recognize that fact, and to treat him accordingly. In no sense is he to be classed with his criminal brother in black. It is unjust to do so. It is to destroy in him every incentive to high endeavor.

And now let me come to the point that I have particularly in mind. What shall we say to our brethren in the South in view of their environments—in view of the perils that constantly beset them? There are three things, I think, we ought to say to them:

1. *Don't be discouraged.* Continue to do your utmost to develop yourselves along all lines—material, intellectual, moral, spiritual. Continue to buy farms; continue to go into business; continue to work at your trades; continue to send your children to school; continue to sustain your churches, and to insist upon filling them with clean, pure men. Whatever your hands find to do, that is just and pure and lovely, and of good report, do with your might. Do your level best to make the most of yourselves, and of your children. Leave no stone unturned; be alive, wide awake; let no opportunity pass, unimproved. Work, work, hard persistent work, day in and day out, week in and week out, during all the months and years, is the course that must be pursued; is the course that you have been pursuing. Continue to pursue it; continue to apply yourselves earnestly, faithfully in all the avenues of honorable endeavor, in which you are engaged. You have done well; and all the evidences indicate that each decade will find you still farther up the scale of progress. We

rejoice with you, in all the efforts that you have made, and are still making to develop yourselves, to improve your condition. The struggle is a hard one, and it is going to be a long one; but success is bound to crown your efforts. You cannot fail as long as you are determined to succeed.

2. *Be discreet; be cautious; be very careful of what you say and do.* Jesus, in sending his disciples forth, said to them, you will remember: *"Behold, I send you forth as sheep in the midst of wolves: be ye therefore wise as serpents, and harmless as doves."* What He meant was that they were to keep steadily in mind the fact that they were in the midst of wolves, among those who would be only too glad of the slightest pretext to ill-treat them, to violently assail them; and therefore they were to be wise, prudent, careful not to give unnecessary offense; not to expose themselves to unnecessary danger. This is the principle upon which the apostle Paul always acted in his contact with men of various races and conditions; and it is one which is important for us, as a race, to lay to heart. I do not mean by this that we are to surrender a single principle; that we are to efface ourselves; that we are to sacrifice our manhood—our self-respect—by no means. Our manhood, our self-respect must be maintained at all times, under all circumstances; but at the same time, we must be cautious; we must not needlessly expose ourselves to danger. The wisdom of the serpent did not always save the apostles from violence, from brutal assault; and it won't always save us; but it is the course, nevertheless, to be pursued. On the whole, it decreases friction; it lessens the evil. It gives a better opportunity for things to adjust themselves, a better opportunity for us to hold our own while we are strengthening ourselves from within. The wisdom of the serpent is what our people need all over the southland if they are to come out of the struggle in which they are engaged with the least harm to themselves and are to work from the point of greatest advantage to themselves.

3. *Be prepared to defend yourselves, if necessary.* I know the meaning of these words. I have carefully weighed them; and, before God, I believe in the message which they contain. To every black man throughout the whole southland, I say, and say deliberately, *Be prepared to defend yourself if necessary.*

    By this I do not mean that black men should go around with chips on their shoulders seeking a quarrel, seeking to foment strife and dissension. That is the last thing that they should think of doing, that they should permit themselves to engage in. If they are wise, they will cultivate the spirit of peace, peace, peace. Their aim always should be to avoid strife. But if, through no fault of theirs, if, without any just provocation on their part, they are assaulted with murderous intent by individuals or by mobs, they should be prepared to defend themselves. The only defense which a black man in the South has against the mob is the defense which he throws around himself. He has no protection from the civil authorities. What did the civil authorities amount to in the bloody riot at Atlanta? Although the city was in the clutches of a set of fiends, hunting and shooting down Negroes indiscriminately, the Governor was asleep in his bed, and no one thought of waking him until the mob had spent its fury. And the Mayor, we are told, pleaded with the mob; and the mob took it only as a joke, knowing too well where the sympathy of the authorities usually is. *Pleading with a mob!* Who ever heard of pleading with a mob! There is only one effective way of dealing with a mob and that is to shoot it to death; to meet it in the same spirit of violence in which it comes. But there is no disposition on the part of the civil authorities in the South to meet it in that spirit when it is organized for the purpose of lynching Negroes. And therefore Negroes must be prepared to defend themselves. The men who usually compose mobs are nothing but a set of cowards; they are ready to join in murderous assaults because they think that they can do it with impunity, without incurring any danger. The duty of the Negro, therefore, in seeking to protect himself from such violent outbreaks, is to

> make it as perilous as possible for the mob. When the mob understands, and understands from actual experience, that there are blows to take as well as blows to give, it will not be so quick to organize. The only thing which these cowards respect who organize mobs is force, brute force. The only thing which makes them think twice before acting is the fear of being injured, of being hurt. If the civil authorities will not deal with mobs as they ought to be dealt with, then it is the duty of the Negro, in seeking to protect himself from these organized assaults upon his life, to do what he can to remedy the evil. There is but one way, as I have already said, to deal with a mob; and that is to shoot it to death; to riddle it with bullets or dynamite it. And the Negro will be doing himself and the whole South a service by being prepared to make it as perilous as possible for the mob.
>
> Now, do not misunderstand me. Bear in mind the point which I am discussing. I am not urging colored men in the South to make war on white men. I am simply saying it is their duty to be prepared to defend themselves against such organized and murderous assaults as were made upon them in Atlanta.

These are the thoughts that have been running in my mind for the last ten days; these are the things that I have felt like saying to our brethren in the South. *Don't be discouraged.* Continue to do your utmost to develop yourselves along all lines, material, intellectual, moral, spiritual. *Be discreet, be cautious, be very careful of what you say or do.* Keep the peace: do all you can to preserve it: but at the same time, be prepared to defend yourselves if necessary. This, I think, is good advice. It is the advice that ought to be given. I don't think anyone can take any just exception to it. I believe it is sound, through and through; that it is in harmony with the dictates of nature, and of morality, and of religion. If the Negro is not prepared to defend himself, he will be without defense. He will die as the fool dieth.

Let us hope that this reign of terror in the South will not always last. That a change will come and come soon for the better. God hasten the time in this land when the spirit of fraternity, of brotherhood, shall prevail everywhere; when men of all races and colors shall mingle freely together, without bitterness or hatred toward each other. May this land of ours, blessed as it is in so many ways, be an example to all the nations of the earth in justice, in humanity, in all the elements that go to make up a truly Christian civilization. The black man is here to stay; and the white man is here to stay; and there is no reason why they shouldn't live in peace and amity, if they will both do right; if they will both fear God, and keep his commandments; if they will both set up the golden rule, and settle all of their differences in the spirit of him who came not to be ministered unto, but to minister, and gave himself for others. Let us all pray that this spirit may descend upon us all, black and white alike.[9] The prayer of old Governor Hampton, on his death-bed, was: *"God bless all my people, black and white alike."* And that is the spirit that is needed; that is the prayer that will bring peace, lasting peace.

When Russia was in one of her great wars the suffering of the soldiers had been long and bitter, and they were waiting for the end of the strife. One day a messenger in great excitement ran among the tents of the army shouting: Peace! Peace! The sentinel on guard asked: 'Who says peace?' and the sick soldier turned on his hospital mattress and asked: 'Who says peace?' and all up and down the encampment of Russians went the question: 'Who says peace?' The messenger responded: 'The Czar says

[9] This excerpt encapsulates Grimké's EEH through the Bebbington Quadrilateral's core emphases. *Biblicism* is present as Grimké invokes scripture's "golden rule" and Christ's model of servanthood to frame a reconciliatory ethos. *Conversionism* emerges through his appeal for heart transformation across races, urging Black and White Christian communities to embody a Christ-like humility and repentance. *Activism* is implied as Grimké stresses the societal impact achievable through shared adherence to divine commandments. Lastly, *Crucicentrism* is reflected in his call to embody a Christ-centered ethic grounded in selfless service and peace as central to an authentic Christian community. This vision echoes Paul's instruction in Galatians 3:28, which emphasizes unity in Christ beyond social and ethnic divisions, advocating a reconciliatory praxis grounded in justness and mutual respect.

peace!' That was enough. That meant going home. That meant the war was over. No more wounds and no more long marches.

And so, when the Czar in this country, when public sentiment—black public sentiment, and white public sentiment, public sentiment among the best of both races, shall say peace, there will be peace. Our duty, therefore, is to set ourselves earnestly to work to make such a sentiment. We can all lend a hand; we can all do something; we can make the effort, at least. And if the same thing is going on among the whites, soon there will be no more bloody massacres; there will be no more race conflicts.

Sermon 5

The Paramount Importance of Character, or Character, the True Standard by Which to Estimate Individuals and Races[10]

The subject upon which I am to speak is, to my mind, one of very great importance, and one that has always needed to be emphasized, but never more so than today. As a basis for what I have to say, I have selected a passage of Scripture, not only because it is always well to have back of us the Word of God, but especially because, in this particular instance, the passage selected defines or expresses more clearly than elsewhere exactly what I have in mind. The passage is to be found in Romans 2:11: "For there is no respect of persons with God." The subject, if I were to give it a name, would be *The Paramount Importance of Character, or, Character the True Test or Standard by Which to Estimate Individuals or Races.*

In the words, "For there is no respect of persons with God," a great principle of the Divine government is enunciated, which it is important for us to understand, in order that we may know what to expect from God, and in order that it may also become a governing principle in our own lives, in our dealings with others.

In the statement, attention is directed to the manner in which God, the great being who created all things, and by whom all things consist, deals with men. It doesn't say, mark you, that God has no respect for men, that He looks down upon them with contempt, that He regards them as beneath His notice. God is a wonderful being, immeasurably great, infinite in all His perfections—in wisdom, power, holiness, justice, goodness, and truth. He is without beginning of days or end of years. He is sometimes represented as sitting upon the circle of the earth, and the inhabitants thereof appearing as grasshoppers to Him. We are also told that all nations are as nothing before Him. In view of the greatness of God and our littleness, it has sometimes been thought that we are too insignificant to claim His attention. The deistic theory of the universe has some such idea as

---

[10] Grimké, *Works I*, 473–89. Delivered October 27, 1911.

this back of it: God is too great, too exalted to be concerned in human affairs. And, even in the mind of the psalmist, some such thought as this seemed to have flashed for a moment:

> When I consider thy heavens, the work of thy fingers,
> The moon and stars which thou hast ordained;
> What is man that thou art mindful of him?
> And the son of man, that thou visitest him?

What is man? He asks. How little, how insignificant he is. That man is little, infinitely little, as compared with God, is true; but nowhere in the Scriptures are we taught that because of his littleness, he is thereby put beyond the reach of the divine notice. The very opposite of this is true. God is not only represented as thinking of man but as constantly thinking of him and planning for his good. We have the great statement, "God so loved the world that He gave His only begotten Son, that whosoever believeth on Him should not perish, but have everlasting life." It Is also recorded—"The very hairs of your head are all numbered. Not a sparrow falls to the ground without His notice; and ye are more than many sparrows."

No, It isn't stated here that God has no respect for man. The statement is, "For there is no respect of persons with God," which is a very different thing.

No respect of persons! What does that mean? In general, it means that God deals impartially with men; that He has no favorites; that He is not swayed by any bias, either for or against anyone. What is meant here may be seen still farther from the following statements gathered from a few of the commentaries and other sources:

- To regard the person or respect the person is, in the scriptures, uniformly used to denote partiality, or being influenced in a decision not by truth, but by previous attachment to a person or one of the parties—by friendship, or bias, or prejudice.

- To respect the person is to suffer our opinion or judgment to be influenced or biased by the outward circumstances of a person to the prejudice of right and equity.
- To respect persons is to be swayed unduly by social station; to yield to personal considerations at the expense of right and high-mindedness.

There can scarcely be any doubt as to what, in general, was in the mind of the apostle in the use of the expression, "respect of persons." In order, however, that we may see in particular, exactly what is comprehended under it, it will be necessary for us to take up and consider certain passages of Scripture bearing upon the subject. Among such passages, the following may be cited:

- Ye shall do no unrighteousness in judgment: thou shalt not respect the person of the poor, nor honor the person of the mighty; but in righteousness shalt thou judge thy neighbor. (Lev. 19:15)
- Ye shall not respect persons in judgment; ye shall hear the small and great alike. (Deut. 1:17)
- For Jehovah your God, He is God of gods, and Lord of lords, the great God, the Mighty, and the terrible, who regardeth not persons, nor taketh reward. (Deut. 10:17)
- Him that saith to a king, Thou art vile, or to nobles, Ye are wicked; That respecteth not the person of princes, nor regardeth the rich more than the poor. (Job 34:19)
- Of a truth I perceive that God is no respecter of persons; but in every nation, he that feareth Him, and worketh righteousness, is acceptable to Him. (Acts 10:35)
- And, ye masters, do the same things unto them, and forbear threatening; knowing that He who is both their master and yours is in heaven, and there is no respect of persons with Him. (Eph. 6:9)
- For he that doeth wrong shall receive again for the wrong that he hath done; and there is no respect of persons. (Col. 3:25)
- And if ye call on Him as Father, who without respect of persons judgeth according to each man's work, pass the time

of your sojourn in fear: knowing that ye were redeemed not with corruptible things. (I. Pet. 1:17)

- My brethren, hold not the faith of our Lord Jesus Christ, the Lord of glory, with respect of persons. For if there come into your synagogue a man with a gold ring, in fine clothing, and there come in also a poor man in vile clothing: and ye have regard to him that weareth the fine clothing, and say, Sit thou here in a good place; and say to the poor man, Stand thou here, or sit under my footstool; do ye not make distinctions among yourselves, and become judges with evil thoughts? (Jas. 2:1–4)
- Bring forth therefore fruit worthy of repentance; and think not to say within yourselves, We have Abraham to our father. (Matt. 3:8, 9)

In the first of these passages, the exhortation is, "Ye shall do no unrighteousness in judgment." This has reference to the administration of justice, to judicial officers, to those to whom have been committed the settlement of differences between man and man; and the meaning is, the judge in rendering a decision must not be influenced by the outward condition or circumstances of those who may appear before him. In this particular passage, attention is called to two classes of persons—the poor and the mighty, or the poor and the rich—the word mighty is here used as equivalent to rich. The fact that a man is poor, in adjudicating his case, should not militate in the least against him, and vice versa, the fact that he is rich, should not in the least weigh in his favor. The relative financial standing of the individuals involved should be entirely eliminated and should play no part in reaching a decision. The decision should be based upon the merits of the case, upon the actual facts, irrespective of who the litigants are.

When these words were written, such was not the case, however; the judges, as a general thing, were corrupt, they were easily bribed, they expected to be bribed. In a contest between a rich man and a poor man, the poor man, therefore, had no chance whatever. Hence in the Old Testament, especially, there is the constant admonition against receiving gifts, against accepting presents as bribes or rewards. And in the New Testament times, the same condition of things largely prevailed, as is clear from what is said of Felix in connection with the trial of the apostle Paul. As the apostle reasoned of righteousness, and temperance, and the judgment to come, Felix was terrified and answered, "Go thy way for this time; and when I have a convenient season, I will call thee unto me." The record goes on to say, "He hoped withal that money would be given him of Paul; wherefore also he sent for him the oftener, and communed with him." In Cicero's first oration against Verres occurs this passage, which gives us an insight into the condition of things that prevailed in his time: "For an opinion has now become established, pernicious to us, and pernicious to the republic, which has been the common talk of every one, not only of Rome, but among the foreign nations also; that in the courts of law as they exist at present, no wealthy man, however guilty he may be, can possibly be convicted." The same condition of things, to some extent, prevails today. The poor man, in the administration of justice, is at a decided disadvantage as compared with the rich man. The rich man has a standing which the poor man has not: the rich man has considerations shown him that are not shown to the poor man; the rich man wields an influence which the poor man does not wield in some of our courts, at least. According to the passage we are considering, we are not to respect the person of the poor, nor honor the person of the mighty, of the rich; we are not to take the part of the poor, because he is poor, against the rich; nor are we to take the part of the rich because he is rich, against the poor. We should take the part of neither, but should deal out even justice to both.

In the second passage, the thought is about the same, though looked at from a little different standpoint: "Ye shall not respect persons in judgment; ye shall hear the small and great alike." The small are those of lowly origin, or humble birth—the common people, those who move in the humbler walks of life; they are small in the sense that they are not looked upon as of very great importance, as carrying much weight, as wielding much influence. The great are those who move in the upper circles, who have wealth, position, influence, who are looked upon by themselves and by others as being somebody. We speak, ordinarily, of high and low, of the upper and the lower classes of society, we speak of Patricians and Plebeians. These are distinctions that exist in society, as we find it today, and as it has always existed. And those in the so-called upper classes feel, as a general thing, that they are entitled to greater consideration than those in the so-called lower classes. Both, however, according to the principle laid down in this passage in Deut. 1:17, are to receive the same consideration, are to stand on precisely the same footing in the matter of judgment. The great, because of his greatness, of his superior position or standing, is not to be allowed to influence us in his favor; nor ought the small, because he is small, because his circumstances are what they are, be allowed to influence us against him. Both alike are to be heard, and heard with the same impartiality; both alike are to be judged, and to be judged without fear or favor. The distinction between great and small is not to be taken into consideration in the administration of justice, or in our moral estimates of men.

In the passage in Ephesians 6:9, the subject is looked at from still another standpoint: "And ye masters, do the same thing unto them, and forbear threatening, knowing that He who is both their master and yours is in heaven, and there is no respect of persons with Him." That is, God, in dealing with men, holds the master and servant alike to the same standard of morals; because a man is in the position of master, God isn't going to be more lenient with him, is not going to hold him to a less rigorous standard, than the one who is in the position of servant. He has no more regard for the master than for the servant and will show him no more consideration. They are both only men and stand before Him on precisely the same footing; what He exacts of the one, He exacts of the other.

In the passage in James 2:1–4, we have still another aspect of the subject: "My brethren, hold not the faith of the Lord Jesus Christ, the Lord of glory, with respect of persons. For if there come into your synagogue a man with a gold ring, in fine clothing, and there come in also a poor man in vile clothing; and ye have regard to him that weareth the fine clothing, and say, Sit thou here in a good place, and say to the poor man, Stand thou here, or sit under my footstool; do ye not make distinctions among yourselves, and become judges with evil thoughts?" Here it is to the well-dressed man, the man in costly apparel, and the poorly dressed man, the man plainly attired, in common, ordinary, inexpensive clothing, such as John the Baptist wore, such as the apostles wore, and such as Jesus Himself wore, attention is here directed. And the evil complained of is that the basis of judgment, the principle upon which these people acted in the treatment that was accorded to visitors who came to their synagogue, was founded entirely upon outward appearance. They assumed that the man who was the best dressed was the best man, the most worthy man; and accordingly, treated him with greater consideration, gave him a better seat, a more comfortable seat, in a more desirable part of the building. It would be all right to discriminate in this way if what is here assumed to be true was actually true, but we know that such is not the case. It is not true that those who wear the best clothes, the most costly apparel, are the best people in point of character. All that is necessary to dress expensively, to array oneself in fineries, is money; and we may have money, and a plenty of it, without having much character. The costliness of the apparel we wear is no evidence of moral worth. We may dress in purple and fine linen, and fare sumptuously every day, and yet be utterly unworthy of the respect of decent people; and, vice versa, we may be clothed in the plainest and least expensive garments, and yet be radiant and beautiful in soul—fit for the society of angels. We can't judge by the quality of the clothes one wears, as to whether he is a good man, or a bad man, whether he is upright in character or not. All judgments, based upon such a standard, therefore, are false, and should be everywhere discarded.

In the passage in Matthew 3:8, 9, the matter is considered from still another standpoint. "Bring forth therefore fruit worthy of repentance, and say not within yourselves, 'We have Abraham to our father.'" The Jew prided himself on the fact that he was a Jew, that he was a descendant of Abraham, and felt that that was the decisive thing, in virtue of which everything else followed: being a Jew was the thing that counted. The purpose of John the Baptist here is to prick that bubble, to destroy that illusion. "The axe lieth at the root of the trees: every tree therefore that bringeth not forth good fruit is hewn down, and cast into the fire." Every tree: there is to be no exception. The tree that does not bring forth good fruit is to be hewn down. The important thing, the decisive thing, is the character of the fruit. It isn't to what race or nationality one belongs—whether he is a Jew or a

Gentile—but what his character and conduct are. It was this thought which John the Baptist wanted to burn into the consciousness of the men who had come to his baptism, and who were listening to his words. The apostle Paul, in Romans 2:28, 29, seeks to impress the same great lesson: "For he is not a Jew who is one outwardly; neither is that circumcision which is outward in the flesh: but he is a Jew who is one inwardly; and circumcision is that of the heart in the spirit and not in the letter; whose praise is not of men, but of God." The important thing to him as a Jew was not his genealogy, was not his descent from Abraham, but the state of his heart, his individual character, as evidenced by his daily walks.

The delusion under which the Jews labored is not confined to the Jews; others are afflicted with the same malady and arrogate to themselves the same flattering assumption. Especially is this true in this country, cursed as it is, by race prejudice. The fact that a man belongs to the white race makes him, according to the notion that prevails in this country, better than the man who belongs to the black race, or to any of the races of darker hue. Independent of his character, irrespective of what his personal worth is, the fact that he is white puts him above the man who is black, however superior, as a matter of fact, the black man may be to him in point of moral and spiritual worth. The white man, living in the slums of our cities, utterly degraded, carries with him this consciousness, this sense of superiority to everything that is black. The feeling is, because a man is of one race, he is not as good as a man of another race; because a man is of one race, he is not entitled to the same consideration as a man of another race. It ignores entirely the personal element and substitutes something else in its place in estimating character, in determining the treatment to be accorded to the individual. The Jew, because he was a Jew, felt that that fact in and of itself, made him superior to men of other races. And the white American feels the same in regard to the color of his skin—the mere fact that he possesses a white skin, in and of itself, he thinks, makes him superior to all who are black or brown, or of any darker hue. That the possession of a white skin in the United States does give a man a decided advantage over a man with a dark skin, is true, in that the white man has privileges, opportunities, advantages open to him that are not open to the man of darker hue;

but that does not affect in the least the fact that with God a white skin carries no more weight than a black skin, or a skin of any other hue. With Him, race, color, makes neither for nor against an individual or race.

God is no respecter of persons also in the matter of sex. Male and female are both alike to Him; He is not disposed to deal any more leniently with the one than the other; both are judged by the same standard, and with the same rigid adherence to what is right. The Ten Commandments, and every other law promulgated by Him apply equally to both. Adultery, fornication, uncleanness, drunkenness, murder, theft, untruthfulness, dishonesty, are just as heinous in His sight in a man as in a woman. What is wrong for the one, is wrong for the other, and equally wrong in His estimation. On this point, He has expressed Himself so clearly that no one can be in doubt as to what His attitude is. The difference which society makes in the judgment which it passes upon the conduct of men and women, has absolutely no warrant in the Word of God and should be everywhere discontinued. Believing firmly in the soundness of the principle which insists upon a single standard of morals for men and women alike, one of the trustees, in a matter of discipline, in one of our institutions of learning, took the position that whatever in a female teacher is sufficient ground for making it necessary to drop her or for requesting her resignation, is also a sufficient ground for doing the same in case of a male teacher. And in this, he was right. It is the only sound, the only safe, the only proper position to be taken in all of our schools of learning. We have no right to set up one standard of character for female teachers, and another and inferior one for male teachers. The same standard should be applied to both alike.

In Job 34:17, 19, there is also this passage:

> And wilt thou condemn him that is righteous and mighty?
> Him that saith to a king, Thou art vile, Or to nobles, Ye are wicked;
> That respecteth not the person of princes?

The reference here is to God; and what it affirms of Him is that where kings are vile, where nobles are wicked, where princes are not what they ought to be, God deals with them regardless of the fact that they are kings, princes, nobles; He says to the king, Thou art vile, to the nobles, Ye are wicked—He puts them where they belong, treats them according to their moral desert. The fact of their high position does not, in the least, blind His eyes to their real character, or affect, in the least, His estimate of them. There is only one thing that counts with God, and that is character; there is only one thing that will pass muster with Him, and that is moral worth, purity of heart and life. It doesn't make any difference what else we may have—money, high social standing, position, or, to what race we belong, it all goes for naught with God unless there is a sound moral basis unless at the center there is purity of heart and life. Everything else is dross and will be cast as rubbish to the void.

Without taking more time in examining other passages of Scripture, those already examined are sufficient to show us clearly what is meant by the expression, "God is no respecter of persons." It means that in His dealing with men, in His estimate of men, in His treatment of them, certain things have no weight with Him, do not give them a better standing with Him, do not lead Him to look more favorably upon them, or to hold them in higher estimation. These things are wealth, position, high social standing, sex, race identity. God doesn't think any more of a rich man, merely because he is rich, than He does of a poor man; He doesn't think any more of a man in high official position, simply because of the position which he occupies, than of one who fills no position of honor or trust; He doesn't think any more of a man who is high-born, who belongs to what is called the upper circles of society, merely because of that fact, than of a man who moves in a lower social stratum; He doesn't think any more of a white man, merely because of his race identity, than He does of a man of any other race. Such considerations do not weigh with Him, are elements that do not affect, in the least, His judgment, are things that lie outside of the factors that count with Him.

And this brings us, very naturally, in this discussion to the question: If such things have no weight with God, what are the things that have? The things that count with Him, that He takes into consideration? A most important question; and one that should claim our closest attention. While God has no respect to the outward appearance and circumstances of the individual, He has respect to his inward condition—to the state of his heart, to his character, to his moral qualities. And we know this to be true, not only from the character of God, but also from many expressed declarations of His Word. When He sent Samuel to the house of Jesse to anoint David king instead of Saul, you remember what occurred. The record is: "And he" i.e., Samuel, "sanctified Jesse and his sons, and called them to the sacrifice. And it came to pass, when they were come, that he looked on Eliab, and said, Surely Jehovah's anointed is before me. But Jehovah said unto Samuel, Look not on his countenance, or on the height of his stature; because I have rejected him: for Jehovah seeth not as man seeth; for man looketh on the outward appearance, but Jehovah looketh on the heart." Samuel thought only of the outward appearance—of the height of his stature, and of the beauty of his countenance, and concluded that he must be the Lord's choice; but the Divine selection was based upon other considerations entirely—God was thinking of the quality of the man—of his moral and spiritual make-up, and not of his physical appearance. So when Peter was sent down to Caesarea to break to Cornelius the bread of life, to give him the information that was necessary to set him right, you remember that among the things that he said, after having been expressly directed to go with the men who were sent to him from Cornelius, was "Of a truth I perceive that God is no respecter of persons; but in every nation, he that feareth Him, and worketh righteousness, is acceptable to Him. In every nation, among all races of men, the thing that counts with God, that makes a man acceptable to God is not his nationality, is not his race; but his personal character: it is the man that feareth God and worketh righteousness that is acceptable to Him." "Of a truth," Peter says, "I perceive: i.e., I understand now: I did not before, that it is character that tells with God and not race or nationality." Let us hope that the time is not far distant when all like Peter will wake up to the same great truth.

There is still another thought here, and it grows naturally out of what has just been said. If outward conditions—the matter of race, affiliation, of wealth, of position, of high or low social standing, as these terms are popularly understood, play no part in the Divine estimate of individuals; neither should they play any part in our estimate of them. The same standard that God follows is the standard that we should follow. The things that count with Him are the things that should count with us. The things that He prizes, that He takes into consideration in estimating the worth of individuals, are the things that we should prize, that we should take into consideration in estimating their worth, and in determining the treatment that should be accorded to them.

This, unfortunately, is not what is done, however. This is not the standard that is followed in the generality of cases. In the estimation of the world, a man morally is judged very much more leniently than a woman. A man is allowed to do things that no woman would be allowed to do and maintain her good name. Whatever one's principles may be, whatever one's personal habits may be, if what the world values is possessed—if there be wealth and position, the way to recognition, to honor, is wide open. In every possible way, the world is putting the emphasis upon the things which are outward, which lie merely on the surface, which appeal simply to what is vain, and empty, and unsatisfying—to our vanity, our self-conceit, our love of display, of pleasure; and is putting little or no emphasis upon the things that are inward and abiding—upon the great and enduring elements of character. The great principle with which we are dealing here is one therefore that should be proclaimed, and proclaimed over and over again, with ever-increasing emphasis, with a view of arousing men everywhere to a sense of the importance of acting upon it, of making it a lamp to their feet, and a light to their path. God is no respecter of persons: and neither should we be. God doesn't care any more for a man than He does for a woman, any more for a rich man than He does for a poor man, for a white man than He does for a black man, for a man in office than for a man out of office, for a man of high birth than for a man of lowly origin; and neither should we. He does care, however, a great deal for character; He does respect the man of moral and spiritual worth—the man whose heart is pure, whose life is clean: and so should we. We should act on this principle ourselves, and train our children to act on it, and organize society in accordance with it.[11]

If we have wealth, position, high social standing, all right; but we should understand ourselves, and we should make our children understand, that although we may possess these things, only as we have better principles than others, only as we live on a higher moral plane than others, only as we are actuated by nobler ambitions, and aspirations than others, are we better than others, are we superior to others.

And so, if those about us have wealth, position, high social standing, occupy places of honor and trust—all right; but unless along with these is conjoined high character, solid, substantial moral worth, they are entitled to no special consideration at our hands, and should receive none. Unless the moral standing of an individual is good, is beyond question, that individual, whatever else he may possess in the way of gifts, endowments, or possessions, cannot be accorded any special consideration, cannot have conferred upon him any special honor without lowering the moral tone of society, without putting a premium upon immorality, upon looseness of living. And this, I am afraid, is often done; I am afraid, as a race, we are too prone to do. Not infrequently we see unworthy men—men of bad repute, of unsavory reputation, exalted to positions of honor, received with applause, handed round from one to another, invited to make addresses on public occasions, and other considerations shown them. The gift of gab, a little public position, the reputation of being smart, or eloquent—anything is sufficient to atone for a lack of character,

---

[11] In this excerpt, and Pauline echo, Grimké's EEH integrates *Biblicism* through a clear reference to the scriptural imperatives of God's impartiality, emphasizing that "God is no respecter of persons." *Activism* and *Conversionism* emerge in Grimké's challenge to model and reform societal values to prioritize moral character above race or wealth, calling for an internalized transformation that respects all individuals equally. *Crucicentrism* underpins his exhortation for "moral and spiritual worth," encouraging alignment with Christ's ethic of impartial love and justness.

anything out of the ordinary is sufficient to make up for a lack of moral worth. I saw a statement the other day, in one of our own papers, to the effect that "in the death of Mr. so and so, known in public life, as so and so, the race loses one of its most loyal and devoted members." As I read it, I said to myself, How can a man be loyal and devoted, in any true sense of the term, to his race, especially, at this stage of its development, when it needs everything that will help to make a favorable impression in its behalf, while he lives a life that is morally a disgrace to it? How can a man who lives a fast life—burning the candle at both ends—whatever his talents may be, be hailed as loyal and devoted to a race that needs more than anything else to be strengthened along moral lines, to be built up in character, except upon the theory that character, upright living, counts for nothing in comparison with the possession of a little talent or of some other possession?

A short while ago, I met a fellow clergyman who said to me with no little enthusiasm: "We had with us in our town the other day Mr. . We got up a big meeting and sent for him. We wanted to hear him. We gave him a great ovation. Isn't he a grand old man!" I was so astonished that I blurted out at once: "What! Do you know what kind of a man he is? What an unenviable reputation he bears?" This man happened to be one of the most notoriously notorious of our public men. I told him that I was surprised at him; and that he might be in better business.

If men of this stamp are to be handed around and great public demonstrations made over them, what possible incentive can there be to the young people who are coming up to be pure and upright in character and conduct? Every such invitation, every such recognition on the part of schools, colleges, universities, and other organizations and communities, is a virtual endorsement of the character and conduct of such men. It says to the young people, in the most effective way possible, Go, and do likewise; if you live in the way these men live, it will be no impediment to you, it will work no disadvantage to you in the struggle of life—certainly, not in our estimation; we won't think any less of you for it. Is that the way to build the race up, to push it forward, to lift it to higher levels, is that the way to train the kind of men and women that we ought to be training if we are to play a great part in the history of the world?

I have been greatly surprised and pained also at times, at the character of the men invited to address meetings under the auspices of Young Men's Christian Associations. I recall the case now of a man who was notorious for his drinking habits, who almost lived in saloons, whose breath was rarely ever free from the smell of liquor. And yet that man, because he occupied a public position, notwithstanding the fact that his drinking habit was known to the officers of the Association, and notwithstanding the fact that they also knew that it was known to the young men who attended the meetings of the association, was placed upon their program of speakers, and the same advertised by them in printed circulars and through the churches. Can Young Men's Christian Associations hope to command the respect of young men, and to be of any real service to them in pointing out the way to higher things, when, in the selection of their speakers, they show that they themselves attach no importance to high character? One of the young men, who was asked if he was going the next day to hear Mr. , said very emphatically, "No; I don't want to hear him. I was with him only last night in a saloon." If he felt that way in reference to the man who was to address the meeting, how must he have felt towards the men who selected him? How much respect could he have had for them? There was only one reason why this man was invited to speak, and that was because he was a public official. That fact, let it be said to the shame of the directors of that association, counted for more than the matter of character, more than counterbalanced his bad record.

It is against that kind of thing that I am protesting. It is for a standard that will keep character ever to the front, that will put the emphasis where God puts it, that I am pleading. And it is in the hope that the men and women who are in positions where they can help to mold public sentiment will see to it that the standard which demands high character as one of the indispensable conditions of public recognition is never lowered out of deference to official position, whether high or low, or anything else which is not in harmony with what is morally and spiritually helpful.

Until we begin to build our own lives, and the lives of our children, to build our homes, and the whole social fabric, in accordance with the great principle which we are here endeavoring to emphasize, and which God is represented as acting upon, we cannot hope for the best results, we cannot hope to have things as they ought to be. People who are deficient in character, who are careless as to how they live, whose lives are not in accordance with strict principles of morality, whose examples cannot be commended to the young—whatever else they may possess, whatever may be their attainments, whatever position they may occupy, they should be treated in such a way as to make them feel the high estimate that we put upon character, the paramount importance that we attach to character; we should treat them in such a way as to make them feel that no mere appendage of wealth, or position, or ability can atone for a lack of moral worth.

Nor should we estimate ourselves by any lower standard than the one that is here set up. We should not permit ourselves to feel that because we are not of a certain race, or color, or of a certain class, or because we can't live as well, dress as well, make as great a display as A and B, that therefore we are not as good as they are. As to whether we are as good as they are does not depend upon whether we are financially equal to them or not, whether we are in the same social circle with them or not, whether we belong to the same race as they do or not. And this we should understand; and train our children to understand.

Nor should we permit others to estimate us by any lower standard than the one set up here—to assume that because we are not like them in the above-named particulars, that therefore we are not as good as they are. They may so estimate us, but it should never be accepted by us; we should never permit ourselves to feel that lack of these things makes us less worthy, puts us on a lower plane.

Nor should we permit others to estimate themselves by any lower standard—to assume that, because in these mere externals or adventitious circumstances they differed from others, they are therefore better than others. We should not permit this, I say, not in the sense that we can prevent them from so regarding themselves, but in the sense that in our dealings with them, in our contact with them, our estimate of them and our treatment of them will be always based upon the higher standard of moral worth. Never, under any circumstances, should we permit ourselves, in our contact with others, to act so as to make them feel that any deference that we may pay them, any respect which we may show them, any desire which we may manifest to be with them, is due to what they have—to their worldly possessions, or to their position or to their race affiliation. The value that we attach to their friendship, to contact and association with them, we should find in other and better things, and should make them feel that it is for these things that we value them and not for the others. The children who are coming up, the boys and girls, the young men and women, and the older men and women too—all should walk according to the high standard here set up—should hold themselves to it and hold others to it.

Is this being done? Alas, there is reason to believe that this noble principle is not very largely followed, that not a great many are walking according to it. The opposite principle, the principle that takes into consideration the things that are merely outward, that lie on the surface, is the one that influences us most, that most largely controls our actions. We have respect to persons; we estimate unduly a great many things that are of minor or secondary importance, and underestimate a great many things that are of paramount importance. The call that comes to all today—to white men and to black men, to men of all races and classes and conditions, is a call to a saner principle of living, to a higher, purer, nobler standard of life—individual life, family life, community life. God is no respecter of persons: He looks through a man's race, color, position—looks behind his riches or poverty, to his character, and estimates him accordingly. And this is the principle by which all should be guided. There is no warrant for setting up any other standard—any lower standard, and it cannot be done without resulting in serious injury to those who do it, and without entailing a curse upon those who come after them. The gospel which seeks to exalt character, to keep character ever to the front, as the test by which to estimate individuals and races, may not be popular, but it is the only gospel that has any saving power in it; the only gospel through which an individual or a race can hope to maintain its own self-respect, and to win and hold the respect of others; the only gospel through which an individual or race can hope to make for itself an honorable record, or to work out for itself a worthy destiny.

Any other standard set up by an individual or a race is bound to result in evil. In the long run, deterioration is sure to set in. The poet says—

And come he slow, or come he fast,
It is but Death who comes at last.

And so here, come it slow or come it fast, a disregard of the great principle we are discussing is sure to work to the disadvantage of the race or individual who offends against it. And the more persistently it is offended against, the more certain is it to bring disaster, to result in moral decay.

There is a warning here for both races in this country—for the white race, in its rabid color-phobia tendencies, in its blind and unreasoning adherence to the color line, in its subordination of everything to the test of color as paramount, in its dealings with the colored race; and a warning also to the colored race, in its materialistic, mammon-loving, and pleasure-seeking tendencies, to the neglect of, or undervaluation of higher and more important things. For the white man, and for the black man, in their relations with the members of their own race, and in their relations with each other, the only wise, the only sensible course to pursue, is that of having no respect of persons, of dealing with all men on the basis of individual personal worth regardless of the accident of birth, or of any other merely adventitious circumstance. This is the principle upon which God acts, and it is the principle upon which men everywhere should act, and must act if they are to realize the best results for themselves and for others.

Sermon 6

Evangelism and Institutes of Evangelism[12]

We have just closed in our city an Institute on Evangelism, held in the New York Avenue Presbyterian Church under the direction of the General Assembly's Permanent Committee on Evangelism. The purpose of these institutes is to stimulate an interest in the work of evangelism. What is evangelism? It is preaching the gospel with a view of getting men at once to accept Jesus Christ. The evangelism that is current in this country, however, does not mean accepting Jesus Christ in the sense of adopting His standard of living, His principles of conduct; it does not mean an earnest and honest effort to conform the character and life to the spirit and teachings of Jesus Christ.

The men and women who come into the church through these evangelistic efforts (I am speaking now particularly of the white people) in the great majority of cases, have no more idea or intention of doing what Jesus wants them to do, except qualifiedly, than they have of butting their heads against a stone wall. They come into the church and bring with them all their colorphobia. Their acceptance of Jesus Christ does not change, in the least, their attitude towards the Negro; their prejudice towards him continues just the same as before they made a profession of religion. And they do not feel, in accepting Jesus Christ, that a change in this regard is necessary; nor does the evangelism that is preached by the white people in this country assume that a change is necessary.

It is an evangelism that makes them feel that they can still hold on to their prejudice and yet be good Christians, yet be followers of the Lord Jesus Christ. Evangelism of that kind is of no real value, counts for nothing in the sight of God; evangelism of that kind is an insult to Jesus Christ; accepting Jesus Christ in that way is nothing but sheer hypocrisy—hypocrisy on the part of those who profess to

---

[12] Grimké, *Works I*, 523–28. Delivered in 1916.

accept, and on the part of those who are content with that kind of acceptance.

There is an evangelism that is genuine, an evangelism for which the great Presbyterian Church in the United States of America should stand, but for which it does not stand—an evangelism that means accepting Jesus Christ in reality and not in pretense—an evangelism that carries along with it brotherhood, that so presents Jesus Christ that men see, and see plainly, what is involved in accepting Him. The Apostle Paul, who understood what was involved in it, and who preached the true evangel, says: "Seeing that ye have put off the old man with his doings, and have put on the new man, that is being renewed unto knowledge after the image of Him that created him: where there can not be Greek and Jew, circumcision and uncircumcision, barbarian, Scythian, bondman, freeman; but Christ is all, and in all." An evangelism that permits men to believe that they can be Christians without making an earnest and honest effort to rid themselves of race prejudice is a spurious evangelism. How few of these men who are evangelists, and those who are back of these evangelistic movements, seem to realize what evangelism really is, what accepting Jesus Christ really involves.

I have a friend who is at the head of an educational work. In the interest of his school, he had occasion some time ago to travel a little in seeking to raise funds. During this tour, he stopped at a certain town and called upon one of the wealthiest, if not the wealthiest, man in the town, who is also a prominent member and officer in one of the churches of the town. This friend is a college graduate and an alumnus of one of the leading theological seminaries of the country; his manner and bearing are also those of a gentleman. He finally succeeded in getting an interview with this wealthy church member, and, in introducing himself said, "I am Mr. B of such a city," and proceeded to state the purpose of his mission. When he was through, this Christian gentleman said to him, "I must tell you frankly that I am losing my interest in your race. Most of the leaders of your people are very assertive; they want to be the social equals of the white people. You have come here, and look how you have introduced yourself to me. You said, 'I am Mr. B.' Now what do you mean by that? You mean simply that you are my social equal, and I don't care to have anything to do with a colored man who feels that way." This friend said, for a moment he was dumb with astonishment, but soon recovered himself and, although he felt at first like telling him just what he thought of him and leaving his house, he held his temper, and finally told him that if it was more pleasing to him to have him drop the word "Mr." in speaking of himself, in the future he would do so.

The point particularly to which I want to direct attention is that this Christian gentleman who could not bear to have a colored man use the word "Mr." in speaking of himself, was at that very time being considered for the chairmanship of the General Evangelistic Committee of one of the greatest denominations in the country, and was afterward appointed its chairman. Now I am not holding the denomination responsible for that appointment, for it knew nothing of this incident of which I am speaking, but think of the man himself, feeling as he did, acting as he did, permitting himself to be considered for the chairmanship of such a committee. Before God, I ask, Was that man fit to be at the head of an evangelistic committee—a committee that sought to hold up Jesus Christ before men with a view of accepting Him, of following Him?

At this Institute on Evangelism, among the speakers was the Rev. J. Ross Stevenson, DD, now Moderator of the General Assembly, and President of Princeton Seminary. I remember Dr. Stevenson very well in connection with the Assembly that met at Buffalo. It was the assembly that had to do with the Separate Presbytery Overture, which overture seemed to me then, and still seems to me, was nothing but an ignoble concession on the part of a great church, to the Negro-hating spirit of the South, in order to effect a union with the Cumberland Church. Among the few strong men of that Assembly who stood up, and in a Christian and manly way protested against drawing the color line in the church, was Dr. Stevenson. I have never lost sight of him since. So that when he was elected President of the Seminary, it was with my hearty approval. I still have confidence in him. I believe at heart he is all right; and therefore I am not disposed at this time to hold him responsible for what I am about to speak of, since he has but recently entered upon his duties as President of the seminary. The fact that Dr. Stevenson was one of the speakers at this Institute on Evangelism, and that he is President of Princeton Seminary, are the things that led me to think of this particular matter that is on my mind.

Princeton is not only the oldest, but the greatest of our theological schools. The work to which it is especially devoting itself is the preparation of men for the gospel ministry—the preparation of men to go out and proclaim the unsearchable riches of grace in Christ Jesus to a perishing world. In a school like that, you would expect to find the highest type of Christianity, the finest expressions of the spirit and teachings of Jesus Christ; you would expect, if anywhere in all the world, men of all races would be received on terms of perfect Christian equality, it would be in a theological seminary—in one of the schools of the prophets. And yet, what is the fact as to this seminary? The color line is drawn in it, so far as the dormitories are concerned. There is no disposition now to allow colored students to occupy rooms within these buildings. It did not use to be so. Forty years ago, when I entered the seminary, there were three other colored students, making four in all, and we all occupied rooms within the dormitories. Things have since changed; prejudice has so increased that the color of a man's skin now shuts him out of these buildings. It is a shame that it should be so. It is a shame that, at the very fountain head of theological training in the great Presbyterian Church, race prejudice should be allowed to assert itself, and to thrive. Who is responsible for this? Is it the President of the seminary? Then he is not fit to be President. Are the professors responsible for it? Then they are not fit to be professors. They may have the scholarship, the technical knowledge, but the higher qualification, the mind that was in Jesus, the spirit and temper of the great Teacher, without which mere scholarship counts for nothing, they are sadly lacking in. Are the Directors responsible for it? Then they are not fit to be Directors in a school of this kind.

How can we consistently go around holding institutes on evangelism when at the head of our great Evangelistic Committee is a man who takes offense at a colored man, an educated, refined colored gentleman, for using the term "Mr." in speaking of himself; and when, in our oldest and greatest theological school, the color line is drawn?

Away with all this hypocrisy! Let us get down to bedrock, to fundamentals, to essential principles of Christianity. Let us have an evangelism, a straightforward, simple preaching of the gospel that will keep off evangelistic committees, and out of theological seminaries, as students and as professors, men who are so unchristian as to be influenced by this wicked and contemptible spirit of race prejudice.[13]

After Naboth had been murdered, Ahab went down to take possession of his vineyard and God sent Elijah down to meet him. And when Ahab saw him, he said, "Hast thou found me, O mine enemy?" He thought he had gotten rid of Elijah. And so it does not make any difference how many evangelistic institutes we may hold, or how many evangelistic campaigns we may begin, in self-complacency, with a view of persuading ourselves that we are very religious, God will always raise up some Elijah to hold up before us this great sin of race prejudice, and burn it into our consciousness until we see the evil of our ways, and repent, and bring forth fruits, meet for repentance. This sin of race prejudice cannot be covered up or salved over, and God is determined that it shall not be covered up or salved over.

---

[13] This excerpt typifies Grimké's EEH by integrating *Biblicism*, emphasizing a return to a Christian witness grounded in the impartial love commanded by scripture. *Conversionism* is expressed in his call for genuine conversion that will not suffer race prejudice in evangelistic spaces. *Activism* is evident as he calls for structural change within church institutions, advocating for a gospel that challenges oppressive social norms. *Crucicentrism* is foundational, as Grimké centers the way of Christ as the true model, opposing superficial displays of faith that exclude racial justice. This stance resonates with Paul's admonition in Romans 12:9, where he urges believers to "abhor what is evil; hold fast to what is good," emphasizing sincerity and justice as inseparable from authentic Christian discipleship.

> Away with the multitude of your burnt offerings and sacrifices. Wash you, make you clean; put away the evil of your doings before mine eyes.
>
> If ye fulfil the royal law according to the Scriptures, Thou shalt love thy neighbor as thyself, ye do well; but if ye have respect to persons, yet commit sin, being convicted by the law as transgressors.
> —James 2:8–9

This message God is going to keep on thundering into the ear of white American Christianity, with this leprous taint of race prejudice running through it, until it heeds the message and frees itself from this abomination.

This is put in tract form because it is now almost impossible to get a matter like this into the religious press. There seems to be a conspiracy of silence, or a secret understanding to choke off discussions of this kind. Darkness is preferred to light.

Sermon 7

The Race Problem as it Respects the Colored People and the Christian Church, in the Light of the Developments of the Last Year[14]

Oh, give thanks unto the Lord, call upon His name; Make known among the peoples His doings.
—Psalm 105:1

We have met here today, in compliance with the request of the President of the United States, to render thanks to Almighty God. That this service may be something more than a mere formality there must be something to be thankful for, and that something we must be conscious of, and conscious that we are in some sense beneficiaries. We naturally ask, therefore, in a service like this, *What is there, in the year that has just passed, to be thankful for?*

I. This question may be asked of us as a nation. In attempting to answer it, I am going to mention only a few of the many things for which we should be thankful:

1. We should be thankful that the bloody war, which for more than four years convulsed the world, and into which we were drawn, is now over. The two great opposing forces, the Allies and the Central Empires, are no longer marshalling their forces, one against the other. Things are not fully settled yet, it is true; the world is still topsy-turvy, everything is in a state of unrest; everywhere agitation in some form is going on, with no certainty as to what the ultimate outcome is going to be. But the great war precipitated by Germany's senseless ambition for world domination, as such, is over—over, certainly for the present. And when we remember what its continuance for another year would have meant in blood and

[14] Grimké, *Works* I, 600–18. Delivered at a Union Thanksgiving Service held at the Plymouth Congregational Church, Washington, DC, November 27, 1919.

treasure, it is certainly a ground for national thanksgiving that the whole horrible business is over.

2. We ought to be thankful also that our casualty list, due to the fact that we went late into the conflict, is much smaller than some of the other nations, certainly smaller than that of France, England, Italy, or Russia. Of the seven million who perished, some were Americans, it is true, but not as many as of the nations that I have just mentioned. There are, in our own land, many, many homes draped in mourning; many, many sad hearts who said goodbye to loved ones as they started for the battlefields of Europe, who will never see their loved ones again in this life. All that is mortal of them is now resting in the sacred, blood-stained soil of France. It is sad to think of these desolate homes and hearts in our own land; but how many, many more there are in other lands, caused by the same great calamity. That there are not more of these desolate homes among us is certainly a ground of national thanksgiving. There might have been a great many more.

3. We ought to be thankful also, for another aspect of the same subject, for the large number of homes that have been made glad by the return of their loved ones—some of them badly maimed, it is true, but so many of them unhurt, and apparently in better physical condition than when they went abroad. The discipline of the army seemed to have rendered them more rugged, to have given them a more vigorous grip upon life. During this last year, during the last few months, how many have been made glad—fathers, mothers, sisters, wives, sweethearts, friends, by the return of their loved ones.

4. We ought to be thankful also that we were enabled to render some substantial aid in arresting, and, for the time being at least, overthrowing the effort on the part of Germany to fasten upon the world its iron heel of military autocracy. There are grave reasons to doubt whether the Allies, unassisted by the United States, could have overthrown Germany. The indications were when we entered the war

> that the Allies were very near exhausted, and that without aid from over this side of the water they would not have been able to hold out much longer. And while that may have been also true of the Central Powers, without our aid, even if the contest had ended in a drawn battle, the principle underlying the great struggle would still have been unsettled, the conflict between autocracy and democracy. Our going into it threw the balance in favor of democracy. And for this we ought to be thankful. If we had stayed out and allowed the nations of Europe to wage the great war alone, it would have been to our everlasting shame—conduct utterly unworthy of our traditions, of our avowed principles, and of our boast of being the great champion of democracy, though in perfect accord with our practice, as seen in the treatment which we accord to our twelve million colored citizens.

II. Leaving now the thought of the nation as a whole: we are here also, not only as American citizens, but as colored American citizens—as citizens, and yet not citizens—citizens with rights guaranteed to us in the Constitution, but with those rights but very imperfectly recognized. On an occasion like this, it is well for us, therefore, to ask ourselves the question, *What reason or reasons have we, as an oppressed, aggrieved, circumscribed class in this country, in the midst of this great white population, to be thankful during the past year?* Are there any reasons, any things as a race, in the events or happenings of the last year, for which we should be thankful?

Notwithstanding many discouragements that meet us almost everywhere and every day; notwithstanding lynchings—the crowning glory of American democracy—still goes on unchecked; notwithstanding race prejudice has grown and is growing with a rapidity unparalleled before, not only in the wide extent of it over the country, but also in its virulence; notwithstanding there is no abatement of segregation in the departments of the general Government under the, shall I say, humane and Christian leadership of our good President who has been so awfully afraid that the heart of the world will be broken if something wasn't done pretty soon for the oppressed millions in other lands; notwithstanding the race riots that have disgraced the land; notwithstanding, I say, these discouragements and others, there are, in the midst of the gloom and darkness, some things for which we should be thankful. And among them:

The evidences of a growing sense, within the race, that it has rights under the Constitution, and of the value and importance of those rights in a republic like this. There was a time when there was a disposition even on the part of some of our leaders to pooh-pooh the idea of our rights; that, it was said, if we concerned ourselves about our duties, our rights would take care of themselves; that when we were worthy of them, they would come to us unsolicited. Thank God that time has passed. Nobody now with a particle of sense or self-respect talks such nonsense. As a race we are not insensible of our duties, nor are we averse to the consideration of our duties. I think the colored man is about as anxious to do his duty as the white man is; neither of them seems to be overburdened with a sense of what Carlyle calls the everlasting yea, and the everlasting nay—with a sense of the binding force of moral obligation. It is well for both races to give attention, and very close attention, to what each ought to do, to be ever looking out for, and to be ever pursuing, the straight and narrow way of what is true, just, pure, lovely and of good report.

No one attaches greater importance to the idea of duty than I do. For years I have loved, as I have loved few poems in the English language, and have read almost oftener than I have any other, Wordsworth's *Ode to Duty:*

Stern Daughter of the voice of God!
O Duty! if that name thou love
Who are a light to guide, a rod
To check the erring, and reprove;
Thou, who are victory and law
When empty terrors overawe;
From vain temptations dost set free;
And calm'st the weary strife of frail humanity.

So have I also for years admired Tennyson's noble lines to the great Duke, "The path of duty is the way to glory."

While it is important for us as individuals and as a race to keep steadily before us the path of duty, turning neither to the right nor to the left; it is no less important that we should keep also just as steadily before us, what our rights are, which means simply that we shall not lose sight of the fact that we are human beings and American citizens, and that as such we are entitled to be treated in a certain way—to enjoy the same rights, the same privileges, that other citizens enjoy, to be accorded the same considerations, neither more nor less than are accorded to others. A man, white or black, living in a community, who is unconcerned about his rights, who doesn't care how he is treated, is lacking in self-respect, and is worthy of no better treatment than he is sure to get. A man who doesn't respect himself can hardly expect others to respect him. And therefore this matter of rights is a vital one, not only to the individual, but to the race. There can be no falling down here, no quiet acquiescence in the deprivation of our rights without serious injury to the race in its character building, and in its efforts to forge forward. We must not forget, both for ourselves and for the sake of the white race, that we have rights; that as American citizens we are entitled to the same treatment as other citizens. Never mind who preaches another gospel, this is the gospel that we must never forget. And one of the encouraging things of the year—one of the things for which we should be particularly thankful, is the manifest growth of sentiment in this respect within the race. No previous year, it seems to me, has shown such a decided advance in the race's consciousness of what it is entitled to as a part of the body politic, as a part of the community. Heretofore there has been among the leaders, among the radical leaders, a vivid consciousness of the fact that we were not getting what we are entitled to as men, and as American citizens. And this group has been steadily growing, so that there are more colored newspapers and more prominent colored people speaking out today in behalf of our rights than ever before. The truckler, the time-serving type of leaders is growing steadily less, and the other, the manly, self-respecting type, is growing steadily larger and larger, for which we should be thankful.

The point, particularly, however, to which I am calling attention is as to the growth of this sentiment among the masses of the colored people. More interest has been manifested by a larger number of colored people, covering a larger area of territory, than in any previous year that I can recall. Never before has there been such a wide-spread interest on the part of the race as a whole in regard to its rights. There are more colored people thinking about their rights today than ever before. They are alive, wide awake, as never before: are not only interested in their rights as never before, but back of their interest there is a purpose, a resolute determination that is also new, and that will some day have to be reckoned with. Anyone who is at all in touch with Negro thought and sentiment, with what is going on among colored people all over the country, cannot fail to be impressed with the fact that this matter of their rights is gripping them now as never before in all their past history. You see it in the large number of organizations that are coming into being, whose specific object is the securing of our rights and the increased activity of those already in existence; you see it in the number of meetings that are being held with this object in view; you see it in the nature of the declarations that are made at great public gatherings and by organizations of one kind or another, even where they are not specifically organized for securing our rights. Thus in the great meeting of the Colored Knights of Pythias at Atlantic City in August, the head of that organization, Major General Robert R. Jackson, in an address which he delivered before that body said: "Dollars or other material gains count for little compared to the realization of our sacred constitutional rights in the mighty struggle in which we, a suffering people, now are enlisted. This is no common task. It is a gigantic struggle and should be accepted by all."

How different that sounds from what used to be said years ago. The emphasis then used to be laid on material things, on the getting of farms and bank accounts as of paramount importance. Now, what do we hear? "Dollars and other material gains count for little compared to the realization of our sacred constitutional rights." And what he says is true. Of what value are material gains if we have no rights which white men are bound to respect: if we can be shot down, murdered, burnt to death, our property destroyed with impunity?

The founders of our great Republic saw very clearly the place which rights should occupy and the importance of keeping the thought ever in mind, for they placed in the Declaration of Independence the immortal statement: "We hold these truths to be self-evident, that all men are created equal; that they are endowed by their Creator with certain inalienable rights; that among these are life, liberty, and the pursuit of happiness. That to secure these rights, governments are instituted among men, deriving their just powers from the consent of the governed." Material gains certainly counted for but little with the founders of the Republic without the enjoyment of rights. And yet some of us are fools enough to decry agitation for our rights. Did I say fools? Yes, that is the only word that expresses it.

Continuing, the speaker at the Atlantic City meeting goes on: "Let me say to the world that the twelve million people of our race kept the fires of Americanism burning. Let us keep them burning until we burn up every Jim Crow sign and every Jim Crow car in this country." And that is the way every manly, self-respecting Negro feels.

This extract that I have given from Gen. Jackson's address is but a sample of how the colored people are speaking and thinking today, but a sample of what is going on to an extent never before equaled. And for it, I say, we ought to be thankful to Almighty God. And thankful because it is one of the hopeful signs of a better day. And it is hopeful because whatever may be said about patiently waiting for our oppressors of their own volition to give us our rights, the simple fact is, a fact confirmed by all experience, as long as we ourselves are willing to be deprived of our rights; as long as we ourselves are inactive in securing our rights, as long as we ourselves are not thoroughly alive to the value and importance of these rights, we will never get them. The more we ourselves are interested in securing them, the sooner they will come. Don't let us fool ourselves here; don't let us imagine for a moment that our rights are going to be secured in any other way except mainly through our own exertions, assisted, of course, by our white friends, but principally through our own efforts. We must bear the burden mainly, and must feel most keenly the responsibility of bringing it about, if the obstacles that now bar our way are to be removed. Our white friends have been of great service to us, and can still be; but we must, in ever increasing measure, come to realize that the more we rely upon ourselves the stronger we will become, and the sooner will we reach the goal.

This widespread and ever-increasing interest in our rights, civil and political, is therefore a most hopeful sign, and one that should bring joy to all of our hearts. This kind of thing can't be going on as it has been going on for the past year, within the race, without producing some very positive results, and results not unfavorable to the race. When the white man comes to realize that the Negro is a man just as he is, having the same capacities, the same desires, the same aspirations, the same desire to be respected as he has; and that what he, under like conditions, would not be willing to submit to, the Negro is not going permanently to submit to, he will see the folly of attempting to proscribe him, to segregate him, to set him apart in a sphere by himself, and so stop his foolish, senseless, wicked opposition.

2. Side by side with this growing interest, on the part of the race in securing its rights, there is another thing for which we should also be thankful as we think of the developments of the last year; and that is the evident purpose of the race, which has never before so clearly revealed itself as during the past few months, no longer to accept quietly, no longer to submit quietly to the acts of violence that a certain class of whites have felt free to inflict upon them, knowing that those in authority would never call them to account, and because of their numbers there would be no danger of being hurt by the victim or victims of their violence. Thank God that time has passed! The Negro has come at last, after years of patient suffering; after years of patient waiting for the civil authorities, both state and national, to throw around him the strong arm of official protection, to the realization of the fact, that there is such a thing as self-protection—a right, inherent in every human being, a right, God-given, God conferred, and a right to be exercised when there is no other way of escaping the danger which threatens. This law of nature, by circumstances over which he has had no control,

has been forced upon his attention as his last and only refuge in the midst of a set of savages. And he has now made up his mind, and that mind is becoming more and more the mind of an ever-increasing number of the race, that since this great white race with all the machinery of government in its hands will not protect him, he will protect himself. Notice what I am saying, *PROTECT* himself. It is not his purpose to become the aggressor; but when he is assaulted it is no longer his purpose to fold his arms and allow the mob to shoot him down, to burn his home, and destroy his property; he is going to do what he can to protect himself and family, even though he may lose his own life in so doing. Even where a Negro commits an offense, the most heinous, he has a right to the protection of the law—a right to be tried and his guilt established according to the forms of law, and, if found guilty, to be punished by those who are officially entrusted with the execution of the law, and not by irresponsible mobs.

This new spirit that is taking possession of the Negro is very clearly and forcibly brought out by Claude McKay, one of the real poets of the race, in a little poem of his, entitled, *If We Must Die.* It was published in the July number of the *Liberator,* and is as follows:

If we must die—let it not be like hogs,
Hunted and penned in an inglorious spot,
While round us bark the mad and hungry dogs,
Making their mock at our accursed lot.
If we must die—oh, let us nobly die,
So that our precious blood may not be shed
In vain; then even the monsters we defy
Shall be constrained to honor us though dead
Oh, kinsmen! We must meet the common foe;
Though far outnumbered, let us still be brave,
And for their thousand blows deal one death-blow!
What though before us lies the open grave?
Like men we'll face the murderous, cowardly pack,
Pressed to the wall, dying, but—fighting back.

There is no mistaking the spirit reflected in this poem that comes straight from the heart. It has been a long time coming, but it has come at last, as is evident from all the recent race riots.

In an article, written by Mr. Charles Edward Russell, on the Chicago race riot, in the October number of *Reconstruction,* I was particularly struck with this paragraph:

> *Throughout the disturbances it was noted that the Negroes did not run. They were expected to run, but did not. They stood and fought, often with astonishingly cool and desperate courage.*

In the November issue of the *Crisis* I find also these words, part of a letter written by a colored woman from the South:

> A week ago an old friend of mine whom I had not seen for twenty years came to see me. After talking of old school days and friends, both of us asking and answering many questions, my friend asked, "And what did you think of the Washington and Chicago riots?"
>
> When I had answered that question she said, "I wish you would send that answer to the *Crisis*, just as you have told it to me, so that our men may know how we women have felt and how we feel now."
>
> I said this: "The Washington riot gave me the thrill that comes once in a lifetime. I was alone when I read between the lines of the morning paper that at last our men had stood like men, struck back, were no longer dumb, driven cattle. When I could no longer read for my streaming tears, I stood up, alone in my room, held both hands high over my head and exclaimed aloud, 'Oh, I thank God, thank God!' When I remembered anything after this, I was prone on my bed, beating the

> pillow with both fists, laughing and crying, whimpering like a whipped child, for sheer gladness and madness. The pent-up humiliation, grief and horror of a lifetime—half a century—was being stripped from me."

The Negro is no longer running as he used to do. A new spirit is taking possession of him. He is now standing; and will stand in his own defense in the future. And the men are not standing alone, the women are back of them.

This change in his mental and moral attitude towards his assailants is, I say, a ground for thanksgiving; and for the simple reason, when the white man gets firmly fixed in his mind, as he will after a few sad experiences, that the Negro is not going to run, but is going to defend himself, there won't be so many lynchings: there will be a growing disposition to allow the law to take its course, to act like civilized beings, and not like savages. These men who go in crowds to lynch a lone Negro are all cowards. Not one of them would go if he thought there was any danger of his being harmed, or of his losing his life. The firm resolve on the part of the Negro to protect himself is the only way now, so far as I can see, that seems to offer any hope of checking this spirit of lawlessness that is rampant in the South, and that is steadily spreading all over the country. The United States Government, as well as the State governments, have no wish to suppress such outrages, judging from the mild, the pusillanimous manner in which they deal with them, or else they are powerless to do so, which is not true. It is not from lack of power, but from lack of disposition on the part of most of the public officials, as well as of the people who are responsible for the election of and continuance of such officials. When lynchings become so dangerous that those who take part in them can hardly hope to escape unscathed, there will be less disposition to engage in them. The Negro ought therefore to be encouraged, as long as the State is powerless to protect him, or is unwilling to protect him, to protect himself not only for his own sake, but also for the sake of the community; for a spirit of lawlessness is a disgrace to any community. And whatever helps to prevent that disgrace or to restore ordered government in the community is or ought to be a ground for thanksgiving. We ought to rejoice therefore because of this new force which is now coming into play, in what has hitherto seemed a hopeless situation.

3. There is still one other thing that I want to mention in the events of the past year for which, as a race, we ought to be thankful: I refer to the appeal that has been sent out by the Federal Council of the Churches of Christ in America.

   Much time, we are told, was given to a full and free discussion of the racial situation, out of which came this address, which represents, we are told, "the thought of these leaders, and the deliberative judgment of the Administrative Committee of the Federal Council of the Churches of Christ in America." This Federal Council of Churches represents practically all of the Protestant churches in the United States and therefore the great bulk of white Christians.

   I want to quote a few paragraphs from this address and then follow with some observations on the address as a whole. It begins:

   > *The recent race conflicts in some of our cities challenge the attention of the Churches of Jesus Christ to their responsibility respecting an amicable adjustment of race relations in America.*
   >
   > *The present situation is a challenge to the churches charged with the promotion of the brotherhood of man, which look upon all men as entitled to a footing of equality of opportunity. This calls for preaching the duty of economic and community justice for the colored man, thus securing peace and good will between the races. Beyond all else the present situation calls for confession on the part of Christian*

> *men and women of failure to live up to the standard of universal brotherhood taught by Jesus Christ.*
>
> *The actual practice of the principles of brotherhood can prevent race conflicts and nothing else will. The Church must offer ideals, the programme and the leadership in this crisis. The Church must meet its obligation, or leadership will pass not only to secular agencies, economic or socialistic, but to forces that are destructive of civilization.*

The simple fact is, it is already passing to forces that are destructive of civilization. These forces and agencies have been actively at work, while the Church has been looking idly on.[15]

The address continues:

> *We must confess that the church and its ministry, as related to the welfare of the colored people, has been too little inspired by the fundamental principles and ideals of Jesus Christ. Communities that have expressed horror over atrocities abroad, have seen, almost unmoved and silent, men beaten, hanged and burned by the mob.*

It then goes on to outline a programme embracing some eight different items, all of which are important, and which,

---

[15] Grimké, quoting the Federal Council of Churches, engages his EEH by anchoring Biblicism in a call for a responsive Christian witness rooted in social action predicated upon the scripture's mandates. This passage reflects Conversionism in its appeal for believers to embody a "universal brotherhood taught by Jesus Christ." Activism emerges as Grimké calls the church to economic and community justice—addressing racial inequality as an essential indicative of the gospel. Finally, Crucicentrism is evident in his appeal to Christ's redemptive work, admonishing Christians to reflect Christ's reconciliation in their actions. This echoes Paul's counsel in Galatians 3:28, which proclaims unity in Christ that transcends ethnic and social hostilities.

if carried out, will result in great good, in bettering immensely, present conditions. I am not going to stop, however, to discuss this very excellent programme, to take up the separate items embraced in it. Time will not permit. There are one or two things in regard to it, however, to which I do desire at this time to direct attention as specially significant, and as forming a ground for thanksgiving on our part, as a race.

1. This address, coming as it does from the representatives of the Federal Council of the Churches of Christ in America, shows that the so-called Christian church in this country, that white American Christianity, has at last awakened to a realization of the fact that the religion of Jesus Christ has something to do with this race question in this country. It has been so difficult, difficult to get our white brethren to see that it had. For years I have been hammering away at it, endeavoring in every possible way to arouse them from their stupor, from their insensibility, their blindness, on this matter. I have spoken on it; I have written on it; I have sent articles to religious journals on it; I have published tracts and circulated them on it, all with this end in view. The very first time Rev. Billy Sunday was announced to visit our city, before he began his revival campaign here, I wrote him: I said to him, "I notice you are to be in our city. Race prejudice is rampant in this city; it flaunts itself everywhere. Has Christianity no message on the subject? Is this evil, this ever-growing evil that is doing almost more than anything else to destroy the self-respect and to increase the burdens of ten million colored people in this country, to go unrebuked by the representatives of religion? Will you not say a word on the subject while you are in our midst? I notice that you have been striking with sledge-hammer blows some of the great evils of today—intemperance, impurity, gambling, the lust for gold, frivolity, political corruption, the tobacco habit, and the like. Will it be asking too much of you to turn for a moment to this gigantic evil, *RACE PREJUDICE,* and deal it

also one of those sledge-hammer blows? It is difficult to get anyone to speak on the subject. All seem to be afraid."

After the close of a great BIBLE CONFERENCE in our city, the purpose of which was to magnify the Bible and Christianity, at which there were several distinguished men, not only from our own country, but from abroad, I wrote an article to the *New York Independent,* which, however, was not published; it was after that intrepid leader and tried friend of the race, Dr. William Hayes Ward, ceased to be connected with the paper. It was afterwards published in tract form and widely circulated. In that article, among other things, I said:

> The colored people here, after such a conference, after such a flood of light upon the Word of God from so many eminent preachers and teachers, ought to see the effect of it in lessening race prejudice, in creating a more friendly feeling towards them; but it will have no such effect. Race prejudice will be just as strong, just as pronounced and aggressive in the community and in the churches as before. The wonderful enthusiasm with which these meetings were attended, in view of the little effect which they will have upon the moral and spiritual life of the community, makes them seem almost like a farce. The best way to teach people the value of the Bible and of Christianity is not by holding Bible conferences, but by living the truths of the Bible, by exemplifying the spirit of its Founder. The cause of Christianity and of the Bible is not to be helped by verbal eulogies, but by eloquent examples of Christly living.
>
> *Of what value is a Bible conference in a community, cursed by race prejudice, that begins and closes with not one word on the subject? If it were a little evil, hid out of sight, scarcely perceptible, there might be some excuse: but when it stinks to heaven, when it flaunts itself everywhere, when the very churches are full of it, what possible excuse can there be for silence? Think of a Bible conference aiming to magnify*

> *the Bible and Christianity, and yet afraid to deal with one of the greatest evils in the land today! Instead of magnifying the Bible and Christianity, it is the best way to bring them into contempt. The whole thing looks like a sham, a make-believe effort with no real, earnest, honest purpose of carrying out the principles of Christianity. We need everywhere, not Bible conferences that will pass over in silence a sin like race prejudice, but Bible conferences that will lift up a standard for the people; that will cry aloud and spare not.*

Only last summer, in an article on the race riots that was published in *The Evening Bulletin* at Philadelphia, I said:

> *The thing that astonishes me most is that this vile treatment of colored people goes on, and goes on unchecked, in democratic and Christian America. What becomes of our boast of making the world safe for democracy? Where are the forty million professing Christians in this land? The so-called Christian Church, that ought to have the greatest influence in molding public sentiment in the right direction; that ought to be the greatest militant force against evil (and what greater evil is there than race prejudice?) is resting on its arms, is doing nothing, or comparatively nothing to arrest the evil and to lift up the true standard of brotherhood. We talk about sending missionaries abroad to convert the heathen, where is there in all the world a greater field for Christian missionaries of the right stamp than here in these United States? If every church in this land could be made a missionary center, as it should be, and every minister and Sunday school teacher and church official would become real missionaries after the pattern of Jesus Christ, for one year only, I cannot help feeling that there would be a decided change for the better all over the land. The trouble is the church itself is in the grip of this awful race-hating spirit, and, unfortunately, and to its shame, is doing little or nothing to counteract this evil, but is throwing the weight of its influence rather in favor of it.*

And so I might go on, filling page after page with things that I have been saying on the subject for years. And resulting in what? In simply getting myself written down by the whites as a fanatic, as a man who is clamoring for social equality, as a pessimist, as one who is all the time looking on the dark side. I received a letter once from a man by the name of the Rev. Sol. C. Dickey, DD, the leading spirit in Winona Park, a great religious center in the West, in which he said: "I wish you would let me know what you consider the Negro problem, and if you really insist on social equality, by which is meant inter-marriage of the races." My reply to him, in part, was: "Why do you ask that question? Have you ever seen any statement of mine, in any shape or form, intimating in any way that such a thought was even remotely in my mind? Instead of facing the issue squarely that is involved in this so-called Negro question, and handling it fearlessly in the light of Christian principles, the whole tendency is to evade the question, to dodge the issue, as you are doing by mixing it up with the matter of social equality and the inter-marriage of the races. A Christian man ought to be ashamed to deal with a great issue like this in the pusillanimous spirit in which you are attempting to deal with it. Isn't it time to end this pitiable exhibition of weakness and cowardice." I never heard from him afterwards.

There used to be a man connected with Howard University—he may still be connected with it—in many respects a very good man, who, after reading one of my tracts (it was handed to him by one of the colored professors), said, "Grimke used to be a very nice fellow, but he seems in these late years to have gotten soured for some reason." Instead of weighing carefully what I was saying in the tract which he read, in dealing with the subject of race prejudice, all that he could see in it was that I was getting soured, which simply meant that I didn't see things as he saw them, which simply meant that the prejudice against which I was complaining and which I asserted was contrary to Christian principle, to the spirit and teachings of Jesus Christ, he didn't object to, nor did he see any inconsistency between it and the principles of the Christianity in which he believed.

And that, unfortunately, has been the attitude of the so-called Christian Church all along. Its record on the race question has been anything but creditable to it. The weight of its great influence has been steadily thrown in favor of race discrimination. It has never attempted in any serious way to register its disapproval. Its representatives in the pulpits of the land have, mostly, been silent on the subject. The whole matter of the relation of the races has been ignored by the church, or treated as a matter with which Christianity had no necessary connection. So that the intolerable treatment to which colored people are subjected, the humiliating and debasing discriminations have not only gone on unrebuked by the church, but among those who practice these discriminations, who are guilty of these meannesses, are to be found in large numbers, members of Christian churches. And where they are not, they are rarely or never rebuked by those who are church members about them. The simple fact is the masses of so-called Christian people are the very ones who are the guilty parties, or who quietly acquiesce in what others are doing, and so are, in a measure, responsible for conditions as they at present exist, and have existed for a long time.

And this has arisen from the fact that the Church has never seriously sought to guide the people aright in this matter, to give them the proper instruction, from the pulpit and in the Sabbath school in the great principle of brotherhood, in the proper relation that should exist between man and man, regardless of race or color. It has simply been afraid to touch the subject, and because of its cowardice, its unfaithfulness to the plain teaching of the Word of God, it more than any other single agency, is responsible for present conditions, for the unfortunate race relations now existing in this country and which has now reached such a crisis that something will have to be done.

Such has been its past record; but now what do I see? If I may judge from the tenor of this address, sent out by the representatives of practically the whole of white Protestant Christianity in this country, it looks as if the scales are really beginning at last to fall from the eyes of the church; and that it means, in the future, to be true to its great mission as the representative of Jesus Christ on the earth; as the fearless and uncompromising exponent of Christian principles and ideals; as the living representative of a brotherhood that knows no man by the color of his skin, or by his race identity. It looks that way, I say; that is what it seems to mean.

And, if that is what it really means; if this noble declaration of principle is to be followed by a campaign of education, begun at once, and carried on in all the churches, in all the Sabbath schools, in all the endeavor societies, in all the homes, represented in all these churches included in the Federal Council of Churches in America, in every city, town, hamlet, village, and rural district, with a view of realizing in the actual every-day life of the people the principles and ideals of Christianity set forth in this address, then is there not only reason for us as a race to rejoice, but a ground of rejoicing and thanksgiving for all, white as well as black. A great organization like the Christian Church cannot address itself seriously to the solution of any problem without bettering conditions. It is the best, the most fitting instrument to deal with this race problem, as with every other problem, if it will only be true, and true always to Christian ideals and principles, giving itself no concern as to results. Whatever the results may be, whatever consequences may flow from loyalty to the spirit and teachings of Jesus Christ, will always be in the line of progress, will always be to the best interest of the individual and of the community. All it needs to be concerned about, if it is to fulfill its high mission as the light of the world, as the salt of the earth, is to see to it that it turns a deaf ear to every other voice except the voice of God, and that it goes forward fearlessly, courageously under its direction.

And, it looks, as I have said, as if this is about what it has made up its mind to do.

In reading recently Dr. Cornelius H. Patton's admirable volume, *World Facts and America's Responsibility,* I was very much impressed, deeply touched, by a paragraph which occurs in the chapter entitled, *"The East and the West Fight for a Common Cause."* This is the paragraph:

> *Nothing that came out of France is more reassuring than that extract from a letter of an American Negro soldier to his mother at home, which caught the eye of a thoughtful censor and so was given to the public. What he said was this: 'I tell you, mammy, they treat us fine. There's plenty of fighting, but we's jest as good as anybody else. We don't ever know we's black unless we look in the glass.' Still better is this incident from our own Southland. In a certain aristocratic home of the South when the colored houseboy entered the Army, in recognition of the event, the lady of the house hung a service flag in the kitchen window, having previously hung a service flag in the parlor window in honor of her son's enlistment. Later the son returned home and inquired what the flag in the kitchen meant. When he was told that it stood for Jim, their servant, he said, "Mother, no service flag shall hang in the kitchen of this house. Jim and I are fighting side by side in this war." And, taking the colored servant's flag, he placed it in the parlor window beside his own.*

After I had finished reading these lines I said to myself, *that is just as it should be.* As that American Negro soldier and his comrades were treated fine by the French people; as they were made to feel that they were as good as anybody else; as they were never made conscious of the color of their skins, so ought it to be in this country. Every American citizen, white or black, ought to be made to feel, and would be made to feel, if America lived up to its professed democratic principles, the same sense of equality as every French citizen feels, white or black, with nothing in any part of the French Republic to remind them of anything different.

And so the spirit exhibited by this white southern aristocrat in refusing to permit a distinction to be drawn between himself and the colored man who had been a servant in his family, since they were both American citizens, and were both fighting side by side under the same flag, is the new spirit that must take the place of the old Bourbon spirit represented by his mother. Under the flag there must be no distinction between citizens, based on race or color. Men who fight side by side under the same flag, and upon whom the same duties and responsibilities are imposed, there never can be any good or sufficient reason why the one should be accorded rights, privileges not accorded to the other. Duties and responsibilities of citizens cannot be made the same, without according to each the same rights and privileges, except by an act of injustice, by the exercise of arbitrary and despotic power.

These two incidents clearly indicate what the problem is which confronts us in this country in dealing with this race question. And, if the Church is worth its salt; if it means business; if these declarations, as embodied in this address to the country, are not mere camouflage, but the expression of a real, earnest purpose on its part to live out the principles and ideals of Christianity as set forth in the life, character and teachings of Jesus Christ, in the course of time there is bound to be a decided change for the better. There would have been a change long ago for the better if the Church had done its duty, if it had not, in so many respects, played false to its great Head and to its avowed principles. But I must stop. I have spoken quite long enough.

We can all, I am sure, not only as American citizens, but as colored Americans, lift up our hearts today in gratitude to God. We thank Him, that the great war is over; we thank Him, that so few of our soldiers, as compared with other countries, perished during the great conflict; we thank Him for the many homes in our land that have been made glad by the return of loved ones out of the blood and smoke of battle; we thank Him for the part which, as a nation, we were permitted to play in the momentous struggle between autocracy and democracy in the great world contest.

And we thank Him also and especially for the clear and unmistakable evidences of a growing, ever-deepening interest of the race in its rights—in the estimate it puts upon them; we thank Him for the new spirit that is taking possession of the race—the spirit that is no longer running away from its assailants, but is now standing in its own defense, since the law is powerless to defend it, or is unwilling to do so; we thank Him that the so-called Christian Church in this land is at last awaking to a sense of its shortcomings, and of its responsibilities in properly expounding and in worthily living out the principles of Christianity. For all these things we thank Him.

And, as a race, in the future as in the past, as an expression of our gratitude to Him, let us resolve to continue unfalteringly to trust Him and His Son, Jesus Christ, remembering, never forgetting the great truth,

> *Except the Lord build the house, They labor in vain that build it: Except the Lord keep the city, The watchman waketh but in vain.*

Whatever other races may do, or other individuals may do, let us make up our minds that we will serve the Lord, and that we will train our children to do the same. Linked with God; yielding ourselves in loving obedience to God, the gates of hell, all the powers of darkness, in high places as well as low places, will not be able to prevail against us; we will still be pressing on the upward way, as we have been doing ever since Lincoln's great Emancipation Proclamation was issued and the three great war amendments to the Constitution were ratified.

Let us be thankful; let us be ever praising the Lord!

BIBLIOGRAPHY

Abelard, Peter. *Ethica*. Translated by D. E. Luscombe. Oxford: Clarendon Press, 1971.

Agnon, Shmuel Yosef. *Days of Awe*. New York: Schocken Books, 1965. Originally published in 1948.

Alcántara, Jared E. *The Practices of Christian Preaching: Essentials for Effective Proclamation*. Grand Rapids, MI: Baker Academic, 2019.

Anderson, Gary A. *That I May Dwell Among Them*. Grand Rapids, MI: Eerdmans, 2023.

Aquinas, Thomas. *Commentary on Saint Paul's Letter to the Romans*. Translated by F. R. Larcher and Edward C. Miller. Steubenville, OH: Emmaus Academic, 2018.

———. *Commentary on the Letters of Saint Paul to the Corinthians*. Translated by Fabian Larcher and Daniel Keating. Steubenville, OH: Emmaus Academic, 2018.

Artemi, Eirini. "John of Damascus and the Use of the Letters of Paul in His Writing: An Exact Exposition of the Orthodox Faith." *Mirabilia* 24 (2017): 23–39.

Augustine. *On Nature and Grace*. Translated by Peter Holmes. In *Nicene and Post-Nicene Fathers, First Series*, Vol. 5, edited by Philip Schaff. Buffalo, NY: Christian Literature Publishing Co., 1887.

———. *The City of God*. Translated by Marcus Dods. New York: Modern Library, 1950.

———. *Expositions of the Psalms 1–32*, III/15. Introduction by Michael Fiedrowicz, translation and notes by Maria Boulding,

OSB, edited by John E. Rotelle, OSA. Hyde Park, NY: New City Press, 2000.

———. *Confessions.* Translated by Henry Chadwick. Oxford: Oxford University Press, 2009

Barth, Karl. *The Epistle to the Romans*, translated by Edwyn C. Hoskyns. 6th ed. London: Oxford University Press, 1933.

———. *Homiletics.* Translated by Geoffrey W. Bromiley and Donald E. Daniels. Louisville: Westminster John Knox Press, 1991.

Bass, Carole. "John Hollander, Poet & Professor." *Yale Alumni Magazine*, August 19, 2013. Accessed August 7, 2024. https://yalealumnimagazine.org/blog_posts/1543-john-hollander-poet-professor.

Bauckham, Richard. "Reading Scripture as a Coherent Story." In *The Art of Reading Scripture*, edited by Ellen Davis and Richard Hays, 38–53. Grand Rapids, MI: Eerdmans, 2003.

Bebbington, D. W. *Evangelicalism in Modern Britain: A History from the 1730s to the 1980s*. Revised ed. London: Taylor & Francis Group, 2005.

Berkowitz, Matthew. "A Psalm of Repentance." *JTS*, August 28, 2004/5764. Accessed July 11, 2024. https://www.jtsa.edu/torah/a-psalm-for-repentance.

Berlin, Adele. *The Dynamics of Biblical Parallelism.* Revised and expanded ed. Grand Rapids. MI: Eerdmans, 2007. Originally published in 1985.

Berlin, Ira, ed. *The Destruction of Slavery*. Vol. 1 of *Freedom: A Documentary History of Emancipation, 1861–1867.* Cambridge: Cambridge University Press, 1985.

Blum, Edward J. *Reforging the White Republic: Race, Religion, and American Nationalism, 1865–1898*. Baton Rouge: Louisiana State University Press, 2005.

Broadus, John A. *On the Preparation and Delivery of Sermons*. Kindle. Auckland: Titus Books, 2014.

Bruce, Dickson D. *Archibald Grimké: Portrait of a Black Independent*. Baton Rouge: Louisiana State University Press, 1993.

Buttrick, George A. *Jesus Came Preaching*. New York: Scribner, 1931.

Calloway, Carolyn R. "A Rhetorical Analysis of the Persuasion of Francis J. Grimké." PhD diss., Indiana University, 1976. Xerox University Microfilms.

Calvin, John. *Commentaries on the Epistle of Paul the Apostle to the Hebrews*. Translated and edited by John Owen. Edinburgh: Calvin Translation Society, 1853.

———. *Commentaries on the Epistles of Paul to the Galatians and Ephesians*. Translated by William Pringle. Grand Rapids, MI: Eerdmans, 1948.

———. *Commentary on the Epistle of Paul to the Romans*. Translated by John Owen. Grand Rapids, MI: Christian Classics Ethereal Library, 1947.

———. *Commentary on the Epistle of Paul to the Ephesians*. Translated by William Pringle. Grand Rapids, MI: Christian Classics Ethereal Library, 1947.

———. *Commentary on the Book of Psalms*. Translated by James Anderson. Grand Rapids, MI: Christian Classics Ethereal Library, n.d.

———. *Commentary on the Epistle to the Romans*. Translated by John Owen. Whitefish, MT: Kessinger, 2010.

Cameron, Michael. *Christ Meets Me Everywhere: Augustine's Early Figurative Exegesis*. Oxford: Oxford University Press, 2012.

Campbell, James T. *Songs of Zion: The African Methodist Episcopal Church in the United States and South Africa*. Chapel Hill: University of North Carolina Press, 1998.

Canellos, Peter S. *The Great Dissenter: The Story of John Marshall Harlan, America's Judicial Hero*. New York: Simon & Schuster, 2021.

Carroll, Charles. *The Negro Beast, or In the Image of God*. St. Louis, MO: American Book and Bible House, 1900.

Chapell, Bryan. *Christ-Centered Preaching: Redeeming the Expository Sermon*. 2nd ed. Grand Rapids, MI: Baker Academic, 2005.

Chesterton, G. K. *Saint Thomas Aquinas: The Dumb Ox*. New York: Image Books, 1974.

Chrysostom, John. *Homilia II de laudibus sancti Pauli*. In *Patrologiae Cursus Completus: Series Graeca*, Vol. 50, edited by J.-P. Migne, 477–480. Paris: Garnier Fratres, 1857.

Collins, Patricia Hill. *Black Feminist Thought: Knowledge, Consciousness, and the Politics of Empowerment*. New York: Routledge, 2000.

Cone, James H. *A Black Theology of Liberation*. Maryknoll, NY: Orbis Books, 1990.

Cooper, Alan, and Elaine Ravich. "Psalm 27: The Days of Awe." Jewish Theological Seminary. Last modified August 25, 2012. Accessed July 12, 2024. https://www.jtsa.edu/torah/psalm-27-the-days-of-awe.

Copeland, Rita. *Pedagogy, Intellectuals, and Dissent in the Later Middle Ages: Lollardy and Ideas of Learning*. Cambridge: Cambridge University Press, 2001.

Cormode, Scott. "Innovation that Honors Tradition: The Meaning of Christian Innovation." *Journal of Religious Leadership* 14, no. 2 (Fall 2015): 99–102.

Costley, Clare L. "David, Bathsheba, and the Penitential Psalms." *Renaissance Quarterly* 57, no. 4 (Winter 2004): 1244–71. https://www.jstor.org/stable/4143695.

Cribb, Bryan, and Channing Crisler. *The Bible Toolbox.* Nashville: B&H Academic, 2019.

Crisler, Channing L. *An Intertextual Commentary on Romans. Volume 1: Romans 1:1–4:25.* Eugene, OR: Pickwick Publications, 2021.

———. *An Intertextual Commentary on Romans, Volume 3: Romans 9:1–11:36.* Eugene, OR: Pickwick Publications, 2022.

———. *Reading Romans as Lament: Paul's Use of Old Testament Lament in His Most Famous Letter.* Kindle. Eugene, OR: Pickwick, 2016.

———. "Interview 1." Interviewed by Eric J. Freeman, May 19, 2023.

———. "Interview 2." Interviewed by Eric J. Freeman, June 22, 2023.

———. "Interview 3." Interviewed by Eric J. Freeman, November 16, 2023.

———. "Interview 4." Interviewed by Eric J. Freeman, June 13, 2024.

———. "Interview 5." Interviewed by Eric J. Freeman, October 24, 2024.

Crummell, Alexander. *The Greatness of Christ and Other Sermons.* New York: Thomas Whitaker, 2 and 3 Bible House, 1882.

Davidson, Richard M. "A Song for the Sanctuary: Celebrating Its Goodness, Its Truth, Its Beauty." *Adventist Review*, July 2, 1992, 704–07.

Davis, Ellen F., and Richard B. Hays, eds., *The Art of Reading Scripture*. Grand Rapids, MI: Eerdmans, 2003.

Dickerson, Dennis. *African American Preachers and Politics: The Careys of Chicago*. Jackson: University Press of Mississippi, 2011.

Diehl, Judy. "Empire and Epistles: Anti-Roman Rhetoric in the New Testament Epistles." *Currents in Biblical Research* 10, no. 2 (2012): 217–63.

Donfried, Karl. "The Relationship between Paul and John Chrysostom." Lecture at the 2008 Pauline Symposium, Istanbul, Turkey, October 9–17, 2008. Accessed August 9, 2024. https://www.youtube.com/watch?v=FoI5MAawd7M.

Du Bois, W. E. B. *The Souls of Black Folk*, unabridged ed. Mineola, NY: Dover, 2016. Originally published in 1903.

Dunn, James D. G. *The Theology of Paul the Apostle*. Grand Rapids, MI: Eerdmans, 2006.

Du Toit, Philip la Grange. "Paul, Empire and Eschatology." *HTS Teologiese Studies/Theological Studies* 77, no. 4 (2021): 1–10. https://doi.org/10.4102/hts.v77i4.6904.

Dyson, Walter. *Howard University: The Capstone of Negro Education, A History: 1867–1940*. Washington, DC: Graduate School, Howard University, 1941.

Edwards, O. C. *The History of Preaching*. Vol. 1. Kindle. Nashville: Abingdon Press, 2004.

Ehrman, Bart D. "The Apostle Paul: Polling Our Sources." In *Peter, Paul, and Mary Magdalene*, 89–100. New York: Oxford University Press, 2006.

Elliott, Neil. *The Arrogance of Nations: Reading Romans in the Shadow of Empire*. Minneapolis: Fortress Press, 2018.

Felder, Cain Hope. *Stony the Road We Trod: African American Biblical Interpretation*. Minneapolis: Fortress Press, 1991.

Ferris, William Henry. *Alexander Crummell: An Apostle of Negro Culture*. Boston: Pilgrim Press, 1920.

———. *The African Abroad*. Vol. 2. New Haven, CT: Tuttle, Morehouse & Taylor, 1913.

Ferry, Henry Justin. "Francis James Grimké: Portrait of a Black Puritan." PhD diss., Yale University, 1970. University Microfilms.

———. "Francis James Grimké: Prophet on a Tightrope." Lecture notes, Reformed Institute of Metropolitan Washington, n.d. Accessed August 8, 2024. https://reformedinstitute.org/resources/.

———. "Patriotism and Prejudice: Francis James Grimké on World War I." *Journal of Religious Thought* 32 (Spring–Summer 1975): 86–94.

Foley, Malcolm. "The Only Way to Stop a Mob: Francis Grimké's Biblical Case for Lynching Resistance." In *Every Leaf, Line, and Letter: Evangelicals and the Bible from the 1730s to the Present*, edited by Timothy Larsen, 196–217. Downers Grove, IL: InterVarsity Press, 2021.

Foner, Eric. *Give Me Liberty! An American History*. Vol. 1. 6th ed. New York: W. W. Norton & Company, 2020.

Foner, Philip S., and Robert James Branham, eds. *Lift Every Voice: African American Oratory, 1787–1900*. Tuscaloosa: University of Alabama Press, 1998.

Forbes, James. *The Holy Spirit & Preaching*. Nashville: Abingdon Press, 1989.

Forten, Charlotte L., and Anna J. Cooper. *Life and Writings of the Grimke Family*. Published by Anna J. Cooper, 1951. Accessed August 18, 2024. https://xtf.lib.virginia.edu/xtf/view?docId=chadwyck_aap/uvaGenText/tei/chaap_D045.xml.

Fortune, T. Thomas. "Howard's Next President." *New York Age* 19, no. 19, January 4, 1906, 4. Accessed August 18, 2024. https://dds.crl.edu/crldelivery/8217.

Franklin, V. P. *Black Self-determination: A Cultural History of the Faith of the Fathers.* Westport, Conn.: L. Hill, 1984.

Fredrickson, George M. *Black Liberation: A Comparative History of Black Ideologies in the United States and South Africa.* New York: Oxford University Press, 1995.

Fredriksen, Paula. *Augustine and the Jews: A Christian Defense of Jews and Judaism.* New Haven, CT: Yale University Press, 2010.

Freeman, Kathryn, Elise M. Edwards, Bertis D. English, and Stephanie C. Boddie. "Pandemics, the Rev. Francis J. Grimké, and Life Lessons." In *Racialized Health, COVID-19, and Religious Responses: Black Atlantic Contexts and Perspectives*, edited by R. Drew Smith, Stephanie C. Boddie, and Bertis D. English, 99–109. New York: Routledge, 2022.

Freire, Paulo. *Pedagogy of the Oppressed.* New York: Bloomsbury, 2000.

George, Carol V. R. *Segregated Sabbaths: Richard Allen and the Emergence of Independent Black Churches, 1760–1840.* New York: Oxford University Press, 1973.

Green, Maxine. *The Dialectic of Freedom.* New York: Teachers College Press, 1988.

Grimké, Angelina Weld. "A Biographical Sketch of Archibald H. Grimke." *Opportunity* 3 (February 1925): 44–47.

Grimké, Archibald H. "Alumni Petition Trustees: Indict Gordon and Pray for His Dismission." *New York Age* 18, no. 43, June 8, 1905, 1. https://dds.crl.edu/crldelivery/8217.

———. "Colorphobia in Howard: Under New Pilot, Old Ship Now Heads Due South." *New York Age* 18, no. 40, May 18, 1905, 1.

———. "Dr. Gordon Faces a Crisis: Said He Should Right-About-Face or Abdicate." *New York Age* 18, no. 42, June 1, 1905, 1.

———. "A Madonna of the South." *Southern Workman* 29, no. 7 (July 1900): 391–96.

———. "Memoirs of Archibald H. Grimké." In *Archibald H. Grimké Papers*, Box 2, Folder 47. Washington, DC: Moorland-Spingarn Research Center, Howard University, n.d.

———. "Snubbed Coleridge-Taylor: His Reception at Boston and Howard Contrasted." *New York Age* 18, no. 41, May 25, 1905, 1.

———. "Troubles of Howard: Executive Raids Upon Other Departments' Finances." *New York Age* 18, no. 39, May 11, 1905, 1.

Grimké, Francis James. *Meditations on Preaching*. Minneapolis: Log College Press, 2018.

———. "Mr. Moody and the Color Question in the South." *Independent* 38, no. 1964, Thursday, July 22, 1886, 7.

———. *The Works of Francis J. Grimke*. Vol. 1, edited by Carter G. Woodson. Washington, DC: Associated, 1942.

———. *The Works of Francis J. Grimke.* Vol. 2, edited by Carter G. Woodson. Washington, DC: Associated, 1942.

———. *The Works of Francis J. Grimke.* Vol. 3, edited by Carter G. Woodson. Washington, DC: Associated, 1942.

———. "Letter to 'Dear Bro,'" January 24, 1887. In *Francis Grimké Papers*, Box 1, Folder 1.

Grimké, Henry. "Letter to 'Dear Boys,'" n.d. In *E. Montague Grimké Papers.*

Gutman, Herbert G. "Protestantism and the American Labor Movement: The Christian Spirit in the Gilded Age." *American Historical Review* 72, no. 1 (1966): 74–101. https://doi.org/10.2307/1848171.

Gwaltney, Grace R. "The Negro Church and the Social Gospel from 1877 to 1914." MA thesis, Howard University, Washington, DC.

Haar, James. "Orlande de Lassus." In *The New Grove High Renaissance Masters: Josquin, Palestrina, Lassus, Byrd, Victoria*, edited by Stanley Sadie, 157–227. New York: W. W. Norton & Company, 1984.

Harding, Vincent. *There is a River: The Black Struggle for Freedom in America.* New York: Harcourt Brace Jovanovich, 1981.

Hays, Richard B. *Echoes of Scripture in the Gospels.* Waco, TX: Baylor University Press, 2016.

———. *Echoes of Scripture in the Letters of Paul.* New Haven, CT: Yale University Press, 1989.

———. *Echoes of Scripture in the Letters of Paul.* New ed. New Haven, CT: Yale University Press, 1993.

Heilig, Christoph. *Hidden Criticism? The Methodology and Plausibility of the Search for a Counter-Imperial Subtext in Paul.* Tübingen, Germany: Mohr Siebeck, 2015.

Heisler, Greg. *Spirit-Led Preaching: The Holy Spirit's Role in Sermon Preparation and Delivery.* Nashville: B&H Academic, 2007.

Herrmann, Erik. "Luther's Journey with Paul." *Lutheran Witness*, June/July 2008. Accessed May 3, 2024. https://witness.lcms.org/2008/luthers-journey-with-paul-6-2008/.

Hesselink, I. John. *Calvin's First Catechism: A Commentary.* Louisville KY: Westminster John Knox Press, 1998.

Hesseltine, W. B. "Some New Aspects of the Pro-Slavery Argument." *Journal of Negro History* 21, no. 1 (1936): 1–59.

Hobson, Christopher Z. *The Mount of Vision: African American Prophetic Tradition, 1800–1950.* New York: Oxford University Press, 2012.

Hollander, John. *The Figure of Echo: A Mode of Allusion in Milton and After.* Berkeley: University of California Press, 1981.

Hopkins, Charles H. *The Rise of the Social Gospel in American Protestantism 1865–1915.* New Haven, CT: Yale University Press, 1967.

Horton, Michael. *Calvin on the Christian Life: Glorifying and Enjoying God Forever.* Wheaton, IL: Crossway, 2014.

John of Damascus. *Expositio Accurata Fidei Orthodoxae.* Patrologia Graece 94:961.

———. *On the Divine Images: Three Apologies Against Those Who Attack the Divine Images.* Translated by David Anderson. Crestwood, NY: St. Vladimir's Seminary Press, 1980.

———. *Pro Sacris Imaginibus Orationes Tres.* Patrologia Graece 94:1227–419

Johnson, Todd M., and Gina A. Zurlo. *World Christian Encyclopedia.* 3rd ed. Edinburgh: Edinburgh University Press, 2019.

Kautsky, Karl. *The Dictatorship of the Proletariat,* translated by H. J. Stenning. London: Forgotten Books, 2018. Originally published in 1918.

Keener, Craig S. *The Gospel of Matthew: A Socio-Rhetorical Commentary.* Grand Rapids, MI: Wm. B. Eerdmans, 2009.

———. *The Historical Jesus of the Gospels.* Grand Rapids, MI: Eerdmans, 2009.

———. "Romans Session 1: Introduction." Lecture series produced by Ted Hildebrandt from biblicalelearning.org, February 15, 2016. YouTube video, 1:04:37. Accessed July 9, 2023. https://www.youtube.com/watch?v=hPQZOexILag

Keesmaat, Sylvia. "Exodus and the Intertextual Transformation of Tradition in Romans 8:14–30." *Journal for the Study of the New Testament* 54 (1994): 29–56.

King'oo, Clare Costley. *Miserere Mei: The Penitential Psalms in Late Medieval and Early Modern England, Reformations: Medieval and Early Modern.* Notre Dame, IN: University of Notre Dame Press, 2012.

Klink, Edward W., III, and Darian R. Lockett. *Understanding Biblical Theology: A Comparison of Theory and Practice.* Grand Rapids, MI: Zondervan, 2012.

Koester, Craig R. *Revelation and the End of All Things.* 2nd ed. Grand Rapids, MI: Wm. B. Eerdmans Publishing Co., 2018.

Kowalski, Marcin. "The Lion Against the Eagle: A Critical Appraisal of the Anti-Imperial Reading of Paul." *Collectanea Theologica*

93, no. 2 (2023): 57–103. https://doi.org/10.21697/ct.2023.93.2.03.

Kristeva, Julia. "The Bounded Text." In *Desire in Language: A Semiotic Approach to Literature and Art*, edited by Leon S. Roudiez, translated by Thomas Gora, Alice Jardine, and Leon Roudiez, 36–63. New York: Columbia University Press, 1980. Originally published 1969.

———. *Revolution in Poetic Language*. New York: Columbia University Press, 1984.

Langley, Kenneth J. *How to Preach the Psalms*. Dallas: Fontes Press, 2021.

Larsen, Timothy. *Every Leaf, Line, and Letter: Evangelicals and the Bible from the 1730s to the Present*. Downers Grove, IL: IVP Academic, 2021.

LaRue, Cleophus James. *The Heart of Black Preaching*. Louisville, KY: Westminster John Knox Press, 2000.

Levering, Matthew. *Paul in the Summa Theologiae*. Washington, DC: Catholic University of America Press, 2014.

Levine, Lawrence W. *Black Culture and Black Consciousness: Afro-American Folk Thought from Slavery to Freedom*. New York: Oxford University Press, 30th anniversary ed., 2007.

Leyerle, Blake. *The Narrative Shape of Emotion in the Preaching of John Chrysostom*. Berkeley: University of California Press, 2020.

Liddell, Henry George, and Robert Scott. *A Greek-English Lexicon*. 9th ed. Revised by Henry Stuart Jones and Roderick McKenzie. Oxford: Clarendon Press, 1996.

Lippmann, Walter. *A Preface to Morals*. New York: Routledge, 2017. Originally published 1929.

Litfin, Duane. *Paul's Theology of Preaching: The Apostle's Challenge to the Art of Persuasion in Ancient Corinth*. Downers Grove, IL: IVP Academic, 2015.

Lockwood, Lewis, and Jesse Ann Owens. "Giovanni Pierluigi da Palestrina." In *The New Grove High Renaissance Masters: Josquin, Palestrina, Lassus, Byrd, Victoria*, edited by Stanley Sadie, 93–153. New York: W. W. Norton & Company, 1984.

Louth, Andrew. *St. John Damascene: Tradition and Originality in Byzantine Theology*. Oxford: Oxford University Press, 2002.

Luker, Ralph. *The Social Gospel in Black and White: American Racial Reform, 1885–1912*. Chapel Hill: University of North Carolina Press, 1991.

Luscombe, David. *The School of Peter Abelard: The Influence of Abelard's Thought in Medieval Europe*. Cambridge: Cambridge University Press, 1969.

Luther, Martin. *Commentary on Romans*. Translated by J. Theodore Mueller. Grand Rapids, MI: Kregel Publications, 1976.

———. *Lectures on Romans*. In *Luther's Works*, vol. 25. Edited by Hilton C. Oswald. St. Louis: Concordia Publishing House, 1972.

———. *Commentary on Paul's Epistle to the Galatians*, translated by Theodore Graebner. Grand Rapids, MI: Zondervan, 1949.

Marenbon, John. *The Philosophy of Peter Abelard*. Cambridge: Cambridge University Press, 1997.

Martin, Andrew. "The Civil, Political, Religious, and Moral: Francis Grimké, W.E.B. Du Bois, and the Early NAACP." Paper presented at the 73rd annual meeting of the Evangelical Theological Society, Fort Worth, TX, November 16–18, 2021. 00:40:23 on audio. Accessed August 17, 2024, https://www.wordmp3.com/details.aspx?id=40528.

Mayer, Wendy, trans. *The Cult of the Saints: John Chrysostom's Homilies on Saints*. Crestwood, NY: St. Vladimir's Seminary Press, 2006.

McKee, Elsie Anne, and B. A. Gerrish. *John Calvin: Writings on Pastoral Piety*. New York: Paulist Press, 2002.

McKnight, Scott. "The Apostle Paul: 'No One Knows the Trouble I've Seen.'" Lecture given at Lanier Theological Library Lecture Series, Houston, TX, October 26, 2019. YouTube, 1:11:41. Accessed July 12, 2023. https://youtu.be/TC3eqZbTkos.

———. *Reading Romans Backward: A Gospel of Peace in the Midst of Empire*. Waco, TX: Baylor University Press, 2019.

Meagher, John C. "John 1:14 and the New Temple." *Journal of Biblical Literature* 88, no. 1 (1969): 57–68. https://doi.org/10.2307/3262833.

Meier, John P. *A Marginal Jew: Rethinking the Historical Jesus*. 5 vols. New Haven, CT: Yale University Press, 1991-2016.

Mews, Constant J. *Abelard and Heloise*. Oxford: Oxford University Press, 2005.

Miller, A. G. *Elevating the Race: Theophilus G. Steward, Black Theology, and the Making of an African American Civil Society, 1865–1924* Knoxville: University of Tennessee Press, 2003.

Mitchell, Margaret M. *The Heavenly Trumpet: John Chrysostom and the Art of Pauline Interpretation*. Louisville, KY: Westminster John Knox Press, 2002.

———. *John Chrysostom on Paul: Praises and Problem Passages*. Atlanta: SBL Press, 2022.

Moo, Douglas J. *The Epistle to the Romans*. Grand Rapids, MI: Eerdmans, 1996.

Mortimer, Alfred G. *Notes on the Seven Penitential Psalms, Chiefly from Patristic Sources*. London: Joseph Master & Co., 1889.

Moses, Wilson J. *Alexander Crummell: A Study of Civilization and Discontent*. New York: Oxford University Press, 1989.

Müller-Bloch, C., and J. Kranz. "A Framework for Rigorously Identifying Research Gaps in Qualitative Literature Reviews." In *Proceedings of the International Conference on Information Systems*, edited by T. Carte, A. Heinzl, and C. Urquhart, Fort Worth, TX, December 16, 2015.

Murray, Andrew E. *Presbyterians and the Negro: A History*. Philadelphia: Presbyterian Historical Society, 1966.

Neuhaus, John. *Freedom for Ministry*. Grand Rapids, MI: Eerdmans, 1979.

Newman, Richard S. *Freedom's Prophet: Bishop Richard Allen, the AME Church, and the Black Founding Fathers*. New York: New York University Press, 2009.

Nickel, Mary. "Incorporating Intimacy: The Evocative Story of Francis J. Grimké." *Journal of Black Religious Thought* 1, no. 2 (2022): 196–227. https://doi.org/10.1163/27727963-01020005.

Noll, Mark A. *God and Race in American Politics: A Short History*. New York: Oxford University Press, 2001.

———. "Theology, Presbyterian History, and the Civil War." *Presbyterian History* 89, no. 1 (Spring/Summer 2011): 5–15.

———. "Still Under a Bushel." In *America's Book: The Rise and Decline of a Bible Civilization, 1794–1911*, 642–64. New York: Oxford University Press, 2022. https://doi.org/10.1093/oso/9780197623466.003.0031.

Oakes, Peter. *Reading Romans in Pompeii: Paul's Letter at Ground Level.* Kindle. Minneapolis: Fortress Press, 2009.

Obituary for George van Deurs. *Philadelphia Inquirer*, September 17, 1906, 2. Accessed August 18, 2024. https://www.newspapers.com/article/the-philadelphia-inquirer-obituary-for-g/83378023/.

O'Reilly, Graham. *Allegri's Miserere in the Sistine Chapel.* New York: Oxford University Press, 2020.

Parker, T. H. L. *Calvin's Preaching*. Edinburgh: T&T Clark, 1992.

Payne, Daniel. *Recollections of Seventy Years.* Nashville: Publishing House of the A.M.E. Sunday School Union, 1888.

Pennington, Jonathan T. *Reading the Gospels Wisely: A Narrative and Theological Introduction.* Grand Rapids, MI: Baker Academic, 2012.

Piper, John. *The Future of Justification: A Response to N. T. Wright.* Wheaton, IL: Crossway, 2007.

Pipes, William H. *Say Amen, Brother! Old-Time Negro Preaching: A Study in African American Frustration.* Detroit: Wayne State University Press, 1951.

Plett, Heinrich F. "Intertextualities." In *Intertextuality*, 3–29. Berlin: de Gruyter, 1991.

Porter, Stanley E. "Allusions and Echoes." In *As It Is Written: Studying Paul's Use of Scripture*, edited by Stanley E. Porter and Christopher D. Stanley, 29–40. Atlanta: Society of Biblical Literature, 2008.

———. "Further Comments on the Use of the Old Testament in the New Testament." In *The Intertextuality of the Epistles: Explorations of Theory and Practice*, edited by Thomas L.

Brodie, Dennis R. MacDonald, and Stanley E. Porter, 98–110 Sheffield: Sheffield Phoenix Press, 2006.

———. "The Use of the Old Testament in the New Testament: A Brief Comment on Method and Terminology." in *Early Christian Interpretation of the Scriptures of Israel: Investigations and Proposals*, edited by Craig A. Evans and James A. Sanders, 79–96. Sheffield: Sheffield Academic Press, 1997.

———. "Wittgenstein's Classes of Utterances and Pauline Ethical Texts." *Journal of the Evangelical Theological Society* 32, no. 1 (March 1989): 85–97.

Porter, Stanley E., and Jason C. Robinson. *Hermeneutics: An Introduction to Interpretive Theory*. Grand Rapids, MI: Eerdmans, 2011.

Porter, Stanley E., and Cynthia Long Westfall. "Paul Confronts Caesar with the Good News." In *Empire in the New Testament*, 90–105. Eugene, OR: Pickwick, 2011.

Punt, Jeremy. "Paul the Jew, Power of Evil and Rome." *Scripture* 117 (2018): 1–17. https://doi.org/10.7833/117-1-1389.

Quicke, Michael J. *360-Degree Leadership*. Grand Rapids, MI: Baker Books, 2006.

Raboteau, Albert J. *Slave Religion: The "Invisible Institution" in the Antebellum South*. Updated ed. New York: Oxford University Press, 2004.

Ramsey, Bonaventure. *Beginning to Read the Fathers*. New York: Paulist Press, 1985.

Ravenel, Harriott H. *Charleston: The Place and the People*. New York: Macmillan, 1906.

Reed, Trudie Kibbe. *The Caring Community: A Journey into the Spiritual Domain of Transformative Leadership*. Bloomington, IN: iUniverse, 2010.

Rothenbuhler, Eric W., Lawrence J. Mullen, Richard DeLaurell, and Choon Ryul Ryu. "Communication, Community Attachment, and Involvement." *J&MC Quarterly* 73, no. 2 (Summer 1996): 445–66.

Rylaarsdam, David. *John Chrysostom on Divine Pedagogy: The Coherence of His Theology and Preaching*. Oxford: Oxford University Press, 2014.

Sanders, E. P. *Jesus and Judaism*. Philadelphia: Fortress Press, 1985.

———. *Paul and Palestinian Judaism*. Minneapolis: Fortress Press, 1977.

Sanlon, Peter. "Depth and Weight: Augustine's Sermon Illustrations." *Churchman* 122, no. 1 (Spring 2008): 61–76.

Schwarzwalder, Robert F., Jr., "'For a Real, Not a Sham Christianity': Francis J. Grimké on Racial Strife and World Peace in the Early Twentieth Century." *Fides et Historia* 53, no. 2 (Summer/Fall 2021): 17–33.

Seifrid, Mark A. "Paul's Approach to the Old Testament in Rom 10:6-8." *Trinity Journal* 6, no. 1 (Spring 1985): 3–37.

Shrock, Joel. *The Gilded Age*. Westport, CT: Greenwood Press, 2004.

Sidwell, Mark. "Francis Grimké and the Value and the Limits of Carter Woodson's Model of the Progressive Black Pastor." *Fides et Historia,* 32, no. 1 (Winter/Spring 2000): 99–117.

Smith, Robert, Jr., "Clamp Preaching Lectures 2014, Part 1." Clamp Divinity School. Accessed October 10, 2022. https://youtube.com/playlist?list=PLWAWCkW7P-ezi6bui45FJE7uMRY0BeXmW.

Smitherman, Geneva. *Word from the Mother: Language and African Americans*. 1st ed. London: Routledge, 2021.

Spurgeon, Charles Haddon. *The Treasury of David*, vols. 1–6. London: Marshall Brothers, n.d.

Stanley, Christopher D. "The Social Environment of 'Free' Biblical Quotations in the New Testament." In *Early Christian Interpretation of the Scriptures of Israel: Investigations and Proposals*, edited by Craig A. Evans and James A. Sanders, 18–27. Sheffield: Sheffield Academic Press, 1997.

Steinmetz, David C. *Calvin in Context*. 2nd ed. Oxford: Oxford University Press, 2010.

———. *Luther in Context*. Bloomington: Indiana University Press, 1986.

Stendahl, Krister. "The Apostle Paul and the Introspective Conscience of the West." *Harvard Theological Review* 56, no. 3 (July 1963): 199–215.

Stewart, C. F. *Soul Survivors: An African American Spirituality*. Louisville, KY: Westminster John Knox Press, 1997.

Sunquist, Scott W. *The Unexpected Christian Century: The Reversal and Transformation of Global Christianity, 1900–2000*. Grand Rapids, MI: Baker Academic, 2015.

Thomas Aquinas. *Commentary on the Letters of Saint Paul*, translated by Fabian Larcher, OP, edited by J. Mortensen. Lander, WY: Aquinas Institute, 2012.

———. *Commentary on the Letters of Saint Paul: Complete Set (Latin–English Opera Omnia)*, edited by the Aquinas Institute. Steubenville, OH: Emmaus Academic, 2012.

———. *Summa Theologica, Pars Prima Secundae*, eBook #17897. Salt Lake City: Project Gutenberg Literary Archive Foundation, 2006.

Tise, Larry E. *Proslavery: A History of the Defense of Slavery in America, 1701–1840*. Athens: University of Georgia Press, 1987.

Travers, Michael E. "Severe Delight: The Paradox of Praise in Confession of Sin." In *The Psalms: Language for All Seasons of the Soul,* edited by Andrew Schmutzer and David Howard. Chicago: Moody, 2013.

Turner, Lorenzo Dow. *Africanisms in the Gullah Dialect*. Chicago: University of Chicago Press, 1949.

Waters, Guy Prentiss. *Justification and the New Perspectives on Paul: A Review and Response*. Phillipsburg: P&R, 2004.

Watson, Francis. *Paul, Judaism and the Gentiles: A Sociological Approach*. Cambridge: Cambridge University Press, 1986.

Wawrykow, Joseph. *The Westminster Handbook to Thomas Aquinas*. Louisville, KY: Westminster John Knox Press, 2005.

Weima, Jeffrey A. D. *Paul, The Ancient Letter Writer*. Grand Rapids, MI: Baker Academic, 2016.

Weld, A. G. "Letter to Mr. Grimkie" [*sic*], February 15, 1868. *Grimké Papers*, Howard University.

Wendland, Ernst. "Text Analysis and Genre of Jonah (Part 2)." *JETS* 39, no. 3 (September 1996): 373–95.

West, Rebecca. *The Court and the Castle: Some Treatments of a Recurrent Theme*. New Haven, CT: Yale University Press, 1957.

Westerholm, Stephen. *Perspectives Old and New on Paul: The "Lutheran" Paul and His Critics.* Grand Rapids, MI: Eerdmans, 2003.

———. *Romans: Texts, Readers, and the History of Interpretation.* Grand Rapids, MI: Eerdmans, 2022.

Williams, George W. *A History of the Negro Troops in the War of the Rebellion.* New York: Harper and Brothers, 1888.

Williamson, Joel. *After Slavery: The Negro in South Carolina During Reconstruction, 1861–1877.* Chapel Hill: University of North Carolina Press, 1965.

Wilmore, Gayraud S. *Black Religion and Black Radicalism: An Interpretation of the Religious History of African Americans.* Maryknoll, NY: Orbis Books, 1998.

Witvliet, John D. *The Biblical Psalms in Christian Worship: A Brief Introduction and Guide to Resources.* Grand Rapids, MI: Eerdmans, 2007.

Woodson, Carter G. *The History of the Negro Church.* Washington, DC: Associated Publishers, 1921.

———. "Fifty Years of Negro Citizenship as Qualified by the United States Supreme Court." *Journal of Negro History* 6, no. 1 (January 1921): 1–53. https://www.jstor.org/stable/271387.

———. ed., *The Works of Francis J. Grimké.* 4 vols. Washington, DC: Associated, 1942.

Work, Monroe N. "The Passing Tradition and the African Civilization." In *Journal of Negro History* 1, no. 1 (January 1916): 34–41. https://www.jstor.org/stable/2713514.

Wright, N. T. *Justification: God's Plan and Paul's Vision.* Downers Grove, IL: IVP Academic, 2009.

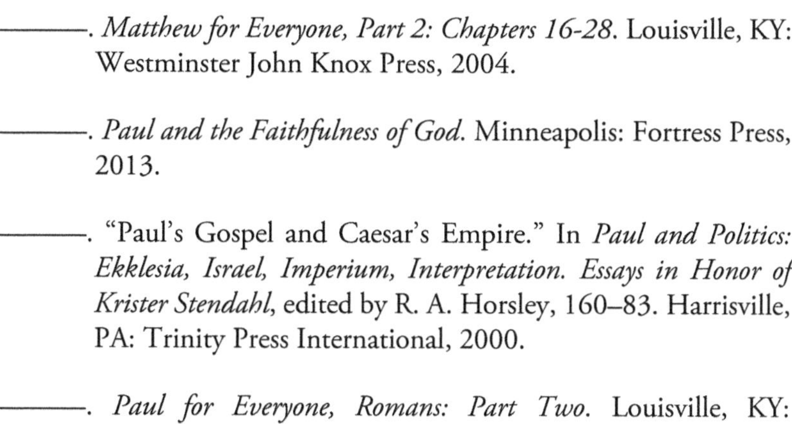

———. *Matthew for Everyone, Part 2: Chapters 16-28*. Louisville, KY: Westminster John Knox Press, 2004.

———. *Paul and the Faithfulness of God.* Minneapolis: Fortress Press, 2013.

———. "Paul's Gospel and Caesar's Empire." In *Paul and Politics: Ekklesia, Israel, Imperium, Interpretation. Essays in Honor of Krister Stendahl*, edited by R. A. Horsley, 160–83. Harrisville, PA: Trinity Press International, 2000.

———. *Paul for Everyone, Romans: Part Two*. Louisville, KY: Westminster John Knox Press, 2004.

Ultima Sententia

Drawing from Grimké's witness and Paul's legacy, it is my prayer that this work has blazed a path where evangelical doctrine and the struggle against ethnic prejudice unite in a harmonious voice through an emancipatory homiletic—a homiletic echoed throughout my journey as a clergyman in the heart of the Old Confederacy.

+Eric J. Freeman

About the Author

Eric J. Freeman is a scholar-practitioner whose work bridges homiletics, social ethics, and pastoral leadership. He holds a PhD in Homiletics

and Social Ethics from Anderson University, an MA in Theological Ethics from Lutheran Theological Southern Seminary, and a BSBA from the University of Florida. With more than 30 years of ministry experience, Dr. Freeman serves as Senior Pastor of The Meeting Place Church of Greater Columbia and as a bishop within the Christian Covenant Fellowship of Ministries.

As founder of The Freeman Institute for Integrative Research, Dr. Freeman developed the *Evangelical Emancipatory Homiletics™* framework—a preaching model that integrates biblical theology, doctrinal fidelity, and contextual awareness to confront social injustice. His academic and ministerial contributions reflect a lifelong commitment to gospel-centered engagement with pressing societal issues. In recognition of his leadership and impact, he was named Humanitarian of the Year (2023) by the South Carolina State Conference of the NAACP.

Dr. Freeman lives in Columbia, South Carolina, with his wife, Coleen. They are the proud parents of two adult children.

The Freeman Institute

FOR INTEGRATIVE RESEARCH

www.ingramcontent.com/pod-product-compliance
Lightning Source LLC
Chambersburg PA
CBHW032304280326
41932CB00009B/690